Table of Contents

Consumption   189

FOOD

Colorado State University | Fort Collins

Hannah Caballero
Amanda Memoli
Sue Doe

FOUNTAINHEAD
PRESS

Cover artwork and Archival photos provided by University Historic Photograph Collection, Colorado State University, Archives and Special Collections

Cover Design by Doris Bruey
Book Design by Susan Moore

For information, please call or write:

1-800-586-0330
Fountainhead Press
Southlake, TX 76092
Web Site: www.fountainheadpress.com
E-mail: customerservice@fountainheadpress.com

1st Edition

ISBN: 978-1-68036-332-6

Printed in the United States of America

Student Essay Contest
Topic: Food

Who:
CSU Students (only) completing CO150 in good standing during the 2016–17
Academic Year in sections addressing the course topic of Food

What:
Contest for "Best CO150 Essays of 2016" on the topic of FOOD and
approaching any issue relating to the topic from any angle.

What to Include:

Submit

- a researched (source-based) argumentative essay or a Photo Essay with
  accompanying Rhetorical Analysis done for CO150 on the topic of
  Food to sue.doe@colostate.edu

- a letter of transmittal that explains your audience and purpose for
  the text you're submitting and your willingness to be included among
  contestants and willingness to be published in the next reader

- a letter of support from your CO150 instructor, verifying the essay's
  completion in CO150 and your completion of the course in good
  standing (passing with a C or better)

- reliable contact information for you so that we may reach you after the
  end of the semester/school year

When:
By not later than May 22, 2017. Winners will be announced in late May or
early June 2017.

Where:
Colorado State University –Fort Collins

Why:
Awards of $125 (1st place), $75 (2nd place) and $50 (3rd place) AND
publication of your award-winning essay in the next reader. Possible public
readings in 2017-18 school year.

Introduction
The Food, Energy & Water Nexus: or It's Gonna be a *Wicked* Problem to Sustain the Planet in the 21st Century

"Globally, today's food system has major weaknesses: nearly 800 million people are left hungry, one-third of the human race is malnourished, over half of some crops never make it to the table, and the planet is ravaged from environmentally unfriendly agricultural practices. As the global population is expected to soar exponentially in the coming years, we must examine ways to feed more people efficiently and sustainably, while combatting climate change."[1]

Food, Energy and Water (FEW) are the essential ingredients for sustaining human life on the planet. Over time and space, these resources are finite. Their sustainability, and by association the sustainability of the human species, depends on upon how wisely they are used and consumed. That's the macro-scale. On a regional scale, people in first-world countries like the U.S. struggle with different food issues than do people in other parts of the world.

Further, despite society's significant technological advances in food production during the post-industrial era, the consumption, production, and distribution of food poses one of the most difficult problems of the 21st century. To support a burgeoning world population that is expected to grow to 9.6 billion by 2050[2], and especially to support it equitably, we are going to need some very good thinking and responsible living. Rittel, Horst, and Webber call the kind of challenge that demands such thinking a "wicked problem," by which they mean "thorny" and "difficult" as opposed to morally flawed![3] Yet as you consider the readings in this Food reader, which in subsequent years will be followed by readings addressing Energy and Water, you might consider the dimensions that connect and extend scientific consideration of limited resources to the human dimensions of nurturing resources and addressing scarcity. Indeed, as you read, you will see that our relationship to food is deeply connected to culture and ties to emotion as well as to the religious and spiritual.

---

1 International Food Policy Research Institute: https://www.ifpri.org/news-release/why-middle-east-hungry-blame-armed-conflict

2 Pew Research Center: http://www.pewresearch.org/fact-tank/2014/02/03/10-projections-for-the-global-population-in-2050/

3 Rittel, Horst, and Melvin Webber; "Dilemmas in a General Theory of Planning," pp. 155–169, *Policy Sciences*, Vol. 4, Elsevier Scientific Publishing Company, Inc., Amsterdam, 1973.

As the range of readings here suggest, we cannot divorce the scientific from the lived, the experienced, and the felt!

The complex challenges posed by food production, consumption, and distribution for a growing world population are both ecological and human, and solutions depend on understanding human and ecological connections, the complexity of systems, and the limitations of every solution. Solutions, after all, like problems themselves, are reflective of values and are simultaneously personal and societal, individual and governmental. Good efforts are also inevitably flawed but that doesn't excuse us from undertaking them.

What is it about food that makes it a difficult, thorny, or "wicked" problem? Rittel and Webber say that the most important problems of our day are "wickedly complex" because they involve

- different stakeholders with different views on the topic
- solutions that themselves contain the seeds of new problems and consequences
- changing characteristics
- differing locations and hence differing contexts
- the use and abuse of political, social, and economic power

So what is the point of addressing such problems if they defy solution? And what can you offer as a first-year composition student to such complex discussions? First, we do not consider difficult topics in order to sit around and lament the challenges! Rather, we recognize that difficult problems require nuanced responses rather than knee-jerk reactions and you can be part of that. As a college student and the next generation who will inherit these problems, you will soon be expected to not only critique ideas on such topics but to contribute ideas in new and educated ways. You will be expected to show an awareness and appreciation for the perspectives and potential biases of stakeholders who generally act with partial knowledge and in their own self-interest. Moreover, when Rittel and Webber describe problems as wickedly difficult, they mean that such problems demand not only the best of our rationality but collaborative, innovative, flexible responses that take into account the human dimensions that are involved. Strategies that are needed for addressing such complex problems are:

- holistic rather than linear thinking
- action, experimentation and evaluation of approaches
- collaborative effort

- engagement of stakeholders
- development of higher order competencies such as big picture thinking and effective communication
- capacity for envisioning futures
- understanding of both human and natural world behaviors

One difficulty of our food, water and energy (FEW) systems begins with the fact that they are interconnected by geography and ecosystems. Variations in climate (precipitation and temperature regimes) and the distribution of continents across the globe from the Equator to the Poles fundamentally determine the availability of these key resources. Upon this ecosystem framework, the distribution of human populations and the degree of technological advancement of societies are overlaid, contributing to how limited resources are distributed to meet societal needs. At all scales, from local neighborhoods to continents, there are issues of quantity, quality and justice/equity in regard to food (as well as energy and water). These issues are driven as well by the social, technical and economic systems in place. In turn, societal issues of poverty, hunger, disease, human migration, security, and conflict are all linked to FEW systems. Africa, the most undernourished region of the world, is where half the world's population growth will occur between now and 2050, according to a 2015 report of the United Nations.[4] Will there be food to support such growth? And in the U.S., where food, energy and water problems might be considered less likely and infrastructure safely in place, problems still exist and weaknesses in structures are revealed when we consider food deserts and lead in water pipes. An uneven access to high quality food, energy, and water exists even within U.S. borders.

In the end, the magnitude and nature of food-related problems may seem overwhelming, but the old charge of think globally, act locally carries weight here. In striving to be problem solvers, we might begin at home, where most of us were first introduced to food. What is your understanding of your own, local relationship to food and how does food, even on the campus of Colorado State University, reflect the values and beliefs, as well as the resource management and technical solutions applied to production, consumption, and distribution of food?

You may still be wondering why we chose food, energy and water as topics for CO150. Consider that you are now a CSU Ram and part of the long history of the "ag school," of Colorado—hence the "A" emblazoned on the foothills just to the west of campus. In fact, you are now officially associated with the land grant tradition of Colorado and the United States. In 1862 when the Morrill Act

---

4 *World Population Prospects: Key Findings and Advance Tables.* United Nations Report 2015: http://esa.un.org/unpd/wpp/Publications/Files/Key_Findings_WPP_2015.pdf

provided the allocation of land for creation of at least one land grant college or university per state, the seeds for our topic selection were sewn. Land grant colleges and universities were charged with addressing issues of practical study such as agriculture, engineering, and military science. Part of the idea was to extend the idea of university learning to a broad public, educating farmers, merchants, and other everyday people so that they might vote intelligently and participate effectively in society. Then in 1890, subsequent to the Civil War, the second Morrill Act required former Confederate states to demonstrate that race was not a criterion for admission to land grant institutions, which led to the development of historically black colleges and universities. In 1994, the land grant mission was extended even further to explicitly include the original residents of these United States, the Native peoples, thus establishing the 31 tribal colleges of the American Indian Higher Education Consortium. The proud history of the land grant institution has been to be increasingly inclusive of diverse people's voices.

And where does writing fit in? To be an effective communicator on any topic, but perhaps particularly on difficult ones, you must be able to read and write critically, understand not only what texts say but why they say it, where they come from, and the perspectives they represent, and be informed enough to contribute. In order to be this informed contributor, you must understand the contexts that writing occurs in as well as the values and beliefs of those who are writing and those who are reading. But you cannot wait to know everything before contributing because that day will never come; we all must function and contribute, even though we do so from a position of partial understanding. And then we seek always to learn more and act in accordance with revised understanding.

In CO150, we talk a great deal about the rhetorical situation and the rhetorical triangle, the combination of which help us to understand the context of written texts. We seek to understand how the texts we read and the texts we write are reflective of values, beliefs, contexts and "exigencies" (needs that emerge and require a response). As you consider the rhetorical situations you confront throughout CO150, consider how these central notions of communicating might assist you in all the years ahead as you consider your own and others' purposes for writing:

The Rhetorical Situation –

According to Lloyd Bitzer, the rhetorical situation is comprised of a combination of *exigence* (a problem exists in the world and is in need of response), *audience* (those who might be able to have an influence on the problem) and *constraints* (the factors, including people and events, that limit efforts, decisions, and action).[5]

---

5   Lloyd Bitzer, "The Rhetorical Situation," *Philosophy & Rhetoric* 1.1 (January 1968): 1-14.

The Rhetorical Triangle –

This model suggests that a combination of factors contributes to the creation of an effective communication "event." We should consider context (rhetorical situation) and utilize our resources, which include our own authorship and credibility, the needs of our audience, and our choices in terms of text or message which can include images, numbers, and other symbols in addition to words.

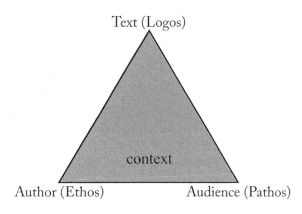

We hope that you will keep these concepts in mind as you take up the readings in this reader, *FOOD: Part I of Food, Energy, and Water,* which responds to existing exigencies related to food. The readings in this book are classified under the categories of production, consumption, and distribution. In many cases, you may wish to challenge this categorization since all organizational approaches are to some degree inadequate. However, we wanted to organize the conversation in a meaningful way so that you, too, could consider additional approaches. We especially set out to represent the work of our own colleagues here at CSU, so we have selected some of the important work that's being done at CSU as part of the land grant mission. We also wanted to represent some local, non-academic efforts in regard to food, so while this reader represents some resources, our links from the CANVAS course page provide even more. We are conscious, however, that we have missed important contributors, many from our local context. We have left out far more than we could include! However, our selected texts represent not only disciplinary variety but also diverse viewpoints of various groups who are involved in conversations about food—people who elsewhere in the course we will describe as "stakeholders."

In the weeks ahead, we hope that CO150 will do its part to prepare you for the hard work you will face in addressing and articulating positions on the difficult, thorny, and, yes, even "wicked" problems your generation will face.

We hope that CO150 and this reader will help you to see how writing works not only as a means for conveying ideas but as a means for discovering and developing them. We encourage you to think about the varied ways that different modes of thinking and discovery address the challenges around food and hence the challenges associated with any area of human concern. That is, as you consider the topic of food, are you more drawn toward scientific investigation, toward policy development, toward community outreach to underserved populations, toward poetry? CO150 and this reader, with its wide range of source types, offer you the opportunity to consider the differences in ways of examining difficult topics and hence to begin to consider your major and your future career path.

Through it all, we hope that you will consider the consequences of the choices that we make in regard to food, both in terms of human dimensions and more broadly in terms of the impact of food choices on the planet. We hope that you will see writing and rhetorical choices not as either empty or conspiratorial words on a page but as prompts for action and even as action itself. Writing, after all, is one way that we inscribe ourselves upon the world. And with an education, we learn to frame an argument and back it up with solid evidence clearly explained, rather than just stating our right to an opinion.

In keeping with CO150's broad theme of "entering the conversation," which you will learn about in the course, we encourage you to enter the conversation not only as informed and critical consumers of texts and ideas but as knowledgeable contributors as well. That will take hard work, research of various kinds, and a willingness to step up and speak out, knowledgeably, rationally, and yet with conviction. As students and future alums of Colorado State University, we know you are up to the challenge, and we look to you as our best hope for the future.

—The Composition Program, Colorado State University

If you have questions, suggestions, or concerns, please email sue.doe@colostate.edu

A National Food Policy for the 21st Century

Mark Bittman, Michael Pollan, Ricardo Salvador, Olivier De Schutter

Medium, October 2015

According to their websites, Mark Bittman and Michael Pollan are journalists and authors on topics concerning food and agriculture. Ricardo Salvador is the director and senior scientist at the UCS Food and Environment Program, and Olivier De Schutter is a professor and member of the UN Committee on Economic, Social, and Cultural Rights. This text was originally published on the website *Medium*, which the publication claims "is not for everybody, but it's open to everybody. It encourages participation and a diversity of opinion. Anyone can earn influence on *Medium* via the value of their ideas, thoughtfulness of their responses, or quality of their rhetoric." This article was published in October 2015, so the 2016 presidential race greatly shaped its context and exigence.

A memo to the next president

"Thanks to the productivity of our farmers, the United States has led the world in agriculture for generations. But it's time to recognize that the challenges facing our food system have shifted; we need to do more than produce an abundance of cheap calories. Too many of our children are struggling with obesity and type 2 diabetes, while many adults struggle with chronic preventable diseases linked to diet, costing us more than $500 billion a year. We must commit not just to feeding but to nourishing our citizens, especially our children. We can do this by honoring our great tradition of small family farms, and by building a food system that works with nature while continuing to be productive and profitable. To that end, I'm announcing the creation of a task force reporting directly to me and charged with developing the nation's first National Food Policy. This policy will be organized around the paramount objective of promoting health—that of our citizens and of the environment—at each link in the food chain, from the farm to the supermarket, to our schools, home tables, and even restaurants.

With the development of this policy, we will demonstrate that the American food sys-
tem can continue to be a model the rest of the world can follow."

— America's next president
A scenario for the State of the Union address, January 28, 2017

The Opportunity

The current and future well-being of the nation can be significantly improved by creating a National Food Policy (NFP). Such a policy, if properly conceived and implemented, will result in a healthier population, a reduction in hunger, mitigation of (and adaptation to) climate change, decreases in energy consumption, improved environmental conservation, rural and inner city economic development, a reduction in socioeconomic inequality, a safer and more secure food system, and savings to the federal budget, especially in spending on health care.

How could a single innovation such as the NFP possibly deliver on such a broad spectrum of our major contemporary challenges? Because these various issues are currently addressed through piecemeal and often contradictory approaches, whereas they are interlocking problems that can best be addressed through a unified and coordinated policy focused on their common denominator: the food system.

The very idea of a comprehensive "food system" is new. The next administration has an opportunity to innovate and lead on the major issues of our times, nationally and internationally, by demonstrating its grasp of this reality. Previous administrations have failed to appreciate the linkages between farming, diet, public health, and the environment, with the result that the food system has never been effectively overseen, administered, or regulated. This in turn has resulted in severe market failures that we call by other names: the obesity crisis, runaway hunger, epidemics of chronic disease, the ethanol bubble, surface water contamination and hypoxia, soil degradation, food safety scares and recalls, rural economic decline, inner city food deserts, labor exploitation, rising economic inequality, and the federal fiscal crisis. By attending to the food system, it is possible to connect all these dots and begin to address them in a coordinated and effective way.

The situation we face reflects, in large part, the unintended consequences of the last fundamental shift in agricultural policies, implemented by President Nixon in the early seventies. In an effort to combat a spike in food prices, the Nixon Administration abandoned supply controls and used the policy tools at its disposal to boost farm production by subsidizing, and encouraging, the industrialization and consolidation of commodity agriculture. This "productivist paradigm"—heavily dependent on fossil fuel inputs and a small number of crops grown in monoculture—succeeded in producing an abundance of cheap calories. But this was achieved at a price to the health of the population, the environment, and rural economy that is no longer sustainable.

The food system resulting from these policies has created economic and path dependencies that complicate reform, leaving us with a set of institutions and policy vehicles that are incapable of tackling the problems of the food system— problems that go far beyond food and farming. Today, policies are needed that respond to the evolution and actual structure and function of the contemporary food system. A coherent NFP must therefore replace obsolete conceptions, policies, tools, and institutions with new ideas and processes to address current challenges and prevent similar market failures from occurring in the future.

Public support for this bold action will come from uniting traditional constituencies in the labor, social justice, environmental, alternative energy, and public health sectors with those in the food movement. The various constituencies composing food system activism, from field to plate, are acquiring greater public visibility and political power. This is attested by the successful mobilization of groups such as the Coalition of Immokalee Workers[1], the Food Chain Workers Alliance, Restaurant Opportunities Center, Farm to School, FoodCorps, Real Food Challenge, the Partnership for Healthier America, the new emphasis on food and farming among the leading environmental organizations (including the Natural Resources Defense Council, Environmental Defense Fund, Environmental Working Group, and Union of Concerned Scientists), and the broad coalition of organizations that has forced Big Food and Big Ag to spend nearly $100 million since 2012 to resist calls for GMO[2] labeling. The NFP could be the organizing principle that galvanizes this nascent movement and its emerging political power. A new political constituency is forming around food issues. The old "farm vote" will soon be overtaken by a "good food" vote comprised not only of a new generation of young farmers, but also of the people they feed, a rapidly growing segment of the population who have begun to vote with their dollars— and their actual votes—for a healthier, less exploitative, more humane food system[3]. Leadership and vision from the president would be commensurate with the stakes, and would provide the administration with an opportunity for landmark executive action and historical legacy.

The Agenda

The United States has been the global leader in creating and establishing a large-scale and productive food system. It therefore falls to the U.S. to continue its leadership role by rectifying the shortfalls of that system, demonstrating how to reshape it for the 21st century so that it meets its reason for being. That reason is to produce a wholesome and healthful food supply for people of all socioeconomic backgrounds, while treating humans and animals fairly and compassionately and nurturing the ecosystems on which we depend.

For the foreseeable future, food system reform initiatives will have trouble surviving in a Congress heavily influenced by agribusiness interests[4]. Thus most of the goals set forth here can be best achieved using existing federal and executive tools, repurposing existing resources and institutions, and enforcing existing laws and regulations. The immediate objective would be to monitor and coordinate the components of the food value chain to better match the desired criteria. The executive has the authority and therefore the opportunity to oversee each link in the food chain:

- Production (labor and environment standards)
- Processing and distribution (antitrust and food safety)
- Retail and institutional delivery (wages and economic inequality)
- Healthcare and public health (prevention via public education, medical and healthcare incentives—including appropriate incentives for healthy food—and policies ensuring availability of that food).

Public support for bold executive actions will be necessary, and the mobilization and organization of that support will take money. But there are philanthropies that focus on food, health, and equity issues[5]; their funding, along with support from individual citizens, will follow when they see a clear vision and agenda around food, such as the NFP.

The Action

Production: Ideally, our agricultural policies will align with our public health goals, using policies that encourage the system to produce more of the kind of food recommended by leading nutritionists from the government, private sector, and academia[6],[7],[8]. Current government policies and incentives reward production of too much of the wrong stuff and encourage production to supply the export market, at great cost to natural resources and public health domestically, and to developing markets and agricultural systems internationally[9],[10]. Policy should push the system to favor quality of diets over quantity of calories. This transformation can be accomplished by coordinating the vast federal machinery to undertake the following steps:

1. **Develop** a roadmap[11] to "re-solarize" the production system. There are many moving parts to this agenda, but this core idea unifies most of them: To the extent that we wean American agriculture from its heavy 20th-century diet of fossil fuel and put it back on one of contemporary sunshine captured through photosynthesis, we can solve several problems at once, including improving the American diet and mitigating climate change. The problem, in a nutshell, is that we grow too much of our food in vast monocultures, which depend on applications of fossil fuel fertilizer, fossil fuel pesticides, and energy-intensive processing and transport. These monocultures produce more calories per farmer, yet they survive only as long as fossil energies are available and cheap, and only because society is willing to let those farmers externalize heavy environmental, health, and socioeconomic costs[12],[13]. They also lead directly to a fast-food diet based on the building blocks of commodity corn (for cheap sweeteners and meat) and commodity soy (for cheap oil and meat). The more diversified a farm production system is, the more it relies on free contemporary sunlight rather than fossil fuels and fertilizers. A more diversified agriculture would at the same time help diversify the American diet and sequester significant amounts of carbon in the soil. Relocalizing the food system contributes to this objective. This will reduce energy consumption and improve food safety and security, while at the same time improving the quality of calories produced, since the less food is processed for national distribution the fresher and more nutritious it is[14]. A long-term policy to resolarize U.S. agriculture by promoting diversification will bring many benefits that can be achieved by:

    A. **Direct** USDA research and extension programs to investigate, develop, promote and support regionally appropriate, regenerative, diversified farming systems. The potential of these agro-ecological systems to produce yields and profits comparable to so-called conventional agriculture, especially in the face of drought and other climate disruptions, is now well established[15].

    B. **Support** and reorient the Land Grant University system so that it serves local and regional constituencies and their needs[16]. Reduced public funding has made these institutions increasingly reliant on industry, thus turning public investment into private profit[17],[18]. Recently, the President's Council of Advisors on Science and Technology (PCAST) proposed dealing with this quandary through "rebalancing the U. S. Department of Agriculture's research portfolio" and creating "innovation institutes" funded through public/private partnerships[19]. PCAST recommended this strategy to overcome "congressional constraints" in funding, and the capture of the land grant system by private sector interests, which raises the question: Why should a public system created to serve the public interest be co-opted in this way?

C. **Launch** a "Farmer Corps" to educate a new generation of "sun farmers" and help put them on the land. The federal government should reverse historical course and embrace the goal of increasing the number of farmers, as part of its push for full employment. No young generation of farmers will emerge under the present conditions; while the average U.S. farmer was 50 years old in 1982, he or she was 58 in 2012[20].

2. **Encourage** and promote the reintegration of animals on farms by ending federal subsidies and regulatory indulgence for confined animal feed operations (CAFOs). These operations must be recognized and regulated as the factories that they are, with the same standards, regulations, and penalties applied to other industries emitting noxious products. This can be done by enforcing existing environmental laws[21], and by requiring waste treatment (and a halt to using EQIP[22] funds to subsidize this negative externality). Essayist Wendell Berry, honored recently by President Obama with the National Humanities Medal[23], has best expressed the logic of this measure: "Once plants and animals were raised together on the same farm—which therefore neither produced unmanageable surpluses of manure, to be wasted and to pollute the water supply, nor depended on such quantities of commercial fertilizer. The genius of America farm experts is very well demonstrated here: they can take a solution and divide it neatly into two problems[24]."

3. **Eliminate** the routine non-medicinal use of antibiotics in animal agriculture. Relevant authority lies with the Food and Drug Administration. The science supports the imperative of this measure to preserve the effectiveness of antibiotics for human medicine and to slow the spread of the "superbugs" responsible for MRSA[25] and other antibiotic-resistant infections. European Union experience demonstrates that this is feasible without a productivity tradeoff. (Furthermore, fewer CAFOs will mean fewer antibiotics in animal production, and vice versa.)[26] The FDA should immediately announce that it will move to regulate animal antibiotics; it's already clear that its voluntary guidelines have had no appreciable effect[27].

4. **Support** the Environmental Protection Agency in its recent rethinking[28] of the Renewable Fuel Standard[29] (the "ethanol mandate"). The mandate originally intended to support transition to sustainable cellulosic biofuels. Yet, since its implementation a decade ago, this federal subsidy to corn producers has only entrenched the dominance of corn in the Midwest. Layered over crop insurance and other direct and hidden subsidies, the Renewable Fuel Standard has generated biofuel so soaked with fossil fuel inputs that its modest energy benefits scarcely begin to cover the environmental and social harm caused by intensive corn monocultures: consolidation and increase of farm size, displacement of farmers via creation of barriers for entry into farming, and making farmland too expensive to use for actual food, further linking the food and energy markets, so that the volatility of the price of oil creates havoc in agricultural commodities' markets. If biofuels are to be supported at all, such support should be reserved for sustainable cellulosic biofuels, particularly those made from perennial grasses that reduce fossil fuel dependence while playing a complementary role in diverse, modern multifunctional agricultural systems[30]. (fix footnotes on this page: 26, 29, 30)

5. **Promote** greater production of actual food, especially seasonal fruits and vegetables for regional markets, by providing equitable access to farm credit and loan guarantees for all farmers, particularly for young, beginning, and organic farmers who have historically encountered barriers to access to government programs. Such measures would create at minimum 189,000 new jobs in local food systems and $9.5 billion in new revenue for healthy foods[31].

6. **Take** a firm stance to reform agricultural subsidies in the next Farm Bill, and ensure that public investment supports beginning farmers and those who produce actual food using sustainable practices[32]. Current policy perversely rewards farmers who have not practiced conservation agriculture, as opposed to those who have; and it overwhelmingly supports large-scale monocultures, the exact opposite from what we need to promote[33],[34].

7. **The president** should work with Congress and all relevant agencies to fully fund and implement programs that encourage diversified farming, rewarding food production and diversification rather than monocultures of industrial and export crops; ecological services (including carbon sequestration) rather than overproduction; and quality rather than quantity of production[35].

8. **To close** nutrient cycles at scale, make municipal and institutional composting of food and yard waste mandatory, and give the compost to farmers and ranchers.

9. **Ensure** that wages for farm labor are fair and sufficient to permit workers who harvest, process, prepare, and serve our food to have access to the food they have helped to produce and deliver.

10. **Generally**, preserve and enhance the social safety net, so that fairer wages and benefits for workers in all economic sectors increase wealth and economic stability among the most vulnerable. This will reduce hunger in the world's largest economy, where currently 49 million citizens (one in six) are food insecure[36], and should be a prominent part of any president's commitment to battling economic inequality[37].

The Marketplace:

1. **Enforce** anti-trust laws currently on the books to restore competition to food markets at every level: seeds, grain trading, animal feeding, meatpacking, and supermarkets[38]. This problem is so well known that in 2010 the Antitrust Division of the Department of Justice, together with the USDA, held five joint public workshops on how concentration in the food industry was hurting both suppliers and consumers. However, apart from a report, nothing came out of these hearings. The middle of the chain (processing and marketing), it seems, still holds a veto power on any reform of the food chain that would tackle the issue of bargaining power—with the two ends negatively affected (farming and eating)[39].

2. **Establish** a federal grain reserve, modeled on the Strategic Petroleum Reserve, to cushion destructive swings in commodity prices[40]. Price volatility in agricultural markets has been increasing significantly in recent years, in part as a result of financial speculation (the excessive weight of derivatives in shaping prices on the spot markets), and in part because of the merger between the food and the energy markets: Because small-size production units are the least able to cope with these price swings, this is one more threat to the survival of small farms and the local markets on which they sell their produce.

3. **Provide** grants to towns and cities to build year-round, indoor/outdoor farmers markets, especially in underserved urban neighborhoods, under an enhanced Farmers Market Promotion Program[41]. These will draw farmers and real food into cities, revitalize rural, and urban economies (restaurants and others businesses sprout up around farmer's markets) and would become one of the signature public-works legacies of any presidential administration.

4. **Coupled** with prescriptions and programs administered by hospitals seeking to comply with the Affordable Care Act's mandate to prioritize preventive

treatments[42], distribute farmer's market vouchers for healthy fruits, vegetables, and lean meat to Women, Infants and Children (W.I.C.[43]), and Food Stamp (SNAP[44]) recipients. This will improve access to healthful food and the diet of recipients while driving growth in the regional farm economy[45]. The disconnection between food and health is a critical dysfunction targeted by the Affordable Care Act, and one that has been pointedly described by Wendell Berry: "People are fed by the Food Industry, which pays no attention to health, and healed by the Health Industry, which pays no attention to food[46]."

5. **Increase** the SNAP program's objectives and effectiveness by reforming the system so that its subsidies are directed toward the purchase and consumption of healthy foods, in harmony with recommendations from leading health authorities (cf., footnote 6), thereby protecting against both hunger and obesity[47].

6. **Direct** the USDA to support regional slaughterhouses and meat processing facilities. Establish a local meat inspection corps to nurture burgeoning local meat production. The dominant position of the "big four" meatpackers (Tyson, Cargill, JBS and National Beef), who together corner two thirds of the markets[48], can only be addressed by decentralizing processing facilities. This will also strengthen the bargaining position of hog, cattle, and poultry farmers.

7. **Enforce** worker safety rules already on the books throughout the food system. Give the Occupational Safety and Health Administration the resources it needs to protect food workers, from field to factory.

8. **Mandate** that federal food procurement (in the military, national parks, schools, prisons, etc.) prioritize the purchase of food from regional producers. Pattern on the successful work of the National Farm to School Network[49] and School Food Focus[50], organizations that have created working business models to connect regional supply with institutional demand for healthful food.

9. **Create** a federal definition of good food, based on health and nutrition, and apply it to all federal nutrition programs. Encourage states to adopt it for sales tax purposes[51]. What Mexico has done with some success[52]—raising value added taxes on sugary soda drinks to discourage consumption—can be achieved on an even larger scale in the U.S.

The Food Culture:

In many ways, the Obama family has set an example that the next presidency could expand on. It did so by establishing the first producing kitchen garden on White House grounds since the FDR Administration, by modeling healthful eating, and by patronizing and promoting local farmers markets. It established programs such as Let's Move[53] and the Partnership for a Healthier America[54]. It promoted reforms in key social welfare programs such as the Child Nutrition Act[55], it set up the Childhood Obesity Task Force[56] and it challenged the Grocery Manufacturers Association to produce and advertise healthful foods in pursuit of their own economic interests[57]. It reformed the healthcare system along preventive principles through the Affordable Care Act. This platform provides a strong basis for the next president to build on the Obama Administration's demonstration of the importance of food, health, equity, and sustainability. This can be accomplished through measures such as the following:

1. **President** Kennedy made physical education an accepted part of the school curriculum; the next president should do the same for "edible education." Build gardens in schools, patterned after the White House garden and programs such as Edible Schoolyard, which can be used to infuse food and health throughout the curriculum. Introduce cooking lessons in schools, including cooking of vegetarian dishes, and explicitly targeted to both boys and girls. Boost the Child Nutrition Act so that school lunch spending increases by $1 a day per pupil to underwrite healthy, sustainably grown food, a sizable portion of which should be purchased locally (a model successfully implemented by the Province of Ontario in 2013[58]). Rebuild cafeterias, many of which are equipped only to microwave processed food, by funding programs to upgrade kitchens and dining areas[59]. Increase funding for USDA competitive grants targeted to build Farm to Cafeteria value chains[60]; raise the eligibility threshold for free and reduced school meals to 200 percent of the poverty rate[61].

2. **Support** expansion of the successful FoodCorps program[62], established by an AmeriCorps grant and matching philanthropic funding, to place college graduates in schools to support teachers' efforts to include food in curricula and promoting health through programs such as school gardens and healthier cafeteria choices. Forgive federal student loans in exchange for two years of service in the program, and provide a path to formal institutionalization of the program in schools and within the Department of Agriculture.

3. **Support** the burgeoning market for health, fairness, and sustainability through food by providing maximum transparency in food labeling. Make it simple to determine that food is healthful, fair, and sustainable through re-

conceived labels conveying what we now know to be important about our food[63].

4. **Enlist** the advertising industry in a public service campaign to promote the consumption of vegetables in place of junk food and water in place of soda, particularly for children. Nothing would do more to reduce rates of Type 2 diabetes—and the federal spending required to treat it—than a reduction of soda consumption by children[64]. To prevent the taste  preferences of children being shaped by the advertising campaigns of food companies, tax advertising for junk food and soda and use the revenue to fund public campaigns on healthy foods.

5. **Partner** and coordinate with NGOs as they develop a tough food industry pledge governing marketing to children, and then through the Partnership for a Healthier America, single out for recognition those food companies that sign it.

Administrative

This is obviously a large undertaking, and one that will require not just political will—but also authority, coordination, and continuous monitoring. Many of the issues discussed here are now administratively intractable because purview over issues that need to be managed in tandem is distributed across various jurisdictions. Establishment of effective oversight to enable reform will mean restructuring the politics of food and agriculture; it would be foolish to underestimate the size of that task.

The Department of Agriculture (USDA) is large and saddled with disparate and often conflicting goals. It manages subsidy and trade promotion programs that incentivize production of the industrial commodities underpinning the global junk food culture, the very culture that it theoretically opposes by recommending healthful eating and administering the SNAP program[65]. USDA should be reconstituted as a new entity, with a name that clearly identifies what must become its foremost mission. (We propose "The U.S. Department of Food, Health and Well-being.") This measure would represent more than a ceremonial renaming but a broad reconceptualization of the purpose, structure, programs, and operations of the department, entailing elimination of obsolete and unaligned components, and recombination with functions currently established in separate agencies, such as HHS, EPA, and DOE. The rationale and framing for such government reform can be solidly based upon updating the agency, eliminating waste, and declaring victory where missions have been fulfilled.

For example: It may have made sense for USDA to administer anti-hunger programs when the leading public health issue was a lack of calories. But now that obesity is an even bigger problem than hunger in the U.S., the quality of nutrition assistance matters as much as its quantity, and when SNAP funding constitutes 80 percent of the Farm Bill budget, food and health should be preeminent in the objectives, expertise, programming, and directives of the department. The interests of production agriculture should be subordinated to the goals of nutrition and health. These meaningful reforms would encompass and inform institutional purchasing throughout all government agencies and programs, including SNAP, Women, Infants and Children, and the School Lunch Program. Nor are these reforms trivial: Increasing national consumption of fruits and vegetables to meet MyPlate[66] recommendations would save more than 100,000 lives and $17 billion annually in health care costs *from heart disease alone*[67]. Additionally, such actions would be more than prudent health management, constituting as they do more responsible public expenditure, and as such have broad public and non-partisan support, including from fiscal conservatives[68].

An example in the category of declaring victory for a mission fulfilled is the Foreign Agricultural Service, which functions to promote, develop, and maintain export markets for U.S. agricultural products, using mechanisms such as credit guarantees for U.S. exports coupled with favorable credit terms for foreign buyers. This aligns the agency with the interests of productivism; thus some of the world's most profitable corporations receive public subsidy for their global business models. When U.S. production began to outstrip domestic demand this function might have made sense, but now this program serves overproduction, environmental degradation, and ill health. Clearly this is a case where a mature industry can compete without aid.

A critical factor making farm subsidy programs difficult to reform is the alliance of commodity groups with the "hunger lobby," an alliance that once served the interests of the urban poor. No longer, as demonstrated by the debate and negotiations over the 2014 Farm Bill, which occasionally raised the possibility of eliminating or severely underfunding SNAP. Today there is far more political support for nutrition programs than for crop subsidies, reflective of the demographic and democratic reality that there are many more hungry non-farming citizens than farmers. Breaking up the Farm Bill might be the best way to break the farm lobby's stranglehold on our food policies[69],[70]. As an initial step to enable this necessary shift to more effective farm policy deliberations in the future, the president should encourage House and Senate Leadership to reconstitute their respective "Agriculture Committees" as "Food and Health Committees," with membership representative of the appropriate expertise and geographical diversity, on the irrefutable logic that the purview and mandate of these committees is too important to be left in the hands of a narrowly defined regional business interest group[71].

Whether or not expanding the mission of the Department of Agriculture to take in food and health is politically feasible, the next president should appoint a National Food Policy Advisor, charged with:

Coordinating food policy across all government departments[72] to ensure that agriculture policies no longer undercut (but instead support) public health, energy, climate change, and our professed foreign policy goals to help low-income countries to feed themselves.

Working to rationalize our dangerously fragmented food safety system, now divided across several different departments.

Working to incorporate agriculture into climate change policy, by rewarding farmers for sequestering carbon and treating animal factories that contribute to climate change like any other polluting industries.

Lobbying Congress for the necessary policies and reforms (e.g., conservation compliance, Child Nutrition Act, committee restructuring, etc.).

In summary

The U.S. government has never before had a national food policy, let alone one that seeks at the highest level to align federal agricultural policies with our public health and environmental objectives. Were the next president to inaugurate such a policy, and by executive action establish the mechanisms for its implementation, the potential would dramatically increase to drive long-term change in three critical issues of our times: health care, climate change, and economic equality. Sustained progress on all three of these issues will be limited unless progress is made in addressing a fourth, seemingly less salient issue: the health, sustainability, and fairness of the food system.

The National Food Policy is therefore not simply about food. It's about health, it's about rural landscapes, it's about the environment, it's about education, and it's about poverty. It is also, ultimately, about whether democracy can respond—about our ability to move away from the policies we've been trapped in since the 1970s. The problems have changed since then; the change in policies to meet the new challenges we face is long overdue.

Appendix 1: Successful Existing Food Policy Models

The president can point to a number of working examples of successful municipal and regional programs, with robust business models, upon which federal programs can be patterned:

The City of Los Angeles' "Good Food Pledge"[73]

The state of Michigan's "Good Food Charter"[74]

The state of Pennsylvania's Fresh Food Financing Fund[75] (made possible in part by the American Recovery and Reinvestment Act[76])

North Carolina State's Center for Environmental Food Systems[77], which has generated knowledge, businesses and jobs to supply the state's demand and capacity to produce

Endnotes

1. Recognized by President Obama as "one of the great human rights causes of our time."
2. Genetically modified organism
3. Gould, D. 2013. "Food Trends Get Technical, Sustainable and Healthy," 28 Dec 2012, Forbes
4. Gilens, M., & Page, B. I. (2014). Testing Theories of American Politics: Elites, Interest Groups, and Average Citizens. Perspectives on Politics, 12(3), 564–581. doi:10.1017/S1537592714001595
5. Sustainable Agriculture and Food Systems Funders; Grantmakers in Health; the Global Alliance on the Future of Food
6. Food and Nutrition Service (Department of Agriculture), Office of Disease Prevention and Health Promotion (Department of Health and Human Services), Institute of Medicine (National Academies), Division of Nutrition, Physical Activity and Obesity (Centers for Disease Control), National Prevention Strategy-Healthy Eating (Office of the Surgeon General), Nutrition Source (Harvard School of Public Health)
7. "The Healthy Farmland Diet," Union of Concerned Scientists
8. Economics Research Service (Department of Agriculture), Americans' at-home food spending out of sync with dietary recommendations
9. "Trends in the United States and Abroad Affecting the Food & Ag System," AGree
10. "Toward Healthy Food and Farms," Union of Concerned Scientists
11. Jackson, W. and W. Berry. A 50-Year Farm Bill, January 2009
12. Godfrey, H. C. J. et al. "The Future of the Global Food System," Philosophical Transactions of the Royal Society, August 16, 2010
13. "The Healthy Farm: A Vision for U. S. Agriculture," Union of Concerned Scientists
14. Pollan, M. Unhappy Meals, 28 Jan 2007. The New York Times Magazine
15. De Schutter, Olivier. Agroecology and the Right to Food, December 2010
16. "Kellogg Commission on the Future of State and Land-Grant Universities"

17. Rausser, G., Simon, L., & Stevens, R. (2008). Public vs. Private Good Research at Land-Grant Universities. Journal of Agricultural & Food Industrial Organization, 6(2)

18. Pardey, P. G., J. M. Alston and C. Chan-Kang. "Public Food and Agricultural Research in the United States: The Rise and Decline of Public Investments, and Policies for Renewal," AGree, April 2013

19. President's Council of Advisors on Science and Technology, Report to the President on Agricultural Preparedness and The Agriculture Research Enterprise, Dec. 2012

20. Farm Demographics

21. Clean Water Act, Clean Air Act Amendments, Comprehensive Environmental Response, Compensation, and Liability Act ("Superfund")

22. Environmental Quality Incentives Program, Natural Resource Conservation Service, Department of Agriculture

23. National Medal of Arts and National Humanities Medal Ceremony, The White House, March 2, 2011

24. The Unsettling of America: Culture & Agriculture (1996), p. 62

25. Methicillin Resistant Staphylococcus aureus

26. Kennedy, D. 2013. Science 342:777

27. Bittman, M. The FDA's Not-Really-Such-Good-News. Opinionator, The New York Times, December 17, 2013

28. "Renewable Fuels: Regulation and Standards," EPA

29. Renewable Fuel Standard

30. Smart Bioenergy, Union of Concerned Scientists

31. "Plant the Plate," Union of Concerned Scientists

32. "2014 Farm Bill Drill Down: Conservation—Crop Insurance Linkages," National Sustainable Agriculture Coalition

33. Taxpayers for Common Sense, Senate's New Way to Lock in Unlimited Farm Subsidies, July 4, 2012

34. "The Farm Bill Still Gives Wads of Cash to Agribusiness. It's Just Sneakier About it," New Republic, Feb 4, 2014

35. "The Case for Ending Crop Subsidies," Environmental Working Group

36. Food Security, Key Statistics and Graphics, Economics Research Service

37. "Remarks by the President on Economic Mobility," The White House

38. Ikerd, J. "Corporitization of Agricultural Policy." Small Farm Today, 2010

39. Our 21st Century Economy, US Department of Justice

40. Ray, D. "Producers Leery of Grain Reserve: The Concept or the Implementation?" University of Tennessee Agricultural Policy Analysis Center

41. Agricultural Marketing Service, US Department of Agriculture

42. "Hospitals may be markets for healthier food to satisfy Obamacare," Fresh Advantage

43. Women, Infants and Children Program

44. Supplemental Nutrition Assistance Program

45. Fruit and Vegetable Prescription Program, Wholesome Wave

46. Berry, W. "Sales Resistance for Beginners," IN: Sex, Economy, Freedom and Community, 1994

47. The Hamilton Project/Brookings Institution, Strengthening SNAP for a More Food-Secure, Healthy America. Policy Brief 2013–6

48. The Big Four Meatpackers, High Country News

49. Farm to School,

50. School Food Focus

51. De Schutter, Olivier. The Right to an Adequate Diet: The Agriculture-Food-Health Nexus, 2012

52. Reducción en el consumo de bebidas, Instituto Nacional de Salud Pública

53. Let's Move

54. A Healthier America

55. History of National School Lunch Program, US Department of Agriculture

56. Solving the Problem of Childhood Obesity Within a Generation, Let's Move, May 2010
57. "Remarks by the First Lady at a Grocery Manufacturers Association Conference," March 16, 2010
58. Legislative Assembly of Ontario, Bill 36, Local Food Act
59. Robert Wood Johnson Foundation, Pew Charitable Trusts, Serving Healthy School Meals, U.S. Schools Need Updated Kitchen Equipment, Dec 2013
60. Food and Nutrition Service (Department of Agriculture), Farm to School Program
61. Assistant Secretary for Planning and Evaluation (Department of Health and Human Services), 2013 Poverty Guidelines. One Version of the [U.S.] Federal Poverty Measure
62. Food Corps
63. Bittman, M. "My Dream Food Label," Opinionator, The New York Times, October 13, 2012
64. DeBoer, M. et al. 2013. Sugar-Sweetened Beverages and Weight Gain in 2- to 5-Year-Old Children, Pediatrics 132(3)
65. Supplemental Nutrition Assistance Program
66. MyPlate, USDA FNS
67. "The $11 Trillion Reward," Union of Concerned Scientists
68. Bittman, M. "$11 Trillion Reasons," Opinionator, August 6, 2013, The New York Times
69. Together with the American public, we support farmers and their interests. Sadly, it is not these people and their interests who are served by the cynically named corporate "farm lobby." "Farm lobbyists strike back against push to split House farm bill," The Hill
70. Shearn, I. "Whose Side is the American Farm Bureau On?" The Nation, July 6, 2012
71. Bellemare, Marc F., and Nicholas Carnes (2015). "Why Do Members of Congress Support Agricultural Protection?," Food Policy 50: 20–34
72. Building upon precedent established by the President's Childhood Obesity Task Force, which established in 2010 a concrete action plan of 5 goals and enjoined 7 Executive offices to work in coordination
73. Good Food LA
74. Michigan Food
75. Pennsylvania Fresh Food Financing
76. ARRA, Federal Funds Information for States
77. Center for Environmental Farming Systems

Questions for Discussion

1. How could a national food policy "drive long-term change in three critical issues of our times: health care, climate change, and economic equality"?

2. Why do you think the authors chose to begin their article with a hypothetical speech by the next president? How effective was this strategy?

3. Which of the initiatives that the authors discuss do you think would make the biggest impact on American citizens' general wellbeing? Why?

Counting the Hungry

Martín Caparrós

The New York Times, September 2014

> As stated by his publisher, Simon and Schuster, Martín Caparrós is an Argentinian novelist, essayist, and travel writer. Additionally, he has worked as a journalist for television, radio, and print. He won the 2004 Planeta Prize for his book, *Valfierno,* about the 1911 Mona Lisa heist. It was published in over a dozen languages. In addition to extensive books and essays, he is the author of a book about global hunger, entitled *El Hambre.* According to *The New York Times* website, this article was translated from Spanish by Kristina Cordero, and was published as on op-ed in 2014.

We don't know who they are. The people suffering from hunger are not our relatives, friends, co-workers; they probably don't read this paper. We don't know them, but at the very least we ought to know how many of them there are, because policy and aid decisions depend on that number; because very often their lives depend on that number. But we don't know, because the hunger statistics reported by the United Nations Food and Agriculture Organization are flawed.

Every year, around this time, in collaboration with the International Fund for Agricultural Development and the World Food Program, the F.A.O. publishes its report on hunger—or, as it is now called, "food insecurity." What most people remember are the numbers: whether hunger went up or down, and by how much. But hunger statistics are confusing. It is very hard to calculate with precision how many men and women do not eat enough. Most live in countries where weak states are incapable of accounting for all their citizens, and the international organizations that try to come up with head counts must use statistical calculations instead of detailed census reporting.

The F.A.O. makes an effort: by studying agricultural inventories; food imports and exports; the local uses of food; economic hardship and social inequality. From there it determines the estimated availability of food per capita. The difference between required and available calories gives the F.A.O. its number of undernourished people. This sounds like a sensible method, but it is entirely malleable. And so its results can be adjusted according to the needs of the moment.

This month, the F.A.O. reported jubilantly that the total number of chronically undernourished people went down to 805 million—209 million fewer than in 1990-92. These numbers carry a particular weight: They will be the last published before 2015, when the United Nations Millennium Development Goals are supposed to be completed. According to the report, these new numbers show that the organization's aspiration "of halving the proportion of undernourished people in developing countries by 2015 is within reach."

This sounds like great news, but it's not so simple. According to the development goals, the rate of hunger in 1990 is the one that's supposed to be halved. But that 1990 number has been adjusted several times, usually making the current numbers look more favorable by comparison.

It's a long story. At the World Food Conference in Rome, in 1974, when Henry A. Kissinger famously stated that "within a decade, no child will go to bed hungry," F.A.O. experts estimated that the number of hungry people in developing regions was close to 460 million, and that in 10 years it could reach 800 million. That prediction was close: In a 1992 report, the F.A.O. stated that there were 786 million hungry people in 1988-90. It was a dramatic increase, a serious blow.

In that report, the F.A.O. revised its previous calculations, saying that its statistical method had been wrong. Now, the F.A.O.'s experts said, they believed that in 1970 there weren't 460 million hungry people in the developing world, but more than twice that number, 941 million. This, in turn, allowed them to say that the 1989 figure of 786 million did not represent a dramatic increase but, in fact, a decrease of 155 million: quite an achievement.

The changes kept coming. In 2004, the F.A.O. said that the number of undernourished people in developing regions had reached 815 million. This would have seemed like a disappointing increase from the 786 million figure. But in that same report, the F.A.O. revised its 1990 numbers once again, and stated that in 1990 there hadn't been 786 million but rather 823 million hungry people. So hunger had gone down after all.

In the F.A.O.'s 2011 report, the number of hungry people in the developing world in 1990 was 833 million—20 percent of the developing world's population. Then it was 980 million in the 2012 report, after the F.A.O. experts revised their methodology once again. By 2013, those 980 million hungry people had become 995 million—23.6 percent of the population—who, along with the 20 million undernourished people in the developed world, added up to a staggering total of 1.015 billion.

Revisiting the Past

The United Nations has often revised its estimate for the number of hungry people in the developing world in 1990. Many of the changes have made it look as if there has been more progress in reducing hunger.

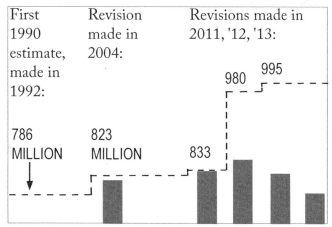

First 1990 estimate, made in 1992:

Revision made in 2004:

Revisions made in 2011, '12, '13:

980   995

786 MILLION   823 MILLION   833

Source: author's analysis of data from the Food and Agriculture Organization of the United Nations

This is the 1990 number that the F.A.O. now uses to explain how we have won a new battle against hunger. It also means that, to reach the United Nations' goal of halving the proportion of the hungry in the developing world by 2015, we don't need to go down to 10 percent of the population (half of that 20 percent), but to "only" 11.8.

It is possible to assume that statistical methods—factoring in new population, caloric and economic data—may be much better now than 30 years ago. It is harder to imagine that they have changed so much in the last three years as to add more than 160 million people who had previously stayed under the radar. We know that there is nothing more variable than the past, but it is unusual to watch it changing so fast, so visibly. You could say they are just numbers, abstractions; they wouldn't really matter much if they were just bad propaganda figures. The problem is that they are, in fact, canonical figures: the kind that are used to determine funds and priorities.

This is not conscious corruption. It's a symptom of an institutional culture that has to prove it is achieving important progress. The 1990 change justifies the United Nations' efforts and jobs, as much as it quiets our consciences. And it has a double economic effect: It convinces donors that their money has been fruitfully invested, and it justifies the reductions of these investments. International food aid, after peaking at $5.5 billion in 2008, decreased to $4 billion in 2012, according to the Organization for Economic Cooperation and Development.

So maybe next time, when we are told that hunger is being defeated, it would be wise to keep asking where and how and whose. After all, these figures help define the lives of hundreds of millions—wait, how many hundreds of millions?—of the victims of persistent hunger, the greatest outrage of our time.

Questions for Discussion

1. What specific flaws does Caparrós point out when critiquing the FAO's recounting of world hunger?

2. Caparrós begins his paper by stating, "We don't know who they are. The people suffering from hunger are not our relatives, friends, co-workers; they probably don't even read this paper." Based on this opening statement, what can we assume about Caparrós' intended audience?

3. At the end of his article, Caparrós claims, "This is not conscious corruption. It's a symptom of an institutional culture that has to prove it is achieving important progress." Do you agree with Caparrós' critique of western aid?

Prayer after Eating

Wendell Berry

Poetry Magazine, 1971

> Wendell Berry is, according to his profile on the Poetry Foundation's
> website, a poet, novelist, and environmentalist. In addition to
> his work as a writer, Wendell Berry has maintained a farm in rural
> Kentucky for over 40 years. His profile claims that despite his ability
> to work in a number of genres, "his message is essentially the same:
> that humans must learn to live in harmony with the natural rhythms
> of the earth or perish." His book, *The Unsettling of America: Culture and
> Agriculture*, is considered an instrumental text in the environmental
> movement. A proponent of small-scale farming, Berry is considered
> a political maverick because of the criticisms that he levels toward
> both environmentalists and large-scale corporate farms. This poem
> was first published in *Poetry Magazine* in 1971.

For purposes of allowing the poem to stand on its own and not be affected by
surrounding text, it is shown on the next page.

I have taken in the light

that quickened eye and leaf.

May my brain be bright with praise

of what I eat, in the brief blaze

of motion and of thought.

May I be worthy of my meat.

Helpful Texts on Writing

How to Turn Debate Into Dialogue

Deborah Tannen

The Argument Culture: Stopping America's War of Words, 1989

Balance. Debate. Listening to both sides. Who could question these noble American traditions? Yet today, these principles have been distorted. Without thinking, we have plunged headfirst into what I call the "argument culture."

The argument culture urges us to approach the world, and the people in it, in an adversarial frame of mind. It rests on the assumption that opposition is the best way to get anything done: The best way to discuss an idea is to set up a debate; the best way to cover news is to find spokespeople who express the most extreme, polarized views and present them as "both sides"; the best way to settle disputes is litigation that pits one party against the other; the best way to begin an essay is to attack someone; and the best way to show you're really thinking is to criticize.

More and more, our public interactions have become like arguing with a spouse. Conflict can't be avoided in our public lives any more than we can avoid conflict with people we love. One of the great strengths of our society is that we can express these conflicts openly. But just as spouses have to learn ways of settling their differences without inflicting real damage, so we, as a society, have to find constructive ways of resolving disputes and differences.

The war on drugs, the war on cancer, the battle of the sexes, politicians' turf battles—in the argument culture, war metaphors pervade our talk and shape our thinking. The cover headlines of both *Time* and *Newsweek* one recent week are a case in point. "The Secret Sex Wars," proclaims *Newsweek.* "Starr at War," declares *Time.* Nearly everything is framed as a battle or a game in which winning or losing is the main concern.

The argument culture pervades every aspect of our lives today. Issues from global warming to abortion are depicted as two-sided arguments, when in fact most Americans' views lie somewhere in the middle. Partisanship makes gridlock in Washington the norm. Even in our personal relationships, a "let it all hang out" philosophy emphasizes people expressing their anger without giving them constructive ways of settling differences.

Sometimes You Have To Fight

There are times when it is necessary and right to fight—to defend your country or yourself, to argue for your rights or against offensive or dangerous ideas or actions. What's wrong with the argument culture is the ubiquity, the kneejerk nature, of approaching any issue, problem or public person in an adversarial way.

Our determination to pursue truth by setting up a fight between two sides leads us to assume that every issue has two sides no more, no less. But if you always assume there must be an "other side," you may end up scouring the margins of science or the fringes of lunacy to find it.

This accounts, in part, for the bizarre phenomenon of Holocaust denial. Deniers, as Emory University professor Deborah Lipstadt shows, have been successful in gaining TV air time and campus newspaper coverage by masquerading as "the other side" in a "debate." Continual reference to "the other side" results in a conviction that everything has another side—and people begin to doubt the existence of any facts at all.

The power of words to shape perception has been proved by researchers in controlled experiments. Psychologists Elizabeth Loftus and John Palmer, for example, found that the terms in which people are asked to recall something affect what they recall. The researchers showed subjects a film of two cars colliding then asked how fast the cars were going; one week later they asked whether there had been any broken glass. Some subjects were asked, "How fast were the cars going when they bumped into each other?" Others were asked, "How fast were the cars going when they smashed into each other?"

Those who read the question with "smashed" tended to "remember" that the cars were going faster. They were also more likely to "remember" having seen broken glass. (There wasn't any.) This is how language works. It invisibly molds our way of thinking about people, actions, and the world around us.

In the argument culture, "critical" thinking is synonymous with criticizing. In many classrooms, students are encouraged to read someone's life work, then rip it to shreds.

When debates and fighting predominate, those who enjoy verbal sparring are likely to take part —by calling in to talk shows or writing letters to the editor. Those who aren't comfortable with oppositional discourse are likely to opt out.

How High-Tech Communication Pulls Us Apart

One of the most effective ways to defuse antagonism between two groups is to provide a forum for individuals from those groups to get to know each other personally. What is happening in our lives, however, is just the opposite. More and more of our communication is not face to face, and not with people we know. The proliferation and increasing portability of technology isolates people in a bubble.

Along with the voices of family members and friends, phone lines bring into our homes the annoying voices of solicitors who want to sell something—generally at dinnertime. (My father-in-law startles phone solicitors by saying, "We're eating dinner, but I'll call you back. What's your home phone number?" To the non-plused caller, he explains, "Well, you're calling me at home: I thought I'd call you at home, too.")

It is common for families to have more than one TV, so the adults can watch what they like in one room and the kids can watch their choice in another—or maybe each child has a private TV.

E-mail, and now the Internet, are creating networks of human connection unthinkable even a few years ago. Though e-mail has enhanced communication with family and friends, it also ratchets up the anonymity of both sender and receiver, resulting in stranger-to-stranger "flaming."

"Road rage" shows how dangerous the argument culture—and especially today's technologically enhanced aggression—can be. Two men who engage in a shouting match may not come to blows, but if they express their anger while driving down a public highway, the risk to themselves and others soars.

The Argument Culture Shapes Who We Are

The argument culture has a defining impact on our lives and on our culture.

It makes us distort facts, as in the Nancy Kerrigan-Tonya Harding story. After the original attack on Kerrigan's knee, news stories focused on the rivalry between the two skaters instead of portraying Kerrigan as the victim of an attack. Just last month, *Time* magazine called the event a "contretemps" between Kerrigan and Harding. And a recent joint TV interview of the two skaters reinforced that skewed image by putting the two on equal footing, rather than as victim and accused.

It makes us waste valuable time, as in the case of scientist Robert Gallo, who co-discovered the AIDS virus. Gallo was the object of a groundless four-year investigation into allegations he had stolen the virus from another scientist. He was ultimately exonerated, but the toll was enormous. Never mind that, in his words, "These were the most painful and horrible years of my life." Gall spent four years fighting accusations instead of fighting AIDS.

It limits our thinking. Headlines are intentionally devised to attract attention, but the language of extremes actually shapes, and misshapes, the way we think about things. Military metaphors train us to think about, and see, everything in terms of fighting, conflict and war. Adversarial rhetoric is a kind of verbal inflation—a rhetorical boy-who-cried-wolf.

It encourages us to lie. If you fight to win, the temptation is great to deny facts that support your opponent's views and say only what supports your side. It encourages people to misrepresent and, in the extreme, to lie.

End the Argument Culture by Looking at All Sides

How can we overcome our classically American habit of seeing issues in absolutes? We must expand our notion of "debate" to include more dialogue. To do this, we can make special efforts not to think in twos. Mary Catherine Bateson, an anthropologist at Virginia's George Mason University, makes a point of having her class compare three cultures, not two. Then, students are more likely to think about each on its own terms, rather than as opposites.

In the public arena, television and radio producers can try to avoid, whenever possible, structuring public discussions as debates. This means avoiding the format of having two guests discuss an issue. Invite three guests—or one. Perhaps it is time to re-examine the assumption that audiences always prefer a fight.

Instead of asking, "What's the other side?" we might ask, "What are the other sides?" Instead of insisting on hearing "both sides," let's insist on hearing "all sides."

We need to find metaphors other than sports and war. Smashing heads does not open minds. We need to use our imaginations and ingenuity to find different ways to seek truth and gain knowledge through intellectual interchange, and add them to our arsenal—or, should I say, to the ingredients for our stew. It will take creativity for each of us to find ways to change the argument culture to a dialogue culture. It's an effort we have to make, because our public and private lives are at stake.

Responding—Really Responding—to Other Students' Writing

Richard Straub

The Subject is Writing, 1999

Okay. You've got a student paper you have to read and make comments on for Thursday. It's not something you're looking forward to. But that's alright, you think. There isn't really all that much to it. Just keep it simple. Read it quickly and mark whatever you see. Say something about the introduction. Something about details and examples. Ideas you can say you like. Mark any typos and spelling errors. Make your comments brief. Abbreviate where possible: *awk, good intro, give ex., frag.* Try to imitate the teacher. Mark what he'd mark and sound like he'd sound. But be cool about it. Don't praise anything really, but no need to get harsh or cutthroat either. Get in and get out. You're okay. I'm okay. Everybody's happy. What's the problem?

This is, no doubt, a way of getting through the assignment. Satisfy the teacher and no surprises for the writer. It might just do the trick. But say you want to do a *good* job. Say you're willing to put in the time and effort—though time is tight and you know it's not going to be easy—and help the writer look back on the paper and revise it. And maybe in the process learn something more yourself about writing. What do you look for? How do you sound? How much do you take up? What exactly are you trying to accomplish? Here are some ideas.

How Should You Look at Yourself as a Responder?

Consider yourself a friendly reader. A test pilot. A roommate who's been asked to look over the paper and tell the writer what you think. Except you don't just take on the role of The Nice Roommate or The Ever-Faithful Friend and tell her what she wants to hear. *This all looks good. I wouldn't change a thing. There are a couple of places that I think he might not like, but I can see what you're doing there. I'd go with it. Good stuff.* You're supportive. You give her the benefit of the doubt and look to see the good in her writing. But friends don't let friends think their writing is the best thing since *The Great Gatsby* and they don't lead them to think that all is fine and well when it's not. Look to help this friend, this roommate writer—okay, this person in your class—to get a better piece of writing. Point to problems and areas for improvement but do it in a constructive way.

See what you can do to push her to do even more than she's done and stretch herself as a writer.

What Are Your Goals?

First, don't set out to seek and destroy all errors and problems in the writing. You're not an editor. You're not a teacher. You're not a cruise missile. And don't rewrite any parts of the paper. You're not the writer; you're a reader. One of many. The paper is not yours; it's the writer's. She writes. You read. She is in charge of what she does to her writing. That doesn't mean you can't make suggestions. It doesn't mean you can't offer a few sample rewrites here and there, as models. But make it clear they're samples, models. Not rewrites. Not edits. Not corrections. Be reluctant at first even to say what you would do if the paper were yours. It's not yours. Again: Writers write, readers read and show what they're understanding and maybe make suggestions. What to do instead: Look at your task as a simple one. You're there to play back to the writer how you read the paper; what you got from it; what you found interesting; where you were confused; where you wanted more. With this done, you can go on to point out problems, ask questions, offer advice, and wonder out loud with the writer about her ideas. Look to help her improve the writing or encourage her to work on some things as a writer.

How Do You Get Started?

Before you up and start reading the paper, take a minute (alright, thirty seconds) to make a mental checklist about the circumstances of the writing, the context. You're not going to just read a text. You're going to read a text within a certain context, a set of circumstances that accompany the writing and that you bring to your reading. It's one kind of writing or another, designed for one audience and purpose or another. It's a rough draft or a final draft. The writer is trying to be serious or casual, straight or ironic. Ideally, you'll read the paper with an eye to the circumstances that it was written in and the situation it is looking to create. That means looking at the writing in terms of the assignment, the writer's particular interests and aims, the work you've been doing in class, and the stage of drafting.

- *The assignment*: What kind of writing does the assignment call (or allow) for? Is the paper supposed to be a personal essay? A report? An analysis? An argument? Consider how well the paper before you meets the demands of the kind of writing the writer is taking up.

- *The writer's interests and aims*: What does the writer want to accomplish? If she's writing a personal narrative, say, is she trying to simply recount a past experience? Is she trying to recount a past experience and at the same time amuse her readers? Is she trying to show a pleasant experience on the surface, yet suggest underneath that everything was not as pleasant as it seems? Hone in on the writer's particular aims in the writing.

- *The work of the class*: Try to tie your comments to the concepts and strategies you've been studying in class. If you've been doing a lot of work on using detail, be sure to point to places in the writing where the writer uses detail effectively or where she might provide richer detail. If you've been working on developing arguments through examples and sample cases, indicate where the writer might use such methods to strengthen her arguments. If you've been considering various ways to sharpen the style of your sentences, offer places where the writer can clarify her sentence structure or arrange a sentence for maximum impact. The best comments will ring familiar even as they lead the writer to try to do something she hasn't quite done before, or done in quite the same way. They'll be comforting and understandable even as they create some need or do more, a need to figure out some better way.

- *The stage of drafting*: Is it an early draft? A full but incomplete draft? A nearly final draft? Pay attention to the stage of drafting. Don't try to deal with everything all at once if it's a first, rough draft. Concentrate on the large picture: the paper's focus; the content; the writer's voice. Don't worry about errors and punctuation problems yet. There'll be time for them later. If it's closer to a full draft, go ahead and talk, in addition to the overall content, about arrangement, pacing, and sentence style. Wait till the final draft to give much attention to fine-tuning sentences and dealing in detail with proofreading. Remember: You're not an editor. Leave these sentence revisions and corrections for the writer. It's her paper. And she's going to learn best by detecting problems and making her own changes.

What to Address in Your Comments?

Try to focus your comments on a couple of areas of writing. Glance through the paper quickly first. Get an idea whether you'll deal mostly with the overall content and purpose of the writing, its shape and flow, or (if these are more or less in order) with local matters of paragraph structure, sentence style, and correctness. Don't try to cover everything that comes up or even all instances of a given problem. Address issues that are most important to address in this paper, at this time.

Where to Put Your Comments?

Some teachers like to have students write comments in the margins right next to the passage. Some like to have students write out their comments in an end note or in a separate letter to the writer. I like to recommend using both marginal comments and a note or letter at the end. The best of both worlds. Marginal comments allow you to give a quick moment-by-moment reading of the paper. They make it easy to give immediate and specific feedback. You still have to make sure you specify what you're talking about and what you have to say, but they save you some work telling the writer what you're addressing and allow you to focus your end note on things that are most important. Comments at the end allow you to provide some perspective on your response. This doesn't mean that you have to size up the paper and give it a thumbs up or a thumbs down. You can use the end comment to emphasize the key points of your response, explain and elaborate on issues you want to deal with more fully, and mention additional points that you don't want to address in detail. One thing to avoid: plastering comments all over the writing; in between and over the lines of the other person's writing—up, down, and across the page. Write in your space, and let the writer keep hers.

How to Sound?

Not like a teacher. Not like a judge. Not like an editor or critic or shotgun. (Wouldn't you want someone who was giving you comments not to sound like a teacher's red pen, a judge's ruling, an editor's impatience, a critic's wrath, a shotgun's blast?) Sound like you normally sound when you're speaking with a friend or acquaintance. Talk to the writer. You're not just marking up a text; you're responding to the writer. You're a reader, a helper, a colleague. Try to sound like someone who's a reader, who's helpful, and who's collegial. Supportive. And remember: Even when you're tough and demanding you can still be supportive.

How Much to Comment?

Don't be stingy. Write most of your comments out in full statements. Instead of writing two or three words, write seven or eight. Instead of making only one brief comment and moving on, say what you have to say and then go back over the statement and explain what you mean or why you said it or note other alternatives. Let the writer know again and again how you are understanding her paper, what you take her to be saying. And elaborate on your key comments. Explain your interpretations, problems, questions, and advice.

Is It Okay to Be Short and Sweet?

No. At least not most of the time. Get specific. Don't rely on general statements alone. How much have generic comments helped you as a writer? "Add detail." "Needs better structure." "Unclear." Try to let the writer know what exactly the problem is. Refer specifically to the writer's words and make them a part of your comments. "Add some detail on what it was like working at the beach." "I think we'll need to know more about your high school crowd before we can understand the way you've changed." "This sentence is not clear. Were *you* disappointed or were *they* disappointed?" This way the writer will see what you're talking about, and she'll have a better idea what to work on.

Do You Praise or Criticize or What?

Be always of two (or three) minds about your response to the paper. You like the paper, but it could use some more interesting detail. You found this statement interesting, but these ideas in the second paragraph are not so hot. It's an alright paper, but it could be outstanding if the writer said what was really bothering her. Always be ready to praise. But always look to point to places that are not working well or that are not yet working as well as they might. Always be ready to expect more from the writer.

How to Present Your Comments?

Don't steer away from being critical. Feel free—in fact, feel obligated—to tell the writer what you like and don't like, what is and is not working, and where you think it can be made to work better. But use some other strategies, too. Try to engage the writer in considering her choices and thinking about possible ways to improve the paper. Make it a goal to write two or three comments that look to summarize or paraphrase what the writer is saying. Instead of *telling* the reader what to do, *suggest* what she might do. Identify the questions that are raised for you as your reader:

- Play back your way of understanding the writing:
  This seems to be the real focus of the paper, the issue you seem most interested in.
  So, you're saying that you really weren't interested in her romantically?

- Temper your criticisms:
  This sentence is a bit hard to follow.
  I'm not sure this paragraph is necessary.

- Offer advice:
  It might help to add an example here.
  Maybe save this sentence for the end of the paper.

- Ask questions, especially real questions:
  What else were you feeling at the time?
  What kind of friend? Would it help to say?

- Do you need this opening sentence?
  In what ways were you "a daddy's little girl"?
  Explain and follow up on your initial comments:

You might present this episode first. This way we can see what you mean when you say that he was always too busy. How did you react? Did you cry or yell? Did you walk away? This makes her sound cold and calculating. Is that what you want?

- Offer some praise, and then explain to the writer why the writing works:
Good opening paragraph. You've got my attention.
Good detail. It tells me a lot about the place.
    I like the descriptions you provide—for instance, about your grandmother cooking, at the bottom of page 1; about her house, in the middle of page 2; and about how she said her rosary at night: "quick but almost pleading, like crying without tears."

How Much Criticism? How Much Praise?

Challenge yourself to write as many praise comments as criticisms. When you praise, praise well. Think about it. Sincerity and specificity are everything when it comes to a compliment.

How Much Should You Be Influenced by What You Know About the Writer?

Consider the person behind the writer when you make your comments. If she's not done so well in class lately, maybe you can give her a pick-me-up in your comments. If she's shy and seems reluctant to go into the kind of personal detail the paper seems to need, encourage her. Make some suggestions or tell her what you would do. If she's confident and going on arrogant, see what you can do to challenge her with the ideas she presents in the paper. Look for other views she may not have thought about, and find ways to lead her to consider them. Always be ready to look at the text in terms of the writer behind the text.

Good comments, this listing shows, require a lot from a reader. But you don't have to make a checklist out of these suggestions and go through each one methodically as you read. It's amazing how they all start coming together when you look at your response as a way of talking with the writer seriously about the writing, recording how you experience the words on the page and giving the writer something to think about for revision. The more you see examples of thoughtful commentary and the more you try to do it yourself, the more you'll get a feel for how it's done.

Here's a set of student comments on a student paper. They were done in the last third of a course that focused on the personal essay and concentrated on helping students develop the content and thought of their writing. The class had been working on finding ways to develop and extend the key statements of their essays (by using short, representative details, full-blown examples, dialogue, and multiple perspectives) and getting more careful about selecting and shaping parts of their writing. The assignment called on students to write an essay or an autobiographical story where they looked to capture how they see (or have seen) something about one or both of their parents—some habits, attitudes, or traits their parents have taken on. They were encouraged to give shape to their ideas and experiences in ways that went beyond their previous understandings and try things they hadn't tried in their writing. More a personal narrative than an essay, Todd's paper looks to capture one distinct difference in the way his mother and father disciplined their children. It is a rough draft that will be taken through one or possibly two more revisions. Readers were asked to offer whatever feedback they could that might help the writer with the next stage of writing (Figure 1).

This is a full and thoughtful set of comments. The responder, Jeremy, creates himself not as a teacher or critic but first of all as a reader, one who is intent on saying how he takes the writing and what he'd like to hear more about:

> Good point. Makes it more unlikely that you should be the one to get caught.
> Great passage. Really lets the reader know what you were thinking.
> Was there a reason you were first or did it just happen that way?
> Would he punish you anyway or could you just get away with things?

He makes twenty-two comments on the paper—seventeen statements in the margins and five more in the end note. The comments are written out in full statements, and they are detailed and specific. They make his response into a lively exchange with the writer, one person talking with another about what he's said. Well over half of the comments are follow-up comments that explain, illustrate, or qualify other responses.

The comments focus on the content and development of the writing, in line with the assignment, the stage of drafting, and the work of the course. They also view the writing rhetorically, in terms of how the text has certain effects on readers. Although there are over two dozen wording or sentence-level errors in the paper, he decides, wisely, to stick with the larger matters of writing. Yet even as he offers a pretty full set of comments he doesn't ever take control over the text. His comments are placed unobtrusively on the page, and he doesn't try to close things down or decide things for the writer. He offers praise, encouragement, and direction. What's more, he pushes the writer to do more than he has already done, to extend the boundaries of his examination. In keeping with the assignment and the larger goals of the course, he calls on Todd in several comments to explore the motivations and personalities behind his parents' different ways of disciplining:

Figure 1

Jeremy
Todd
ENG 1
Rick Straub
Assign 8b

Uh, oh

like this paragraph. It immediately puts the reader close to you and also produces a picture in the reader's mind

When I called home from the police station I was praying that my father would answer the phone. He would listen to what I had to say and would react comely, logical, and in a manner that would keep my mother from screaming her head off. If my Mother was to answer the phone, I would have to explain myself quickly in order to keep her from having a heart attached.

When I was eleven years old I hung out with a group of boys that were almost three years older than me. The five of us did all the things that young energetic kids did playing ball, riding bikes, and getting in to trouble. [Because they were older they worried less about getting in trouble and the consequences of there actions than I did.]

Good point, makes it more unlikely that you should be the one to get caught

what other things did you do to get into trouble? Or is it irrelevant?

My friends and I would always come home from school, drop our backpacks off and head out in the neighborhood to find something to do. Our favorite thing to do was to find construction cites and steal wood to make tree forts in the woods or skateboard ramps. So one day, coming home from school, we noticed a couple new houses being built near our neighborhood. It was a prime cite for wood, nails, and anything else we could get our hands on. We discussed our plan on the bus and decided that we would all meet there after dropping our stuff off at home. [I remember being a little hesitant at first because it was close to my house but beyond the boundaries my parents had set for me. Of course I went because I didn't want to be the odd man out and have to put up with all the name calling.] I dropped my bad off and I headed to the construction cite.

great passage really lets the reader know what you were thinking

I meet my friends there and we began to search the different houses for wood and what not. We all picked up a couple of things and were about to leave when one of my friends noticed what looked to be a big tool shed off behind of the houses. It looked promising so we decided that we should check it out. Two of the boys in the group said they had all the wood they could carry and said they were going home. The rest of us headed down to the shed to take a look.

was there a reason you were there first or did it just happen that way?

Once there we noticed that the shed had been broken in to previously. The lock on it had been busted and the hinges were bent. I opened the door to the shed and stepped inside to take a look around while my friends waited outside. It was dark inside but I could tell the place had been ransacked, there was nothing to take so I decided to leave. I heard my friends say something so I turned back around to site of them running away.

I thought that they were playing a joke on me so I casually walked out one to see a cop car parked near one of the houses under construction. As soon as I saw that cop car I took off but was stopped when a big hand pulled at the back of my shirt. I watched my friends run until they were out of cite and then I turned around.

The cop had me sit in the cop car while he asked my questions. He asked me if I know those kids that ran off and I said "Nnnnnoooooooo". The cop asked me if I had broken into that shed and I said "Nnnnnoooooo". The cop wrote down what I was saying all the while shaking his head. Then he told me that I wasn't being arrested but I would have to go down to the station to call my parents and have them pick me up. Upon hearing that I nearly soiled my undershorts. "My God, I'm dead. My mom is going to kill me."

what else happened at the police station? how long were you there?

At the station the officer showed me the whole station, jail cells and everything. An obvious tactic to try and scare me, which worked. That plus the thought of my mom answering the phone and my trying to explain what happened nearly made me sick.

"Wwwwhhhaatttt? You're where?" She would say.

"The police station mom," uh oh, hear it comes.

"Ooooohhhh my God, my son is a criminal," so loud I would have to pull the phone away from my ear.

maybe you could say more as to why you think your mom is like this

She had this uncanny ability to blow things out of proportion right from the start. She would assume the worse and then go from there. This was a classic example of why I could never go to her if I had any bad news. She would start screaming, get upset, and then go bitch at my father. My father is a pretty laid back but when ever my mother started yelling at him about me, he would get angry and come chew me out worse than if I had just gone to him in the first place.

If my father were to answer the phone he would respond with out raising his voice. He would examine the situation in a logical manner and make a decision from there.

"Uhmmm (long pause). You're at the police station."

"Yeah dad. I didn't get arrested they just had me come down here so I had to tell you."

"Uhm, so you didn't get arrested (long pause). Well (long pause). I'll come pick you up and will talk about it then."

I like the way you use dialogue in this section to illustrate how each of your parents would react an then explain to the reader what each of them are like. It works well.

id your Dad
et into trouble
s a kid so he
nows what it's
ke? Explain
hy he reacts as
e does

I feel like I can relate to my father much better than I can to my mother. He has a cool and collective voice that can take command of any situation. I always feel like he understands me, like he knows what I'm thinking all the time. This comes in real handy when I get in trouble.

would he punish
you anyway
or could
you just get
away with
things

I called home. Sweat beading on my lip.

"Hello", my mom said. Oh geez, I'm dead.

"Mom can I talk to dad?"

"Why, what's wrong?"

"Oh nothing, I just need talk to him, yes, this is going to work!"

"Hold on," she said.

"Hello," my father said.

"Dad, I'm at the police station." I told him the whole story of what happened. He reacted exactly as I expect he would.

"Uhhmmm (long pause). You're at the police station...

really like the ending, it tells the reader what is going to happen without
aving to explain it step by step. Good paper, I like the use of dialogue.
erhaps more on your understanding of why your parents react as they do

Maybe you could say more as to why you think your mom is like this. Did you dad get into trouble as a kid so he know what it's like? Explain why he reacts as he does.

He is careful, though, not to get presumptuous and make decisions for the writer. Instead, he offers options and points to possibilities:

Perhaps more on your understanding of why your parents react as they do.
What other things did you do to get into trouble? Or is it irrelevant?

From start to finish he takes on the task of reading and responding and leaves the work of writing and revising to Todd.

Jeremy's response is not in a class by itself. A set of comments to end all commentary on Todd's paper. He might have done well, for instance, to recognize how much this paper works because of the way Todd arranges the story. He could have done more to point to what's not working in the writing or what could be made to work better. He might have asked Todd for more details about his state of mind when he got caught by the policeman and while he was being held at the police station. He might have urged him more to make certain changes. He might even have said, if only in a brief warning, something about the number of errors across the writing. But this is moot and just. Different readers are always going to pick up on different things and respond in different ways, and no one reading or response is going to address everything that might well be addressed, in the way it might best be addressed. All responses are incomplete and provisional—one reader's way of reading and reacting to the text in front of him. And any number of other responses, presented in any number of different ways, might be as useful or maybe even more useful to Todd as he takes up his work with the writing.

All this notwithstanding, Jeremy's comments are solid. They are full. They are thoughtful. And they are respectful. They take the writing and the writer seriously and address the issues that are raised responsibly. His comments do what commentary on student writing should optimally do. They turn the writer back into his writing and lead him to reflect on his choices and aims, to consider and reconsider his intentions as a writer and the effects the words on the page will have on readers. They help him see what he can work on in revision and what he might deal with in his ongoing work as a writer.

Letter from Birmingham Jail

Martin Luther King, Jr.

16 April 1963

My Dear Fellow Clergymen*:

While confined here in the Birmingham city jail, I came across your recent statement calling my present activities "unwise and untimely." Seldom do I pause to answer criticism of my work and ideas. If I sought to answer all the criticisms that cross my desk, my secretaries would have little time for anything other than such correspondence in the course of the day, and I would have no time for constructive work. But since I feel that you are men of genuine good will and that your criticisms are sincerely set forth, I want to try to answer your statement in what I hope will be patient and reasonable terms.

I think I should indicate why I am here in Birmingham, since you have been influenced by the view which argues against "outsiders coming in." I have the honor of serving as president of the Southern Christian Leadership Conference, an organization operating in every southern state, with headquarters in Atlanta, Georgia. We have some eighty five affiliated organizations across the South, and one of them is the Alabama Christian Movement for Human Rights. Frequently we share staff, educational and financial resources with our affiliates. Several months ago the affiliate here in Birmingham asked us to be on call to engage in a nonviolent direct action program if such were deemed necessary. We readily consented, and when the hour came we lived up to our promise. So I, along with several members of my staff, am here because I was invited here. I am here because I have organizational ties here.

But more basically, I am in Birmingham because injustice is here. Just as the prophets of the eighth century B.C. left their villages and carried their "thus saith the Lord" far beyond the boundaries of their home towns, and just as the Apostle Paul left his village of Tarsus and carried the gospel of Jesus Christ

---

* Highlighted areas are of particular interest as illustrations of particular forms of appeal that you may discuss in class.

to the far corners of the Greco Roman world, so am I compelled to carry the gospel of freedom beyond my own home town. Like Paul, I must constantly respond to the Macedonian call for aid.

Moreover, I am cognizant of the interrelatedness of all communities and states. I cannot sit idly by in Atlanta and not be concerned about what happens in Birmingham. Injustice anywhere is a threat to justice everywhere. We are caught in an inescapable network of mutuality, tied in a single garment of destiny. Whatever affects one directly, affects all indirectly. Never again can we afford to live with the narrow, provincial "outside agitator" idea. Anyone who lives inside the United States can never be considered an outsider anywhere within its bounds.

You deplore the demonstrations taking place in Birmingham. But your statement, I am sorry to say, fails to express a similar concern for the conditions that brought about the demonstrations. I am sure that none of you would want to rest content with the superficial kind of social analysis that deals merely with effects and does not grapple with underlying causes. It is unfortunate that demonstrations are taking place in Birmingham, but it is even more unfortunate that the city's white power structure left the Negro community with no alternative.

In any nonviolent campaign there are four basic steps: collection of the facts to determine whether injustices exist; negotiation; self purification; and direct action. We have gone through all these steps in Birmingham. There can be no gainsaying the fact that racial injustice engulfs this community. Birmingham is probably the most thoroughly segregated city in the United States. Its ugly record of brutality is widely known. Negroes have experienced grossly unjust treatment in the courts. There have been more unsolved bombings of Negro homes and churches in Birmingham than in any other city in the nation. These are the hard, brutal facts of the case. On the basis of these conditions, Negro leaders sought to negotiate with the city fathers. But the latter consistently refused to engage in good faith negotiation.

Then, last September, came the opportunity to talk with leaders of Birmingham's economic community. In the course of the negotiations, certain promises were made by the merchants—for example, to remove the stores' humiliating racial signs. On the basis of these promises, the Reverend Fred Shuttlesworth and the leaders of the Alabama Christian Movement for Human Rights agreed to a moratorium on all demonstrations. As the weeks and months went by, we realized that we were the victims of a broken promise. A few signs, briefly removed, returned; the others remained.

As in so many past experiences, our hopes had been blasted, and the shadow of deep disappointment settled upon us. We had no alternative except to prepare for direct action, whereby we would present our very bodies as a means of laying our case before the conscience of the local and the national community. Mindful of the difficulties involved, we decided to undertake a process of self purification. We began a series of workshops on nonviolence, and we repeatedly asked ourselves: "Are you able to accept blows without retaliating?" "Are you able to endure the ordeal of jail?" We decided to schedule our direct action program for the Easter season, realizing that except for Christmas, this is the main shopping period of the year. Knowing that a strong economic-withdrawal program would be the by product of direct action, we felt that this would be the best time to bring pressure to bear on the merchants for the needed change.

Then it occurred to us that Birmingham's mayoral election was coming up in March, and we speedily decided to postpone action until after election day. When we discovered that the Commissioner of Public Safety, Eugene "Bull" Connor, had piled up enough votes to be in the run off, we decided again to postpone action until the day after the run off so that the demonstrations could not be used to cloud the issues. Like many others, we waited to see Mr. Connor defeated, and to this end we endured postponement after postponement. Having aided in this community need, we felt that our direct action program could be delayed no longer.

You may well ask: "Why direct action? Why sit ins, marches and so forth? Isn't negotiation a better path?" You are quite right in calling for negotiation. Indeed, this is the very purpose of direct action. Nonviolent direct action seeks to create such a crisis and foster such a tension that a community which has constantly refused to negotiate is forced to confront the issue. It seeks so to dramatize the issue that it can no longer be ignored. My citing the creation of tension as part of the work of the nonviolent resister may sound rather shocking. But I must confess that I am not afraid of the word "tension." I have earnestly opposed violent tension, but there is a type of constructive, nonviolent tension which is necessary for growth. Just as Socrates felt that it was necessary to create a tension in the mind so that individuals could rise from the bondage of myths and half truths to the unfettered realm of creative analysis and objective appraisal, so must we see the need for nonviolent gadflies to create the kind of tension in society that will help men rise from the dark depths of prejudice and racism to the majestic heights of understanding and brotherhood.

The purpose of our direct action program is to create a situation so crisis packed that it will inevitably open the door to negotiation. I therefore concur with you in your call for negotiation. Too long has our beloved Southland been bogged down in a tragic effort to live in monologue rather than dialogue.

One of the basic points in your statement is that the action that I and my associates have taken in Birmingham is untimely. Some have asked: "Why didn't you give the new city administration time to act?" The only answer that I can give to this query is that the new Birmingham administration must be prodded about as much as the outgoing one, before it will act. We are sadly mistaken if we feel that the election of Albert Boutwell as mayor will bring the millennium to Birmingham. While Mr. Boutwell is a much more gentle person than Mr. Connor, they are both segregationists, dedicated to maintenance of the status quo. I have hope that Mr. Boutwell will be reasonable enough to see the futility of massive resistance to desegregation. But he will not see this without pressure from devotees of civil rights. My friends, I must say to you that we have not made a single gain in civil rights without determined legal and nonviolent pressure. Lamentably, it is an historical fact that privileged groups seldom give up their privileges voluntarily. Individuals may see the moral light and voluntarily give up their unjust posture; but, as Reinhold Niebuhr has reminded us, groups tend to be more immoral than individuals.

We know through painful experience that freedom is never voluntarily given by the oppressor; it must be demanded by the oppressed. Frankly, I have yet to engage in a direct action campaign that was "well timed" in the view of those who have not suffered unduly from the disease of segregation. For years now I have heard the word "Wait!" It rings in the ear of every Negro with piercing familiarity. This "Wait" has almost always meant "Never." We must come to see, with one of our distinguished jurists, that "justice too long delayed is justice denied."

We have waited for more than 340 years for our constitutional and God given rights. The nations of Asia and Africa are moving with jetlike speed toward gaining political independence, but we still creep at horse and buggy pace toward gaining a cup of coffee at a lunch counter. Perhaps it is easy for those who have never felt the stinging darts of segregation to say, "Wait." But when you have seen vicious mobs lynch your mothers and fathers at will and drown your sisters and brothers at whim; when you have seen hate filled policemen curse, kick and even kill your black brothers and sisters; when you see the vast majority of your twenty million Negro brothers smothering in an airtight cage of poverty in the midst of an affluent society; when you suddenly find your tongue twisted and your speech stammering as you seek to explain to your six year old daughter why she can't go to the public amusement park that has just been advertised on television, and see tears welling up in her eyes when she is told that Funtown is closed to colored children, and see ominous clouds of inferiority beginning to form in her little mental sky, and see her beginning to distort her personality by developing an unconscious bitterness toward white people; when you have to concoct an answer for a five year old son who is asking: "Daddy, why do white people treat colored people so mean?"; when you take a cross county drive and find it necessary to sleep night after night in the uncomfortable corners of your automobile because no motel will accept you; when you are humiliated day in and day out by nagging signs reading "white" and "colored"; when your first name becomes "nigger," your middle name becomes "boy" (however old you are) and your last name becomes "John," and your wife and mother are never given the respected title "Mrs."; when you are harried by day and haunted by night by the fact that you are a Negro, living constantly at tiptoe stance, never quite knowing what to expect next, and are plagued with inner fears and outer resentments; when you are forever fighting a degenerating sense of "nobodiness"—then you will understand why we find it difficult to wait. There comes a time when the cup of endurance runs over, and men are no longer willing to be plunged into the abyss of despair. I hope, sirs, you can understand our legitimate and unavoidable impatience.

You express a great deal of anxiety over our willingness to break laws. This is certainly a legitimate concern. Since we so diligently urge people to obey the Supreme Court's decision of 1954 outlawing segregation in the public schools, at first glance it may seem rather paradoxical for us consciously to break laws. One may well ask: "How can you advocate breaking some laws and obeying others?" The answer lies in the fact that there are two types of laws: just and unjust. I would be the first to advocate obeying just laws. One has not only a legal but a moral responsibility to obey just laws. Conversely, one has a moral responsibility to disobey unjust laws. I would agree with St. Augustine that "an unjust law is no law at all."

Now, what is the difference between the two? How does one determine whether a law is just or unjust? A just law is a man made code that squares with the moral law or the law of God. An unjust law is a code that is out of harmony with the moral law. To put it in the terms of St. Thomas Aquinas: An unjust law is a human law that is not rooted in eternal law and natural law. Any law that uplifts human personality is just. Any law that degrades human personality is unjust. All segregation statutes are unjust because segregation distorts the soul and damages the personality. It gives the segregator a false sense of superiority and the segregated a false sense of inferiority. Segregation, to use the terminology of the Jewish philosopher Martin Buber, substitutes an "I it" relationship for an "I thou" relationship and ends up relegating persons to the status of things. Hence segregation is not only politically, economically and sociologically unsound, it is morally wrong and sinful. Paul Tillich has said that sin is separation. Is not segregation an existential expression of man's tragic separation, his awful estrangement, his terrible sinfulness? Thus it is that I can urge men to obey the 1954 decision of the Supreme Court, for it is morally right; and I can urge them to disobey segregation ordinances, for they are morally wrong.

Let us consider a more concrete example of just and unjust laws. An unjust law is a code that a numerical or power majority group compels a minority group to obey but does not make binding on itself. This is difference made legal. By the same token, a just law is a code that a majority compels a minority to follow and that it is willing to follow itself. This is sameness made legal.

Let me give another explanation. A law is unjust if it is inflicted on a minority that, as a result of being denied the right to vote, had no part in enacting or devising the law. Who can say that the legislature of Alabama which set up that state's segregation laws was democratically elected? Throughout Alabama all sorts of devious methods are used to prevent Negroes from becoming registered voters, and there are some counties in which, even though Negroes constitute a majority of the population, not a single Negro is registered. Can any law enacted under such circumstances be considered democratically structured?

Sometimes a law is just on its face and unjust in its application. For instance, I have been arrested on a charge of parading without a permit. Now, there is nothing wrong in having an ordinance which requires a permit for a parade. But such an ordinance becomes unjust when it is used to maintain segregation and to deny citizens the First-Amendment privilege of peaceful assembly and protest.

I hope you are able to see the distinction I am trying to point out. In no sense do I advocate evading or defying the law, as would the rabid segregationist. That would lead to anarchy. One who breaks an unjust law must do so openly, lovingly, and with a willingness to accept the penalty. I submit that an individual who breaks a law that conscience tells him is unjust, and who willingly accepts the penalty of imprisonment in order to arouse the conscience of the community over its injustice, is in reality expressing the highest respect for law.

Of course, there is nothing new about this kind of civil disobedience. It was evidenced sublimely in the refusal of Shadrach, Meshach and Abednego to obey the laws of Nebuchadnezzar, on the ground that a higher moral law was at stake. It was practiced superbly by the early Christians, who were willing to face hungry lions and the excruciating pain of chopping blocks rather than submit to certain unjust laws of the Roman Empire. To a degree, academic freedom is a reality today because Socrates practiced civil disobedience. In our own nation, the Boston Tea Party represented a massive act of civil disobedience.

We should never forget that everything Adolf Hitler did in Germany was "legal" and everything the Hungarian freedom fighters did in Hungary was "illegal." It was "illegal" to aid and comfort a Jew in Hitler's Germany. Even so, I am sure that, had I lived in Germany at the time, I would have aided and comforted my Jewish brothers. If today I lived in a Communist country where certain principles dear to the Christian faith are suppressed, I would openly advocate disobeying that country's antireligious laws.

I must make two honest confessions to you, my Christian and Jewish brothers. First, I must confess that over the past few years I have been gravely disappointed with the white moderate. I have almost reached the regrettable conclusion that the Negro's great stumbling block in his stride toward freedom is not the White Citizen's Counciler or the Ku Klux Klanner, but the white moderate, who is more devoted to "order" than to justice; who prefers a negative peace which is the absence of tension to a positive peace which is the presence of justice; who constantly says: "I agree with you in the goal you seek, but I cannot agree with your methods of direct action"; who paternalistically believes he can set the timetable for another man's freedom; who lives by a mythical concept of time and who constantly advises the Negro to wait for a "more convenient season." Shallow understanding from people of good will is more frustrating than absolute misunderstanding from people of ill will. Lukewarm acceptance is much more bewildering than outright rejection.

I had hoped that the white moderate would understand that law and order exist for the purpose of establishing justice and that when they fail in this purpose they become the dangerously structured dams that block the flow of social progress. I had hoped that the white moderate would understand that the present tension in the South is a necessary phase of the transition from an obnoxious negative peace, in which the Negro passively accepted his unjust plight, to a substantive and positive peace, in which all men will respect the dignity and worth of human personality. Actually, we who engage in nonviolent direct action are not the creators of tension. We merely bring to the surface the hidden tension that is already alive. We bring it out in the open, where it can be seen and dealt with. Like a boil that can never be cured so long as it is covered up but must be opened with all its ugliness to the natural medicines of air and light, injustice must be exposed, with all the tension its exposure creates, to the light of human conscience and the air of national opinion before it can be cured.

In your statement you assert that our actions, even though peaceful, must be condemned because they precipitate violence. But is this a logical assertion? Isn't this like condemning a robbed man because his possession of money precipitated the evil act of robbery? Isn't this like condemning Socrates because his unswerving commitment to truth and his philosophical inquiries precipitated the act by the misguided populace in which they made him drink hemlock? Isn't this like condemning Jesus because his unique God consciousness and never ceasing devotion to God's will precipitated the evil act of crucifixion? We must come to see that, as the federal courts have consistently affirmed, it is wrong to urge an individual to cease his efforts to gain his basic constitutional rights because the quest may precipitate violence. Society must protect the robbed and punish the robber.

I had also hoped that the white moderate would reject the myth concerning time in relation to the struggle for freedom. I have just received a letter from a white brother in Texas. He writes: "All Christians know that the colored people will receive equal rights eventually, but it is possible that you are in too great a religious hurry. It has taken Christianity almost two thousand years to accomplish what it has. The teachings of Christ take time to come to earth." Such an attitude stems from a tragic misconception of time, from the strangely irrational notion that there is something in the very flow of time that will inevitably cure all ills. Actually, time itself is neutral; it can be used either destructively or constructively. More and more I feel that the people of ill will have used time much more effectively than have the people of good will. We will have to repent in this generation not merely for the hateful words and actions of the bad people but for the appalling silence of the good people. Human progress never rolls in on wheels of inevitability; it comes through the tireless efforts of men willing to be co workers with God, and without this hard work, time itself becomes an ally of the forces of social stagnation. We must use time creatively, in the knowledge that the time is always ripe to do right. Now is the time to make real the promise of democracy and transform our pending national elegy into a creative psalm of brotherhood. Now is the time to lift our national policy from the quicksand of racial injustice to the solid rock of human dignity.

You speak of our activity in Birmingham as extreme. At first I was rather disappointed that fellow clergymen would see my nonviolent efforts as those of an extremist. I began thinking about the fact that I stand in the middle of two opposing forces in the Negro community. One is a force of complacency, made up in part of Negroes who, as a result of long years of oppression, are so drained of self respect and a sense of "somebodiness" that they have adjusted to segregation; and in part of a few middle-class Negroes who, because of a degree of academic and economic security and because in some ways they profit by segregation, have become insensitive to the problems of the masses. The other force is one of bitterness and hatred, and it comes perilously close to advocating violence. It is expressed in the various black nationalist groups that are springing up across the nation, the largest and best known being Elijah Muhammad's Muslim movement. Nourished by the Negro's frustration over the continued existence of racial discrimination, this movement is made up of people who have lost faith in America, who have absolutely repudiated Christianity, and who have concluded that the white man is an incorrigible "devil."

I have tried to stand between these two forces, saying that we need emulate neither the "do nothingism" of the complacent nor the hatred and despair of the black nationalist. For there is the more excellent way of love and nonviolent protest. I am grateful to God that, through the influence of the Negro church, the way of nonviolence became an integral part of our struggle.

If this philosophy had not emerged, by now many streets of the South would, I am convinced, be flowing with blood. And I am further convinced that if our white brothers dismiss as "rabble rousers" and "outside agitators" those of us who employ nonviolent direct action, and if they refuse to support our nonviolent efforts, millions of Negroes will, out of frustration and despair, seek solace and security in black nationalist ideologies—a development that would inevitably lead to a frightening racial nightmare.

Oppressed people cannot remain oppressed forever. The yearning for freedom eventually manifests itself, and that is what has happened to the American Negro. Something within has reminded him of his birthright of freedom, and something without has reminded him that it can be gained. Consciously or un-consciously, he has been caught up by the Zeitgeist, and with his black brothers of Africa and his brown and yellow brothers of Asia, South America and the Caribbean, the United States Negro is moving with a sense of great urgency toward the promised land of racial justice. If one recognizes this vital urge that has engulfed the Negro community, one should readily understand why public demonstrations are taking place. The Negro has many pent up resentments and latent frustrations, and he must release them. So let him march; let him make prayer pilgrimages to the city hall; let him go on freedom rides -and try to understand why he must do so. If his repressed emotions are not released in nonviolent ways, they will seek expression through violence; this is not a threat but a fact of history. So I have not said to my people: "Get rid of your discon-tent." Rather, I have tried to say that this normal and healthy discontent can be channeled into the creative outlet of nonviolent direct action. And now this approach is being termed extremist.

But though I was initially disappointed at being categorized as an extremist, as I continued to think about the matter I gradually gained a measure of satisfac-tion from the label. Was not Jesus an extremist for love: "Love your enemies, bless them that curse you, do good to them that hate you, and pray for them which despitefully use you, and persecute you." Was not Amos an extremist for justice: "Let justice roll down like waters and righteousness like an ever flow-ing stream." Was not Paul an extremist for the Christian gospel: "I bear in my body the marks of the Lord Jesus." Was not Martin Luther an extremist: "Here I stand; I cannot do otherwise, so help me God." And John Bunyan: "I will stay in jail to the end of my days before I make a butchery of my conscience." And

Abraham Lincoln: "This nation cannot survive half slave and half free." And Thomas Jefferson: "We hold these truths to be self evident, that all men are created equal . . ." So the question is not whether we will be extremists, but what kind of extremists we will be. Will we be extremists for hate or for love? Will we be extremists for the preservation of injustice or for the extension of justice? In that dramatic scene on Calvary's hill three men were crucified. We must never forget that all three were crucified for the same crime—the crime of extremism. Two were extremists for immorality, and thus fell below their environment. The other, Jesus Christ, was an extremist for love, truth and goodness, and thereby rose above his environment. Perhaps the South, the nation and the world are in dire need of creative extremists.

I had hoped that the white moderate would see this need. Perhaps I was too optimistic; perhaps I expected too much. I suppose I should have realized that few members of the oppressor race can understand the deep groans and passionate yearnings of the oppressed race, and still fewer have the vision to see that injustice must be rooted out by strong, persistent and determined action. I am thankful, however, that some of our white brothers in the South have grasped the meaning of this social revolution and committed themselves to it. They are still all too few in quantity, but they are big in quality. Some -such as Ralph McGill, Lillian Smith, Harry Golden, James McBride Dabbs, Ann Braden and Sarah Patton Boyle—have written about our struggle in eloquent and prophetic terms. Others have marched with us down nameless streets of the South. They have languished in filthy, roach infested jails, suffering the abuse and brutality of policemen who view them as "dirty nigger-lovers."

Unlike so many of their moderate brothers and sisters, they have recognized the urgency of the moment and sensed the need for powerful "action" antidotes to combat the disease of segregation. Let me take note of my other major disappointment. I have been so greatly disappointed with the white church and its leadership. Of course, there are some notable exceptions. I am not unmindful of the fact that each of you has taken some significant stands on this issue. I commend you, Reverend Stallings, for your Christian stand on this past Sunday, in welcoming Negroes to your worship service on a nonsegregated basis. I commend the Catholic leaders of this state for integrating Spring Hill College several years ago.

But despite these notable exceptions, I must honestly reiterate that I have been disappointed with the church. I do not say this as one of those negative critics who can always find something wrong with the church. I say this as a minister of the gospel, who loves the church; who was nurtured in its bosom; who has been sustained by its spiritual blessings and who will remain true to it as long as the cord of life shall lengthen.

When I was suddenly catapulted into the leadership of the bus protest in Montgomery, Alabama, a few years ago, I felt we would be supported by the white church. I felt that the white ministers, priests and rabbis of the South would be among our strongest allies. Instead, some have been outright opponents, refusing to understand the freedom movement and misrepresenting its leaders; all too many others have been more cautious than courageous and have remained silent behind the anesthetizing security of stained glass windows.

In spite of my shattered dreams, I came to Birmingham with the hope that the white religious leadership of this community would see the justice of our cause and, with deep moral concern, would serve as the channel through which our just grievances could reach the power structure. I had hoped that each of you would understand. But again I have been disappointed.

I have heard numerous southern religious leaders admonish their worshipers to comply with a desegregation decision because it is the law, but I have longed to hear white ministers declare: "Follow this decree because integration is morally right and because the Negro is your brother." In the midst of blatant injustices inflicted upon the Negro, I have watched white churchmen stand on the sideline and mouth pious irrelevancies and sanctimonious trivialities. In the midst of a mighty struggle to rid our nation of racial and economic injustice, I have heard many ministers say: "Those are social issues, with which the gospel has no real concern." And I have watched many churches commit themselves to a completely other worldly religion which makes a strange, un-Biblical distinction between body and soul, between the sacred and the secular.

I have traveled the length and breadth of Alabama, Mississippi and all the other southern states. On sweltering summer days and crisp autumn mornings I have looked at the South's beautiful churches with their lofty spires pointing heavenward. I have beheld the impressive outlines of her massive religious education buildings. Over and over I have found myself asking: "What kind of people worship here? Who is their God? Where were their voices when the lips of Governor Barnett dripped with words of interposition and nullification? Where were they when Governor Wallace gave a clarion call for defiance and hatred? Where were their voices of support when bruised and weary Negro men and women decided to rise from the dark dungeons of complacency to the bright hills of creative protest?"

Yes, these questions are still in my mind. In deep disappointment I have wept over the laxity of the church. But be assured that my tears have been tears of love. There can be no deep disappointment where there is not deep love. Yes, I love the church. How could I do otherwise? I am in the rather unique position of being the son, the grandson and the great grandson of preachers. Yes, I see the church as the body of Christ. But, oh! How we have blemished and scarred that body through social neglect and through fear of being nonconformists.

There was a time when the church was very powerful—in the time when the early Christians rejoiced at being deemed worthy to suffer for what they believed. In those days the church was not merely a thermometer that recorded the ideas and principles of popular opinion; it was a thermostat that transformed the mores of society. Whenever the early Christians entered a town, the people in power became disturbed and immediately sought to convict the Christians for being "disturbers of the peace" and "outside agitators.'" But the Christians pressed on, in the conviction that they were "a colony of heaven," called to obey God rather than man. Small in number, they were big in commitment. They were too God-intoxicated to be "astronomically intimidated." By their effort and example they brought an end to such ancient evils as infanticide and gladiatorial contests.

Things are different now. So often the contemporary church is a weak, ineffectual voice with an uncertain sound. So often it is an archdefender of the status quo. Far from being disturbed by the presence of the church, the power structure of the average community is consoled by the church's silent—and often even vocal—sanction of things as they are.

But the judgment of God is upon the church as never before. If today's church does not recapture the sacrificial spirit of the early church, it will lose its authenticity, forfeit the loyalty of millions, and be dismissed as an irrelevant social club with no meaning for the twentieth century. Every day I meet young people whose disappointment with the church has turned into outright disgust.

Perhaps I have once again been too optimistic. Is organized religion too inextricably bound to the status quo to save our nation and the world? Perhaps I must turn my faith to the inner spiritual church, the church within the church, as the true ekklesia and the hope of the world. But again I am thankful to God that some noble souls from the ranks of organized religion have broken loose from the paralyzing chains of conformity and joined us as active partners in the struggle for freedom. They have left their secure congregations and walked the streets of Albany, Georgia, with us. They have gone down the highways of the South on tortuous rides for freedom. Yes, they have gone to jail with us. Some have been dismissed from their churches, have lost the support of their bishops and fellow ministers. But they have acted in the faith that right defeated is stronger than evil triumphant. Their witness has been the spiritual salt that has preserved the true meaning of the gospel in these troubled times. They have carved a tunnel of hope through the dark mountain of disappointment.

I hope the church as a whole will meet the challenge of this decisive hour. But even if the church does not come to the aid of justice, I have no despair about the future. I have no fear about the outcome of our struggle in Birmingham, even if our motives are at present misunderstood. We will reach the goal of freedom in Birmingham and all over the nation, because the goal of America is freedom. Abused and scorned though we may be, our destiny is tied up with America's destiny. Before the pilgrims landed at Plymouth, we were here. Before the pen of Jefferson etched the majestic words of the Declaration of Independence across the pages of history, we were here. For more than two centuries our forebears labored in this country without wages; they made cotton king; they built the homes of their masters while suffering gross injustice and shameful humiliation -and yet out of a bottomless vitality they continued to thrive and develop. If the inexpressible cruelties of slavery could not stop us, the opposition we now face will surely fail. We will win our freedom because the sacred heritage of our nation and the eternal will of God are embodied in our echoing demands.

Before closing I feel impelled to mention one other point in your statement that has troubled me profoundly. You warmly commended the Birmingham police force for keeping "order" and "preventing violence." I doubt that you would have so warmly commended the police force if you had seen its dogs sinking their teeth into unarmed, nonviolent Negroes. I doubt that you would so quickly commend the policemen if you were to observe their ugly and inhumane treatment of Negroes here in the city jail; if you were to watch them push and curse old Negro women and young Negro girls; if you were to see them slap and kick old Negro men and young boys; if you were to observe them, as they did on two occasions, refuse to give us food because we wanted to sing our grace together. I cannot join you in your praise of the Birmingham police department.

It is true that the police have exercised a degree of discipline in handling the demonstrators. In this sense they have conducted themselves rather "nonviolently" in public. But for what purpose? To preserve the evil system of segregation. Over the past few years I have consistently preached that nonviolence demands that the means we use must be as pure as the ends we seek. I have tried to make clear that it is wrong to use immoral means to attain moral ends. But now I must affirm that it is just as wrong, or perhaps even more so, to use moral means to preserve immoral ends. Perhaps Mr. Connor and his policemen have been rather nonviolent in public, as was Chief Pritchett in Albany, Georgia, but they have used the moral means of nonviolence to maintain the immoral end of racial injustice. As T. S. Eliot has said: "The last temptation is the greatest treason: To do the right deed for the wrong reason."

I wish you had commended the Negro sit inners and demonstrators of Birmingham for their sublime courage, their willingness to suffer and their amazing discipline in the midst of great provocation. One day the South will recognize its real heroes. They will be the James Merediths, with the noble sense of purpose that enables them to face jeering and hostile mobs, and with the agonizing loneliness that characterizes the life of the pioneer. They will be old, oppressed, battered Negro women, symbolized in a seventy two year old woman in Montgomery, Alabama, who rose up with a sense of dignity and with her people decided not to ride segregated buses, and who responded with ungrammatical profundity to one who inquired about her weariness: "My feets is tired, but my soul is at rest." They will be the young high school and college students, the young ministers of the gospel and a host of their elders, courageously and nonviolently sitting in at lunch counters and willingly going to jail for conscience' sake. One day the South will know that when these disinherited children of God sat down at lunch counters, they were in reality standing up for what is best in the American dream and for the most sacred values in our Judaeo Christian heritage, thereby bringing our nation back to those great wells of democracy which were dug deep by the founding fathers in their formulation of the Constitution and the Declaration of Independence.

Never before have I written so long a letter. I'm afraid it is much too long to take your precious time. I can assure you that it would have been much shorter if I had been writing from a comfortable desk, but what else can one do when he is alone in a narrow jail cell, other than write long letters, think long thoughts and pray long prayers?

If I have said anything in this letter that overstates the truth and indicates an unreasonable impatience, I beg you to forgive me. If I have said anything that understates the truth and indicates my having a patience that allows me to settle for anything less than brotherhood, I beg God to forgive me.

I hope this letter finds you strong in the faith. I also hope that circumstances will soon make it possible for me to meet each of you, not as an integrationist or a civil-rights leader but as a fellow clergyman and a Christian brother. Let us all hope that the dark clouds of racial prejudice will soon pass away and the deep fog of misunderstanding will be lifted from our fear drenched communities, and in some not too distant tomorrow the radiant stars of love and brotherhood will shine over our great nation with all their scintillating beauty.

Yours for the cause of Peace and Brotherhood,

Martin Luther King, Jr.

Shitty First Drafts

Anne Lamott

Bird by Bird, 1995

Now, practically even better news than that of short assignments is the idea of shitty first drafts. All good writers write them. This is how they end up with good second drafts and terrific third drafts. People tend to look at successful writers, writers who are getting their books published and maybe even doing well financially, and think that they sit down at their desks every morning feeling like a million dollars, feeling great about who they are and how much talent they have and what a great story they have to tell; that they take in a few deep breaths, push back their sleeves, roll their necks a few times to get all the cricks out, and dive in, typing fully formed passages as fast as a court reporter. But this is just the fantasy of the uninitiated. I know some very great writers, writers you love who write beautifully and have made a great deal of money, and not one of them sits down routinely feeling wildly enthusiastic and confident. Not one of them writes elegant first drafts. All right, one of them does, but we do not like her very much. We do not think that she has a rich inner life or that God likes her or can even stand her. (Although when I mentioned this to my priest friend Tom, he said you can safely assume you've created God in your own image when it turns out that God hates all the same people you do.)

Very few writers really know what they are doing until they've done it. Nor do they go about their business feeling dewy and thrilled. They do not type a few stiff warm-up sentences and then find themselves bounding along like huskies across the snow. One writer I know tells me that he sits down every morning and says to himself nicely, "It's not like you don't have a choice, because you do—you can either type or kill yourself." We all often feel like we are pulling teeth, even those writers whose prose ends up being the most natural and fluid. The right words and sentences just do not come pouring out like ticker tape most of the time. Now, Muriel Spark is said to have felt that she was taking dictation from God every morning—sitting there, one supposes, plugged into a Dictaphone, typing away, humming. But this is a very hostile and aggressive position. One might hope for bad things to rain down on a person like this.

For me and most of the other writers I know, writing is not rapturous. In fact, the only way I can get anything written at all is to write really, really shitty first drafts. The first draft is the child's draft, where you let it all pour out and then let it romp all over the place, knowing that no one is going to see it and that you can shape it later. You just let this childlike part of you channel whatever voices and visions come through and onto the page. If one of the characters wants to say, "Well, so what, Mr. Poopy Pants?," you let her. No one is going to see it. If the kid wants to get into really sentimental, weepy, emotional territory, you let him. Just get it all down on paper, because there may be something great in those six crazy pages that you would never have gotten to by more rational, grown-up means. There may be something in the very last line of the very last paragraph on page six that you just love, that is so beautiful or wild that you now know what you're supposed to be writing about, more or less, or in what direction you might go—but there was no way to get to this without first getting through the first five and a half pages.

I used to write food reviews for *California* magazine before it folded. (My writing food reviews had nothing to do with the magazine folding, although every single review did cause a couple of canceled subscriptions. Some readers took umbrage at my comparing mounds of vegetable puree with various ex-presidents' brains.) These reviews always took two days to write. First I'd go to a restaurant several times with a few opinionated, articulate friends in tow. I'd sit there writing down everything anyone said that was at all interesting or funny. Then on the following Monday I'd sit down at my desk with my notes, and try to write the review. Even after I'd been doing this for years, panic would set in. I'd try to write a lead, but instead I'd write a couple of dreadful sentences, xx them out, try again, xx everything out, and then feel despair and worry settle on my chest like an x-ray apron. It's over, I'd think, calmly. I'm not going to be able to get the magic to work this time. I'm ruined. I'm through. I'm toast. Maybe, I'd think, I can get my old job back as a clerk-typist. But probably not. I'd get up and study my teeth in the mirror for a while. Then I'd stop, remember to breathe, make a few phone calls, hit the kitchen and chow down. Eventually I'd go back and sit down at my desk, and sigh for the next ten minutes.

Finally I would pick up my one-inch picture frame, stare into it as if for the answer, and every time the answer would come: all I had to do was to write a really shitty first draft of, say, the opening paragraph. And no one was going to see it. So I'd start writing without reining myself in. It was almost just typing, just making my fingers move. And the writing would be terrible. I'd write a lead paragraph that was a whole page, even though the entire review could only be three pages long, and then I'd start writing up descriptions of the food, one dish at a time, bird by bird, and the critics would be sitting on my shoulders, commenting like cartoon characters. They'd be pretending to snore, or rolling their eyes at my overwrought descriptions, no matter how hard I tried to tone those descriptions down, no matter how conscious I was of what a friend said to me gently in my early days of restaurant reviewing. "Annie," she said, "it is just a piece of *chicken*. It is just a bit of *cake*."

But because by then I had been writing for so long, I would eventually let myself trust the process—sort of, more or less. I'd write a first draft that was maybe twice as long as it should be, with a self-indulgent and boring beginning, stupefying descriptions of the meal, lots of quotes from my black-humored friends that made them sound more like the Manson girls than food lovers, and no ending to speak of. The whole thing would be so long and incoherent and hideous that for the rest of the day I'd obsess about getting creamed by a car before I could write a decent second draft. I'd worry that people would read what I'd written and believe that the accident had really been a suicide, that I had panicked because my talent was waning and my mind was shot.

The next day, though, I'd sit down, go through it all with a colored pen, take out everything I possibly could, find a new lead somewhere on the second page, figure out a kicky place to end it, and then write a second draft. It always turned out fine, sometimes even funny and weird and helpful. I'd go over it one more time and mail it in. Then, a month later, when it was time for another review, the whole process would start again, complete with the fears that people would find my first draft before I could rewrite it.

Almost all good writing begins with terrible first efforts. You need to start somewhere. Start by getting something—anything—down on paper. A friend of mine says that the first draft is the down draft—you just get it down. The second draft is the up draft—you fix it up. You try to say what you have to say more accurately. And the third draft is the dental draft, where you check every tooth, to see if it's loose or cramped or decayed, or even, God help us, healthy.

What I've learned to do when I sit down to work on a shitty first draft is to quiet the voices in my head. First there's the vinegar-lipped Reader Lady, who says primly, "Well, that's not very interesting, is it?" And there's the emaciated German male who writes these Orwellian memos detailing your thought crimes. And there are your parents, agonizing over your lack of loyalty and discretion; and there's William Burroughs, dozing off or shooting up because he finds you as bold and articulate as a houseplant; and so on. And there are also the dogs; let's not forget the dogs, the dogs in their pen who will surely hurtle and snarl their way out if you ever stop writing, because writing is, for some of us, the latch that keeps the door of the pen closed, keeps those crazy ravenous dogs contained.

Quieting those voices is at least half the battle I fight daily. But this is better than it used to be. It used to be 87 percent. Left to its own devices, my mind spends much of its time having conversations with people who aren't there. I walk along defending myself to people, or exchanging repartee with them, or rationalizing my behavior, or seducing them with gossip, or pretending I'm on their TV talk show or whatever. I speed or run an aging yellow light or don't come to a full stop, and one nanosecond later am explaining to imaginary cops exactly why I had to do what I did, or insisting that I did not in fact do it.

I happened to mention this to a hypnotist I saw many years ago, and he looked at me very nicely. At first I thought he was feeling around on the floor for the silent alarm button, but then he gave me the following exercise, which I still use to this day. Close your eyes and get quiet for a minute, until the chatter starts up. Then isolate one of the voices and imagine the person speaking as a mouse. Pick it up by the tail and drop it into a mason jar. Then isolate another voice, pick it up by the tail, drop it in the jar. And so on. Drop in any high-maintenance parental units, drop in any contractors, lawyers, colleagues, children, anyone who is whining in your head. Then put the lid on, and watch all these mouse people clawing at the glass, jabbering away, trying to make you feel like shit because you won't do what they want—won't give them more money, won't be more successful, won't see them more often. Then imagine that there is a volume-control button on the bottle. Turn it all the way up for a moment, and listen to the stream of angry, neglected, guilt-mongering voices. Then turn it all the way down and watch the frantic mice lunge at the glass, trying to get to you. Leave it down, and get back to your shitty first draft.

A writer friend of mine suggests opening the jar and shooting them all in the head. But I think he's a little angry, and I'm sure nothing like this would ever occur to you.

Beyond Black and White: Document Design and Formatting in the Writing Classroom

Martin J. Klein and Kristi L. Shackleford

Writing in Spaces, 2011

You've received your first assignment in a college writing course[1] You've created an outline, done the necessary research, and written a first draft of your paper. Now it's time for you to revise your work so you can submit the paper. However, writing a paper for a course involves more than simply generating content and turning it into your instructor. Equally important as the words you write is how the appearance of your document influences the way readers interpret your ideas.

Most people think of design as the arrangement of images on the page. This is only half true: Graphics can convey concepts that you can't express in writing. If you were writing an article about an oil spill and the damage it caused, one powerful photograph could make your point more persuasively than pages of writing. Good document design integrates the words on the page with appropriate imagery to fully illustrate your meaning. An image of the Deep Horizon oil spill won't have the same impact if the image isn't coupled with a sentence about the scope of the spill.

An often-overlooked element of design is the visual treatment of text itself. In this definition of text, text does not include your word choice or the structure of your argument. Instead, it refers to the look of the words on the page. Are all the fonts the same? Are key ideas written in a text larger than other text? Are some words in bold? All of these choices influence the way your document looks and is perceived by your readers. Depending on the type of paper your instructor has assigned and the preparation rules or style guide required, subtle variations in text might be your only design option.

In a typical first year writing course, you'll be focusing—of course—on writing. If the intent of writing is to communicate an idea, the way you present your writing is also important. You can greatly improve a standard research paper on climate change with the addition of an image showing differences in ice caps over a period of years. You can strengthen data supporting your position in an opinion paper if you present it in a graph rather than a narrative format. However, include graphics in written assignments with care: they should supplement, not replace, your writing. When you are creating, don't think of design features as only images. Remember that visual design applies to the style of the text you use to convey ideas. The remainder of this chapter focuses on the use of text as a design element.

What You Should Know about Design Choices and Elements

You can talk about design in a multitude of ways. What some designers call white space, for example, others call negative space. In both cases, they are referring to areas of a page free from text or objects, such as the white space that makes up the margins around the text of this paragraph. A designer may talk about the use of alignment in a design, while someone else will describe how textual elements "line up" on a page. All theories and methods of design include the same basic ideas, just expressed in different terms. The names of elements on a page are much less important than their function. The definitions below will help you understand the way we use these terms.

Text and Type

Typeface refers to the look of your text. It typically includes the font family (e.g., Times New Roman), the type size (e.g., 12 point) and type emphasis (e.g., bold). Spacing is the amount of space around a line of text within a document. The amount of space between lines of text is called leading (pronounced *led*) or line spacing. Leading is typically the size of the font plus two points. For example, standard leading for 12-point type is 14 points, indicated as 12/14 point: this paragraph uses 11 point Adobe Garamond Pro with 13.2 point leading. Increasing the amount of leading, or size of line spacing, can increase readability. Large amounts of text are often set with a leading of twice the text (12/24 point), also called double-spacing.

Images

The visual elements of a design range from simple boxes to the use of color photographs. Designers often use the term "images" to refer to the wide range of visual elements available—photographs, line drawings, technical illustrations, graphs, charts, and so on. Not all images are appropriate for all uses. A color photo of the beach, for instance, may have more persuasive power than a black-and-white drawing because the photograph evokes a more complete and personal reaction. A technical illustration that allows a reader to see the inside of a device can demonstrate the proper assembly of equipment in more detail than an actual photograph. In some cases, though, images can distract from the meaning of your text. You should not include random clip art of a tree, for example, to supplement a paper on the importance of environmental sustainability. In contrast, you may strengthen your position on environmental sustainability with a graph showing the cumulative effects of non-recycled materials.

Design Elements

Like the combination of text and images, the integration of four key design elements—Contrast, Repetition, Alignment, and Proximity—gives a design power. You can remember these elements by the acronym CRAP. Don't let the name influence you, though—following these principles is one of the best ways to ensure your document looks its best. It is sometimes difficult to differentiate among these concepts because they influence each other.

Contrast

Contrast refers to the visual differences in elements on a page. These differences highlight the significance of the individual items, as well as draw the reader's attention to different areas of a page. In a magazine layout, for example, the largest photograph is more noticeable because of its larger size in comparison to others on a spread. Color in a design can also provide noticeable contrast.

In text, you see contrast through different uses of formatting options. This might include choosing different typefaces to visually separate headings from your main text. Contrast may also be visible in the differing sizes or emphasis applied to a text. If you apply bold formatting to keywords in your document, they stand out from others and indicate that they are significant. If every other word in your document is bold, however, the effect of the contrast is lost. A similar effect occurs when you overuse a highlighter when marking a textbook: important information gets lost rather than being easier to find.

Look at the first page of this chapter. You can immediately see the name "Beyond Black and White" and recognize that it is the title of the chapter. Your eye is immediately drawn to it because it is the biggest item on the page. Just below the title, the authors' names are in smaller, bold text. The contrast between the size and emphasis in the two lines of text quickly illustrates that they are providing different information.

Repetition

Repetition involves the use of consistency to visually group multiple items that express similar ideas or are somehow related. You can apply this design element to graphics, including the use of shapes and color. For example, many of your textbooks may include a section summarizing key ideas from the text. By placing all summaries in a similarly shaped box or highlighted by the same color, you can tell that these items have something in common. Once you realize that all summaries in your political science textbook are in green boxes, you can find them at a glance.

You can apply repetition simply by formatting text in different ways. When you look at a restaurant menu, you'll see that the larger categories—like "Appetizers" and "Desserts"—are presented in the same font and size as each other, which is different from the listing of the food items themselves. This repeated format shows that those categories are equivalent. It also indicates that a new section is beginning, as do the headings that divide sections of this chapter. In papers written for a class, you express repetition in text primarily through placement, such as always putting page numbers in the same place on the page. On a Works Cited page, the organization of citation materials (such as the author's name and book title) makes information easier to locate. Repetition makes your intent more obvious to readers.

Repetition lets you quickly glance through this book and find information, even in sections you haven't already read. To find the first page of a chapter, you look for a large title with lots of white space above it. If you're looking for a specific page in the book, you know to look at the outside corners to locate the page numbers.

Alignment

In design, alignment refers to the placement of elements on a page. While everything on a page is aligned in that it has been placed somewhere, some alignment strategies are better than others. You can think of it as asking a sick friend, "Do you have a temperature?" Of course, everyone has a temperature; what you're asking is if your friend has an elevated or abnormal temperature. In the same way, when document designers talk about alignment, they typically mean consistent alignment. For example, text that is left justified or graphics that run along the edge of the page are considered properly aligned.

Aligning elements creates a cleaner, more attractive design and emphasizes the consistency of information on a page. Alignment also helps readers access and process information in a publication. Appropriately aligned text clarifies for the reader where ideas begin and end. It also increases readability by allowing the reader's eye to return to a consistent location on the page while reading. Breaking the alignment scheme is also a valuable design tool. When a block quote is indented, it is quickly apparent that the text has a slightly different meaning than the text above and below it.

The text alignment throughout this chapter indicates when a topic is changing and how a large piece of text (the chapter) can be broken into smaller chunks (the sections). Main headings within the text are centered over justified body text. To find the idea you're looking for, you can look for the centered text and know that a new idea is being introduced.

Proximity

Proximity is the grouping of elements that have something in common. Often a layout involves a single idea, and the designer uses the entire page to place thematically related text and graphics. When multiple ideas are included on a single page, the reader can tell which are related based on how close—or how far—they are from each other. An obvious example is a box including a photo and its caption.

In academic writing and formatting, the placement of text often illustrates proximity. You place headings that identify the content of a section directly above that section, cuing the reader to a shift. This proximity also allows readers to quickly find related information based on the heading of a section.

Look at the image labeled as Fig. 1. As soon as you see the graphic, you can look immediately below it, see what it is named and why it is included. What if that label was on the next page? Placing related elements together is an efficient way to make sure they are properly understood.

For More Information

Design texts aren't just for professional designers! You can find examples of the principles discussed here in a variety of design books. Look for a basic book that covers designing with images and text to learn more. A good one to start with is Robin Williams *Non-Designer's Design Book*; many of the ideas in this chapter are based on ones presented in her book.

How You Can Apply These Design Principles

Incorporating design principles into a publication has an immediate and compelling effect. Even text-heavy documents, such as academic papers or resumes, become more appealing and comprehensible with even minor restructuring.

Mathew J. Kraft
225 Ingram Road
Harrisonburg, VA 22807
kraft@hotmail.com
555-555-4321

Education 2008 – Bachelor of Arts, University of Arizona, Tucson, AZ Major:
Creative Writing Minor: Political Science
Courses: Creative Writing Workshop, Genre Theories, Technology and Writing,
Publication Management

2004 – Honors Diploma
University High School, Phoenix, AZ

Employment
2007 – current   Editorial Assistant, Political Science Summary, Tucson, AZ
                        Managed day-to-day activities of a monthly journal in
                        political science. Tracked manuscript submissions and kept
                        in contact with authors and publisher.
2006 – 2007   Graphic Design Intern, University of Arizona Marketing
                        and Communications, Tucson, AZ
                        Designed and produced marketing brochures, pamphlets,
                        and catalogs.
                        Maintained websites for participating clients.
2002 – 2004   Server, Phoenix Café, Phoenix, AZ
                        Took customer orders Managed nightly restaurant closing
                        Prepared bank deposits

Software Skills
Adobe: InDesign, Illustrator, Dreamweaver
Microsoft: Word, Excel, PowerPoint
Operating Systems: Macintosh and Windows

Clubs and Organizations
Alpha Beta Fraternity (President)
Student Ambassadors

Fig. 1. An unformatted resume.

The example in Fig. 1 shows an unformatted resume. The lack of repetition, contrast, alignment, and proximity make the document unattractive as well as difficult to follow. There is no way to easily distinguish important information, like the applicant's name and contact information. Sections run together, and no key ideas are clear.

Mathew J. Kraft

225 Ingram Road   kraft@hotmail.com
Harrisonburg, VA 22807   555-555-4321

Education

2008 – Bachelor of Arts, **University of Arizona**, Tucson, AZ
    Major: Creative Writing Minor: Political Science
    Courses: Creative Writing Workshop, Genre Theories, Technology and
    Writing, Publication Management

2004 – Honors Diploma, **University High School**, Phoenix, AZ

Employment

2007 – current   Editorial Assistant, **Political Science Summary**, Tucson, AZ
- Managed day-to-day activities of a monthly journal in political science.
- Tracked manuscript submissions and kept in contact with authors and publisher.

2006 – 2007   Graphic Design Intern, **University of Arizona Marketing and Communications**, Tucson, AZ
- Designed and produced marketing brochures, pamphlets, and catalogs.
- Maintained websites for participating clients.

2002 – 2004   Server, **Phoenix Café**, Phoenix, AZ
- Took customer orders
- Managed nightly restaurant closing
- Prepared bank deposits

Software Skills

    Adobe: InDesign, Illustrator, Dreamweaver
    Microsoft: Word, Excel, PowerPoint
    Operating Systems: Macintosh and Windows

Clubs and Organizations

- Alpha Beta Fraternity (President)
- Student Ambassadors

Fig. 2. A formatted resume.

Fig. 2 shows the same content using the previously discussed design elements. The document is more visually appealing as well as being easier to review. Each individual design principle is involved, and their combination leads to a stronger design.

Repetition is shown through the consistent emphasis and text used in the various sections of the resume. There is contrast between the size of the author's name and the contact information, clearly highlighting the most significant information. School and business names shown in bold create strong contrast within lines of text. Text is firmly and consistently aligned. Text is easy to read from the left justification, and the author's name is highlighted as the only centered text on the page. Proximity makes finding information simple, as section headings are placed directly above their supporting information.

The Basics of Style Guides

Style guides are collections of conventions on everything from word choice to format gathered into one place and used in writing. Their primary purpose is to ensure that all documents in a given environment adhere to a certain look and consistent use of language, but they serve a much broader purpose.

Style guides eliminate the guesswork in areas of writing that have multiple options. For example, both advisor and adviser are accurate spellings of a word; a style guide specifies which instance is preferred for the document you are writing. Style guides assure consistence in an organization's publications, such as placing the titles and page numbers in the same area of the page for all documents. Finally, they make reading and comprehension easier for the audience by presenting similar information in similar ways. Readers who want to view the source material you've used in a paper, for example, will refer to your list of authors and publications. The format and even the title of this section will vary depending on the style guide you've chosen. The "Works Cited" or "Reference" pages provide the information on all referenced documents in a presentation different from the main text, making it easy to identify.

Most academic disciplines follow a style guide. In addition, many companies and academic institutions establish their own style guides to supplement established style guides. In most writing courses, as well as other courses in the humanities, we use the Modern Language Association (MLA) style.

A Primer of MLA Style

The Modern Language Association produced their first "MLA style sheet" in 1951 as a way to ensure consistency within documents shared in the academic community. The style sheet evolved into the first edition of the *MLA Handbook* in 1977. Now in its seventh edition, the *MLA Handbook* is the primary source for stylistic choices made in writing for the humanities.

Style guides reflect the items of importance in writing for a particular community. The types and structure in information shown in the MLA style guide differ from those in other disciplines. For example, the American Psychological Association (APA)—used by many of the sciences—has its own style guide. Even popular media, including newspapers and magazines have their own style guide: the Associated Press (AP) guide.

Writers using a specific style guide will emphasize different pieces of information. For example, citations in MLA emphasize the author as primary focus, while the APA style guide features dates (see Fig. 3).

Style guides are dynamic documents, and they change to reflect evolutions in technology for both research and production. When MLA style was first developed, it did not include a style for referencing Internet sources. As online media became an increasingly significant means of sharing resources, the style guide was adapted to incorporate references for websites, online journals, and print journals retrieved online. Changes in production options for writers and publishers also influenced changes to style guides. When authors typed papers using traditional typewriters, they were unable to use italics to indicate the name of a publication; instead, the underlining of text indicated these documents. Modern word processing programs allow the author to control type at a much more precise level, allowing italics as well as control of spacing and line breaks.

MLA Style In-Text Citation	**APA Style In-Text Citation**
Johnson felt that "there was a lack of trust amongst people when it came to money" (234).	Johnson (2003) felt that "there was a lack of trust amongst people when it came to money" (p. 234).
Some researchers argue that money creates "a lack of trust amongst people" (Johnson 234)	Some researchers argue that money creates "a lack of trust amongst people" (Johnson, 2003, p. 234).
MLA Style Works Cited	**APA Style Reference**
Crowley, Sharon, and Debra Hawhee. Ancient Rhetorics for Contemporary Students. 3rd ed. New York: Pearson Education, 2004.	Crowley, S. & Hawhee, D. (2004). Ancient rhetorics for contemporary Students. (3rd ed.) New York, NY: Pearson Education.

Fig. 3. MLA and APA emphasize different citation elements.

Like most style guides, MLA style changes over time. The guideline presented here are appropriate for the seventh edition of the MLA Style Guide. You should check to make sure you are using the most current version. In the college courses you take, your individual instructors may impose additional style choices or ones that conflict with the style guide for the academic discipline. Be sure to follow the special style instructions for the assignments in that course.

Applying MLA Style in Your Own Papers[2]

The way you use words and place text on a page influence the audience's ability to comprehend information. Much the way the shape of a stop sign indicates the same meaning as "STOP" to a driver, readers understand information in part through its placement and format. As a result, there is consistency among the papers submitted within a writing classroom and established journals in an academic field. This consistence allows readers to become accustomed to certain conventions and increases readability. When a professor reviews multiple papers formatted in the same way, for example, she can easily find the author's name and class section on all of the papers. Likewise, students in an English class will be able to find a source from the information given in an academic journal because they can understand in-text citation and bibliographic reference.

MLA-formatted papers for a class rarely include graphic elements, like illustrations or tables. In fact, MLA style limits the use of design in formatting to ensure that the focus remains on the text. Settings specified by MLA incorporate the design principles reviewed above. The remainder of the chapter discusses MLA formatting of academic papers, like the research papers you'll develop in your writing classes, as opposed to writing for publication, such as professional journals.

The primary use of repetition in MLA format is to indicate that text formatted in the same way throughout a paper signifies a similar use. Contrast is important in separating distinct sections of a paper from one another. Alignment in MLA increases readability by providing a common starting point for the reader. Proximity helps readers follow related ideas. For example, section headers are located directly over the text they introduce, allowing readers to quickly find information.

Margins

Margins are the distance from the edge of the paper to where the text starts. They define the amount of white space around the text on the page. They are important because they emphasize the text through contrast (black text on a white page) and increase readability through consistent alignment (headings and text line up to the left margin). Margins also contribute to readability by providing a place for the reader's eyes to rest: they ensure appropriate white space to prevent a page from becoming too dense with text.

The MLA style guide requires specific margins of one inch (1") on all four sides of a page (see Fig. 4).

---

2 As this reader went to press, the MLA released the 8th edition—though too late to make changes to this reader. As this event suggests, no style guide is stable and "rules" are merely conventions, not unchanging regulations

See section 4.1 of the *MLA Handbook* for information on margins.

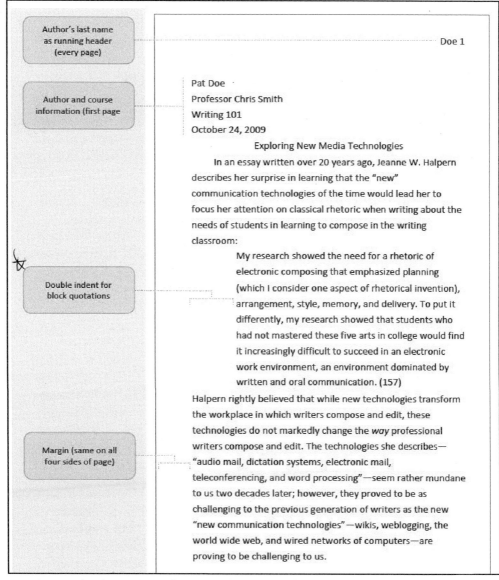

Fig. 4. The first page of a paper formatted according to MLA Style.

Typeface and Spacing

Appropriate typeface usage involves all design elements. The repetition of a single font throughout a document shows the reader that each section of the paper is part of a single whole. The strong visual color contrast of black text on a white background increases readability. Black text, for example, is easier to read than gray text, a difference you may notice when your printer is low on ink. Alignment indicates a separation of ideas or the introduction of a new concept. The title of the paper centered over the left-aligned text shows the beginning of the paper's content. The placement of a section title illustrates proximity. Each one is adjacent to its respective text directly above the first paragraph of a section.

MLA requires a serif font (like Times New Roman) in 12-point type. A serif font is one that has edges or "feet" on the ends of the letters. A sans-serif font (like Arial) is straighter, without edges or flares as part of its shape. Serif fonts are traditionally easier to read, though this distinction has decreased as desktop publishing programs and font qualities have improved.

All text, from the initial header through the reference page, must be double-spaced (see Fig. 5). There is no additional spacing before or after headings. Each new paragraph is indented by ½ inch. The consistent spacing within the document makes reading easier as well as providing a reviewer with room for notes. The indention of each paragraph clearly indicates the beginning of a new idea.

See section 4.2 of the *MLA Handbook* for information on typeface and spacing.

Titles and Headings

A title and internal headings help to separate the body of the paper into smaller, more specific, sections. They break text into shorter, more readable sections, or chunk information in the paper into reasonable portions. In addition, headings allow the reader to quickly skim through a document in search of specific ideas. Headings are described in levels, meaning their hierarchal structure in the paper. A second level heading must follow a first level heading. For example, after reading this entire chapter, you can easily find information on a specific element by looking for the appropriate heading.

Within MLA style, the title refers to the entire paper, while headings refer to individual sections within the paper. The contrast in MLA titles and headings comes mainly from alignment. Both students writing in the classroom and professionals writing for publication use MLA style. Limiting the amount of formatting—like adding italics or bold for emphasis—and focusing on alignment helps ensure that headings remain consistent when different fonts are used. The title is centered over the main text; headings are left justified over body text that is indented (see Fig. 5).

See section 4.3 of the *MLA Handbook* for information on titles and headings.

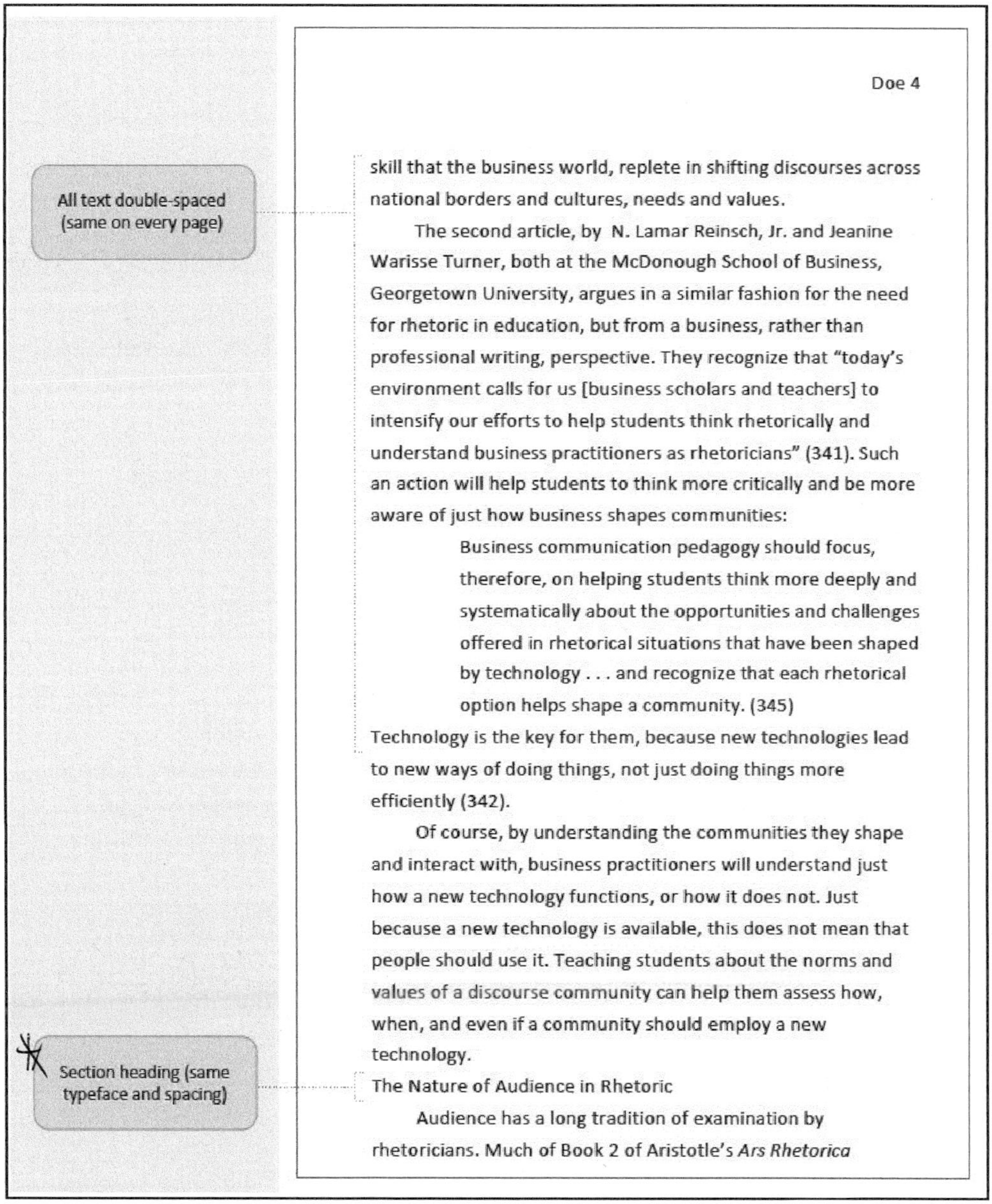

Doe 4

skill that the business world, replete in shifting discourses across national borders and cultures, needs and values.

> All text double-spaced (same on every page)

The second article, by N. Lamar Reinsch, Jr. and Jeanine Warisse Turner, both at the McDonough School of Business, Georgetown University, argues in a similar fashion for the need for rhetoric in education, but from a business, rather than professional writing, perspective. They recognize that "today's environment calls for us [business scholars and teachers] to intensify our efforts to help students think rhetorically and understand business practitioners as rhetoricians" (341). Such an action will help students to think more critically and be more aware of just how business shapes communities:

> Business communication pedagogy should focus, therefore, on helping students think more deeply and systematically about the opportunities and challenges offered in rhetorical situations that have been shaped by technology . . . and recognize that each rhetorical option helps shape a community. (345)

Technology is the key for them, because new technologies lead to new ways of doing things, not just doing things more efficiently (342).

Of course, by understanding the communities they shape and interact with, business practitioners will understand just how a new technology functions, or how it does not. Just because a new technology is available, this does not mean that people should use it. Teaching students about the norms and values of a discourse community can help them assess how, when, and even if a community should employ a new technology.

> Section heading (same typeface and spacing)

The Nature of Audience in Rhetoric

Audience has a long tradition of examination by rhetoricians. Much of Book 2 of Aristotle's *Ars Rhetorica*

Fig. 5. A page formatted in MLA style showing double-spacing and a section heading.

Headers and Page Numbers

Headers are a user service, providing information to readers regarding their location in the text. The header includes the author's last name and the page number (see Fig. 4). Because the header information is formatted consistently and places in the exact location on each page, this use of repetition helps readers easily find and identify document information.

On the initial page of a research paper, the header also includes the author's name, the date of submission, course instructor's name and course designation, usually left justified (see Fig. 4). This information, but not its placement, may vary depending on your course. Always check with your professor or refer to handouts provided in class for specifics.

Subsequent pages of the paper require that the author's last name and page number be placed in the upper, right-hand corner of the page, one-half inch (0.5") from the top edge of the page and one inch (1") from the right edge of the paper.

See section 4.4 of the *MLA Handbook* for information on page numbers.

Illustrations

Illustrations, including photographs, line drawings, maps, or graphs, help your readers better understand the information you are communicating. Sometimes illustrations support the function of the text. For example, we use the illustrations in this chapter to help you better understand the concepts we are writing about. Understanding the importance of graphics would be much harder with no illustrations as support. In other instances, the illustrations themselves are the primary pieces of information. For instance, a simple graph can be far more dramatic and comprehensible than a long paragraph full of numbers and percentages.

With MLA style, illustrations should be labeled *Figure* (usually abbreviated as *Fig.*), numbered consecutively, and given a brief caption following the label. As we have done with the illustrations in this chapter, the caption should readily identify the key feature of the illustration. Place the illustration as close as possible to the text where you first reference it to help readers understand why you included it.

Writers frequently use illustrations created by others to supplement their writing. If you find an image on a website, you cannot use it without permission. And while some websites explicitly give permission to use their images, you must still cite the source in your own work.

While you can use others' properly attributed illustrations, sometimes you will create the illustrations yourself. For example, you may want to capture an image of your computer's desktop to add to a document about computer systems.

To copy a screen shot of your computer to the clipboard, press <Ctrl-Shift-Command> (Apple)-3 on Mac OS X or <Print Screen> on Windows. Once on the clipboard, the image will be available for you to manipulate with an image editing software or paste unaltered into almost any type of graphics program.

While some images may already be exactly the way you need them, most of the time you will need to make changes to images before you can use them. Two free image editing software packages are GIMP—the GNU Image Manipulation Program—for Mac OS X and Windows systems (available at http://www.gimp.org/) and Paint.NET for use only on Windows systems (available at <getpaint.net>).

Other things to remember when using illustrations:

- *Always use visuals of good quality.* A bad illustration can distract your reader and lessen the credibility of your argument.

- *Don't distort the image.* Keep the image in proportion by holding the <Shift> key as you are adjusting the image in your word processor.

- *Make sure the image is of the right quality and resolution.* An image that looks great on a website may not look as good when printed. Check the resolution of the image before enlarging it so there is no loss of quality.

- *Use the image at the appropriate size.* Don't try to force a full-page Power-Point slide into a one-inch square space.

- *Crop images to remove extraneous material.* Keep the focus on the important part of the illustration just like you do with text. For example, if including a web browser screenshot of a web page in a paper, readers do not need to see the browser window from or your favorites/bookmarks menu in the visual used in the document.

See section 4.5 of the *MLA Handbook* for information on working with illustrations.

Conclusion

While not every class, assignment or topic lends itself to the inclusion of graphics, you can still design your documents to be appealing to your reader. Good design choices can also make your document more accessible to your readers. A clean design with graphic and typographical indicators of content gives your readers more opportunities to engage with and understand your intention.

Style guides define typographical and design rules for you as a writer and a reader. MLA is the most commonly used style guide in first-year writing, but most disciplines have their own. All style guides answer the questions you commonly encounter as a writer—Should page numbers be at the top or bottom of the page? How do I cite an article from a magazine's website? When you answer these questions, you can concentrate on the writing itself and developing your ideas. As a reader, you will be able to identify an established style and use it to your advantage. Finding the information you want (paper topics, authors cited) is easier when you know where to look (headings, reference pages). While the reasoning behind the rules in a style guide may not be intuitive, following them leads to better-designed documents.

WORKS CITED

Modern Language Association of America. *The MLA Handbook for Writers of Research Papers.* 7th ed. New York: MLA, 2009. Print.

Production

"The action of making or manufacturing from components or raw materials, or the process of being so manufactured"

– Oxford English Dictionary

Listening to the Conversation

"We are coming to an end of cheap, plentiful water. Most of the food companies assume that water will remain cheap, and for investors that assumption is dangerous in terms of the companies' long term profitability, We feel that most [food] companies are not addressing these risks adequately."

– Brooke Barton, author and director the Ceres Water & Food Programs

"Think about that: The U.S. Department of Justice and the FBI now contend, in effect, that the theft of genetically modified corn technology is as credible a threat to national security as the spread to nation-states of the technology necessary to deliver and detonate nuclear warheads. Disturbingly, they may be right."

– Ted Genoways, author and contributing editor of *The New Republic*

"We need to reduce our meat consumption. That's very important in all of this: (per capita) meat consumption today is about 170 pounds of meat per year in the U.S. That's not including fish, eggs or milk. If we include all of these it becomes around 300 or so pounds a year. It's extremely unsustainable. It's unprecedented, such an extreme demand for meat being supplied on a daily basis. It's inhumane, it's unsustainable, and it's also unnecessary."

– Sonia Faruqi, freelance journalist and investment banker

Local people who regularly hunted or fished or foraged or walked or played in the local countryside served the local economy and stewardship as inspectors, rememberers, and storytellers. They gave their own kind of service to the eyes-to-acres ratio. Now most of those people are gone or absent, along with most of the farming people who used to be at work here.

– Wendell Berry, farmer, conservationist, and writer

"I think using animals for food is an ethical thing to do, but we've got to do it right. We've got to give those animals a decent life and we've got to give them a painless death. We owe the animal respect."

– Temple Grandin, professor and consultant to the livestock industry

If we are to create a society that values black life, we cannot ignore the role of food and land. I believe that black people's collective experience with slavery and sharecropping has created an aversion to the land and a sense that the land itself is an oppressor. The truth is that without good land and good food we cannot be truly free... Owning our own land, growing our own food, educating our own youth, participating in our own healthcare and justice systems—this is the source of real power and dignity.

– Leah Penniman, high school teacher and owner of Soul Fire Farm.

Lack of Food Means Syrian Children Face 'Irreversible' Health Issues, says UN

Harriett Grant

The Guardian, December 2015

> According to her website, Harriet Grant is a freelance journalist who often writes for *The Guardian* and *BBC*. Much of her writing concerns humanitarian issues ranging from the UK to Syria to Bangladesh. Her piece here about the Syrian Civil War illustrates how the conflict has impacted the health and food supply of Syrians. The *BBC* explains how the civil war began in March 2011, and though a number of ceasefires have been attempted, the war continues unresolved as of Summer 2016. The conflict has claimed the lives of at least 250,000 Syrians, and 11 million more have fled their homes. The war started when several Syrian teens were arrested and tortured for writing "revolutionary slogans" on a wall and then police shot several protesters. It has continued as a complicated situation involving parties who are loyal to President Bashar al-Assad, those who oppose him, jihadist militants who are taking advantage of the chaos, and many outside nations who seek a resolution to the war. Underlying tensions also stem from ideological differences between the Sunni majority and the Shia Alawite sect to which the President belongs.

The UN's World Food Programme warns that funding problems mean vulnerable groups in Syria and neighbouring countries are not getting critical nutrients

Syrian children across the Middle East are facing "irreversible" health problems caused by severe food shortages, as the World Food Programme (WFP) continues to struggle to meet the needs of even the most vulnerable refugees.

Dina El Kassaby, a spokeswoman for WFP, says ongoing funding problems mean the agency can't ensure that young children are getting sufficient nutrients or that pregnant women are getting the nutrition they need to give their children a healthy start in life. The organisation provides rations and food aid to 4 million people within Syria and another 1.5 million who are displaced across the region.

Syrian boys help make a fire to boil water at a refugee camp in the Bekaa valley, Lebanon. Among Syrian infants aged six to 17 months in the country, only 3% had a 'minimum acceptable diet'. Photograph: Hassan Ammar/AP

She said: "We are seeing now that families are eating less nutritious food. Rather than fresh foods they are buying rice and pasta, food that will fill them for longer—but this means they aren't getting the level of micronutrients they need. Nearly all the mothers I met are skipping meals so their children can have more food."

WFP tries to ensure that breastfeeding and pregnant women get extra vouchers so they can buy fresh food or meat. But El Kassaby says this is not always possible. "The value of the vouchers was reduced several times in 2015, so many families coped by purchasing less expensive staple food items to ensure that the value of the voucher would stretch to cover a longer period of time.

"This is a major cause of concern for us. The first 1,000 days of a child's life, from conception to the end of the second year, is absolutely critical. Malnutrition in those early years can be largely irreversible and causes delays in growth as well as mental health problems."

Of a population of around 22 million, 6.3 million Syrians are food insecure. This means they don't have sufficient access to nutritious food. The UN children's agency, Unicef, warned in its 2015 report into the vulnerability of Syrian refugees in Lebanon that two-thirds of children under five had less than three cooked meals a day, compared to half in 2014. Only 3% of infants between six and 17 months had a "minimum acceptable diet", mainly because of fewer meals and poor nutritional diversity.

From pregnancy, through breastfeeding and infant diet, malnutrition in the early months and years can damage a child's brain, impair the immune system, and cause stunting, where the child's body stops growing properly.

This year has seen food rations for Syrian refugees seesaw. Cuts, some of which have since been reversed, have left the most vulnerable groups with only $14 a month and removed rations from hundreds of thousands of households altogether. In September, the WFP dropped a third of Syrians from its food assistance programme, including more than 200,000 displaced people living in Jordan.

In October, a donation of $30m from the European Commission meant that WFP could restart funds to those who lost support earlier in the year, and increase provision for the most vulnerable. But that support is only 80% of what nutritional experts say is needed.

El Kassaby says that there is not enough money to keep helping Syrians and vulnerable refugees in neighbouring countries through the first months of 2016.

"Right now, looking ahead to May we are short of $358m out of a total funding requirement of $639m. We have had donors stepping up since September but we really need a predictable and sustainable source of funding. We don't want to send texts to people telling them that this month they will only get half their usual food support. I just feel helpless, knowing that we do our best but it is still not good enough."

WFP is carrying out a special programme within Syria to give children extra vitamins through snacks provided at school. El Kassaby says the programme is vital for children but won't be able to expand unless more funding is found.

"We are buying local dates and making them into fortified high nutrition cookies and it gives the kids they energy they need. These children would have been going without breakfast before this so it's an incentive for their parents to send them in to school.

"We would like to expand this scheme but it's very difficult without funding levels that are predictable and regular."

Henry Sebuliba, a nutritionist with Unicef, adds: "We are so far not seeing levels of malnutrition rising above the dangerous levels of 3% of the child population. But we have to focus on food insecurity—that is the problem for the future."

The food crisis is made worse by the increasing debt levels of many families, as four years of displacement bites heavily into savings. Agencies warn that debt creates a vicious cycle, whereby refugees become more dependent on the fluctuating food vouchers, and less able to cope without them.

An assessment of more than 4,000 refugee households by UNHCR, Unicef and WFP found that nearly 90% are more in debt than they were a year ago.

The percentage of refugee households buying food on credit has jumped to more than 75%, from 30% in 2014.

Experts working with child refugees say that it is not only physical health that is being threatened by the funding crisis. A report out last week by Save the Children highlighted the mental health problems that are being exacerbated by the lack of support services for severely traumatised children.

"The repercussions for the future mental health of an entire generation could be catastrophic," said Ian Rodgers, country director for Save the Children inLebanon.

"In addition to the obvious psychological damage caused by witnessing traumatic events and extreme violence, there are a myriad of secondary, under-funded and often overlooked, daily causes of psychological and social damage once a displaced child arrives in a new community."

Questions for Discussion

1. What are some of the impacts of malnutrition on families?

2. What does the article indicate is the best solution for the malnourished children?

3. What other solutions do you think may help solve the problem (this may include ideas from other articles in this reader)?

'Take My Job!'
Campaign Markets Agricultural Labor

National Public Radio

July 2010

> *National Public Radio* (*NPR*) is a non-profit radio station that focuses on news and cultural stories. Founded in 1970, a telephone survey by Harris found *NPR* to be "the most trusted news source in the United States," as reported by Wikipedia. *NPR's* Michel Martin, the host of the Tell Me More segment on *NPR*, is a regular host on *NPR* and correspondent for *ABC News.* This interview is conducted with the president of the United Farm Workers, a union founded by Cesar Chavez in 1962 to create and protect agricultural workers' rights. The exigence for the discussion is the argument that undocumented workers take American jobs.

One stereotype about undocumented workers in the U.S. is that they occupy agricultural jobs that could be filled by Americans in need of work. The United Farm Workers (UFW) of America labor union is testing that theory. They have launched the "Take Our Jobs!" campaign, which invites unemployed Americans to take a stab at agricultural labor. Host Michel Martin speaks with United Farm Workers President Arturo Rodriguez about the campaign and perceptions about agricultural labor.

MICHEL MARTIN, host:

I'm Michel Martin and this is TELL ME MORE from NPR News.

Coming up, a refuge for the musical genre called deep house. It's under the tracks on the outskirts of Baltimore and its got people all jacked up. That conversation in a few minutes.

But, first, with the national unemployment rate hovering just below 10 percent and polls showing broad support for Arizona's tough new law aimed at driving out illegal immigrants, that's the law that the U.S. Justice Department is now fighting, clearly many Americans believe that undocumented workers are stealing jobs from Americans who would be willing to do them. The United Farm Workers, the UFW, wants to test that theory. The union's Take Our Jobs campaign invites unemployed Americans to take a stab at agricultural labor.

With us to talk about the campaign and the realities of agricultural work in the U.S., we're joined by United Farm Workers' president, Arturo Rodriguez. He joins us from his office in Kern County, California. Also with us is Gabriel Thompson. He's the author of the memoir, "Working in the Shadows: A Year of Doing the Jobs (Most) Americans Won't Do." We talked to him previously because he did just that. He did those jobs that the United Farm Workers is now inviting people to do. And Mr. Thompson joins us from our bureau in New York. Welcome to you both.

Mr. ARTURO RODRIGUEZ (President, United Farm Workers): Thanks for having me.

Mr. GABRIEL THOMPSON (Author, "Working in the Shadows: A Year of Doing the Jobs (Most) Americans Won't Do"): Thank you so much for having us, Michel.

MARTIN: Mr. Rodriguez, let's start with you. You launched this Take Your Jobs campaign. You're scheduled to go on "The Colbert Report" to talk about it. So would it be fair to say that this is actually fairly tongue in cheek or are you serious that you really are inviting people to do agricultural work and you're going to teach them how to do it?

Mr. RODRIGUEZ: Well, we're definitely inviting folks. In fact, we sent letters to every single member of Congress. And as of date we still have not received a response from any of them a positive response, saying that they are willing to go work out in the fields because we're really tired of all the criticism that's been launched against farm workers, immigrants and saying that we're actually there taking their jobs when in fact I don't think people really realize how difficult it is to work in the fields.

MARTIN: Okay, well, presumably members of Congress already have a job, so maybe they wouldn't necessarily be as interested in your offer as other people might be. But are you seriously expecting to and willing to and hoping to train people who are unemployed who say, you know, I can't get a job because somebody illegal is taking my job? Are you really saying, I'm going to train people to do this work?

Mr. RODRIGUEZ: You know, we're actually, what we're doing is that we have a website, takeourjobs.org and people are applying for that and we're then directing them to websites where there are jobs available and assisting them in every particular way possible. And, yes, we are hoping that they come and they apply and that they actually go get the experience of working in the fields and see what it is to become a professional farm worker and work in the conditions that farm workers work in every day.

MARTIN: And you talk a little bit about that on the site. It cautions that duties may include tilling the soil, transplanting, weeding, thinning, picking, cutting, sorting, and packing of harvested produce. May set up and operate irrigation equipment. Work is performed outside in all weather conditions. Summertime, 90-plus degree weather and is physically demanding, requiring workers to bend, stoop, lift, and carry up to 50 pounds on a regular basis. You're not making that sound as appealing as, well, say, being a summer associate in a law firm. I don't know, is that your intention?

Mr. RODRIGUEZ: Well, we just want to paint a real picture for folks. We don't want folks to think something different. Anybody going out there better be ready to really work in severe, difficult conditions.

MARTIN: And how much can people expect to earn?

Mr. RODRIGUEZ: You know, it's minimum wage. And then some jobs call for piece rate, so you maybe make a little bit more if you can pick the crop as fast as they require.

MARTIN: And Gabriel Thompson, let's turn to you. You actually did this of your own volition. And just refresh our memories about this for people who may not have heard our earlier conversation. Why did you decide to do this?

Mr. THOMPSON: I think first it was that so much of the talk around immigration and so much demonizing of immigrants is done by people in air conditioned offices that were completely removed from the reality on the ground of what it's like to do the work that everyone depends upon. So my mission was pretty simple. It was to go out and do spend two months in each one of these jobs, beginning with cutting lettuce for Dole in Yuma, Arizona.

You know, Yuma has had a high unemployment rate, has one of the highest rates in the state and yet, I never saw another white person in the fields. But the reality of the job is that it is incredibly physically demanding. You come home and you're just—I was at least—completely wiped out. I'd be in bed by 7 PM, 8 PM, right when I got home. But the other piece is that it's very skilled worked and you have to really be able to stick it out for a while before you even get a basic level of, sort of, adequacy in doing the job.

MARTIN: Gabriel Thompson, was it your impression that many of the people you worked with at Dole were undocumented? Because the impression I got from your book is that, in fact, that they were documented. That they had specific visas that allowed them to work there. They crossed freely, back and forth, across the border. What was your impression?

Mr. THOMPSON: Yeah, Yuma's a little bit; it's a different situation than much of the farm work going on around the country because it's right near the border. A lot of the workers on my crew were actually guest workers because the companies that said they couldn't find Americans to fill those jobs. And so, you know, basically any American that showed up at Dole's office, or any of these companies that had guest workers, would be guaranteed a job in the fields.

I showed up on a Friday. I was on the fields on Monday. So there was never a sense that people were taking jobs. And every now and then, you know, I talked to my supervisor in my dorm or the foreman, they would have someone come up and try it for a couple days and very quickly they realized that this type of job, it's not just hard like oh, construction is hard or as some other jobs are hard, which I've done. It's so physically demanding that I actually consider having survived two months and writing a book about it, so it's kind of a huge accomplishment in my kind of life experience to survive two months in the lettuce fields.

MARTIN: And there were workers who were out there in the fields with, who were pregnant, as I recall. There was one woman who was out there who was out-cutting you, as I recall, who was pregnant at the time.

Mr. THOMPSON: Oh, many. The other real clear difference I think is to, that needs to be made is that this is one part of their lives. And they come home from an exhausting day and they're raising families and they're helping their kids with school work.

And for me it was really awe-inspiring to see just how much energy and how much dedication they had to, not only do this work, but then to live sort of full lives as much as possible to help raise their families.

MARTIN: Mr. Rodriguez, is it your sense like Mr. Thompson said, that if you are documented, if you were an American citizen, these jobs are for the taking? Is that your sense as well?

Mr. RODRIGUEZ: Oh definitely. I mean there is no doubt they have a job forever, as long as they can do the work. The reality is, though, Michel, that probably, according to government reports, at least 50 percent if not more farm workers today are undocumented out there.

MARTIN: Well, how do you respond to the sense that many people have. I mean any conversation we have on this topic, any conversation that most people in the media have on this topic, people will call, email and write and say that undocumented workers are not only displacing Americans, but also demanding and using services for which they do not pay.

What is your response to that?

Mr. RODRIGUEZ: Farm workers, they come here really, because they want to realize the American dream like anyone else. And they're not here to take advantage of the system. They're not to, in particular way, hurt America. In fact, they see themselves as really benefiting America. They realize no one else wants to go to work out in the fields. So consequently, they want to be a part of America just like anyone else. They want their children to get educated. So some can work in the fields but they want to see them have opportunities that they didn't have growing up.

MARTIN: But wait, what about those who would argue that if undocumented immigrants were not available to do this work, then the working conditions would improve? That the pay would improve and the conditions would improve. That in effect, you're making it easier for employers to keep these jobs as hard and as grueling as they are instead of looking for ways to make the working conditions better?

Mr. RODRIGUEZ: You know, in reality, farm work has always been a low-paying job with no benefits, no laws covering and protecting them as other workers here in this country. It was not immigrants that were primarily working in the fields at that time. It was American citizens. People that were here that were migrating all over the country. And yet, back then there was a large Anglo population.

In fact, about 40 percent of the farm worker population were people that had migrated from Oklahoma and all over the country to work in the fields.

MARTIN: Go ahead Gabriel.

Mr. THOMPSON: I think too, one important note of and I think the message of Take Our Jobs campaign, is a reflection of the fact that we need to remember how this economy went downhill. It wasn't farm workers in the fields, harvesting lettuce for eight bucks an hour or processing poultry for $7.50 an hour that led to this large unemployment.

I mean, these were people in suits highly educated that dismantled our economy. But I think, inevitably, you're going to start finding people blaming folks that whose voices often aren't heard. And I think then they have this notion that well, immigrants—undocumented immigrants are here and they're really milking the system and doing all these things. And the Take Our Jobs idea sounds essentially like, if you think we are coasting by and not contributing to this country, come check it out. Come see how it feels.

MARTIN: Well, having done that Gabriel, what's the final word from you? What the hardest thing about doing the farm work that you did?

Mr. THOMPSON: I think it's just living with the constant pain.

(Soundbite of laughter)

Mr. THOMPSON: People would say after five days you start getting use to it and the pain goes away. But really what happens is you just you start redefining what constitutes pain. And so you just have to become used to always having your hands swollen, and used to your back going out, and used to falling asleep at the drop of a hat.

I would say, the positive is that, as opposed to some of the other jobs I did, there is a real feeling in the fields—at least where I was—of solidarity among workers—about workers really feeling that the work they're doing has a lot of dignity. And they—even if American consumers in grocery stores don't make the connection, workers in the fields make the connection that they are literally feeding the United States American citizens and doing some of the hardest jobs that exist.

MARTIN: Mr. Rodriguez, I noticed that you laughed when Gabriel mentioned that living with the constant pain and you actually chuckled. Why did you chuckle?

Mr. RODRIGUEZ: No, because it's true. I mean your hands are swollen. They're cut up. They're stained. And the women that oftentimes they'll work on their knees and their knees are brown so they won't wear skirts because they're ashamed of showing that off to people. I mean those are just the realities that farm workers face every single day. So it's a grueling effort, a grueling job that takes place and they get very little recognition for what they do. But the reality is, that if it wasn't for them, we would not have food on our tables every single day.

MARTIN: Arturo Rodriguez is the president of the United Farm Workers. He is launching the Take Our Jobs campaign. He says that he will train, or the UFW will train, Americans who wish to do agricultural work. And he joined us from his office in Kern County, California.

From New York we heard from Gabriel Thompson. He's the author of the memoir *Working in the Shadows: A Year of Doing the Jobs (Most) Americans Won't Do.* And if you want to hear my previous conversation with Gabriel Thompson about his book, you can go to our website. Go to npr.org, click on programs then on TELL ME MORE.

Mr. Rodriguez, Mr. Thompson, thank you so much for joining us.

Mr. RODRIGUEZ: Thank you very much, Michel.

Mr. THOMPSON: Thanks for having me.

Questions for Discussion

1. What is Arturo Rodriquez's primary argument concerning the role that immigrants play in unemployment rates?

2. Which counterarguments does Martin bring up with his guests? How might this appeal to his listeners?

3. How well does Gabriel Thompson's experience in the fields build his ethos?

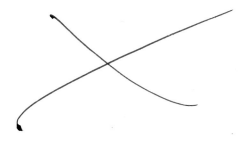

Science Is Warning Us that a Food Crisis Is Coming to Southern Africa. Will We Stop It?

Christopher Groskopf

Quartz, March 2016

According to the website for the news source *Quartz*, "*Quartz* is a digitally native news outlet, born in 2012, for business people in the new global economy. We publish bracingly creative and intelligent journalism with a broad worldview, built primarily for the devices closest at hand: tablets and mobile phones." Groskopf's article discusses climate change's impact on subsistence farming, a widely-used practice in southern Africa in which families grow enough food to feed themselves for the year, and ideally enough to store until the following year's harvest. Problems with this farming method lie in farmers often losing a year's food due to severe weather and farmers having no time to earn additional income because they devote their time to farming.

In April, harvest season begins in Southern Africa. An ongoing drought means the season will yield a historically poor crop. Countries including Malawi, South Africa, and Zimbabwe will have major shortfalls of grain. By one count, more than 20 million people in the region already have limited access to food—notwithstanding the drought. Without intervention, the next year will put those people and millions more at risk of malnutrition or even starvation.

But knowing all this makes intervention more possible than ever.

Famines are a powerful illustration of how suddenly nature can undercut a poor or poorly prepared society. We have paid dearly for our failure to respond to them efficiently. Economist Stephen Devereux has estimated 70 million people were killed by famine in the 20th century alone.

Today, analysts employing new sources of information, better technology, and networks of human monitors have made it possible to foresee agricultural disaster far enough ahead so that resources can be mobilized to prevent starvation.

The impending food crisis in Southern Africa has yet to capture the international media's attention, but it is the subject of ongoing analysis by a network of agriculturists, climatologists and economists. Global monitoring centers, such as the Famine Early Warning Systems Network (FEWS), issue regular updates. If the crisis does devolve into a famine, the world will have known it was coming for at least six months.

How to foresee a crisis

Many different organizations monitor food security around the world. FEWS is a collaboration between five US agencies and two private companies. The UN's Food and Agriculture Organization (FAO) hosts another group called the Global Information and Early Warning System (GIEWS). Each group gathers and analyzes data until they determine it is time to sound the alarm about an impending crisis.

Last year a powerful El Niño smothered Southern Africa with hot, dry air, prompting FEWS to issue just such a warning. Many areas experienced the driest start to the growing season in 35 years. South Africa had the least annual rainfall it's had in a century. The drought delayed planting of crops by up to 50 days in some places. According to Christopher Hillbruner, a food security analyst at FEWS, that makes it impossible for the region to bounce back this year. "Even if tomorrow it rained beautifully for two months, the crops aren't in the ground, so it doesn't matter," he said.

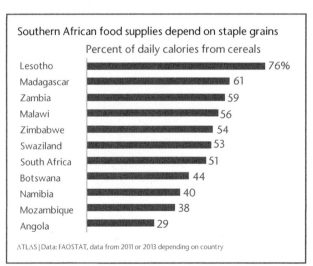

Southern African food supplies depend on staple grains
Percent of daily calories from cereals

Country	Percent
Lesotho	76%
Madagascar	61
Zambia	59
Malawi	56
Zimbabwe	54
Swaziland	53
South Africa	51
Botswana	44
Namibia	40
Mozambique	38
Angola	29

ATLAS | Data: FAOSTAT, data from 2011 or 2013 depending on country

Agriculture provides food, income and employment for 70% of the region's population, according to the Southern African Development Community (SADC). Locally harvested grains, especially corn, are a key staple of regional diets.

The growing season for most grains, including corn, begins between October and December. Farmers harvest those crops between April and June. Any interruption of this cycle can have devastating consequences both for those rural subsistence farmers who feed themselves, as well as for urban residents who rely on food grown in the countryside.

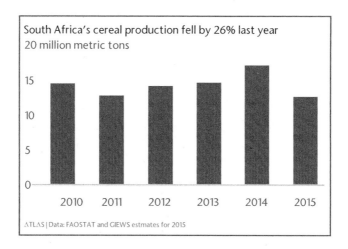

South Africa's cereal production fell by 26% last year
20 million metric tons

ATLAS | Data: FAOSTAT and GIEWS estmates for 2015

Compounding the food supply problem, there was also a drought in the region last year. The cereal harvest in South Africa, the region's largest producer, was down by more than a fourth from the year before.

Measuring a harvest before it happens

Satellite data is used to monitor the drought's impact on agriculture. These "remote sensing" platforms measure changes in the air, land, and water through the spectral properties of the Earth. With decades of such measurements on file, it's now possible not only to chart the temperature, precipitation, and other factors, but also how much today's conditions deviate from historical norms. The following interactive map[1] shows what proportion of normal rainfall Southern Africa has received over the last five months, using data from the National Oceanic and Atmospheric Organization.

Researchers combine basic measurements to create more complex benchmarks of crop health. For example, the FAO uses an indicator called the Agricultural Stress Index (ASI) to quantify the cumu-

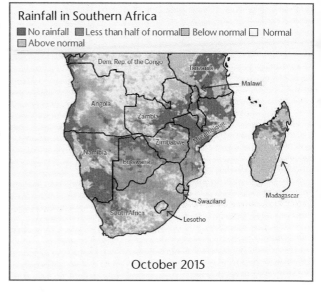

Rainfall in Southern Africa
■ No rainfall ■ Less than half of normal■ Below normal □ Normal
□ Above normal

October 2015

---

1 Please see the original citation for this source to access source-related materials such as the interactive map that's referred to here.

lative stresses on crops. They publish ASI maps of every country in the world, three times a month, allowing for quick comparisons between different times and places. For example, the maps below illustrate the situation in Malawi at the height of the growing season, for each of the last four years.

The Agricultural Stress Index for Malawi for four successive Februaries. Darker shades of gray and black indicate a greater chance of crop failure. (GIEWS)

This kind of climate analysis has developed significantly over the last decade, though Hillbruner is quick to note that improvements to FEWS projections haven't come from big technological breakthroughs, but rather a steady progression of small changes. Their analysis relies on a "convergence of evidence" from many sources, including human monitors, where no single source is treated as authoritative.

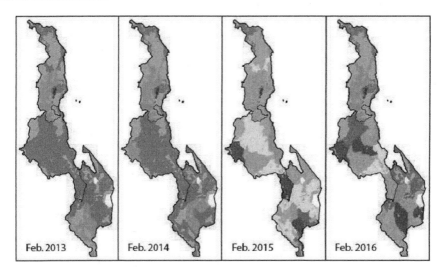

Feb. 2013   Feb. 2014   Feb. 2015   Feb. 2016

Monitoring food economics

Projecting the future of food security requires looking closely at more than just weather. Even when food does make it to markets, it may be too expensive for subsistence farmers who have lost their main source of income to the drought. Economic variables, such as regional food reserves, transportation costs, and local price trends can be as important as crop yields.

Grain reserves will be one major difference between this year's drought and last year's. In 2014, a record harvest flowed into grain silos across Southern Africa. This provided an important buffer against food insecurity. Zambia, in particular, benefited from its reserves. It was able to support itself, while also exporting nearly 500 thousand metric tons to neighboring Zimbabwe.

Unfortunately, the leftovers from 2014's banner year are now almost entirely used up. This year few countries have any significant stockpiles. Those countries that are able are already in the process of negotiating large-scale imports from Europe or South America. Lesotho, Malawi, Swaziland, and Zimbabwe have issued new appeals for humanitarian assistance since the onset of El Niño, according to GIEWS economist Jonathan Pound.

Production levels and stockpiles are the big picture for food security, but they don't guarantee any particular price at the village market. Other factors, such as transportation, can cause local prices to change independent of national trends. Researchers at GIEWS and elsewhere are trying to better understand those local impacts by tracking prices within each country. Analysts monitor that data for sudden spikes and issue alerts when they happen. In response to food shortages and depreciating currencies the FAO issued price warnings for Malawi and South Africa in February (pdf).

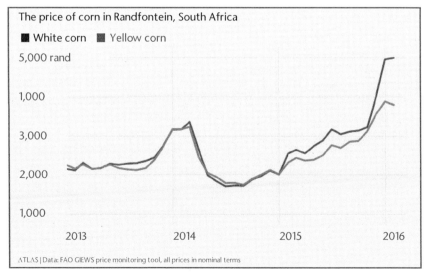

Fortunately, while regional food prices are up, global food prices are way down from their peaks in the last decade. This may help offset some of the cost of large-scale food imports. Low oil prices will also reduce the cost of distributing imported food, which will further drive down prices for consumers.

Early warning provides an opportunity

According to Hillbruner, the worst of the food crisis won't arrive until this time next year—just before harvest, when food stocks are most depleted. In a way, that's good news. "There is an extended period of time before the worst outcomes come to pass, so we have relatively more time to act," he said.

Food for Peace (FFP), an office within USAID, is the funder of FEWS. In an interview with Quartz, acting director Matt Nims said they've been able to make specific preparations based on FEWS projections, including ensuring they have fully-stocked pipelines of emergency food products, and stocking up on specific types of food in their warehouses, such as sorghum, something they wouldn't have done in a 'normal year.'

"It put Southern Africa on the watch as far as how much resources we're going to dedicate," Nims said.

Local organizers are also preparing. In late February, SADC, the World Food Programme, and the FAO agreed on ten short-term objectives, including collecting better data on those being affected and streamlining logistics for food distribution.

There are good reasons to believe that a famine can be prevented. Southern Africa faced a similar drought in 1992 and avoided a famine, despite the loss of more than half of its harvest. Imports and changes in local diets compensated for the diminished local food supply.

However, what is more likely to be the on the mind of humanitarians and policymakers is the 2011 Horn of Africa drought which did cause a famine—the worst to hit any part of Africa in many years. It killed as many as a quarter of a million people in Somalia. Humanitarian groups were widely criticized for reacting too slowly, though interference by the militant group al-Shabaab was also a major factor in keeping aid out of the hardest-hit areas.

Fortunately, Southern Africa's governments are basically stable. Large-scale food imports are already being organized in many places and relief organizations are operating in the regions with the most immediate drought impacts. Unlike other parts of Africa, conflict is not a major barrier to aid distribution.

Even so, preparing for El Niño-related problems is complicated by the need to address more urgent food crises in Ethiopia, South Sudan, and Yemen. Planners worry that sounding the alarm about a future crisis can draw attention away from ones already underway.

In the long run, agricultural modernization, development of local markets, and other efforts to build up countries' resiliency are the best solution to prevent famines. Until those efforts are further along, the world must continue to respond to the crises that inevitably arise.

It's not yet possible to predict every outbreak of hunger before it happens. Wars erupt. Currencies collapse. Harvests fail in corners of world where monitoring programs aren't yet active."The world is a big place. I think we can always be surprised by things," Nims told Quartz.

And yet, the science of famine prediction is the best it's ever been. Year by year, data sources improve, as does understanding of the complex interplay between agriculture, climate, and economics. Advance warning may not be a magical solution that can prevent every famine, but at least in Southern Africa the world has both the knowledge and the capacity to prepare for one, and maybe even prevent it, long before it begins.

Questions for Discussion

1. How is advanced data and technology helping to address famine?

2. How does the use of images help the writer achieve his purpose? How do those images appeal to logos, ethos, and pathos?

3. How are the suggested policies at the end of Groskopf's article similar and/or different to the policies proposed in Bittman et al.'s "A National Food Policy for the 21st Century"?

Factory farming is killing the planet: Why the meat industry's future needs to look more like its past

Lindsay Abrams

Salon, July 2015

Salon is an online magazine which covers topics like news, entertainment, technology, business, and innovation. Their website reveals that they have 17.6 million visitors each month and were at the forefront of being a magazine which exists solely online. Lindsay Abrams is a *Salon* reporter specializing in climate change and environmental issues. She wrote this article in response to growing ag-gag laws which have been issued in several states across the country. An ag-gag law prevents activists and reporters from exposing farm practices by making it illegal to take pictures or videos on factory farms without consent and forcing whistleblowers to turn over all information to authorities rather than reporters.

What happens when you go from never thinking about where your meat comes from to visiting 60 farms across three continents?

One thing's for sure: your food will never again look the same.

That was the case for Sonia Faruqi, whose new book, "Project Animal Farm," documents her journey from a self-described "materialistic investment banker" with an imagination informed by "Little House on the Prairie" to eyewitness to the often unsavory realities of modern-day factory farming. She emerged not just with tales of horrific abuse (although there are certainly plenty of those) but with suggestions for how—with systemic reform and a reconsideration of just how much meat we actually need to be eating—we can still have our meat and sleep at night, too.

"Farms are the modern '1984,'" Faruqi writes. "Official party lines are disseminated to the public and readily accepted by it. At every meal, people swallow small and large doses of lies." With ag-gag laws trying to making visits to factory farms a thing of the past, Salon spoke with Faruqi about why it's not such a bad thing if the truth causes you to lose your appetite. Our conversation has been lightly edited for clarity.

Before you started out on this project, what was the image you had in your mind of farms and where your meat came from?

The image was mixed. I had viewed organic as pastoral and picturesque. Then I learned that it wasn't. As for the rest of the industry, other than organic, I had watched a couple of videos online, but I didn't really know much about it. There was very much a distance. I'd never been to any farm before.

I wanted to ask you about your deconstruction of that organic label: You write about how it can mean vastly different things depending on where you're looking. When we see that label on our food, how much stock can we put in it? Does it really tell us anything?

It does tell us something, but it doesn't tell us as much as we would hope. For instance the outdoor requirement in the U.S. and Canada is 120 days of the year, which translates to one out of three days of the year when animals are supposed to have outdoor access. That's sometimes also treated as a maximum. If it's not organic then the animals would generally have zero days of outdoor access, so this 120 days does make a difference.

Organic is good in areas such as not using antibiotics, chemicals, pesticides and drugs in general. But with animal welfare there does need to be more of a focus. There are some loopholes in it. There's that loophole with dairy cows: in Canada, for two-thirds of the year they can be chained to stalls and that is still called organic. In the U.S. that loophole was closed a few years ago, which is a good thing.

Organic does have some importance as a differentiator between farms, but it hasn't fully reached that potential yet. What would need to happen is stronger regulations and stronger inspections to make that happen.

Are there other labels that you found to be very misleading or not living up to their potential? I know "free range" is one that you mentioned.

Yes. The trouble with free range is that it's hardly defined at all. It has very little meaning. It's completely open to interpretation. In free range we don't know how much outdoor access. Organic means 120 days, but for free range there is no number, the quality of outdoor access, from what age the animal has outdoor access—these important factors are not taken into account. In chapter four you see that I'm at this turkey farm and the fence is broken. That batch of turkeys that I saw would never once step outside. But they would also be described as free range. There are these issues. Fences break, that's fine. But then in my view the animals should no longer be defined and priced as free range. They are not at all.

How does the situation we have in the U.S. compare to what you saw going on in the developing world?

Throughout the book I run to a lot of places: the U.S., Mexico, Canada, Belize, Indonesia, Malaysia, Singapore and the United Arab Emirates. Eight very different countries. Indonesia and Belize were both fascinating. Belize is a small country where most of the farming, almost all of it, is done by Mennonite missionaries. I would describe that farming as small pastoral. These are small pastoral farms where most of the time the animals are outdoors. You constantly see cows grazing in grass fields. It's the sort of system that existed in the U.S. and Canada and other countries about a half to one century ago, and which is very much outdated today.

Indonesia is a country that is very much in transition. It's where the traditional farming is being replaced by the more industrial methods. Indonesia's neighbor Malaysia, for instance, has completely changed its methods of farming from traditional and pastoral to extremely industrial. That has happened largely, or at least partially, because of fast food chains coming into the country. I found that fast food does play a role in how countries farm. As soon as fast food companies like KFC and McDonald's come to other countries they bring with them a whole mindset and a whole method of certain breeds and processes, like antibiotics and artificial insemination, that they just transport over pretty much exactly the same.

So the short answer is different countries are in different states. Some are staying pastoral because they want to. Others are becoming extremely industrial at a very fast and concerning speed and they view it as a sort of development. It's viewed as the same thing as getting a bigger car, getting a bigger house. You are creating more factory farms, you are eating more meat as well.

There's been a big push from fast food companies in the U.S. to rethink the way they produce their food and their meat. Do you see the potential for them to lead that kind of change in the way we raise meat, because they have so much purchasing power, in the same way that they created our current status quo?

I think that while these commitments are helpful and do offer a step in the right direction, sometimes they are reactive. They are reacting to some campaign started by some person or some organization or they are reacting in general to the public perception of fast food. Most people today in the U.S. and Canada know that fast food isn't really good for them or the world. They are reacting to that as well. It's tough to know how much of that is genuine versus more reactionary. But either way these steps are good. They are removing antibiotics and offering free range eggs and things. But there's a long way to go in this line of change.

This example you saw of a pastoral farm, you call it "outdated," but it's still something you think the world can move back towards?

Right. So in "Project Animal Farm" I divide farms into four kinds. There's small pastoral, which I lived at in Belize. I lived with a Mennonite missionary family of women. They had a beautiful farm of a small herd of cows and small flocks of hens. They would sell every weekend at the farmers market. Living there and seeing how they work and how the pastures are managed and how the animals all have names, that was very eye-opening to me. There is a strong relationship among the people and the animals and the land.

Then there's small industrial, which doesn't really make any sense because you don't have economies of scale. It's industrial, but it's not like you are necessarily reducing costs by being industrial.

Then there's large industrial, which is more than 95 percent of the farms in the U.S. and Canada, which are factory farms. It's essentially a large industrial operation.

Then I come up with a fourth part of this, which I believe is the solution to most of the humane and sustainability problems we are seeing. That's large pastoral. In the book I'm not recommending that people go to the past. We move to the future while keeping the past in mind. I've been to a couple of these farms in the U.S. and Canada. It's a large farm and the animals are fully outdoors. It's pastoral, but it has economies of scale and the low costs that producers and consumers want.

It's a little closer to what someone who has never been to a farm might picture, it sounds like.

Yes, I think so. It's a very different experience when you go to a large industrial versus a large pastoral farm. It's completely different. The sensory feelings, which you are seeing and smelling, the conditions of the animals, the conditions of the place itself. It's something that has not been suggested before. I'm the first person to suggest it in the book. The economy today is so global and large and scale really does matter. I think that scale and ethics don't have to be in opposition with each other. We can have both.

Even with the world's rising demand for meat?

Yes, even with that demand. But one of the other points is that we need to reduce our meat consumption. That's very important in all of this: (per capita) meat consumption today is about 170 pounds of meat per year in the U.S. That's not including fish, eggs or milk. If we include all of these it becomes around 300 or so pounds a year. It's extremely unsustainable. It's unprecedented, such an extreme demand for meat being supplied on a daily basis. It's inhumane, it's unsustainable, and it's also unnecessary.

Some people ask me if I'm saying that everybody should be a vegetarian or vegan. It's not a dichotomy. My answer is that everybody can reduce their meat consumption. If a family of four reduces their meat consumption by a quarter, that's equal to one person being vegetarian. I'm not saying that everybody needs to be a vegetarian, but I am saying that everybody should do something, even if not everything. Reducing meat consumption and paying attention to where it's being purchased from and how those animals are treated is very important.

There's one other thing that you call for at the end of the book: increasing gender diversity in farms. Why is that such an important component of reform?

I got that idea at the Mennonite women's farm in Belize. In this family there were sons, but they didn't want to work on the farm. So it was very much a women-run farm. It was extremely different from all the other places, because most of the other places I visited were managed and owned by men. Animal agriculture today is very much a male-dominated industry at both worker levels and senior levels. At senior levels, one out of every 15 to 20 executives is going to be a woman. I wrote a long article in *The Atlantic* a couple of years ago; some of that argument is also in the book. Essentially when it comes to animals and food, men and women are shown scientifically to have different thoughts and opinions. Women are more likely to favor legislation for animals. Women eat less meat. Women eat less fast food. Women pay more attention to food safety. Women are more likely to buy organic. There's all this statistical data, not just in the U.S., but also in Europe and other countries that does show a difference between men and women and attitudes towards food and animals. Gender diversity is something that's good in any field. Any field that's male-dominated we've seen that it should have more women, whether we are talking about science, law, the police force. In agriculture it's perhaps more, or at least as much, as in these areas because the attitudes and opinions toward animals and food issues do vary by gender.

Questions for Discussion

1. What are some of the ways that Faruqi argues for farms to be changed?

2. How do Faruqi's credentials affect her author ethos and your reading of this interview as the audience?

3. How is Faruqi's description of the farms she visited similar or different to your own perception or experience of farms?

A Cow's Eye View

Temple Grandin

Thinking in Pictures, 2006

> Dr. Temple Grandin is a Professor of Animal Science at Colorado State University who is world-renowned for her work in designing humane slaughter facilities for major companies across the United States. She is famous not only for the work in her field, but for her advocacy work for children with autism, as she herself has autism. Her well-known books include *Humane Livestock Handling* and *Thinking in Pictures: My Life with Autism.* The excerpt here is from *Thinking in Pictures*, a book in which she attempts to "see through a cow's eyes" with her unique perspective in order to describe humane and efficient slaughterhouses.

One third of the cattle and hogs in the United States are handled in facilities I have designed. Throughout my career I have worked on systems to improve the treatment of livestock. The principle behind my designs is to use the animals' natural behavior patterns to encourage them to move willingly through the system. If an animal balks and refuses to walk through an alley, one needs to find out why it is scared and refuses to move. Unfortunately, people often try to correct these problems with force instead of by understanding the animal's behavior. My connection with these animals goes back to the time I first realized that the squeeze machine could help calm my anxiety. I have been seen the world from their point of view ever since.

People ask me all the time whether the cattle know they are going to be slaughtered. What I have observed over the years and at many meat plants is that the things that frighten cattle usually have nothing to do with death. It is the little things that make them balk and refuse to move, such as seeing a small piece of chain hanging down from an alley fence. For instance, a lead animal will stop to look at a moving chain and move his head back and forth in rhythm with its swing. He isn't concerned about being slaughtered; he's afraid of a small piece of chain that jiggles and looks out of place.

Most people do not observe these simple things because they get the cattle too excited by poking and prodding them when they refuse to move through an alley or out of a pen. When cattle are excited, it is impossible to determine what is bothering them. They go into antipredator mode and push themselves together in a boiling ball of circling, agitated animals, with their heads toward the center of the group. The smallest distraction can stop a group of cattle moving through an alley. I remember one time when a meat plant became totally chaotic because a plastic juice bottle had fallen into the entrance where the cattle lined up to walk into the plant. They absolutely refused to walk over the white plastic bottle. Anything that causes visual contrast will attract the animals' attention. They fear a drain gate across a concrete floor or a sparkling reflection from a puddle. Sometimes moving an overhead lamp to eliminate a reflection on a floor or wall will make it easier to move cattle and hogs. Poor lighting can cause many problems. Cattle and hogs will not walk into a dark place, so installing a lamp to illuminate the entrance to an alley will entice them to enter. Animals, like people, want to see where they are going.

When I put myself in a cow's place, I really have to be that cow and not a person in a cow costume. I use my visual thinking skills to simulate what an animal would see and hear in a given situation. I place myself inside its body and imagine what it experiences. It is the ultimate virtual reality system, but I also draw on the empathetic feelings of gentleness and kindness I have developed so that my simulation is more than a robotic computer model. Add to the equation all of my scientific knowledge of cattle behavior patterns and instincts. I have to follow the cattle's rules of behavior. I also have to imagine what experiencing the world through the cow's sensory system is like. Cattle have a very wide, panoramic visual field, because they are a prey species, ever wary and watchful for signs of danger. Similarly, some people with autism are like fearful animals in a world full of dangerous predators. They live in a constant state of fear, worrying about a change in routine or becoming upset if objects in their environment are moved. This fear of change may be an activation of ancient antipredator systems that are blocked or masked in most other people.

Fear is a universal emotion in the animal kingdom, because it provides an intense motivation to avoid predators. Fear is also a dominant emotion in autism. Therese Joliffe wrote that trying to keep everything the same helped her avoid some of the terrible fear. Tony W. wrote that he lived in a world of daydreaming and fear and was afraid of everything. Before I started taking antidepressants, minor changes in my daily routine caused a fear reaction. There were times that I was dominated by fear of trivial changes, such as switching to daylight savings time. This intense fear is probably due to a neurological defect that sensitizes the nervous system to stimuli that are minor to normal people.

In order to survive, members of a prey species such as cattle or sheep have to be ever vigilant and flee when they spot a predator. Cattle and sheep have supersensitive hearing, an acute sense of smell, and eyes on the sides of their heads so they can scan the landscape while grazing. They are much more sensitive to high-pitched sounds than people and can hear sounds that are outside the range of human hearing.

High-pitched sounds tend to be more disturbing to them than low-pitched sounds. Tom Camp, a USDA researcher in Texas, found that a loud bell on an outdoor telephone caused a calf's heart rate to jump suddenly by fifty to seventy beats per minute. It's unlikely that anyone but me would have noticed that the sounds that upset cattle are the same kinds of sounds that are unbearable to many autistic children with overly sensitive hearing. A sudden hissing similar to that caused by the air brakes on a semi truck will trigger a strong startle reaction in both calves and cattle. When calves hear this sound, they instantly lay their ears against their heads and back up to get away from the source of the noise. Like cattle, a person with autism has hypervigilant senses.

Even today, a person whistling in the middle of the night will cause my heart to race. High-pitched sounds are the worst. High, rapidly repeated sounds are stimulating to the nervous system. P.B. McConnell and his colleague J.R. Baylis, in Germany, found that dog trainers use high-pitched intermittent sounds to stimulate a dog to do something like fetch, while low sounds are used to make it stop, such as saying "Whoa" to a horse. In tame animals the high-pitched sounds have a mild activating effect, but in wild animals and autistic children they set off a massive fear reaction.

Contrary to popular belief, cattle and other livestock can see color, but their visual system is most attuned to detecting novel movement. Cattle vision is like having wide-angle camera lenses mounted on the sides of your head. The animals have 360 degree vision and can see all around themselves, except for a small blind spot behind their rear ends. However, the price they pay for wide-angle vision is a very narrow field where they can perceive depth. To do that, cattle have to stop and put their heads down. Predatory species, such as lions, dogs, cats, and tigers, have their eyes on the front of their heads, which enables them to perceive depth and accurately judge distances when they leap and bring down their prey. Eyes on the front of the head provide superior binocular vision, whereas eyes on the sides of the head provide the ability to scan the environment and be constantly vigilant.

In the old American West, novelty sometimes triggered stampedes during the great cattle drives. A hat blowing in the wind or a horse bucking would set off the instinct to flee. It is possible to desensitize cattle to novelty, however. For example, calves in the Philippines are grazed along the highways from birth. They learn that all the sights and sounds of the highway will not hut them. These tame, halter-broken animals are not perturbed by anything.

Most cattle on American ranches are exposed to far less novelty. Coats and hats left on fences will often cause them to balk and refuse to walk by. When a steer is calm in its familiar home feedlot pen, the same hat or coat left on a fence may evoke first fear and then curiosity. The steer will turn and look at the coat and then cautiously approach it. If the coat does not move, he will eventually lick it. A coat that is flapping in the wind is more likely to make animals fearful, and they will keep their distance. In the wild, sudden movement is a sign of danger; it may be a lion in a bush or an animal fleeting from a predator.

The reaction of cattle to something that appears out of place may be similar to the reaction of autistic children to small discrepancies in their environment. Autistic children don't like anything that looks out of place—a thread hanging on a piece of furniture, a wrinkled rug, books that are crooked on the bookshelf. Sometimes they will straighten out the books and other times they will be afraid. Their fear reaction may be similar to a cow's reaction to a coffee cup in an alley or a hat on a fence. Autistic children will also notice minor discrepancies that normal people ignore. Could this be an old antipredator instinct that has surfaced? In the wild, a broken branch on a tree or disturbed earth is a possible sign of predator activity in the vicinity. The animal that survives and avoids the lions is the one that has developed the finest abilities in detecting warning signs of changes.

Cattle, deer, and antelope will turn and face a source of potential danger that is not immediately threatening. Cows on a pasture will turn and face an approaching person, and antelope on the African plains will turn toward and sometimes follow a lion they cannot see. The animals will follow the lion but remain at a safe distance, which enables instant flight. This is known as the animal's flight zone.

People working with cattle reared on the open range can use the principles of the flight zone to move groups of animals efficiently and quickly. The size of the flight zone will vary depending on how tame the cattle are. Tame dairy cattle may have no flight zone, and they will approach people for petting. Beef cattle raised on western ranches are not completely tame, and they will move away if people go too close to them. The flight zone can vary from five feet to over one hundred feet. Excited cattle will have a larger flight distance than calm cattle. H. Hedigar stated in his book *The Psychology and Behavior of Animals in Zoos and Circuses* that taming is the artificial removal of the flight distance between animals and people.

It is fairly easy to move groups of cattle in a quiet and orderly manner if people work on the edge of the herd's collective flight zone. Deep invasion of the flight zone, however, may cause cattle to panic. If they are cornered in a pen, they may attempt to jump a fence to increase the distance between themselves and a threatening person.

Therapists have observed that autistic children often lash out when they stand close to other children while waiting in a line. They become tense when other children invade their personal space. Having another child accidentally brush up against them can cause them to withdraw with fear like a frightened animal. A light unexpected touch triggers flight, and a firm touch, similar to the pressure of a tightly bunched herd of cattle, is calming.

A great deal of my success in working with animals comes from the simple fact that I see all kinds of connections between their behavior and certain autistic behaviors. Another example is the fact that both cattle and people with autism can become very set in their habits. A change in a daily routine can cause an autistic person to have a tantrum. Such changes used to make me very anxious. Ranchers have discovered that cattle placed on a new pasture must be encouraged to graze the entire area when they are first put there. I observed a lazy group of bullies that refused to walk less than a quarter of a mile to a good pasture. Why do cattle do this? It may have something to do with instincts to avoid predators. When cattle learn that a certain area is safe, they become reluctant to move to a new area, which may contain danger.

An experiment that Ken Odde and I conducted at Colorado State University indicated the great strength of a bovine's reluctance to change a previously learned safe route. Cattle were given a choice between and alley that led to a squeeze chute and an alley that they could just walk through. The animals quickly learned to avoid the side where they would be restrained in the squeeze chute. When the alleys were switched, most of the cattle refused to switch sides to avoid restraint. Being held in a squeeze chute is slightly uncomfortable, but not so aversive that the animals were willing to change from the previously learned safe route. When something really painful or disagreeable happens, though, most animals will quickly change to avoid it. Mary Tanner, a student at Colorado State University, found that most cows at a dairy were willing to enter both sides of a milking parlor, but a few were very rigid and always entered on the same side.

Preliminary evidence indicates that the more nervous and excitable cows are the ones that are the most reluctant to change a previously learned safe route. Resistance to change may be partially motivated by attempts to reduce anxiety. In my own experience, minor changes in my high school class schedule or switching from daylight savings time to standard time caused severe anxiety. My nervous system and the nervous systems of some other people with autism are in a state of hyperarousal for not good reason. Before I took antidepressant drugs, my nervous system was constantly ready to flee predators. Insignificant little stresses caused the same reaction as being attacked by a lion. These problems were created by abnormalities in my nervous system. Now that the medication has calmed my nerves, I can take small changes in routine in stride.

One of the most stressful events for semiwild cattle is having people deeply invade their flight zone when they are unable to move away. A person leaning over the top of an alley is very threatening to beef cattle that are not completely tame. Cattle will also balk ad refuse to walk through an alley if they can see people up ahead. This is one of the reasons that I designed curved single-file alleys with solid sides. They help keep cattle calmer. The solid sides prevent the animals from being frightened by people and other moving objects outside the alley. A curved alley also works better than a straight one because the cattle are unable to see people up ahead, and each animal thinks he is going back where he came from.

Understanding these kinds of sensitivities made it possible for me to figure out ways to calm flighty antelope at the zoo when other people were convinced that it was impossible to train them to cooperate during veterinary procedures. These procedures were often very stressful, because the animals had to be either shot with a tranquilizer dart or grabbed by people. Antelope can be trained to accept new procedures and novel sights and sounds if those things are introduced gradually and quietly, while the animals are fed treats. I worked with students Megan Phillips, Wendy Grafham, and Mat Rooney to train nyala and bongo antelope to enter a plywood box willingly and stand still during veterinary procedures such as blood testing and injections. The solid sides on the box provided the animals with a sense of safety and security. While they munched on treats, the veterinarian worked on them. During training, we had to take care to avoid triggering a massive fright reaction in these prey-species animals. They had to be carefully desensitized to the sound and movement of the doors on the box, and to people reaching into the box and touching them.

The crafty animals quickly learned to enter the box to get the treats and then kick the moment a blood test was attempted. To stop this, we withheld the treat until the animal stood still and cooperated. Trainers have to discriminate between kicking because of fear and kicking simply to avoid doing something the animal doesn't want to do. Withholding a feed reward will stop learned kicking, but it will have not effect on kicking and thrashing due to fear.

People who work with nonverbal, low-functioning people with autism must similarly be able to determine whether a tantrum or other bad behavior is caused by fear or pain or is a learned avoidance response. Sometimes it's because of pain from sounds that hurt their ears or fear of an unexpected change in routine. Like the cattle and the antelope, autistics are afraid of the unexpected. But sometimes they throw tantrums simply to get attention or to avoid doing a certain activity or school lesson. In one study, aggression and outbursts were greatly reduced in very severely handicapped autistic adults by giving them an object to hold fifteen minutes before they were scheduled to have lunch or ride on the bus. A spoon was used before lunch, and a toy bus was used before riding on the bus. Touch was the only sense that was not confused by sensory jumbling, and holding the object let these people get mentally ready for the next event in their daily routine. There were times when I threw a big tantrum just to watch the grownups react. Observant teachers can tell the difference between a massive fear reaction and the calculated use of bad behavior to avoid tasks the person does not want to do.

People Problems

Mistreatment by people is the number-one cause of animals becoming frightened. The best equipment in the world is worthless unless management controls the behavior of plant employees. When I first started designing equipment, I naively believed that if I could design the perfect system, it would control employee behavior. This is not possible, but I have designed equipment that requires very little skill to operate, provided employees are gentle. Good engineering is important, and well-designed facilities provide the tools that make low-stress, quiet handling at slaughter possible, but employees must operate the system correctly. Rough, callous people will cause distress to animals even if they use the best equipment.

Management attitude is the most important variable that determines how animals are treated. I wouldn't be surprised if this were true of any organization. Livestock handling has greatly improved during the past ten years, and managers are becoming more sensitive about animal welfare, but there still needs to be improvement. It is very painful for me to watch somebody abuse an animal, especially when it happens in one of my systems. Some people buy new equipment and think that it is a substitute for good management. Over the years I have seen animal handling improve with a change in management, and

I have seen it get rough and nasty when a good manager left. A good manager serves as a conscience for the employees. He has to be involved enough to care but not so involved that he becomes numb and desensitized. One cannot rely on the foreman to enforce good behavior. This person often becomes immune to animal suffering on the slaughter floor. The manager who enforces god animal handling is usually most effective if he is at the plant-manager level. Someone in a distant headquarters office is often too detached from the reality of the slaughter floor to be concerned.

Plants that have high standards of animal welfare enforce strict codes of conduct. One manager built his offices so that he could see the stockyards and the cattle ramp that led into the plant. If he saw employees hitting or whipping the cattle, he called the foreman. Employees who handle thousands of animals often become careless and hard. The people who actually kill the animals should be rotated, and complete automation of the actual killing procedure is good for employee well-being. Automation of killing is especially important in very high-speed plants, with rates of over 150 cattle per hour. A person becomes a zombie when he has to shoot thousands of cattle every day. At slower speeds one can take pride in doing the job humanely and treat each animal with respect, but at high speeds it's all one can do to keep up with the relentless movement of the line.

Management also has to be willing to take the time and make the effort to improve handling methods. Employees have to be trained to understand cattle behavior and use the natural instincts of the animals to assist movement. Trained employees learn to time groups of animals so that they will follow the leader. Each group must be driven up to the single-file alley just as the last animal from the previous group is walking into it. If the next group is driven up too quickly, the cattle or hogs will turn around, because there is no place to go. I love nothing more than to watch a plant I've designed run smoothly and efficiently, knowing that the animals are being treated with decency.

I'm always surprised at the number of people who think that the :jungle: still exists at the Chicago stockyards. The Chicago stockyards have been gone for more than thirty years. When I discuss my job with fellow travelers on airplanes, many ask if a sledgehammer is still used. That was banned by the Humane Slaughter Act in 1958 in all meat plants that sold to the U.S. government. In 1978 the act was strengthened to cover all federally inspected plants that sell meat in interstate commerce. The Humane Slaughter Act requires that cattle, pigs, sheep, and goats must be instantaneously rendered insensible to pain prior to slaughter. The act does not cover poultry or ritual slaughter by any religious faith. The law requires that animals are rendered insensible to pain by either captive bolt stunning, electrical stunning, or CO_2 gas. Captive bolt kills the animal instantly by driving a steel bolt into the brain. It has the same effect as a gun. Electrical stunning causes instantaneous unconsciousness by passing a high-amperage electrical current through the brain. It works the same way as electroconvulsive shock treatment in people. If the procedure is done correctly the animal becomes instantly unconscious.

People often ask me if animals are afraid of blood. Again it's the small distractions that scare the animals more than blood. Blood or urine from relatively calm cattle appears to have no effect, but blood from cattle that have become very frightened may contain a "smell of fear" substance. If the cattle remain relatively calm they will voluntarily walk into a chute with blood on it. But if an animal becomes severely stressed for over five minutes the next animal will often refuse to enter.

Design of Restraint Equipment

Many people who design systems to restrain animals don't think about what the device will feel like to the animal. Some engineers are strangely unaware that a sharp edge will dig and hurt. They build devices that mas the animal or dig into it. Restraint equipment used to hold cattle or hogs for either veterinary work or slaughter often squeezes the animal too hard or holds it in an uncomfortable position. One of the reasons I am good at designing this equipment is that I can visualize what the device will feel like. I can put myself into a twelve-hundred-pound steer's body and feel the equipment. What would it be like with a gentle person operating it? What would it be like with a rough person operating it? When I see somebody squeeze and animal too hard in a squeeze chute, it makes me hurt all over.

One of my crusades in the meat industry has been to eliminate shackling and hoisting a method of restraint in kosher slaughter plants. The main animal welfare problem with kosher slaughter is the dreadful methods of restraint used in some plants. The variable of the restraint method must be separated from the variable of the actual shehita kosher cut, which is performed on a fully conscious animal. In kosher slaughter, a special, razor-sharp, long straight knife is used. When the cut is made correctly according to the rules outlined in the Talmud, the animal does not appear to feel it. The Talmud states that there cannot be any hesitation during he cut and the incision must not close back over the knife. The knife must have a perfect blade and be free of nicks, because a nick would cause pain.

I will never forget having nightmares after visiting the now defunct Spencer Foods plant in Spencer, Iowa, fifteen years ago. Employees wearing football helmets attached a nose tong to the nose of a writhing beast suspended by a chain wrapped around one back leg. Each terrified animal was forced with an electric prod to run into a small stall which had a slick floor on a forty-five-degree angle. This caused the animal to slip and fall so that workers could attach the chain to its rear leg. As I watched this nightmare, I thought, "This should not be happening in a civilized society." In my diary I wrote, "If hell exists, I am in it." I vowed that I would replace the plant from hell with a kinder and gentler system.

Ten years ago I was hired by the Council for Livestock Protection in New York to develop a humane upright restraint system for kosher calves. The council was a consortium of major animal advocacy groups such as the Humane Society of the United States, the American Society for the Prevention of Cruelty to Animals, the Fund for Animals, the Massachusetts SPCA, the American Humane Association, and others. It was formed in the early seventies to replace shackling and hoisting with more humane methods of restraint. At this time, upright restraining equipment existed for kosher slaughter of large cattle, but no equipment was available for calves or sheep. When the Humane Slaughter Act was passed in 1958, kosher slaughter was exempted, because no humane alternatives to shackling and hoisting of fully conscious animals existed.

Walter Giger, Don Kinsman, and Ralph Prince, at the University of Connecticut, had demonstrated that a calf can be restrained in a comfortable manner when it straddles a moving conveyor. The animal rides the conveyor like a person riding a horse, supported under the belly and chest. Solid sides on each side of the conveyor prevent it from tilting off. The Connecticut researchers had a good idea, but I had to invent many new components to construct a system that would work in a commercial slaughter plant. To make the new system work, I had to eliminate all pressure points which caused discomfort to the animals. For example, uncomfortable pressure on the leg joints caused calves to struggle and fight the restrainer. Elimination of the pressure points resulted in calm, quiet calves.

One of the advantages of a conveyor restraint system for both conventional slaughter, where cattle are stunned, and ritual slaughter is that the cattle move through it in a continuous line. Each animal has its head on the rear of the animal in front of it. Having observed cattle, I realized that they remain calmer when they can touch each other. Since the cattle were in continuous contact with each other, they remained calmer at the slaughter plant than at the squeeze chute at the Colorado State University Experiment Station. I've also observed that cattle are accustomed to walking in single file. An overview of a cow pasture shows the small, twelve-inch-wide cowpaths. Walking in single file is part of the nature of cattle. This is why a system that handles cattle moving through in single file works well.

Many people do not believe me when I tell them that cattle slaughter can be really calm, peaceful, and humane. In some plants, the cattle remain absolutely calm and the employees are very conscientious. At one large plant, 240 cattle per hour quietly walked up the ramp and voluntarily entered the double-rail conveyor restrainer. It was as if they were going in to get milked. Each fat steer walked into the restrainer entrance and settled down on the conveyor like a little old lady getting on the bus. Most animals entered the restrainer when they were patted on the rear end. Since the cattle move through the system in a continuous line, they are never alone and separated from their buddies. At this plant, the system had been beautifully installed and was brightly illuminated. When slaughter is conducted properly, the cattle experience less stress and discomfort than they experience during handling procedures in the veterinary chute.

Being autistic has helped me to understand how they feel, because I know what it is like to feel my heart race when a car horn honks in the middle of the night. I have hyperacute senses and fear responses that may be more like those of a prey-species animal than of most humans. People often fail to observe animals. Recently I visited a slaughter plant where the cattle were terrified of air that hissed from a pneumatically powered gate. Every time the gate opened or closed, the cattle recoiled and backed down the chute. They reacted as if they had seen a rattlesnake. It was obvious to me that the hissing air scared them, but other people failed to see it. Purchase of a few air silencers solved the problem. With the hissing gone, the animals were no longer afraid of the gate. All it took was a cow's eye view.

Questions for Discussion

1. How does Dr. Grandin use her experience and research with autism to advocate for humanely handling animals in this chapter?

2. Why might Dr. Grandin have chosen to intersperse her description of animal reactions with explanations of how people with autism react to stimuli? How could this appeal to her audience?

3. How do you think Sonia Faruqi, the woman interviewed in Abrams' article, would react to Dr. Grandin's approach to slaughter?

Farmland without Farmers

Wendell Berry

The Atlantic, March 2015

> This article was published in the *Atlantic Monthly* in early 2015. As stated on the publication's website, the *Atlantic Monthly* is a long standing publication that was created in 1857 by renowned poets, Ralph Waldo Emerson and Henry Wadsworth Longfellow. Today, *The Atlantic* describes itself as "a source of opinion, commentary, and analysis for America's most influential individuals who wish to be challenged, informed and entertained." As a publication, it has won more national magazine awards than any other magazine. The article was excerpted from Wendell Berry's recent book, *Our Only World: Ten Essays*, a collection of essays that according to *The Miami Herald*, "convey outrage over environmental and community ruin while also expressing hope that the very species that inflicted such harm is capable of doing better."

As industrial agriculture replaces men with machines, the American landscape loses its stewards, and the culture they built.

The landscapes of our country are now virtually deserted. In the vast, relatively flat acreage of the Midwest now given over exclusively to the production of corn and soybeans, the number of farmers is lower than it has ever been. I don't know what the average number of acres per farmer now is, but I do know that you often can drive for hours through those corn-and-bean deserts without seeing a human being beyond the road ditches, or any green plant other than corn and soybeans. Any people you may see at work, if you see any at work anywhere, almost certainly will be inside the temperature-controlled cabs of large tractors, the connection between the human organism and the soil organism perfectly interrupted by the machine. Thus we have transposed our culture, our cultural *goal*, of sedentary, indoor work to the fields. Some of the "field work," unsurprisingly, is now done by airplanes.

This contact, such as it is, between land and people is now brief and infrequent, occurring mainly at the times of planting and harvest. The speed and scale of this work have increased until it is impossible to give close attention to anything beyond the performance of the equipment. The condition of the crop of course is of concern and is observed, but not the condition of the land. And so the technological focus of industrial agriculture by which species diversity has been reduced to one or two crops is reducing human participation ever nearer to zero. Under the preponderant rule of "labor-saving," the worker's attention to the work place has been effectively nullified even when the worker is present. The "farming" of corn-and-bean farmers—and of others as fully industrialized—has been brought down from the complex arts of tending or husbanding the land to the application of purchased inputs according to the instructions conveyed by labels and operators' manuals.

To make as much sense as I can of our predicament, I turn to Wes Jackson, founder of the Land Institute, in Salina, Kansas, and his perception that for any parcel of land in human use there is an "eyes-to-acres ratio" that is right and is necessary to save it from destruction. By "eyes" Wes means a competent watchfulness, aware of the nature and the history of the place, constantly present, always alert for signs of harm and signs of health. The necessary ratio of eyes to acres is not constant from one place to another, nor is it scientifically predictable or computable for any place, because from place to place there are too many natural and human variables. The need for the right eyes-to-acres ratio appears nonetheless to have the force of law.

We can suppose that the eyes-to-acres ratio is approximately correct when a place is thriving in human use and care. The sign of its thriving would be the evident good health and diversity, not just of its crops and livestock but also of its population of native and noncommercial creatures, including the community of creatures living in the soil. Equally indicative and necessary would be the signs of a thriving local and locally adapted human economy.

The great and characteristic problem of industrial agriculture is that it does not distinguish one place from another. In effect, it blinds its practitioners to where they are. It cannot, by definition, be adapted to local ecosystems, topographies, soils, economies, problems, and needs.

The sightlessness and thoughtlessness of the imposition of the corn-and-bean industry upon the sloping or rolling countryside hereabouts is made vividly objectionable to me by my memory of the remarkably careful farming that was commonly practiced in these central Kentucky counties in the 1940s and 50s—though, even then, amid much regardlessness and damage. The best farming here was highly diversified in both plants and animals. Its basis was understood to be grass and grazing animals; cattle, sheep, hogs, and, during the 40s, the workstock, all were pastured. Grain crops typically were raised to be fed; the farmers would say, "The grain raised here must *walk* off." And so in any year only a small fraction of the land would be plowed. The commercial economy of the farms was augmented and supported by the elaborate subsistence economies of the households. "I may be sold out or run out," the farmers would say, "but I'll not be *starved* out."

My brother recently reminded me how carefully our father thought about the *nature* of our home countryside. He had witnessed the ultimate futility—the high costs to both farmer and farm—of raising corn for cash during the hard times of the 1920s and 30s. He concluded, rightly, that the crop that could be raised most profitably in the long run was grass. That was because we did not have large acreages that could safely be used for growing grain, but our land was aboundingly productive of grass, which moreover it produced more cheaply than any other crop. And the grass sod, which was perennial, covered and preserved the soil the year round.

A further indication of the quality of the farming here in the 40s and 50s is that the Soil Conservation Service was more successful during those years than it would or could be again in the promotion of plowing and terracing on the contour to control soil erosion. Those measures at that time were permitted by the right scale of the farming and of the equipment then in use. Anybody familiar with topographic maps will know that contour lines remain strictly horizontal over the irregularities of the land's surfaces; crop rows cannot be regularly spaced. This variability presents no significant problem to a farmer using one- or two-row equipment in relatively small lands or fields. And so for a while contour farming became an established practice on many farms, and to good effect. It was defeated primarily by the enlargement of fields and the introduction of larger equipment. Eventually, many farmers simply ignored their terraces, plowing over them, the planted rows sometimes running straight downhill. Earlier, a good many farmers had taken readily to the idea of soil conservation. A farmer in a neighboring county said, "I want the water to *walk* off my land, not run." But beyond a certain scale, the farming begins to conform to the demands of the machines, not to the nature of the land.

Within three paragraphs I have twice quoted farmers who used "walk" as an approving figure of speech: Grain leaving a farm hereabouts should *walk* off; and the rainwater fallen upon a farm should *walk*, not run. This is not merely a coincidence. The gait most congenial to agrarian thought and sensibility is walking. It is the gait best suited to paying attention, most conservative of land

and equipment, and most permissive of stopping to look or think. Machines, companies, and politicians "run." Farmers studying their fields travel at a walk.

Farms that are highly diversified and rightly scaled tend, by their character and structure, toward conservation of the land, the human community, and the local economy. Such farms are both work places and homes to the families who inhabit them and who are intimately involved in the daily life of land and household. Without such involvement, farmers cease to be country people and become in effect city people, industrial workers and consumers, living in the country.

I have spoken so far of the decline of country work, but the decline of country pleasures is at least equally significant. If the people who live and work in the country don't also enjoy the country, a valuable and necessary part of life is missing. And for families on farms of a size permitting them to be intimately lived on and from, the economic life of the place is itself the primary country pleasure. As one would expect, not every day or every job can be a pleasure, but for farmers who love their livestock there is pleasure in watching the animals graze and in winter feeding. There is pleasure in the work of maintenance, the redemption of things worn or broken, that must go on almost continuously. There is pleasure in the growing, preserving, cooking, and eating of the good food that the family's own land provides. But around this core of the life and work of the farm are clustered other pleasures, in their way also life-sustaining, and most of which are cheap or free.

I live in a country that would be accurately described as small-featured. There are no monumental land forms, no peaks or cliffs or high waterfalls, no wide or distant vistas. Though it is by nature a land of considerable beauty, there is little here that would attract vacationing wilderness lovers. It is blessed by a shortage of picturesque scenery and mineable minerals. The topography, except in the valley bottoms, is rolling or sloping. Along the sides of the valleys, the slopes are steep. It is divided by many hollows and streams, and it has always been at least partially wooded.

Because of the brokenness and diversity of the landscape, there was never until lately a clean separation here between the pursuits of farming and those of hunting and gathering. On many farms the agricultural income, including the homegrown and homemade subsistence of the households, would be supplemented by hunting or fishing or trapping or gathering provender from the woods and berry patches—perhaps by all of these. And beyond their economic contribution, these activities were forms of pleasure. Many farmers kept hounds or bird dogs. The gear and skills of hunting and fishing belonged to ordinary daily and seasonal life. More ordinary was the walking (or riding or driving) and looking that kept people aware of the condition of the ground, the crops, the pastures, and the livestock, of the state of things in the house yard and the garden, in the woods, and along the sides of the streams.

My own community, centered upon the small village of Port Royal, is along the Kentucky River and in the watersheds of local tributaries. Its old life, before the industrialization of much of the farmland and the urbanization of the people, was under the influence of the river, as other country communities of that time were under the influence of the railroads. In the neighborhood of Port Royal practically every man and boy, some girls and women too, fished from time to time in the Kentucky River. Some of the men fished "all the time" or "way too much." Until about a generation ago, there was some commercial fishing. And I can remember when hardly a summer day would pass when from the house where eventually I would live you could not hear the shouts of boys swimming in the river, often flying out into the water from the end of a swinging rope. I remember when I was one of them. My mother, whose native place this was, loved her girlhood memories of swimming parties and picnics at the river. In hot weather she and her friends would walk the mile from Port Royal down to the river for a cooling swim, and then would make the hot walk back up the hill to town.

Now the last of the habituated fishermen of the local waters are now dead. They have been replaced by fishermen using expensive "bassboats," almost as fast as automobiles, whose sport is less describable as fishing than as using equipment. In the last year only one man, comparatively a newcomer, has come to the old landing where I live to fish with trotlines—and, because of the lack of competition, he has caught several outsize catfish. Some local people, and a good many outsiders, hunt turkeys and deer. There is still a fair amount of squirrel hunting. The bobwhite, the legendary gamebird of this region, is almost extinct here, and the bird hunters with them. A rare few still hunt with hounds.

Most remarkable is the disappearance of nearly all children and teenagers, from the countryside, and in general from the out-of-doors. The technologies of large-scale industrial agriculture are too complicated and too dangerous to allow the participation of children. For most families around here, the time is long gone when children learned to do farmwork by playing at it, and then taking part in it, in the company of their parents. It seems that most children now don't play much in their house yards, let alone in the woods and along the creeks. Many now descend from their school buses at the ends of lanes and driveways to be carried the rest of the way to their houses in parental automobiles. Most teenagers apparently divide their out-of-school time between indoor entertainment and travel in motor vehicles. The big boys no longer fish or swim or hunt or camp out. Or work. The town boys, who used to hire themselves out for seasonal or part-time work on the farms, no longer find such work available, or they don't wish to do the work that is available.

Local people who regularly hunted or fished or foraged or walked or played in the local countryside served the local economy and stewardship as inspectors, rememberers, and storytellers. They gave their own kind of service to the eyes-to-acres ratio. Now most of those people are gone or absent, along with most of the farming people who used to be at work here.

With them have gone the local stories and songs. When people begin to replace stories from local memory with stories from television screens, another vital part of life is lost. I have my own memories of the survival in a small rural community of its own stories. By telling and retelling those stories, people told themselves who they were, where they were, and what they had done. They thus maintained in ordinary conversation their own living history. And I have from my neighbor, John Harrod, a thorough student of Kentucky's traditional fiddle music, his testimony that every rural community once heard, sang, and danced to at least a few tunes that were uniquely its own. What is the economic value of stories and songs? What is the economic value of the lived and living life of a community? My argument here is directed by my belief that the art and the life of settled rural communities are critical to our life-supporting economy. But their value is incalculable. It can only be acknowledged and respected, and our present economy is incapable, and cannot on its own terms be made capable, of such acknowledgement and respect.

Meanwhile, the farmlands and woodlands of this neighborhood are being hurt worse and faster by bad farming and bad logging than at any other time in my memory. The signs of this abuse are often visible even from the roads, but nobody is looking. Or to people who are looking, but seeing from no perspective of memory or knowledge, the country simply looks "normal." Outsiders who come visiting almost always speak of it as "beautiful." But along this river, the Kentucky, which I have known all my life, and have lived beside for half a century, there is a large and regrettable recent change, clearly apparent to me, and to me indicative of changes in water quality, but perfectly invisible to nearly everybody else.

I don't remember what year it was when I first noticed the disappearance of the native black willows from the low-water line of this river. Their absence was sufficiently noticeable, for the willows were both visually prominent and vital to the good health of the river. Wherever the banks were broken by "slips" or the uprooting of large trees, and so exposed to sunlight, the willows would come in quickly to stabilize the banks. Their bushy growth and pretty foliage gave the shores of the river a distinctive grace, now gone and much missed by the few who remember. Like most people, I don't welcome bad news, and so I said to myself that perhaps the willows were absent only from the stretch of the river that I see from my house and work places. But in 2002 for the first time in many years I had the use of a motor boat, and I examined carefully the shores of the twenty-seven-mile pool between locks one and two. I saw a few old willows at the tops of the high banks, but none at or near the low-water line, and no young ones anywhere.

The willows still live as usual along other streams in the area, and they thrive along the shore of the Ohio River just above the mouth of the Kentucky at Carrollton. The necessary conclusion is that their absence from the Kentucky River must be attributable to something seriously wrong with the water. And so, since 2002, I have asked everybody I met who might be supposed to know: "Why have the black willows disappeared from the Kentucky River?" I have put this question to conservationists, to conservation organizations specifically concerned with the Kentucky River, to water-quality officials and to university biologists. And I have found nobody who could tell me why. Except for a few old fishermen, I have found nobody who knew they were gone.

This may seem astonishing. At least, for a while, it astonished me. I thought that in a state in which water pollution is a permanent issue, people interested in water quality surely would be alert to the disappearance of a prominent member of the riparian community of a major river. But finally I saw that such ignorance is more understandable than I had thought. A generation or so ago, when fishing and the condition of the river were primary topics of conversation in Port Royal, the disappearance of the willows certainly would have been noticed. Fishermen used to tie their trotlines to the willows.

That time is past, and I was seeking local knowledge from conservationists and experts and expert conservationists. But most conservationists, like most people now, are city people. They "escape" their urban circumstances and preoccupations by going on vacations. They thus go into the countryside only occasionally, and their vacations are unlikely to take them into the economic landscapes. They want to go to parks, wilderness areas, or other famous "destinations." Government and university scientists often have economic concerns or responsibilities, and some of them do venture into farmland or working forests or onto streams and rivers that are not "wild." But it seems they are not likely to have a particular or personal or long-term interest in such places, or to go back to them repeatedly and often over a long time, or to maintain an economic or recreational connection to them. Such scientists affect the eyes-to-acres ratio probably less than the industrial farmers.

Among the many conservationists I have encountered in my home state, the most competent witness by far is Barth Johnson, a retired game warden who is a dedicated trapper, hunter, and fisherman, as he has been all his life. Barth has devoted much of his life to conservation. Like most conservationists, he is informed about issues and problems. Unlike most, he is exceptionally alert to what is happening in the actual countryside that needs to be conserved. This is because he is connected to the fields and woods and waters he knows by bonds of economy and pleasure, both at once. Moreover, he has lived for thirty years in the same place at the lower end of the Licking River. This greatly increases the value of his knowledge, for he can speak of changes *over time*. People who stay put and remain attentive know that the countryside changes, as it must, and for better or worse.

He tells a story about Harris Creek, a small stream along which he had trapped for many years. It was richly productive, and Barth was careful never to ask too much of it. But in 2007, confident that it would be as it always had been, he went there with his traps and discovered that the stream was dead. He could not find a live minnow or crawfish. There were no animal tracks. So far as he could tell, there could be only one reason for this: In the spring of that year, the bottomland along the creek had been herbicided to kill the grass in preparation for a seeding of alfalfa. In 2008, the stream was still dead. In 2009, there was "a little coon activity." Finally, in 2013, the stream was "close to normal."

I have also learned from Barth that upstream as far as he has looked, to a point two and a half miles above the small town of Boston, the black willows are gone from the Licking River. And in October 2013, he wrote me that the river had turned a brownish "brine" color that he had never seen before.

What happened to the willows? Two young biologists at Northern Kentucky University are now at work on the question, and perhaps they will find the answer. But other scientists have led me to consider the possibility that such questions will not be answered. It may be extremely difficult or impossible to attach a specific effect to a specific cause in a large volume of flowing water.

What killed Harris Creek? Barth's evidence is "anecdotal," without scientifically respectable proof. I have read scientific papers establishing that the herbicide glyphosate and its "degradation products" are present in high concentrations in some Mississippi River tributaries, but the papers say nothing about the effects. I have called up scientists working on water quality, including one of the authors of one of the papers on glyphosate. What about the *effects*? Good question. Nobody knows the answer. It seems that the research projects and the researchers are widely scattered, making such work somewhat incoherent. And besides, there is always the difficulty of pinning a specific cause to a specific effect. To two of these completely friendly and obliging people I told Barth's story of Harris Creek: Does that surprise you? One said it did not surprise him. The other said it was possible but unlikely that the stream was killed by an herbicide. Was an insecticide also involved?

What caused the strange discoloration of the Licking River? Since the discoloration was visible until obscured by mud in the water when the river rose, I suppose that, if it happens again, the odd color could be traced upstream to a source. Will somebody do that? I don't know. Is any scientist from any official body monitoring the chemical runoff from croplands and other likely sources? I have been asking that question too, and so far I have asked nobody who could answer.

In my search for answers, it may be that I have been making a characteristic modern mistake of relying on experts, which has revealed a characteristic modern failure: Experts often don't know and sometimes can never know. Beneficiaries of higher education, of whom I am one, often give too much credit to credentials.

Confronting industrial agriculture, we are requiring ourselves to substitute science for citizenship, community membership, and land stewardship. But science fails at all of these. Science as it now predominantly is, by definition and on its own terms, does not make itself accountable for unintended effects. The intended effect of chemical nitrogen fertilizer, for example, is to grow corn, whereas its known effect on the Mississippi River and the Gulf of Mexico is a catastrophic accident. Moreover, science of this kind is invariably limited and controlled by the corporations that pay for it.

We have an ancient and long-enduring cultural imperative of neighborly love and work. This becomes ever more important as hardly imaginable suffering is imposed upon all creatures by industrial tools and industrial weapons. If we are to continue, in our only world, with any hope of thriving in it, we will have to expect neighborly behavior of sciences, of industries, and of governments, just as we expect it of our citizens in their neighborhoods.

Questions for Discussion

1. What role does Berry believe stories play within a community? How does he believe stories have changed over the last few decades? According to Berry, what effect does this have on the individual's relationship to the land?

2. What kind of evidence does Berry use to support his argument? How does this kind of evidence shape his message? How does it affect his credibility?

3. Berry talks about the importance of the connection between the community and the land. In what way is this sentiment echoed in the Guardian piece?

The Amish Farmers Reinventing Organic Agriculture

Roc Morin

The Atlantic, October 2014

> According to his website, Roc Morin is a journalist, photographer, and multimedia artist based in New York City. He is the curator for the World Dream Atlas, a Facebook page that contains a collection of dreams from around the world. He is also the author of the book, &, which contains stories from his time as a New York City ambulance driver, and a photojournalist. In addition to his work for *The Atlantic*, Morin has also written articles for *NPR, Vice, The Daily Mail,* and *The History Channel.* This article was published in *The Atlantic* in October of 2014, and it centers on the work of John Kempf, and his organization, Advancing Eco Agriculture, a consulting firm whose mission is to "create regenerative farming systems that help farmers grow disease and insect resistant crops with complete plant nutrition."

By studying the immune systems of plants, they've developed a technique that eliminates the need for chemicals.

"In the Second World War," Samuel Zook began, "my ancestors were conscientious objectors because we don't believe in combat." The Amish farmer paused a moment to inspect a mottled leaf on one of his tomato plants before continuing. "If you really stop and think about it, though, when we go out spraying our crops with pesticides, that's really what we're doing. It's chemical warfare, bottom line."

Eight years ago, it was a war that Zook appeared to be losing. The crops on his 66-acre farm were riddled with funguses and pests that chemical treatments did little to reduce. The now-39-year-old talked haltingly about the despair he felt at the prospect of losing a homestead passed down through five generations of his family. Disillusioned by standard agriculture methods, Zook searched fervently for an alternative. He found what he was looking for in the writings of an 18-year-old Amish farmer from Ohio, a man named John Kempf.

Kempf is the unlikely founder of *Advancing Eco Agriculture,* a consulting firm established in 2006 to promote science-intensive organic agriculture. The entrepreneur's story is almost identical to Zook's. A series of crop failures on his own farm drove the 8th grade-educated Kempf to school himself in the sciences. For two years, he pored over research in biology, chemistry, and agronomy in pursuit of a way to save his fields. The breakthrough came from the study of plant immune systems which, in healthy plants, produce an array of compounds that are toxic to intruders. "The immune response in plants is dependent on well-balanced nutrition," Kempf concluded, "in much the same way as our own immune system." Modern agriculture uses fertilizer specifically to increase yields, he added, with little awareness of the nutritional needs of other organic functions. Through plant sap analysis, Kempf has been able to discover deficiencies in important trace minerals which he can then introduce into the soil. With plants able to defend themselves, pesticides can be avoided, allowing the natural predators of pests to flourish.

According to Kempf, the methods he developed through experimentation on his Ohio farm are now being used across North and South America, Hawaii, Europe, and Africa. The entrepreneur promises clients higher-quality crops, bigger yields, better taste, and produce that carries a lucrative "organic" label. Kempf, however, considers his process as an important improvement upon standard organic farming methods. "Organic certification is a negative-process certification," he explained, "You can do nothing to your field and become certified. In contrast, we focus on actively restoring the balance found in natural systems."

I recently sought out Samuel Zook, one of Kempf's earliest converts, at his farm in Lancaster, Pennsylvania to see Advancing Eco Agriculture's practices in action. After trailing a leisurely horse and carriage in my car for several miles, I was greeted at the farm by a bounding dog and Zook's young barefoot son. The boy stared silently with his arms wrapped around a watermelon almost as big as himself. In a straw hat and suspenders, he looked like a miniature version of his father. The elder Zook smiled demurely through a neatly trimmed beard and extended his hand before inviting me on a tour of his fields. A hushed gaggle of children tripped along behind us as we walked among the bales of hay and rows of tomatoes, onions, melons, and squash.

Roc Morin: Can you describe the differences between how you used to farm and how you farm now?

Samuel Zook: The inputs changed drastically. Instead of trying to grow crops that are healthy with fungicides and pesticides, I started to grow crops that are healthy with nutrition.

Morin: What was the hardest part about making the change?

Zook: Well, there was a big psychological block that I had to get through. I'd see a couple bugs out there and feel like I immediately had to do something about it. But, I learned that if I sit back, things will often take care of themselves. That first summer for instance, we saw a lot of horn worms. Before that, I would have sprayed them right away, but this time I waited and a bunch of wasps came along and killed them. Once I saw that, I started getting really excited.

Morin: So, when you use a pesticide you're killing the predators too, right?

Zook: Right. You're killing the entire ecosystem.

Morin: Have all of your problems disappeared?

Zook: I wish I could say that, but not entirely. We're not living in the Garden of Eden yet. The issues I had before have disappeared, but we still have some other issues that we're working on. One of the main things that has improved is how it feels to farm. Before, if I applied fungicide on my tomatoes, I had to wait three to seven days before I could reenter the area. Now, it's so nice to just walk in my field any day of the week and not worry a bit. That in itself is huge. The other thing is, when I used to mix these skull-and-cross-bones chemicals to put in my sprayer, I'd have to be suited up. The children would be around and I'd say, "Now, get in the house. It's not safe." Now though, if the children want to help, it's fine. If I want to mix the solutions better, I'll just put my hand in a stir it around.

Morin: What are some of the problems that you're dealing with now?

Zook: One of my major issues in the greenhouse is spider mites—little insects that just love a warm, dry environment. It's very hard to control them, even conventionally. We usually get them under control, but we often lose some yield.

Morin: How do you get them under control?

Zook: Mainly through applying specific trace minerals like iodine and a whole line of ultra-micronutrients. We analyzed the sap of the plants with the help of a lab and I think we've narrowed the problem down to excessive ammonium nitrates. If ammonia builds up in the plants, it's bug food, so we need to figure out a way to convert ammonia fast. I just spent two days with John [Kempf], and he came up with an enzyme cofactor which we'll use to stimulate that ammonia conversion. We figure things out ourselves now rather than call up the chemical rep.

Morin: What did your chemical rep say when you told him that you didn't need his services anymore?

Zook: Well, that was an interesting summer. He used to come here every week telling me horror stories about all the diseases in the neighborhood. But, I had made up my made up my mind, "No mas." He came back every week for eight weeks telling me what I needed to spray. I said, "I'm fine, thanks." The last time he was here, we were out picking tomatoes and he walked over. He was looking around and talking about this and that, and he didn't even mention pesticides. "Well," he said, "your tomatoes look pretty good." I thought, "Yes!"

Morin: One thing that I immediately noticed is how great everything smells here. Do you still smell it, or are you accustomed to it?

Zook: Oh, I smell it every time I come here. It's exciting. Those aromas are actually compounds the plants produce to defend themselves from insects and disease attacks. A lot of people don't realize that plants have immune systems.

Morin: So, you can smell health—can you smell problems too?

Zook: Yes. There's a real science to walking through a field and pausing to feel what the plants are feeling. There's a huge difference between walking in this field and walking in one that has had six fungicide applications. The plants just don't radiate that same vitality. Another thing I learned is that every time you spray with a fungicide or something, it's actually suppressing the plant as well as the fungi.

Morin: The same way that antibiotics can weaken a person's immune system?

Zook: Yes. It might kill the disease, but then because it has weakened the plant, a week later the plant is much more susceptible to that same disease again. That's the way it is with miticide. If I come in here and spray the mites with it, it would kill some of them, but it kills by messing with their hormones, so the ones that do survive will then mature 50 percent faster. So, it's pretty much guaranteed that I'd have a huge mite outbreak 10 years later. Instead of doing that, let's figure out what this plant wants and provide it. They really do respond.

Morin: What else can you tell by looking at your plants?

Zook: Well, one thing we learn is to read the leaves. This asymmetry here indicates zinc deficiency. The spots over here indicate a phosphorus deficiency. And, this here rippling of the leaf usually indicates excess nitrogen.

Morin: Before you started with this method were you able to read the leaves?

Zook: You know, I barely noticed them at all. I just planted and sprayed. Now, it's much more fun.

Questions for Discussion

1. What methods does Kemft use to help ensure that plants are able to ward off pests? Why are they effective?

2. What does Kempf mean when he says, "organic certification is a negative process certification" ?

3. The article is divided into two sections; it begins with the author offering the reader some context, and later, moves into the format of an interview? Do you find this shift effective? What is the value in using both formats for this text?

4. Do you think Zook's comparison between combat and chemical warfare is a fair one? Why or why not?

Food Companies Are Unprepared for Water Scarcity, Says New Report

Ucilia Wang

The Guardian, May 2015

Currently the assistant editor of Editorial Partnerships at *The Guardian*, Ucilia Wang began working at *The Guardian* in 2003 as a tech and business writer. According to her profile on *The Guardian's* website, she has written for *The Wall Street Journal,* the *U.K. Guardian, MIT Technology Review, GigaOm,* and *Forbes.com.* She writes about topics such as renewable energy, electric cars, water technology, and strategies for lowering the carbon footprint. Additionally, she is the co-founder of Climate Confidential, which publishes reporting on the intersection of environment and technology. The organization's website states that it is funded by readers, "and dedicated to deepening the popular conversation about people, businesses and society reckoning with climate change."

Using public data, a nonprofit ranked the best and worst companies in terms of water use. The results were sobering.

Global food prices, which have been rising since 2012, may be ready for another hike.

In a report released Thursday, Ceres, a sustainable business consortium based in Boston, found that most food companies aren't prepared to deal with the water risks that it expects will lead to higher water and food prices.

"We are coming to an end of cheap, plentiful water. Most of the food companies assume that water will remain cheap, and for investors that assumption is dangerous in terms of the companies' long term profitability," said Brooke Barton, the report's co-author and director of the Ceres water program. "We feel that most companies are not addressing these risks adequately."

Water is a major ingredient in food, from bacon to pizza: growing crops and raising animals account for about 70% of the world's water use, according to the United Nation's Food and Agriculture Organization.

It takes 15,415 liters of water to produce a kilogram of beef, according to the Water Footprint Network, a Netherlands nonprofit that consults on water management and policy. A kilogram of pasta requires 1,850 liters of water.

Moreover, one third of the food production takes place where water is becoming scarce, according to the World Resources Institute, a Washington DC research group that studies water, food, and energy.

Better water management plans by governments and businesses are needed, according to the Ceres report, which ranked 37 companies on their water management.

Scores were based on how the companies track water use and implement conservation plans—and whether their efforts include only their own operations or also their suppliers—as well as what companies are doing to reduce water pollution from fertilizer runoffs and other farming and production processes.

Most of the companies scored poorly. On a scale of zero to 100, 31 companies ranked lower than 50.

Agricultural Products	
Bunge (BG)	29
Chiquita Brands (Private)	20
Cargill (Private)	17
Archer-Daniels-Midland Co (ADM)	10
Fresh Del Monte (FDP)	7
Ingredion (INGR)	5

Beverage	
The Coca-Cola Company (KO)	67
Molson Coors Brewing Company (TAP)	44
Brown-Forman Corporation (BF/B)	29
Constellation Brands (STZ)	24
Dr Pepper Snapple Group (DPS)	15
Monster Beverage (MNST)	1

Meat	
Smithfield Foods (SFD)	33
JBS (JBSS3)	12
Hormel Foods Corp. (HRL)	11
Perdue Farms Inc. (Private)	9
Tyson Foods (TSN)	8
Pilgrim's Pride (PPC)	3

Packaged Food	
Unilever (UN)	70
Nestlé (NSRGY)	64
General Mills (GIS)	57
PepsiCo Inc. (PEP)	55
Kellogg Co. (K)	54
Campbell Soup (CPB)	45
Mondelēz International (MDLZ)	43
ConAgra Foods Inc. (CAG)	31
Keurig Green Mountain (GMCR)	31
J.M. Smucker (SJM)	27
Hershey (HSY)	26
Mead Johnson (MJN)	23
McCormick & Co. (MKC)	14
Dean Foods (DF)	13
WhiteWave Foods (WWAV)	11
Hain Celestial (HAIN)	8
Kraft Foods Group (KRFT)	6
Flowers Foods (FLO)	5
Pinnacle Foods (PF)	1

Companies scored on a 0-100 point basis.

The Ceres report ranked 37 companies on their water management. Photograph: Ceres

Kraft Foods Group, the maker of Cool Whip and Oscar Mayer sandwich meat, scored a mere six points. Tyson Foods, the company behind Jimmy Dean sausage and Sara Lee desserts, got eight. Constellation Brands, supplier of many happy hour staples such as Corona beer and Svedka vodka—and wine producers including Robert Mondavi Winery and Ravenswood—received 24.

The bottom three scorers were Monster Beverage with one point, Pinnacle Foods with one point and Pilgrim's Pride with three points. Meanwhile, Unilever scored the highest at 70, followed by 67 for Coca-Cola, 64 for Nestle, and 57 for General Mills.

Ceres used publicly available data, such as corporate financial and sustainability reports, to make its assessments. Four of its member companies are ranked in the report: General Mills, PepsiCo, Coca-Cola, and Brown Forman.

Where companies fall short

In many cases, companies included in the report aren't tracking water use beyond their own operations, or aren't tracking it well, according to Ceres. That's a problem given that some of the top water uses come from their supply chains.

Most companies also don't have incentives in place—either internally or for their processors or farmers—for improving water conservation or reducing water pollution, the report said.

Kellogg's chief sustainability officer, Diane Holdorf, praised the Ceres report for raising awareness about the challenges companies face and giving examples of practices worth emulating.

Kellogg, which scored 54, plans to do better, Holdorf said. The company's 2014 sustainability report, issued last month, set new goals for 2020. The company is on track to meet its 2015 goal of reducing the amount of water it uses per metric ton of food produced by 15%-20% from 2005 levels.

The 2020 goals include working with farmers to use water and fertilizers more efficiently and protect their watersheds. In February, Kellogg announced several water conservation projects, including one slated to receive $10m in federal funding, on rice farms in Louisiana and wheat farms in Michigan.

"Water is an important issue for us and for the food and beverage sector," Holdorf said. "I think all of us have plenty of work to do."

Packaged food and drink

Drink and snack makers scored the best for their water risk management plans: they tend to have more recognizable brands and are under more pressure from their customers to be good environmental stewards, according to Ceres.

Some have already seen cuts in their sales and expansion plans because of dwindling or polluting water supplies, Barton noted.

Drought punctuated by a short period of intense rain in California contributed to a 28% profit decline in a carrot farming division of Campbell Soup Company during the last quarter of 2014. Last month, Coca-Cola abandoned a project to build a bottling plant in India after a battle from the local community over worries about depleting groundwater supplies.

Overall, packaged food and beverage companies fared better than meat and agricultural product companies such as Chiquita Brands, Archer Daniels Midland, and Fresh Del Monte.

Meat and grains

Jackie Anderson, an ADM spokeswoman, declined to comment on the Ceres assessment, which gives the company a score of 10. Most of the company's processing plants that use high volumes of water are in regions where local water resources are not stressed, she said in an email, adding that ADM surpassed its goal of cutting water use 15% between 2008 and 2018 early, by the end of 2014.

Meat producers face some of the highest water risk because meat production requires so much water. Among the six meat companies included in the report, Smithfield Foods received the highest score—and that's a paltry 33.

Kathleen Kirkham, a spokeswoman for Smithfield, which makes bacon and sausages, emailed to say the company has already exceeded its 2015 goal of reducing water use by 10%, from 2008 levels, per 100 pounds of product produced, and plans to set new goals.

Tyson spokesman Dan Fogleman wrote that the report didn't take into account some of the new technologies the company has been using to conserve and re-use water, leading a 14.7% cut in the gallons of water used per pound of finished product "over the past several years." He said the report also "mischaracterized" the company's North American wastewater discharge as pollution. "The water we release back into the environment has been though a government-permitted treatment process," he said.

Barton said she did consider the water saving technologies in her assessment, but Tyson lost points for not having a publicly stated water reduction goal. Ceres's evaluation—which didn't address the regulatory compliance of waste-water discharge—was based on the most recent public data reported to the US Environmental Protection Agency, according to which Tyson was responsible for the largest wastewater discharge in the US, she said.

"Those discharges are permitted, but are still labeled by the US government as a form of pollution," Barton said.

Some of the companies declined to comment on the report—such as Hormel Foods and Constellation Brands—or didn't respond to requests for comments by press time, such as Dr Pepper Snapple Group.

Best practices and next steps

Ceres also highlighted examples of strong water management policies. For example, Campbell Soup, Dean Foods, Molson Coors, and Unilever offer executives financial incentives for achieving water management goals.

Coca-Cola, General Mills, Kellogg, Nestle, and Unilever have deadline-driven goals to expand sustainable water management practices, which range from planting cover crops to reduce water runoffs and soil erosion to capturing and storing rainfall, across the majority of their suppliers.

The report also recommends several things the industry can do to improve.

While some companies require reporting from their suppliers, it's not clear how they use the data to make better purchasing decisions or to help their suppliers improve. Creating new standards for reporting and data collection could help reduce the amount of time farmers and other suppliers need to spend filling out surveys—and could lead to industry-wide solutions.

Ceres recommends that companies work more closely with their suppliers, including farmers, to collect good data, secure water supplies, and conserve more. Businesses should also support watershed protection and report water risks regularly to their board of directors and shareholders, the group claims.

Meanwhile, investors who want to include water risks in their financial analyses should demand more comprehensive water use reporting from their portfolio companies and make investment decisions accordingly, Ceres suggests. According to the report, they should consider three key factors: how much water is needed, how secure the water supply is, and how the management deals with water scarcity, pollution, and other related risks.

"Right now, a lot of what we are producing is linked to the fact that water is free," Barton said. "We will see a shift."

Questions for Discussion

1. In this article, Wang claims that better water management plans should be put in place by governments and businesses. Why is this the case? What support does she offer for this statement?

2. Consider how Wang chooses to structure her argument. What strategies does she use to make her key points clear to her audience?

3. In many ways, Wang's article highlights the way in which food companies are failing to consider 'the big picture;' in what other ways have we seen individuals or communities failing to recognize 'the big picture' in relation to food?

Corn Wars

Ted Genoways

New Republic, August 2015

Largely considered a left leaning publication, the *New Republic*, according to its website, is an independent journal promoting progressive ideas and championing creative solutions. The publication's mission statement claims, "we don't lament intractable problems; our journalism debates complex issues, and takes a stance. Our biggest stories are commitments for change." The author of this article, Ted Genoways is a contributing editor and the author of the book, *The Chain: Farm, Factory, and the Fate of our Food.* As stated on the book's website, in addition to his work with the *New Republic*, Genoways is a contributing writer at *Mother Jones*, and his essays and poems have been published in *The Atlantic, Bloomberg Businessweek, The New York Times,* and the *Washington Post Book World.* He is a winner of a National Press Club Award and the James Aronson Award for Social Justice Journalism, and he has received fellowships from the NEA and the Guggenheim Foundation.

*The farm-by-farm fight between China and the United States
to dominate the global food supply*

On September 30, 2012, agents from the FBI contacted U.S. Customs and Border Protection at O'Hare International Airport in Chicago with an urgent request. They wanted bags from two passengers on an outbound flight to Beijing pulled for immediate inspection. The passengers didn't track as dangerous criminals: Li Shaoming, president of Beijing Kings Nower Seed Science & Technology, a large Chinese agricultural company that develops corn, rice, cotton, and canola seeds, and Ye Jian, the company's crop research manager.

In Li's luggage, agents found two large Pop Weaver microwave popcorn boxes. Buried under the bags of unpopped snack kernels were roughly 300 tiny manila envelopes, all cryptically numbered—2155, 2403, 20362. Inside each envelope was a single corn seed. In Ye's luggage, agents found more corn seeds hidden amid his clothes, each one individually wrapped in napkins from a Subway restaurant. Customs officers were dispatched to the gate area for the Beijing flight, where they found the two men and conducted body searches. Still more corn seeds, also folded into napkins, were discovered in Ye's pockets.

Meanwhile, at a different gate, Wang Hongwei, another Chinese national believed to be in the employ of Kings Nower (agents never learned if he worked for the company or was related to someone who did), boarded a separate flight for Burlington, Vermont, where he had a car waiting for him to drive to Canada. FBI agents were there to follow him—though Wang, after leaving the airport parking garage, made a series of abrupt turns and managed to give his surveillance team the slip. It didn't matter. Border patrol officers were waiting when Wang pulled up to the Highgate Springs port of entry along the U.S.-Canadian border. He was selected out for a search, which turned up 44 bags of corn seeds under his seat and in his suitcases, as well as a notebook filled with GPS coordinates and a digital camera containing hundreds of pictures of cornfields. Questioned by agents, Wang would say only that he had purchased the seeds from a man named Mo Hailong, the director of international business at the Beijing Dabeinong Technology Group (DBN Group), the parent company of Kings Nower Seed.

Not wanting to alert Mo, agents allowed all three men to leave the country, but their corn seeds were confiscated. Special Agent Mark E. Betten, a 16-year veteran of the FBI specializing in the investigation of intellectual property theft, had the seeds sent to an independent bio-diagnostic testing laboratory, which confirmed that they were proprietary, genetically modified hybrids. Eventually, their genetic sequencing was matched to seeds under development by Monsanto, DuPont Pioneer, and LG Seeds, which, including LG's parent company, Groupe Limagrain, comprise three of the four largest seed companies in the world. The GPS coordinates were found to correspond with farms in Iowa and Illinois, where those companies were testing the performance of new hybrids.

In December 2013, after collecting this evidence, U.S. marshals arrived at Mo's home in Boca Raton, Florida. He was taken into custody and extradited to Iowa, where he has been under house arrest in Des Moines ever since. The FBI also brought charges against five alleged co-conspirators, all Chinese, who remain at large, including the three men stopped by customs agents, and eventually against Mo's sister, Mo Yun, as well. Mo and his sister are scheduled to stand trial before a federal court in Iowa in September on charges of conspiracy to steal trade secrets. If convicted, they face up to ten years in prison and a $5 million fine.

This may seem like a lot of post-September 11 cloak-and-dagger for a few corn seeds, but the U.S. government believes that something much larger is going on. This theft, they argue, stems from an undeniable and dangerous fact: Despite its remarkable landmass, China simply can't grow enough food to feed itself, particularly now that the country's burgeoning middle class has acquired an appetite for meat. (Most corn in China is used as feed for livestock.) Water shortages and lack of arable terrain have forced their government to buy between two and five million metric tons of American corn annually, approximately 94 percent of all corn imported into China each year.

If China hopes to feed (and pacify) its growing population while also loosening the very real stranglehold that America has on its national food supply, its farmers have to start producing a lot more corn—not just enough to meet their domestic demand in good years but enough to maintain a stockpile to offset their global market impact during bad ones. For decades, China has increased corn yields by putting more acres into production, but they're running out of arable land, and the USDA now estimates that Chinese corn consumption will rise by 41 percent by 2023, far outpacing production increases. The only tenable way for China to meet its own demand, then, is by planting high-performance hybrids, which can single-handedly double or potentially even triple per-acre corn production. Chinese scientists haven't developed a significant corn hybrid in years. But Monsanto and DuPont Pioneer, the two American seed giants, have produced so many successful hybrids that they now control 45 percent of all the seed sold in the world.

The Department of Justice maintains that China is quietly permitting and even encouraging companies to steal American agricultural secrets right out of the ground. Acquiring the technology behind these next-generation hybrids could save companies like DBN Group—and the country—as much as a decade, and many millions of dollars, in research. And, plant geneticists familiar with the case told me, the very fact that Kings Nower Seed has brought to market—and intended to bring more—products with stolen genetics hints that the Chinese government is complicit. The theft is not hard to detect or prove; the only way that DBN Group could hope to get away with this scheme is if China were pushing such spying as a matter of policy.

In fact, a 2011 report prepared by the Office of the National Counterintelligence Executive, which advises the president on intelligence matters related to national security, listed "agricultural technology" among the targets "likely to be of greatest interest" to spies from Russia and China. "Surging prices for food," the report stated, "may increase the value of and interest in collecting U.S. technologies related to crop production, such as genetic engineering, improved seeds, and fertilizer." Since that report, the Department of Justice has cracked down, successfully prosecuting Chinese national Kexue Huang for stealing secrets related to organic fertilizer production and an unidentified "new food product" while he was employed at both Dow AgroSciences and Cargill, as well as Weiqiang Zhang, for theft of genetically engineered rice seeds from Colorado-based Ventria Bioscience.

What makes the case against Mo Hailong stand out is that the FBI openly acknowledges that each step of its operation, each escalation of surveillance, was approved by a federal judge under the Foreign Intelligence Surveillance Act (FISA), which requires that the investigating agency provide evidence that wiretapping is "necessary, or relevant, to the ability of the United States to protect against foreign threats to national security, such as attack, sabotage, terrorism, or clandestine intelligence activities." The federal government, thereby, has implicitly acknowledged that it considers agricultural products both an asset and a weapon in a long-range geopolitical chess match with China, a resource of near-military value and importance, one that must be protected by all available means. By that logic, those Chinese nationals stealing corn are spies, no different—and, indeed, perhaps more important—than those who swipe plans for a new weapons system.

This may, at first glance, appear melodramatic—like *Homeland* in the heartland—but it is striking that the Department of Justice did not invoke FISA measures (at least not openly) in carrying out similar investigations into Dongfan Chung, a former Boeing engineer who stole trade secrets related to the Delta IV rocket and the Air Force's C-17 aircraft, or Qing Li, who conspired to procure 30 military accelerometers, which, according to the government, "have applications in smart bombs, missiles, and calibrating g-forces of nuclear explosions." When asked about the extraordinary use of FISA in this case, Nick Klinefeldt, U.S. attorney for the Southern District of Iowa, who is prosecuting Mo, chose his words carefully. "The agriculture industry is important," he said. "It's important not just to the state of Iowa but to the United States." In announcing the charges against Mo last July, Thomas R. Metz, special agent in charge of the Omaha Division of the FBI, went still further, saying that "identifying and deterring those focused on stealing trade secrets, propriety [sic] and confidential information, or national security information is the number two priority for the FBI, second only to terrorism."

Think about that: The U.S. Department of Justice and the FBI now contend, in effect, that the theft of genetically modified corn technology is as credible a threat to national security as the spread to nation-states of the technology necessary to deliver and detonate nuclear warheads. Disturbingly, they may be right. As the global population continues to climb and climate change makes arable soil and water for irrigation ever more scarce, the world's next superpower will be determined not just by which country has the most military might but also, and more importantly, by its mastery of the technology required to produce large quantities of food.

The bureau's investigation of Mo Hailong began only after Mo made a stunning blunder. It was early May 2011, and Mo and Wang Lei, vice chairman of Kings Nower Seed at the time, were driving country roads in Tama County, Iowa, allegedly searching for a DuPont Pioneer test field. But apparently uncertain if he was in the right place or unsure of what kind of seed DuPont Pioneer was testing, Mo had Wang pull to the edge of a field, so they could question a farmer in the midst of spring planting. Mo and Wang told the farmer they had been attending an international agricultural conference at Iowa State and wanted to see someone planting a real cornfield. The farmer was dubious. Ames was nearly an hour away with nothing but expanses of cornfields in between, all at the peak of planting season. How had these two men chanced upon his field on the very day that he happened to be planting an experimental and top-secret seed under development by DuPont Pioneer?

The next day, a DuPont Pioneer field manager spotted the same car. He watched Mo scramble up the ditch bank, and then kneel down in the dirt and begin digging corn seeds out of the ground. When confronted by the field manager, Mo grew flustered and red-faced. He now claimed to be a researcher from the University of Iowa—not Iowa State—on his way to a conference. But before the field manager could question him further, Mo fled. He jumped into the waiting car, and Wang took off, swerving through the grassy ditch before fishtailing onto the gravel road and speeding away.

A few weeks later, agents from the Iowa office of the FBI sat down with DuPont Pioneer representatives for a standing meeting (which itself says something about the importance our law enforcement officials place on our corn) at their corporate headquarters in Johnston, Iowa, a northern suburb of Des Moines. A DuPont Pioneer executive mentioned the incident and explained that the company enters into exclusive contracts with farmers to grow proprietary and often genetically engineered seeds. The exact genetic sequence of successful seeds is a tightly held secret, worth many millions of dollars. The DuPont Pioneer field manager had written down the license plate number and handed it over to company security. Multinational food conglomerates like DuPont Pioneer and Monsanto have sizable security forces and highly efficient investigatory networks. They traced the plates back to a rental car company at the Kansas City airport. Representatives there said the car had been rented by Mo Hailong.

According to court documents, an unnamed vice president and general manager from DuPont Pioneer's Chinese subsidiary told the FBI he already had reason to believe that Kings Nower Seed was somehow stealing the company's experimental seeds in order to raise clones for sale to Chinese farmers. DuPont Pioneer had recently discovered that one of DBN Group's best-selling corn seed products in China shared genetic sequencing with a male parent line that the company had genetically engineered. The executive had confronted a DBN Group executive, sarcastically congratulating him on the success of their product. The Chinese executive had allegedly cracked a knowing smile and nodded, which the DuPont executive had taken as a tacit admission. The FBI agreed to investigate.

Four months later, while the FBI was still looking into the Tama incident, a call came into the sheriff's office in Polk County, Iowa, with a report of three Asian males walking around a cornfield in Bondurant, just outside of Des Moines. Despite the strangeness of such a call, the responding deputy hurried to the field, approached the men, and took down their names: Mo Hailong Robert (Mo occasionally used the alias Robert Mo), Wang Lei, and Li Shaoming, the CEO of Kings Nower Seed. The men acknowledged that they were Chinese seed growers but claimed they were there to offer advice to the owner of the farm. When the FBI learned of the report—and recognized Mo's name—they dispatched an agent from the Omaha field office to interview the farmer. He had never heard of the three men, much less sought their advice. He told the agent he didn't even know what kind of corn he was growing, other than to say he was under contract to Monsanto. Soon after, a Monsanto field representative confirmed that this, too, was a test site for a new parent seed the company had under development.

With an emerging picture of what Mo was up to, the FBI began tracking his movements—and soon discovered that he and Wang were intending to travel together to Des Moines for events held in connection with the World Food Prize. The morning after their arrival, on February 15, 2012, the security team at DuPont Pioneer called the FBI to report "they were confident" (in the words of the subsequent report) that Mo, using an alias and fake corporate affiliation, had joined a delegation visiting their headquarters. The FBI collected the surveillance video of the tour inside DuPont Pioneer's research lab and also identified Mo on corresponding security footage from the delegation's tour of a Monsanto research facility in Ankeny later in the day. That night, agents tracked Mo to a state dinner hosted by Iowa Governor Terry Branstad in honor of Xi Jinping, then the vice president of China and now the president. The next day, Mo and Wang went together to a sports bar near the hotel where they were staying in the Des Moines suburbs. They met up with Xaoming Bao, a Chinese seed executive and former DuPont Pioneer employee whose wife was employed by the company as a corn-genetics researcher.

FBI investigators could now demonstrate that Mo had, on two separate occasions, sought to obtain experimental seeds by collecting them from secret test sites, and furthermore, it appeared he had gained the information about how to find those locations by working with corporate insiders. The FBI also discovered that while he was in Iowa, Mo had shipped hundreds of pounds of packages from a West Des Moines UPS location to his home in Boca Raton. The contents listed on the tracking sheet: "corn samples."

The theft of high-performing corn seeds from a competitor's fields is as old as the cultivation of corn. "They say that a good plant breeder always had lots of pockets," said Donald J. Lee, a professor and plant geneticist in the department of agronomy and horticulture at the University of Nebraska–Lincoln. "And when he would go visit his neighbor's plant breeding fields, they always came back full." Until recently, farmers were their own seed providers. Lee told me his grandfather, a farmer in Iowa a century ago, would select ears from each harvest to provide the seed for planting the next year. He recorded the quality of his yield, slowly identifying a set of seed characteristics that seemed to produce the best crop. In those days, it was not unusual for family and friends to share seed stock. "Maybe a neighbor would say, 'Hey, I really did good with this seed that I got from a cousin in eastern Iowa. You should try a little of this,'" Lee said. "But they were all open-pollinated populations, so those seeds were not genetically identical. In fact, probably every seed was genetically distinct."

So much genetic variability meant that farmers like Lee's grandfather would cross two varieties and get large, robust ears one year, only to find that the same two varieties produced scraggly cobs with missing kernels and dead tips the next. "So if you take a look at the historic yields of corn in Iowa and Nebraska during the teens, the twenties, the thirties—it's flat," he said.

That all changed with the arrival of Henry A. Wallace, the founder of Pioneer Hi-Bred Seeds, who Lee described as "the Bill Gates of the seed industry." Wallace, the son of the longtime president of the Cornbelt Meat Producers, first encountered the problem of genetic variation while studying corn breeding at Iowa State Agricultural College. Rediscovering Gregor Mendel's groundbreaking research on pea pods, Wallace had the key insight that the only solution to producing hearty corn hybrids was to first create genetically pure inbred varieties that could be used as "parents" year after year. Wallace initially worried that such an approach "was probably impractical because of the difficulty of doing the hand-pollinating work," but he was won over by a paper published in 1918 by Donald Jones, a chemist at the Connecticut Agricultural Station's experimental farm. Jones had successfully inbred two separate varieties of corn and then crossed them to produce a durable, high-performing hybrid. Wallace recognized that this was the key to creating seed corn with consistently higher yields, but the old problem remained: Producing these hybrids would be far too complex for the average farmer to undertake alone.

Wallace began to envision an organized way of breeding and distributing high-performing corn seed to farmers across the Midwest. A man of unusual commitment to the common good, he wrote a friend that he did not consider himself a corn breeder but rather "a searcher for methods of bringing the 'inner light' to outward manifestation." So Wallace at first conceived of a nonprofit organization, potentially run with government cooperation and even public funding. In 1921, his father, Henry C. Wallace, was appointed secretary of agriculture and might have helped spearhead such an effort. But after his father died unexpectedly at age 58 and Calvin Coolidge settled into the laissez-faire years of his presidency, Wallace saw little chance of an ambitious national program gaining traction. He decided instead, in May 1926, to start the Hi-Bred Corn Company—the world's first hybrid seed producer.

To interest farmers, Roswell Garst, Wallace's lead salesman, who later became a major seed producer in his own right, went from one farm to the next, across 16 counties in western Iowa, giving away enough eight-pound sample bags of Hi-Bred seeds for farmers to plant half their fields. Whatever additional yield the hybrid corn produced, Pioneer would split fifty-fifty with the farmer. After several years, farmers realized that they would see greater profits by simply buying the bags of seeds, instead of sharing the surplus yield with the company.

Those shared harvests produced something even more valuable than profit for the young company: information about how the seeds performed under different growing conditions. Wallace directed a sizable chunk of his revenue back into research, hiring a team of new corn breeders to devise still more hybrids. In the early 1930s, Perry Collins, one of Wallace's researchers, developed Hybrid 307—the first corn specifically developed and marketed for drought-resistance, hitting seed dealerships just as the country spiraled into the Dust Bowl. And when Wallace was, like his father, appointed secretary of agriculture, by Franklin Roosevelt in 1933, he finally had the resources to nationally evangelize for hybrid seed, which he believed had the potential to rescue the nation from the Great Depression.

The transformation that followed was staggering. When Wallace joined Roosevelt's cabinet, less than 1 percent of America's corn came from hybrid seeds. A decade later, more than three-quarters of all corn was grown from hybrids—nearly doubling the national per-acre yield over the next 20 years. To keep this record output from depressing corn prices, Wallace created the "ever-normal granary," under which the federal government would establish a federal grain reserve. In years of high production, the Department of Agriculture would buy corn and store it to keep prices up. In years of crop loss, the government would release the reserve to keep prices down. Wallace's plan was hugely popular, stabilizing American food prices—and winning him a spot as FDR's running mate in 1940.

But Wallace's remarkable Hi-Bred Corn had one significant drawback: It consumed far more nitrogen compounds from the soil than ordinary corn—more, in fact, than almost any other crop. During the war years, the government solved the problem by simply putting more acres into production, but after World War II, the Department of Agriculture found a different solution. Giant chemical manufacturers, like DuPont and Monsanto, had secured wartime defense contracts to produce ammonia nitrate and anhydrous ammonia to make bombs and other munitions. They had developed an herbicide known as 2,4-D as a potential destroyer of German crops and manufactured the insecticide DDT to prevent the spread of typhus-carrying lice among GIs. As soon as the war was over, DuPont turned to marketing those same chemicals for lawn and garden use as fertilizer, weed killer, and DuPont 5% DDT Insect Spray. Company advertisements from the period touted their products as "Better Things for Better Living … *Through Chemistry.*" But gardens were just the tip of the iceberg. DuPont, along with other giant chemical manufacturers like Dow and Monsanto, teamed up with the grain cartels, including Cargill and Archer Daniels Midland, to lobby for congressional support for producing these compounds as large-scale agri-chemicals.

In 1953, the industry found its greatest ally, when Ezra Taft Benson took over as President Dwight D. Eisenhower's Secretary of Agriculture. (Wallace, by then, had retired from public life. He was briefly the editor of the *New Republic* before making a failed bid for the presidency in 1948.) Benson, a high-ranking member of the Mormon Church and a fanatical Red Scare Republican, immediately informed Eisenhower that he was philosophically opposed to the government price supports developed by Wallace, because, to his mind, they were tantamount to socialism. He publicly referred to small farmers as "irresponsible feeders at the public trough."

Foreshadowing today's aggressive, pro-corporate agricultural policies, Benson argued that the only way to outcompete the collective farms of the Soviet Union and Red China was to use our superior corn and chemical technology to the fullest. The United States could, if it chose, overproduce corn to drive down international prices, and it could use the surplus as a tool of diplomatic leverage in the form of foreign aid. Instead of guns, the United States began to give our allies grain—transforming, for the first time, a food product into a weapon in the national arsenal. The only problem was that by effectively militarizing American agriculture, Benson made agri-tech a target for foreign spying.

In April 2012, Mo flew from his home in Florida to O'Hare International Airport and rented a car. An FBI surveillance team followed him as he drove along back roads through rural Illinois and northern Indiana. After about a week of this, Mo stopped one day at a farm near Monee, Illinois, advertising DuPont Pioneer seeds for sale. The farmer there later told the FBI that Mo had asked about what types of corn and soybeans he could buy, explaining that he had purchased 40 acres nearby and was planning to plant the property. The surveillance team followed Mo to a farm about 15 minutes west of Monee, where, a review of property records soon revealed, Kings Nower Seed had purchased a parcel for $600,000 only the month before.

As agents watched Mo crisscross the Midwest, stopping at seed stores to inquire about different products, they began to suspect that he planned to plant the Illinois acreage by hand. Donald J. Lee, the University of Nebraska professor, compares stealing parent seeds to obtaining programming code without knowing what application it is intended for or what operating system it's meant to run on. Likewise, knowing the genetic structure of a corn seed is just one part of the problem. "You don't know the importance of those genes, unless you have yield data," said Lee. "When did the plant mature? What's its development profile? How did it respond to such-and-such disease?" This is what Mo appeared to be doing: setting up his own covert test farm, one that he could oversee personally.

FBI surveillance teams followed Mo to Crossroads Ag, a DuPont Pioneer seed dealer in Dallas Center, Iowa, and observed him loading bags of seeds into his trunk. When investigators questioned the owner, he said Mo paid in cash—more than $1,500—for six bags of Pioneer Hi-Bred corn seeds. He said Mo had been purchasing seed there for two years, always asking for DuPont Pioneer's "latest products," but this year he had arrived with a detailed list. The owner had told Mo that he wasn't supposed to sell him some of the specific products he was asking for, unless he had a contract agreement with DuPont Pioneer, which the owner knew he didn't. The next day, FBI surveillance watched Mo repeat the process, buying six bags of DeKalb brand seed corn, a Monsanto product, at MFA Agri Services in Pattonsburg, Missouri.

Finally, the team followed Mo back to Adel, Iowa, where Mo unloaded some of the seed bags at a storage facility before driving on to the farm in Illinois where the remaining bags were unloaded and, the FBI believes, seeds may have been planted. About one out of every 200 seeds in a bag of hybrid corn seed is a parent, which can be identified by planting the bag and then collecting kernels from whichever plants look different from the rest. Investigators believe Mo may have been collecting some parent seeds this way. Later, when Mo and two DBN Group employees attempted to FedEx the remaining corn seeds to an associate in Hong Kong, the FBI intercepted the packages and conducted a search of the five boxes. Each contained eight or nine gallon-sized baggies filled with seed corn, along with a handwritten numerical code identifying each hybrid.

The FBI has not revealed exactly when they applied to a FISA court for more broad-ranging investigatory powers, but the FBI's court filings show that their information on Mo and his associates became much more detailed after meetings with DuPont Pioneer executives over the summer. Top executives told agents that "the loss of an inbred line of seed would result in losing approximately five to eight years of research and a minimum of $30 to $40 million dollars, potentially much more." After that, the FBI tapped the men's mobile phones and tracked Mo's bank records. They collected their email from Yahoo, Google, and Hotmail, corporate documents from DropBox, and thousands of files from Mo's Apple iCloud account. The FBI used Mo's mobile phone to track his movements, bugged his rental cars to eavesdrop on his conversations, and installed a video camera outside the storage unit in Adel.

To exercise such investigatory power, the FBI had to argue that Mo was an "agent of a foreign power"—or, in other words, to persuade a judge that Mo might be acting on behalf not just of DBN Group but at the direction of the People's Republic of China. With that, the FBI had the authority to treat Mo as if he were the leader of a state-sponsored Chinese spy ring. (Klinefeldt, the U.S. attorney prosecuting the case, was evasive about whether that suspicion proved substantive. "When you start an investigation," he said, "you don't know exactly where it will lead.")

FBI investigators soon got the explicit evidence they needed to make arrests. Over a listening device installed in an Enterprise rental car, the surveillance team recorded a bizarre and inept conversation between two of Mo's associates from DBN Group, Lin Yong and Ye Jian. In the translated transcript, submitted as part of the government's case, the two men are consumed by worry that they are being followed and about the charges they could face if caught. So, as they drive around rural Illinois looking for DuPont Pioneer and Monsanto test fields from which to steal, they begin making a list of the crimes they have committed. After some back and forth, they come up with trespassing for every time they have slipped onto private property, larceny for the seeds and ears they have been stealing from the fields, and multiple violations of intellectual property protections.

"These are actually very serious offenses," Lin says.

"They could treat us as spies!" Ye interjects.

Lin, exasperated, responds: "That is what we've been doing!"

Soon after, with the harvest season nearly complete, Mo seems to have decided it was time to send to China what corn he and his associates had collected. The group drove back to the secret Illinois farm and began discussing how they would divvy up the seeds. Some would go into checked bags bound for Beijing, others would be carried to a car and driven across the border from Vermont into Canada, and some would go with Mo back to Florida, where he would ship them to China. With tickets booked for departure the following morning, the five men readied their caches of seeds—Li deciding to stash his under packets of Pop Weaver microwave popcorn. The whole group then piled into a white minivan and drove into Monee to eat at the local Subway. On their way out, one of the men, perhaps Ye, must have stuffed his pockets full of napkins.

When Soviet premier Nikita Khrushchev visited the United States at President Eisenhower's invitation in 1959, he specifically requested to see only one man: Roswell Garst, the former Pioneer seed salesman for Henry A. Wallace, who was then head of Garst and Thomas Hi-Bred Corn Company. Khrushchev had met Garst once before, when he visited the Soviet Union, and had become obsessed by the potential of hybrid corn. Khrushchev and his wife spent a day at Garst's farm near Coon Rapids, Iowa. In his memoirs, Khrushchev later wrote, "Garst gave me an entire lecture on agriculture," in which he earnestly explained that American farmers had stopped worrying about crop rotation. "Science today considers that approach outdated. And I think so, too," Garst told the Soviet leader. In past years, planting the same crop repeatedly would have attracted pests and depleted the soil of nitrogen. "Now there is no such problem. We have herbicides and other such chemical substances that make it possible to combat pests," Garst said. And there was no longer any need to plant clover or alfalfa to accumulate nitrogen. "It is more profitable for me to buy nitrogen, potassium, phosphorus, in mix form, and add this fertilizer."

On that same official visit, Ezra Taft Benson led Khrushchev on a tour of the U.S. Agricultural Research Center in Beltsville, Maryland. Benson, in his official remarks, said that there was a "constant give-and-take of information between government scientists and those in private industry," adding that "we are all working together within the framework of our capitalistic free-enterprise society to benefit our farmers, all our citizens, and people throughout the world." He listed hybrid corn first among the achievements of such cooperative efforts and introduced white-coated lab researchers who extolled the virtues of 2,4-D and chemical fertilizers. Khrushchev was unimpressed by a visit he made to a farm owned by President Eisenhower, dismissing it as "not on a scale such as we have at our collective farms and state farms." Benson later remembered that Khrushchev bragged, "We won't have to fight you. We'll so weaken your economy until you fall like overripe fruit into our hands." Benson vowed that American farms would outproduce the Soviets through superior chemistry.

By the end of the Eisenhower era, however, environmentalists began to raise concerns about the hundreds of commercial herbicides and pesticides being applied to American crops in quantities totaling hundreds of millions of pounds. Benson admonished doubters that "abandoning the use of chemicals on farms and in the food industry would result in an immediate decline in the quantity and overall quality of our food supply and cause a rapid rise in food prices paid by the consumer." Even when Rachel Carson documented connections between DDT and 2,4-D and elevated incidence rates of rare forms of cancer in *Silent Spring*, Benson remained unmoved. He is said to have written to Eisenhower wondering "why a spinster with no children was so concerned with genetics," and then, as if to answer his own question, offered that Carson was "probably a Communist." (The Eisenhower Presidential Library, for what it's worth, contains no record of this letter.)

Benson's war on the "socialist" price supports and farm aid programs instituted by Henry A. Wallace stalled out during the liberal-minded 1960s. But at the advent of the new decade, President Richard Nixon appointed Earl Butz, Benson's former assistant, to become the new secretary of agriculture. Butz had grown up on a farm in Indiana and spent 30 years teaching agricultural economics at Purdue before becoming dean of the university's College of Agriculture. Many small farmers hated him, because he had been such a vocal advocate for turning family farming into big business during the Eisenhower administration. His refrain for those families, famously, was: "Get big or get out."

Almost as soon as Butz won approval from Congress, he canceled payments for fallow land and urged farmers to "plant fencerow to fencerow," promising to use the emerging global economy to buttress against low prices. If our supply threatened futures, we would simply go to the world market and use our size and economic might to meet the demand and forge foreign dependence on American food in the bargain. We would defeat the Communists by making them dependent on us to feed themselves. In January 1972, Butz sold what amounted to our entire grain reserve to the Soviets. The following month, Nixon went to China and brokered a deal with Chairman Mao Zedong, allowing the importation of American corn and securing contracts for American companies to build 13 of the world's largest ammonia-processing plants for producing fertilizer on Chinese soil.

America's Communist foes regarded these moves as an agreement not to wage war through food. But Butz discussed these moves in terms of "agri-power," and stated it plainly: "Food is a weapon." To open a new front in the conflict, he supported maintaining American food superiority through yet another innovation: bioengineering feed, such as corn and soybeans. Through the miracle of science, the United States would not only produce more crops than our rivals; we would produce better crops. By 1972, scientists had already developed the ability to cut and splice protein strands in the DNA sequences of bacteria. If they could do the same with plant cells, then they could chemically insert resistance to weeds and insects. Less than five years later, a team from the University of Washington discovered that a bacterium that causes tumorlike growths on plants did so by inserting its own DNA into the cell nuclei of its host plant. What they had discovered was essentially a natural form of gene splicing. By the 1980s, researchers had devised techniques for removing the bacteria genes and inserting desirable DNA sequences.

The U.S. government recognized this as technology the Soviets and Chinese could not match. Monsanto was also quick to see the market opportunity. The company had grown with the production of 2,4-D and its descendant 2,4,5-T, which were then combined to produce Agent Orange to defoliate forest cover during the Vietnam War. In 1970, in an effort to come up with an even stronger plant killer, Monsanto chemist John E. Franz hit upon an herbicide called glyphosate, which was marketed under the trade name Roundup and had seen unmatched growth in broadleaf weed control in the agricultural industry. The only problem with Roundup: It was such an effective herbicide that farmers had to apply it carefully, spraying only early sprouting weeds, to avoid exterminating their crops.

Monsanto's engineers set about searching for a gene that would allow crops to survive exposure to Roundup. They found it in the wastewater-treatment plant of one of their own glyphosate production plants in Louisiana, where workers had noticed a range of bacteria thriving despite exposure to Roundup—and one, under lab testing, displayed total immunity to glyphosate pesticides. By 1996, Monsanto had commercially introduced soybeans that had been genetically modified to resist glyphosate—what the company termed "Roundup Ready."

Next, researchers set to trying to find a genetic-engineering solution to the European corn borer, an insect that inflicted more than $1 billion in losses of corn production in the U.S. and Canada each year. Since the 1960s, endotoxins produced by *Bacillus thuringiensis* (Bt), a common bacteria found in the soil, had been sold as a commercial microbial insecticide to kill moth larvae. If the specific DNA that produced Bt toxins could be isolated and spliced into corn genetic sequences, scientists believed they could create an ear of corn that would be lethal to the European corn borer. Soon, that hurdle had been cleared, and Monsanto began looking for a seed partner to market its pest-resistant corn. If it could marry its genetic modifications with Pioneer's hybrid seeds, Monsanto believed it would have a corn seed with unmatched yield potential.

In the early 1990s, perhaps too eager to demonstrate the effectiveness of its new GMO crops, Monsanto allowed Pioneer to use its biotech to produce Roundup Ready soybeans and Bt corn—asking only for small usage fees and no royalties. For less than $40 million, Pioneer suddenly had the technology and the sales muscle to move toward genetically modified feed crops, a growth market worth many billions of dollars. Rather than partner with Monsanto, Pioneer became its greatest competitor, entering into a joint venture with DuPont, called Optimum Quality Grains. In response, Monsanto launched a series of bitter and protracted lawsuits, and eventually, in 1999, Pioneer sold its entire remaining stock to DuPont (thus changing the name to DuPont Pioneer). In 2002, all eleven lawsuits were settled at once—as DuPont Pioneer realized that it had more to gain by paying for Monsanto's genetics and focusing on capturing the Chinese market.

In the years since, DuPont Pioneer has increased its share of the corn-seed market in China from less than a tenth of a percent to 12 percent. (Monsanto has a 1 percent market share.) DuPont Pioneer has told Chinese officials that they should Americanize their agriculture: consolidate land, plant GMO seed, apply industrial fertilizers, subsidize the sale of planting and harvest equipment. This way, the company argues, China could dramatically increase its per-acre yield. William S. Niebur, who leads DuPont Pioneer's operations in China, told the *Des Moines Register* last year that officials have listened to these recommendations with an "open ear."

In March 2015, Mo Hailong's attorneys filed a motion to suppress all evidence gathered from the secret recordings made of Mo and his associates, arguing that the authorization to gather those materials should never have been granted. In order to legally justify the use of FISA, surveillance must target an "agent of a foreign power," and the purpose of the surveillance must be to gather "foreign intelligence information." Mo's attorneys argue there is no evidence that Mo is an agent of the Chinese government or that his company is backed by China, so for "the first time in the statute's history (as far as our research reveals), the [U.S.] government used FISA to investigate a trade secret dispute between two privately owned companies."

When it comes to the Chinese form of capitalism, the line is undeniably murky. The government has taken a strong hand in recent years in encouraging the growth of China's agricultural sector. In 2013, for example, China's Shuanghui International entered an overvalue bid to buy Smithfield Foods, the world's largest producer of pork. Under questioning by Congress, Smithfield insisted the purchase came without the urging or backing of the Chinese government. But after the purchase received congressional approval, Nathan Halverson at the Center for Investigative Reporting discovered that the Bank of China, the state bank of the Chinese government, had approved the $4 billion loan for Shuanghui to purchase Smithfield in a single day—and in China, Shuanghui has touted the support the government is giving them.

In the wake of that purchase, the Chinese government has been actively consolidating the country's seed companies, which currently number more than 5,000. This consolidation would centralize research, improving China's ability to develop its own hybrids to compete with giants like DuPont and Monsanto, and it would also allow China to mimic the field-to-slaughter vertical integration that has given meat producers like Smithfield and Cargill such an advantage in the United States. DBN Group is a notable example of a seed company that is booming thanks to consolidation and government assistance. Founded in 1994 by seed-tech whiz kid Shao Genhuo, DBN Group has recently acquired more than 30 feed operations from the Chinese government, and the company runs China Farmer University jointly with the Chinese Academy of Agricultural Sciences. By targeting Mo and his sister Mo Yun as the leaders of the spy ring, the FBI may hope to incriminate Shao (who is married to Mo Yun)—and, ultimately, implicate Chinese agriculture ministers. But the U.S. government's argument that the technology behind Roundup Ready soybeans and Bt corn constitutes not just trade secrets but national security secrets is a problematic one.

Companies like DuPont Pioneer and Monsanto like to maintain that they are striving only to feed a burgeoning global population. Last year, Niebur, of DuPont Pioneer China, asked, "Without China's food security, how can we ever imagine an effective, realistic, sustainable global food-security system?" But DuPont Pioneer's goal, of course, is not global food security or feeding the Chinese people, but rather increasing market share and profit by keeping China as a customer. And the Department of Justice has taken up the argument that such a goal is not only of importance to our economy but a matter of national security, an unsettling conflation of the interests of large corporations with that of the country itself.

Today, it's estimated that 92 percent of American corn and 94 percent of American soybeans are GMOs, almost all of it produced by Monsanto or DuPont Pioneer, and again, nearly half of the seed sold globally. Activists in both China and the United States have raised concerns about just two corporations having so much influence over the world food supply, with so little transparency. (Despite repeated requests, DuPont Pioneer declined to participate in this story.)

But these fears, while well founded, miss the larger point of what such companies represent: the intent of the U.S. government to use food as an ever-more powerful point of leverage to wield over large, increasingly hungry nations like China. The prosecution of Mo Hailong and his circle stands as a warning to the Chinese government, issued through its proxy companies. The ears in the field, the seeds in the ground, even the pollen on the wind, are American-owned and American-protected. They are available to the world as food only if you agree to our conditions and are willing to pay our price.

Questions for Discussion

1. Why does Genoways claim that the U.S. Government's handling of the theft of trade secrets is problematic?

2. Genoways spends a lot of time providing context for the 2011 incident. Why is this context important? How does it shape and change audience's understanding of the text?

3. Genoways writes that the U.S. Government contends that the theft of genetically modified food is as credible as a threat to national security, and therefore requires equally drastic measures. Do you agree with this claim? Why or why not?

Radical Farmers Use Fresh Food to Fight Racial Injustice

Leah Penniman

Truth-out.org, February 2015

> This post was published on the Truth-out.org website. Truthout is a non-profit organization that, according to its mission statement, "works to spark action by revealing systemic injustice and providing a platform for transformative ideas, through in-depth investigative reporting and critical analysis." The organization is funded solely by reader support, and accepts no advertising or corporate backing, for the stated purposes of remaining unbiased. The author/ contributor, Leah Penniman, is a local farmer and educator based in Albany, New York. She co-founded Youth Grow in Worcester MA, and she has experience working with farmers in Ghana, West Africa, and Haiti. She splits her time between teaching high school and working on her family farm, Soul Fire Farm, a non-profit "committed to ending injustice in the food system." This article is about her experiences with a new restorative justice program brought about by a partnership between her farm and the County Justice Department. It was originally published in *YES! Magazine*.

In August, five young men showed up at Soul Fire Farm, a sustainable farm near Albany, New York, where I work as educator and food justice coordinator. It was the first day of a new restorative justice program, in partnership with the county's Department of Law. The teens had been convicted of theft, and, as an alternative to incarceration, chose this opportunity to earn money to pay back their victims while gaining farm skills. They looked wary and unprepared, with gleaming sneakers and averted eyes.

"I basically expected it to be like slavery, but it would be better than jail," said a young man named Asan. "It was different though. We got paid and we got to bring food home. The farmers there are black like us, which I did not expect.

"I could see myself having my own farm one day," he added.

As staff at Soul Fire, we were attempting to meet a challenge presented to us by Curtis Hayes Muhammad, the veteran civil rights activist: "Recognize that land and food have been used as a weapon to keep black people oppressed," he said, while sitting at our dinner table months earlier. "Recognize also that land and food are essential to liberation for black people."

Muhammad explained the central role that black farmers had played during the civil rights movement, coordinating campaigns for desegregation and voting rights as well as providing food, housing, and safe haven for other organizers. With his resolute and care-worn eyes, immense white Afro, and hands creased with the wisdom of years, this was a man who inspired us to listen attentively so that we might stand on the shoulders of activists who had gone before.

"Without black farmers, there would have been no Freedom Summer—in fact, no civil rights movement," he said.

Arguably, the seminal civil rights issue of our time is the systemic racism permeating the criminal "justice" system. The Black Lives Matter movement has brought to national attention the fact that people of color are disproportionately targeted by police stops, arrests, and police violence. And once they're in the system, they tend to receive subpar legal representation and longer sentences, and are less likely to receive parole. The deaths of Eric Garner and Michael Brown were not isolated incidents, but part of a larger story of state violence toward people of color.

And yet, that state violence is only one among many dangers. The biggest killers of black Americans today are not guns or violence, but diet-related diseases, including heart disease, cancer, stroke, and diabetes. These illnesses affect minorities at greater rates than white people, in part because of a broken food system that allows only certain populations to access healthy food while subsidizing low-quality food for the rest.

Black youth are well aware that the system does not value their lives.

"Look, you're going to die from the gun or you are going to die from bad food," one young man said while visiting Soul Fire Farm. "So there is really no point."

This fatalism, a form of internalized racism, is common among black youth. It's a clear sign that this country needs a united social movement to rip out racism at its roots and dismantle the caste system that makes these young people unable to see that their beautiful black lives do matter.

Because society's racism is glaringly apparent in the criminal justice system, many activists are building the foundation of the movement we need by starting there.

Combining Prison Visits With Farm-Fresh Food

In 2009, black farmer and prison abolitionist Jalal Sabur helped to start the Freedom Food Alliance, a collective of farmers, political prisoners, and organizers in upstate New York who are committed to incorporating food justice to address racism in the criminal justice system.

Sabur says he was inspired by conversations with the political prisoner Herman Bell, who has been incarcerated 40 years for his role in the Black Liberation Army. He was convicted of killing two police officers, although he continues to maintain his innocence. While incarcerated, Bell collaborated with others to start the Victory Gardens project, which brought urban and rural folks together to plant, grow, tend, and harvest organic fruits and vegetables in Maine.

Between 1995 and 2005, they distributed food for free to political prisoners and community residents around Maine and New Jersey, as well as in Boston, Brooklyn, Harlem, and the Bronx. Bell has said that the Victory Gardens Project is based on the idea that only through collective self-help can people improve their conditions.

"I wanted to find a way to recreate that transformative work," Sabur says.

One of the Freedom Food Alliance's central efforts is Victory Bus Project, a program that reunites incarcerated people with their loved ones while increasing access to farm-fresh food. The New York State Department of Corrections once operated free buses for visitors to all 54 facilities across the state, but shut the program down in 2011 for budgetary reasons, leaving many of its 2,120 monthly passengers with no way to see their family members.

Sabur purchases produce and eggs from local farmers and puts together large food packages, which families of prisoners can purchase for $50 using SNAP/ EBT (formerly known as food stamps). Once they purchase the food, families get a free round trip to visit their loved ones at correctional facilities in upstate New York. Families may choose to give the food to prisoners as a care package, take it home, or both. While on the bus, Jalal facilitates conversations about the prison-industrial complex and food justice, using texts such as Michelle Alexander's *The New Jim Crow*.

For Sabur, one of the most powerful moments in the history of Victory Bus Project was the reunion between political prisoner Robert Seth Hayes and his granddaughter, Myaisha Hayes.

"It was the first time she had seen her granddad in years," Sabur says. "It was really powerful to witness this, not only the connection between them but also knowing he was getting the fresh food that he needed to manage his diabetes."

Teaching Convicted Black Teenagers How to Grow Food

Soul Fire Farm joined the Freedom Food Alliance in 2014, supporting the Victory Bus Project with produce and providing a place to work and learn for young people enrolled in Project Growth, Albany County's new restorative justice program. Advocates of restorative justice argue that incarceration and other forms of punishment brought by the state against an assumed or convicted offender escalate a cycle of violence, and that it makes more sense for a person who has harmed another to restore the relationship. The only problem is that it often means paying out. A teenager who's damaged a vehicle, for example, would need to pay the owner for the cost of repairs. These payments are known as restitution.

A longtime friend of mine and customer of Soul Fire Farm, Jillian Faison works as an attorney for Albany County. She says that restitution was the main sticking point when she advised the county's Department of Law to try out restorative justice. The courts hesitated to require teenagers to pay restitution because they had no means to acquire the funds. It was simpler to mandate more punitive measures.

"There needs to be a way for the youth to earn money to compensate their victims and have a meaningful work experience in the process," Faison explained.

After researching the strongest restorative justice programs in the United States, Jillian helped to create Project Growth in 2013 and brought Soul Fire Farm on as the pilot partner.

The following year, Project Growth brought small groups of convicted teenagers to nonprofit organizations such as Albany City Rescue Mission, Senior Services of Albany, and Soul Fire Farm for internships where they learned job skills and earned money to pay their restitution. Most of them owed their victims less than $500 and kept their wages once those obligations were met. Project Growth's pilot year was funded by the Albany County Legislature and designed by Mission Accomplished Transition Services and Soul Fire Farm.

For the staff at Soul Fire Farm, Project Growth was about more than just restitution. We agreed with the position of Malcolm X in his "Message to Grass Roots," a speech he delivered in 1963. "Revolution is based on land," he said. "Land is the basis of all independence. Land is the basis of freedom, justice, and equality." We saw Project Growth as an opportunity for these young men to heal relationships with their communities, the land, and themselves, as well as to recognize their potential to be agents of change in society. We wanted to make sure the participants knew we saw them as valuable human beings right from the start. So, on the first day, we began by asking for their stories.

"My original charge was loitering, and then once I was in the system, everything got harder and started getting out of control," said a young man named Ben. As others spoke, we learned that his story was not unique—in fact, most of the young men's first arrests had been for loitering. I shared with the group that loitering laws were part of the vagrancy statutes included in the Black Codes. These were laws written to control the black population after Reconstruction, a set of policies that followed the Civil War. The teens started to make eye contact.

I asked the participants to tell me what they thought was broken about the criminal justice system and then co-create a list of suggested policy changes with the New York State Prisoner Justice Coalition, a group that holds its strategic planning meetings here at Soul Fire Farm. Among many suggestions, the participants identified the need for access to good lawyers who actually defend the accused rather than "making them cop a plea" (slang for a plea bargain, an arrangement where the defendant pleads guilty in exchange for a more lenient sentence). The young men also explained that discrimination against people with a criminal record makes it harder to get into college, get a job, or find housing.

Staff members at the farm also did what they could to make sure that the young men in Project Growth gained tangible, land-based skills in addition to the wages they earned. Together we transplanted kale, hand seeded turnips, packed vegetables into boxes for distribution, cooked meals for the farm crew and our guests, and studied the business of running a farm.

We made time for personal reflection and introspection as well. One afternoon, we challenged the participants to sit alone in the farm's forest for 15 minutes making observations and noticing their experience. At first, the young men got up from their spots to seek out the company of others or initiated loud call-and-response games to break the isolation. It took several tries to actualize this activity, so foreign from their daily experience.

"I know we were supposed to be looking at nature or something, but I was just thinking about how I want to be an engineer," Ben said during the conversation afterwards. So we had an impromptu career counseling session for the whole group, which was perfect.

"The most amazing moment for me was when they all took their shoes off and stepped into the mud," says Carmen Duncan, Project Growth's facilitator. "They went from being highly ambivalent at the beginning of the day, then seeing how they weren't being judged and could just be themselves at the end of the day—barefoot. If there was a word for this it would be … fantabulous!"

We plan to bring Project Growth alumni back to the farm this summer as mentors for the newer participants.

Land and Food Essential to Black Lives Matter

For generations, black activists have made sure that farms and food played a role in the struggle for civil rights and dignity. Today, we stand on the shoulders of Fannie Lou Hamer, who created the Freedom Farm Cooperative in Mississippi in 1969 to provide food, housing, and education to families targeted by racism in the Delta. We stand on the shoulders of the Black Panthers, who created free breakfast programs for children and other essential community survival initiatives across the United States in the 1960s. We stand on the shoulders of Dr. Martin Luther King Jr., who both inspired and supported the 1965–1970 Delano Grape Boycott, a campaign to create just working conditions for Latino farmworkers.

But land and food have also been used as a weapon to keep people of color in second-class citizenship. The US government sanctioned the slaughter of buffalo to drive Native Americans off of their land. And the United States Department of Agriculture and the Federal Housing Administration denied access to farm credit and other resources to any black person who joined the NAACP, registered to vote, or signed any petition pertaining to civil rights.

According to the think tank Race Forward, even today, blacks, Latinos, and indigenous people are more likely than whites to earn lower wages, receive fewer benefits, and are more likely to live without access to healthy food. Black people also own less than 1 percent of the nation's farmland, just a fraction of the 14 percent they owned in 1920.

"Police shootings are modern day lynching, and lynching was the tool used by white supremacists to drive black folks off of their valuable land and out of Mississippi," says Dr. Monica White, president of the board at the Detroit Black Community Food Security Network. "We still see a systemic failure to value black lives, in terms of policing, access to food, education transportation, etc. The issue is privilege and oppression. It's the same communities dealing with policing issues and bad food."

White's comments point to an essential truth: If we are to create a society that values black life, we cannot ignore the role of food and land. I believe that black people's collective experience with slavery and sharecropping has created an aversion to the land and a sense that the land itself is an oppressor. The truth is that without good land and good food we cannot be truly free. The Freedom Food Alliance represents one important voice among many insisting that the senseless deaths of our black brothers and sisters by all forms of violence—police shooting, diet-related illness, economic marginalization—must end.

Owning our own land, growing our own food, educating our own youth, participating in our own healthcare and justice systems—this is the source of real power and dignity.

Questions for Discussion

1. In what way does Penniman claim that land and food have been used to oppress Black Americans?

2. What do you know about the author of this text, and her experience with the issue? How does that help to shape your understanding of the message?

3. This article emphasizes the importance that land and food plays in empowering marginalized communities. How else might food be used to empower?

From Working the Farm to Fast Food and Back Again: Rural Mexicans in the Neoliberal Food System

Elizabeth Fitting

Latin@'s Presence in the Food Industry: Changing How We Think About Food, 2016

Elizabeth Fitting Is an anthropologist and an associate professor of sociology and social anthropology at Dalhousie, Nova Scotia, Canada. Her research and teaching focuses on the intersection of food, gender, indigenous peoples, and international development, particularly as it relates to Latin America. Fitting is particularly interested in how economic and agricultural development affect rural and indigenous peoples, including traditional practices of food production. In her consideration of gender, class, race, and intergenerational difference, Fitting contemplates the notion of food justice. She is the author of several articles and one book, *The Struggle for Maize: Compesinos, Workers, and Transgenic Corn in the Mexican Countryside*, Duke University Press, 2011. In this chapter, Fitting uses a research method known as "case study" to examine generational shifts in attitudes toward food production, especially corn production which has a long, rich history in Mexico but also a new unfolding story around the reasons why corn production is on the decline.

You know there's a sick joke amongst older farmers here because the average age of a farmer in the United States is approaching sixty right now…in ten years the average age of the American farmer is going to be dead. Nonetheless, this country is full of farmers! They are standing on street corners looking for work. They come from Mexico, Honduras, Nicaragua, Guatemala, Colombia, Panama. They've been displaced! They mow our lawns, they pump our gas, they cook our food in fancy restaurants, those are farmers. We're surrounded by farmers. They're out of work.

—Eric Holt-Giménez, food scholar, activist, and
executive director of Food First, speaking in Seattle, 1999[1]

---

1 Teresa M. Mares, "Engaging Latino Immigrants in Seattle Food Activism through Urban Agriculture," in *Food Activism: Agency, Democracy and Economy.* Ed. Carole M. Counihan and Valeria Sinischalchi (London: Bloomsbury Publishing, 2014), 31.

Juan is a returned migrant of twenty-six. He left school when he was fourteen to find work in a neighboring town and help support his seven siblings. In the late 1990s, at the age of eighteen, Juan decided to head north to Oregon, where he had an aunt and a cousin who could help him get settled. He borrowed money from a local lender to pay the $1,600 fee to a guide (coyote) to cross the US-Mexico border. The first job he got was washing dishes at a fast food restaurant. Although he had originally planned to work for three years and return home, he decided to stay longer, in part to learn how to speak English. Juan explains that he spent the first four years in the United States working to help support his parents and siblings back in his hometown of San José. He sent $200 a month back to his family to help with their upkeep, his sister's education, a small *milpa* (cornfield), and the cost of building an addition to the house. At his next job, as a waiter, he was able to save for a car and the construction costs of his own house in San José. He also opened a small store that operates out of his house. After traveling back and forth over the years Juan decided to move back to San José in 2004. He now lives with his wife and two children in the house he saved to build. Since he does not grow corn or work in the fields, he purchases his grain from the market in a neighboring town, where it is slightly cheaper. Like other migrants his age, he lacks experience and interest in *maize* agriculture. He is unsure about whether he can support his family without returning to the United States for work in the future.[2]

Rural Mexicans play an integral role in the North American[3] food system. While some grow food for their own communities and even for export, others are immigrant workers on farms, in fast food restaurants, in meat-packing and poultry plants, and staff in restaurants in the United States and, to a lesser extent, Canada. Capitalism, particularly in its neoliberal phase, pushes rural food producers into migrant streams; at home, they face increased usurpation of their resources and mounting environmental and economic hardships, and in response, seek out earnings in urban centers and across national borders. The above quote by Holt-Giménez importantly highlights this process of rural displacement and farmers' search for work abroad. What it does not touch on is what migrant workers desire. Would they rather be farming?

The answer to this question depends on who you talk to and when you talk to them. Base on research in the southern Tehuacán Valley agricultural town of San José Miahuatlán (Puebla) from 2000 to 2008 (for different durations,

---

2   Juan, in discussion with the author, June 8, 2005.
3   North American is used here to refer to Mexico, the United States, and Canada. This paper focuses primarily on valley workers in Mexico and the United States. Only a few residents discussed work in Canada, where Mexicans from other regions are employed in the Seasonal Agricultural Workers Program (see endnote number 5). In the US food sectors, Mexicans work alongside other Latin American immigrants, particularly Central Americans.

with some more recent follow-up interviews),[4] I found that migrants from their teens into their early thirties prefer work in the US for sector rather than in Mexican agriculture despite the considerable risks of undocumented status and employment in the United States. "There is no money in the *milpa*," I was told many times over the years. However, generations differ in their attitudes about, and their knowledge of, agriculture. Young migrants discuss corn agriculture as burdensome work, unprofitable, and even as a backward tradition, while older residents describe agriculture as a dignified livelihood, which is linked to their identities as *campesinos*.[5] Since older residents view the cultivation of maize as a social safety net, the question remains whether or not young migrants will take up agriculture as they age; however, the economic, social, and environmental conditions for them to do so are increasingly difficult.

In this chapter I look at how valley migrants and indigenous campesinos fare under the contemporary food system[6]—or the shift to neoliberal policies and processes related to food and agriculture—and it also attends to the agency of residents in navigating these processes. It illustrates how interconnected the food system is across national borders and across a range of jobs and social locations. In addition to ensuring a steady supply of inexpensive food in the United States,[7] rural Mexicans are integral to the Mexican food supply as peasants

---

4   This paper is based on over seventy interviews with southern valley residents about their livelihoods, as well as participant observation in 2001-2002. I also conducted research during extended summer visits until 2008. My ethnography *The Struggle for Maize: Compesinos, Workers and Transgenic Corn in the Mexican Countryside* (Durham, NC: Duke University Press, 2011) is based on this fieldwork and interviews with participants in the GM corn debates. I remain in contact with several valley residents, receiving occasional updates, and plan to return to conduct a follow-up study.

5   Small and medium-sized farmers often identify as peasants or "campesinos." This has a complex political history in Mexico and other Latin American countries. Although the term carries a lot of conceptual baggage, including over generalized, reified, and romanticized notions of peasant and indigenous communities, I use it here because my interviewees use "compesino" to refer to themselves. I also use "campesino" to mean "petty commodity producer," which I discuss later in this chapter. For a more extensive treatment of the politicized concept and identity of "campesinos" in Mexico, see Christopher Boyer, *Becoming Campesinos: Politics, Identity, and Struggle in Postrevolutionary Michoán, 1920-1935* (Stanford: Stanford University Press, 2003), or my own research on the valley (The Struggle for Maize).

6   The concept of "food system" focuses our attention on policies and practices related to food—its production, provisioning, and consumption. Food systems are embedded in larger social, economic, and ecological contexts and can include alternative or counter practices. Here, for the sake of convenience, I use the term as shorthand to talk about food policies and practices under neoliberal capitalism.

7   Mexicans also work, to a lesser extent, in Canada, where there are important differences from the United States in policies and discourses around immigration. Under the Seasonal Agricultural Workers Program (SAWP), up to 26,000 contracted agricultural workers come to Canada annually, the majority of whom are Mexican. The program is open only to Mexicans and people from the Caribbean (CBC 2012). In the US food system, Mexicans work alongside other Latin American immigrants, particularly Central Americans. See recent research on th4e Canadian SAWP, such as Leigh Binford, *Tomorrow We Are All Going to Harvest* (Austin: University of Texas Press, 2013). For further reading on the anthropology of Mexican immigrants working in different aspects of the US food system, see Steve Striffler, *Chicken: The Transformation of American's Favorite* (New Haven, CT: Yale University Press, 2005) on the poultry industry; Ruth Gomberg-Muñoz, *Labor and Legality: An Ethnography of Mexican Immigrant Network* (Oxford: Oxford University Press, 2011) on restaurant staff; and Patricia Zabella, *I'm Neither Here Nor There: Mexican Quotidian Struggles with Migration and Poverty* (Durham, NC: Duke University Press, 2011), on Californian agriculture, especially strawberry production.

because they produce food, especially maize, for local and—depending on the farmer—national consumption, and they maintain native varieties (*crillos*)[8] of maize in their fields. Peasants and migrant workers typically come from the same rural households; in some cases, they are one and the same, working in different areas of the food system at different moments in their lives. In other cases, migrants are children of campesinos and their earnings help maintain their parents' households or establish their own homes in the valley.

This raises questions about the role of generational groups in social reproduction, or how residents of different age groups maintain and advance their households ("simple" or "expanded" reproduction), and at another level, how their livelihood strategies are a creative response to, and in turn contribute to, the current capitalist food system. Capitalism draws rural agriculturalists into the world of waged labor, but it simultaneously differentiates and segments: within the same communities some benefit more than others, and experiences are shaped by gender, class, ethic, and generational locations. In the valley, indigenous campesinos, depending on their age, resources, and gender, reproduce their households and families through maize agriculture, unpaid labor in the home, work in the valley poultry industry and clothing *maquiladoras* (assembly plants), and migration to the United States (and sometimes Canada) for employment in the restaurant and food processing sectors.[9]

This case study helps to challenge the romantization of rural life, particularly of indigenous and campesino communities, found in some food activism and scholarship.[10] When rural life is romanticized some important dynamics are missed. For example, not enough attention is paid to the pull of capitalism—access to consumer goods and the promise of waged employment or making a profit on agricultural goods, which is, most of the time, not fully realized. Similarly, instead of treating rural communities as homogenous and conflict-free, we should consider how social differences and inequality *within* communities, and even households, are engaged and negotiated as rural populations

8   Native varieties of maize are "*maices navitos*" in Spanish. They are grown, selected, and improved by farmers in their fields, in contrast to scientifically improved or "modern" varieties. However, the term *criollo* is used by interviewees (and is popularly used in the countryside). *Criollo* refers to both native and creolized varieties. Creolized varieties are the result of Intentional of unintentional mixing between native and scientifically improved varieties.

9   Less commonly, valley residents also move to urban centers in Mexico, sometimes as step-migration on the way to the United States. Unlike valley residents who went to the United States as Bracero farm laborers, recent migrants work in food processing and service sectors more frequently than in agriculture.

10   The romanticization of rural communities via calls for food self-sufficiency can be found among some of the En Defensa del Maiz network in Mexico. See Elizabeth Fitting, "The Political Uses of Culture: Maize Production and the GM Corn Debates in Mexico," *Focaal, Journal of Global and Historical Anthropology 48* (2006): 17-34; Fitting, *The Struggle for Maize*, or Henry Bernstein, "Food Sovereignty: A Sceptical View" (Paper presented at the Agrarian Studies Conference, Food Sovereignty: A Critical Dialogue, September 14-15, 2013). http://www.yale.edu/agrarianstudies/foodsovereignty/pprs/1_Bernstein_2013.pdf.

increasingly diversify their livelihoods, relying on the cash markets for goods and labor. Finally, romanticizing rural life can also attribute migrants' hard work to a cultural disposition, which naturalizes their exploitation and subordination.

Corn and Capitalism:

Social Reproduction and Rural Life

> *In times of crisis, when social services collapse or cannot effectively carry out their functions, corn's importance becomes self-evident. Recourse to corn is the last line of defense for security, for hope, for the retreat of lesser units of society in order to defend their very existence.*
>
> —Arturo Warman[11]

In his book *Corn & Capitalism*, Mexican anthropologist Arturo Warman traces the history of maize from Mesoamerica to its emergence as a global staple crop.[12] Corn, he argues, is a particularly important crop for looking at how peasants fared under modern capitalism, as well as its relationship of capital to labor and other resources. Not only was corn the quintessential peasant crop of the Americas, it also was the key crop in the development of the commercial seed industry[13] and remains pivotal to the reproduction of rural life in Mexico today.

Political economy in anthropology, like the work of Warman, approaches capitalism as an economic system that has social, cultural, environmental, and political characteristics that play out in particular ways, in particular places, or as a "history of diversity."[14] While anthropologists have studied food since the emergence of the discipline, the study of food as a commodity—as a good produced for exchange—began later. In the 1950s anthropologists working in Latin America became interested in what commodities tell us about power, particularly unequal social relations and state practices.[15] Commodities embody the labor that went into making them and the system under which they are made. Scholars turn to the work of Karl Marx, who wrote in the nineteenth century, for thinking about commodities. He argues that commodities are

---

11   Arturo Warman, *Corn & Capitalism: How a Botanical Bastard Grew to Global Domination*, trans. Nancy Westrate (Chapel Hill: University of North Carolina Press, 2003 [1998]): 20.
12   Ibid.
13   Jack Ralph Kloppenburg Jr., *The First Seed: The Political Economy of Plant Biotechnology 1492-2000* (New York: Cambridge University Press, 1988).
14   William Roseberry, introduction to *Coffee, Society and Power in Latin America*, ed. William Roseberry, Lowell Gudmundson, and Mario Samper-Kutschback (Baltimore: Johns Hopkins University Press, 1995), 1-37; Eric Wolf, *Europe and the People without History* (Berkeley: University of California Press, 1982).
15   Casey Walsh and Emma Ferry, "Introduction: Production, Power, and Place," in *The Social Relations of Mexican Commodities*, ed. Casey Walsh, Emma Ferry, Gabriela Soto Laveaga, Paula Sesis, and Sarah Hill (San Diego: Center for U.S.–Mexico Studies at the University of California–San Diego, 2003), 1-18.

fetishized under capitalism: that we worship the goods we buy, placing value in them as discrete objects rather than valuing the labor that made them.[16] The market mediates our understanding of where goods come from and, in the process, obscures the unequal and exploitative social relations involved in their making. Commodity fetishism normalizes inequality and exploitative labor conditions, and an important part of this normalization is how commodities, and the system in which they are made, are represented and framed. In recent years, food activism has taken up aspects of this approach—with different degrees of success—asking us to consider where our food comes from and what we know about the lives of those who farm, process, and serve our foods. As part of this line of inquiry, though, we need to understand the broader system of inequality and exploitation in which food producers and workers are located, as well as consider how food workers and producers feed themselves and their families.

Today's food system has its origins in capitalism and colonialism,[17] and it has undergone changes at different historical moments. With the implementation of neoliberal policies in the 1980s, there was an increase in nontraditional food exports from the Global South (fruits, vegetables, and meat), the continued export of subsidized grain from the Global North, the expansion of supermarket chains, the consolidation of agribusiness, the financialization of markets, the liberalization of trade, and the increasing precariousness of rural livelihoods.[18] Today's food system is also characterized by the rise of genetic engineering as the main technology for capitalist agriculture and by changes in regulation at national and international levels, which accommodate this technology.[19]

Agricultural life is always vulnerable to conditions beyond the farmer's control to a degree, like the weather or crop pests. Under capitalism, rural life is precarious in additional ways. As Marx explained, the emergence and expansion of capitalism involved "primitive accumulation," or the expropriation of many farmers' means of production, notably their land.[20] David Harvey refers to this process as "accumulation by dispossession" because it is ongoing in the contemporary world: profit is made from the usurpation and privatization of

---

16   Karl Marx, *Capital: Volume 1*, trans. Ben Fowkers (New York: Vintage Books, 1977 [1866-1867]), 163-77.

17   See Harriet Friedmann, "International Regimes of Food and Agricultural Since 1870," in *Peasants and Peasant Societies*, ed. Theodor Shamin (Oxford: Basil Blackwell, 1987), and Philip McMichael, *Food Regimes and Agrarian Questions* (Halifax: Fernwood Publishing, 2013), on the emergence of the first international food regime with capitalism and British colonialism, as well as for a discussion of the concept of food "regime."

18   Henry Bernstein, *Class Dynamics and Agrarian Change* (Halifax: Fernwood Publishing, 2010); Philip McMichael, "Peasant Prospects in the Neoliberal Age," *New Political Economy 11, no. 3* (2006): 204-418; Philip McMichael, "A Food Regime Genealogy." *Journal of Peasant Studies 36, no. 1* (2009): 139-69.

19   Gabriela Pechlaner and Gerardo Ostero, "The Third Food Regime: Neoliberal Globalism and Agricultural Biotechnology in North America," *Sociologia Ruralis 48, no. 4* (2008): 1-23.

20   Marx, *Capital*, part 8.

resources that were previously in the public domain or held communally, such as land, water, and, today, seeds and genetic resources.[21] This process also involves the commodification of forms of labor that were previously uncommodified or outside the cash nexus. It creates a surplus labor population that is dependent on paid employment but often does not make a living wage. In the valley, such processes have a long history dating back to colonialism, which includes not just the unsurpation of land but also the use and control of spring water.[22] This chapter focuses on the contemporary period in the valley, but agriculture and residents' livelihoods were by no means static in earlier moments.

Scholars of agrarian change argue that accumulation and rural precariousness have intensified with neoliberal capitalism.[23] In Mexico, neoliberal policies involved cuts to rural subsidies, the implementation of counter-agrarian reform policies (such as those which enable communal landholders to sell land), increased corn imports (rather than prioritizing national food self-sufficiency), and exports of fresh fruits and vegetables to Canada and the United States, including organic produce. The country's dependency on corn imports has increased. Mexico now imports its most consumed and most important crop, maize, while its most significant export is labor. Mexico has promoted rural development through modern, commercial agriculture, improved seeds, trade liberalization, and the displacement of what various offices of the state deem "inefficient" campesinos. In this sense, neoliberal policies have sought to transform peasants into new rural subjects: into either agricultural entrepreneurs who produce for export or an inexpensive (and surplus) labor force.[24]

In this neoliberal food system, how do food producers and workers feed themselves? In Mexico, maize remains an important part of the diet, especially in rural locales like the Tehuacán Valley. Women are responsible for cooking, and this includes the preparation of tortillas and other corn-based foods. Women remove the kernels and soak them in limestone,[25] which is then ground to make the *masa* (dough) for tortillas. This process was enormously time consuming until the first corn mill was set up in town in 1953, which shortened the time required to make masa.[26] Meals are considered incomplete without homemade tortillas or tortillas bought fresh from a neighbor. As feminist scholars have rightly pointed out, what is called "reproductive labor"—such as raising children,

21   David Harvey, *The New Imperialism* (Oxford: Oxford University Press, 2003).
22   Discussed in Fitting, *The Struggle for Maize*, ch. 3; and Luis E. Henao, *Techuacán: Campesinado e ir-rigación* (Mexico City: Edicol, 1980).
23   Farshard Araghi, "The Invisible Hand and Visable Foot: Peasants, Dispossession and Globalization," in *Peasants and Globalization*, ed. A. Haroon Akram-Lodhl and Cristóbal Kay (New York: Routledge, 2009), 111-47; Bernstein, *Class Dynamics*, McMichael, *Peasant Prospects*.
24   I expand on this argument elsewhere: Fitting, *The Struggle for Maize*.
25   This is known as nixtamalization, which releases the vitamin niacin and the amino acid tryptophan in the corn. Corn flour that is not nixtramalized lacks this nutritional benefit.
26   Interview, July 2, 2002.

preparing food, and care work—is central to the functioning of capitalism, yet is largely devalued and un- or under-paid. This type of reproductive labor is naturalized as an expression of biological sex, based on ideas about what it means to be a woman, and an innate predisposition for such tasks.

However, daily life complicates conceptualizations of "reproductive" and "productive" labor. The lines between such categories shift and change. In recent years, male migrants from the valley have taken up cooking for themselves and their roommates while living abroad and have remarked to me about the amount of work that goes into food preparation. To a certain extent, these migrants reevaluate assumptions about gendered domestic tasks. Although returned migrants reconsider some expectations about gender, other gender expectations are reinforced. Young women who worked in valley factories continue to contribute to household earnings after having children by staying at home and opening a store, a food stand, or more frequently, taking on piecework for maquilas. Typically, these earnings are seen as supplemental to their husband's or father's wages.

Men and women, teens, and elders work to "reproduce" their households or to secure "the conditions of life and of future production from what is produced and earned now."[27] In the process, their labor—paid and unpaid—contributes to the social reproduction of capitalism, a system in which "daily life depends upon the production of commodities produced through a system of circulation of capital that has profit-seeking as its direct and socially accepted goal."[28] Campesinos in the valley grow maize for reasons other than, or in addition to, profit, but they do so within a wider context of a changing capitalist food system.

As mentioned above, the cultivation of maize is central to the reproduction of rural households because it provides a form of security to older residents who have few sources of income. Maize can either be consumed as tortillas (and other foods) for the household or sold when cash is needed. Warman referred to peasant reliance on the crop as the "recourse to corn."[29] He argues that maize becomes especially important in times of crisis or hardship, when households or communities cope with loss of income or state support, or decide to engage wider markets only selectively. Although historically maize has been an excellent source of economic security, in what ways have valley practices and meaning of maize changed, if at all?

Crisis in the Valley of Corn and Changing Livelihood Strategies

27   Bernstein, *Class Dynamics*, 128.
28   David Harvey, "The Geopolitics of Capitalism," in *Social Relations and Spatial Structures*, ed. Derek Gregory and John Urry (London: Palgrave Macmillan, 1985), 128.
29   Warman, *Corn & Capitalsim*.

The Tehuacán Valley[30] is known as the "cradle of maize" largely due to Richard MacNeish's important archaeological study of the 1960s, which uncovered maize cobs dating back to 5000 BCE,[31] although other regions of Mexico are more likely sites of maize domestication. In addition to Spanish, different dialects of Nahuatl are spoken in the valley's towns.[32] Campesinos and indigenous peoples from the valley and surrounding sierras look to the regional capital of Techuacán for employment. The most commonly grown crops in this semi-arid valley are maize and beans. Garlic, tomatoes, sugarcane, fruits, and flowers, among other crops, are also grown commercially.

When a national economic crisis hit in 1982, and the government began to implement austerity measures followed by neoliberal policies, San José was already suffering from a water drought. Following the escalation of a local conflict over irrigation water, an initial wave of residents left to work in the United States for the first time since the 1950s.[33] In the mid-1990s labor migration from the valley quickly expanded. This was in part due to the implementation of the North American Free Trade Agreement (NAFTA), with its rise in inexpensive US corn exports (which are subsidized in the United States and often sold abroad below cost, or "dumped") and changes to rural subsidies. Local concerns about insufficient irrigation water were also a factor. Valley residents found it increasingly difficult to support their families through farming or selling their maize for income.[34] As one resident in his early forties explained, the earnings and food from agriculture alone were often insufficient. He said, "I work the fields, but five months after harvest, where will my food come from? You can't live off the countryside alone. After the corn runs out, then what?"[35]

---

30   This area is also one of the sites where the Mexican government found evidence of transgenes growing among native varities of maize, contributing to the controversy over transgenic corn that made international headlines beginning in 2001-2002. Because the source of such transgenes is considered to be transgenic corn imported from the United States, this controversy illustrates the interconnectedness of our ostensibly national food systems. Elsewhere, I situate the GM corn controversy in relation to the food system (Fitting, "The Political Uses of Culture: Maize Production and the GM Corn Debates in Mexico," *Focaal, Journal of Global and Historical Anthropology 48* (2006); 17-34; Fitting, *The Struggle for Maize*).

31   Richard S. MacNeish, "Summary of the Cultural Sequence and Its Implications for the Techuacan Valley," in *The Prehistory of the Tehuacan Valley: Excavations and Reconnaissance*, ed. Richard MacNeish (Austin: University of Texas Press, 1972), 496-504.

32   Prior to Spanish conquest, the valley was settled by Nahua, Poploca, Mixteca, Chocho, and Mazateca indigenous groups.

33   In the 1950s up to three dozen residents from San José left to work in the United States as temporary agricultural workers under the Bracero program, the binational treaty between the United States and Mexico, which ran from 1942 to 1964. There were local political struggles over water access during this period also (see Fitting, *The Struggle for Maize*, ch. 3). Close to five million Mexicans sought work in the United States under the program. As Gomberg-Muñoz explains, "As millions of Mexican workers became accustomed to employment practices, lifestyles, and consumption patterns in the United States, they established networks between jobs in the U.S. and friends and family members back home that allowed migratory flows to become self-sustaining in the decades that followed" (Gomberg-Muñoz, *Labor and Legality*, 31).

34   Fitting, *The Struggle for Maize*.

35   Interview, June 23, 2006.

In response, valley residents further diversified their livelihood strategies or the ways they maintain their households, generate income, and produce food for consumption. I use "strategy" intentionally here in order to highlight the agency of residents under discussion. Food producers and workers are not simply pushed and pulled about by larger forces (nor are we as readers, scholars, or activists); rather, they make decisions on how to manage, get ahead, or even challenge, and sometimes change the social and economic conditions in which they find themselves. This response to neoliberal capitalism, and the stresses this type of development places on the environment, especially with declining groundwater levels and soil erosion, is part of a long history of adaption in the region.

The increased diversification of agricultural livelihoods and the expansion (or initiation) of labor migration, which characterized much of rural Mexico in the 1980s, 1990s, and into the new millennium,[36] is experienced in particular ways in particular places. There are also exceptions. For example, in northern Mexico, farmers have taken advantage of changes to policy and the market and have made a profit from converting to maize production.[37] In other regions, some communities have selectively engaged the market by selling peasant crafts and foods like tortillas, strengthening their communities,[38] or organizing oppositional political movements and social alternatives to neoliberal policies (the Zapatista or EZLN movement being a famous example).[39]

In the valley, maize production and off-farm employment constitute part of a local strategy between age groups or generations to maintain or advance the economic position of their families. It is a strategy that embodies tensions, not only between wives and their migrant husbands but also between generations, as children are raised with an absent parent and teen workers, at some stage, reduce their financial contributions to their parents' households.

---

36   Alejandro Nadal, "Corn and NAFTA: An Unhappy Alliance," Seeding: *The Quarterly Newsletter of Genetic Resources Action International 17, no. 2* (2000): 10-17; Antonio Turrent-Fernández, Timothy A. Wise, and Elise Garvey, "Achieving Mexico's Maize Potential: Global Development and Environment Institute" (Working Paper, no. 12-03, Medford, MA: Tufts University, October 2012). http://www.ase.tufts.edu/gdate/Pubs/wp/12-03TurrentMexMaiz.pdf.
37   Hallie Eakin, Julia C. Bausch, and Stuart Sweeny, "Agrarian Winners of Neoliberal Reform: The 'Maize Boom' of Sinaloa, Mexico, "*Journal of Agrarian Change 14, no. 1* (2014): 26-51.
38   J. Samuel Barkin, *International Organization: Theories and Institutions* (New York: Palgrave Macmillan, 2006).
39   The Ejército Zapatista de Liberació Nacionel (EZLN), Zapatista National Liberation Army, made up largely of Mayans, declared war against the Mexican state on the first day of 1994, the day the NAFTA went into effect, from the Lacandon region of Chiapas. Although the movement began as an armed struggle, it became largely civil disobedience against the state's military excursions in the region and neoliberal globalization. This movement has generated enormous international and media attention on the struggles of indigenous peoples in Mexico and beyond, as well as discussions about participatory democracy and alter-globalization.

In a sociological sense, "generation" refers both to one's age group (or stage in the life cycle) and to the sense of identity and meaning shared by an age group at a particular historical moment.[40] Philip Abrams's concept draws our attention to the wider social, political, and economic changes in society and asks whether the sense of being part of a particular age group is static—that is, continuous with the previous age group or groups—or whether it is undergoing change in connection to those wider changes. In the valley, as young people work in maquilas and migrate north to work in the neoliberal food system, and their ideas about rural life and sense of identity distinct from a previous generation?

"We are Campesinos"

Some of us grow corn because there is no other work. Not everyone can get a job or make it across the border.

—Maize farmer, male, June 21, 2006

Maize farmers in San José are generally men who are either (a) in their thirties or forties, have worked in the United States (for periods between months to several years), and often have a small business or income like bus driving in the valley, a corn mill, construction work, and so forth, or who are (b) full-time agriculturalists in their fifties and older who are less likely to find paid employment other than work as local agricultural day laborers.[41] As the interviewee quoted above said to me, "Some of us grow corn because there is no other work." Both men and women of these older generations work in the fields. Women are also food producers and preparers. They

Milpa (maize field) in the southern Tehuacán valley.
Courtesy of author, Elizabeth Fitting, 2008.

---

40   Philip Abrah, *Historical Sociology* (Ithaca, NY: Cornell University Press, 1982), ch. 8.
41   Farmers from San José can be considered "petty commodity producers" in that they own or have usufruct rights to the land, irrigation water, and/or seed; they produce maize for consumption and sale, but the scale of production is relatively small; and they rely on unpaid labor or sharecropping. Those who can afford it hire local day laborers to help with the more arduous parts of planting and harvesting.

farm crops like tomatoes and are responsible for selecting maize seed to save for future replanting; however, agriculture, and maize cultivation in particular, are considered "men's work."

Farmers in the valley refer to themselves as campesinos, a term which has a complex history in a country that experienced a peasant revolution in the early twentieth century and numerous development interventions aimed at improving rural production. In the early to mid-twentieth century, revolutionary leadership and the new state portrayed campesinos as the rightful owners of the land and the heart and soul of Mexico.[42] Such representations were undergirded by redistributive land reform and agrarian policies. While this imagery and discourse was used to generate support for the state, it also resonated with many rural peoples, including indigenous farmers in the Tehuacán Valley.

Husking and sorting dry maize. Courtesy of author, Elizabeth Fitting, 2008.

The term campesino remains in use in the valley today, but the context in which it is used has significantly changed. In addition to some branches of the state portraying campesinos as inefficient and culturally backward producers, agrarian policies and supports have been dismantled or radically transformed. For older residents, the term campesino recalls a past when the state had a responsibility—at least officially—to small-scale farmers. They use the term to signal hard work and a dignified life, which is in contrast to some official state narratives about inefficient peasants. In this sense, campesino as a self-label is one of the ways that residents criticize and sometimes challenge official policy and discourse. They also have refused to sell their communal land to agribusiness and have a history of petitions and conflict with the state (and valley neighbors) over access to spring water.[43]

---

42   Boyer, *Becoming Campesinos*.
43   Explored further in Fitting, *The Struggle for Maize*, ch. 3 and 5.

In addition to signaling a previous era of state obligation to rural folk and a sense of respectable hard work, the term campesino connotes a preference for local or regional criollo corn over yellow industrial corn (grown in the north or the United States). Residents of all ages prefer criollo maize for making tortillas, even though I found that imported or industrial grain was 30 percent cheaper at the local market. When yellow corn is received through government programs or purchased at the local store, it is either fed to farm animals or mixed with local corn to hide its taste and texture. The industrial corn flour, Maseca, and yellow imported corn are seen as "pig food" that is considered not very tasty and not consistent with a dignified rural life. A female storeowner, who also has a small milpa for her household's consumption, told me that people grow corn despite the cost because they prefer the taste of white corn and because it makes tortillas of better quality than those found in cities. As she explains, "We grow corn because we want to have good, soft, white tortillas. They don't turn out the same in the city. In Mexico City, a truck carrying masa comes round as if it were mud. It's even uncovered! They say we live like animals here in the countryside, but in the city, they eat like animals!"[44] Through her comparison between rural and urban tortillas, the storeowner counters urban stereotypes about rural Mexico as backward or uncivilized ("they say we live like animals"). Access to local corn of high quality is connected to the idea that campesinos are hard working and deserving of respect. Ironically, for young migrants from the valley working and living abroad, Maseca, the industrial corn flour, has become a taste of home.[45]

Although maize remains the most cultivated and important crop in San José,[46] agricultural production is on the decline overall. There are now a number of households that no longer grow maize at all. Agricultural fields are transformed into housing for returned migrants, irrigation and rain water levels are reportedly low, and the price of inputs has increased. Indeed, under NAFTA, the cultivation of criollo maize for food in the valley came to cost at least as much as purchasing imported corn.

While male and female residents in their forties and older often view the cultivation of maize as minimizing risk, migrants and maquiladora workers in their teens and twenties do not believe that maize agriculture provides

---

44   Interview, June 20, 2006.
45   Jeffrey Pilcher, "Taco Bell, Maseca, and Slow Food: A Postmodern Apocalypse for Mexico's Peasant Cuisine?" in *Fast Food/Slow Food: The Cultural Economy of the Global Food System*, ed. Richard Wilk (Lanham, MD: AltaMira Press, 2006).
46   Residents grow several varieties of maize. The most common are rain-fed white corn—distinct from industrial, hybrid yellow corn—grown for human consumption and an irrigated white maize for sale on the cob, called elote. Residents have grown this commercial elote since the 1960s. Elote can be sold for a better price than grain because there is a market for it (both in the valley and beyond, in Mexico City), and it can be dried and eaten at home. However, elote required irrigation water and therefore is more costly to produce than rain-fed corn, which means the poorer strata of households either grow rain-fed corn only or they sharecrop elote fields with a relative or neighbor who contributes the irrigation water or some other inputs.

advantages, particularly not for their generation. At this stage of migration and their lives, you migrants have few agricultural skills, prefer nonagricultural work, and view corn agriculture as an unprofitable tradition with few future prospects.

"No hay dinero en la milpa":

US Bound Migration and Back Again

"You can't make any money in the countryside! There is no money in the milpa!"

—Teenage migrant workers discussing maize farming, November 30, 2001

The younger generation has joined wage labor circuits that take them farther afield than previous generations. Most young men now migrate to the United States for work, and this migration is often undocumented and transnational in the sense that residents generally come home to the valley for months and sometimes years at a time, build houses, marry partners from town, and then return to the United States for another stint.

In comparison, young women of the same age tend to travel much shorter distances to work in maquilas and poultry plants within the valley, but they now do so unaccompanied by male relatives. Unaccompanied female travel, at this scale, is fairly new, and it generates discussion and anxiety among some residents. Even though men also work in valley maquilas and, to a lesser extent, women become migrants bound for the United States, these are gendered labor circuits because they are underpinned by assumptions about what is appropriate work for each gender, and because the distances that men and women travel to work differ. These are also transnational circuits: migrants remit money home and live transborder lives, while workers in valley assembly plants generate profit for domestic and foreign consortiums. Participation in these circuits of labor and capital provides much-needed income for rural households, but it also puts stress and strain on families and on the workers involved. Maquila work, for example, is demanding; it involves keeping up with an output quota and working long hours (sometimes in hot factories) for low wages. If and when women marry and have kids, one of the few options for employment is to continue working in the maquila industry as piece-workers from home.[47]

Residents of all ages agree that income from off-farm employment, particularly in the United States where the wages are higher, is key for household maintenance and socioeconomic advancement. The southern valley has become a migrant-sending region. Previously, there had been up to three dozen contracted

---

47   Lourdes Flores Morales, "No me gustaba, pero es trabajo": Mujer, trabajo y desechabilidad en al maquila (Mexico City: Instituto de Ciencias Sociales y Humanidades "Alfonso Vélez Pilego," BUAP/Plaza y Valdés S.A. de C.V., 2008).

agricultural workers from San José under the Bracero Program in the 1950s and 1960s, but most of these contract workers returned home, and migration did not expand significantly. Migration from San José to the United States started up again in the 1980s and increased rapidly in the 1990s. This reflects larger trends in Mexico and the needs of the low-end service economy in the United States. An estimated 1.8 million undocumented migrants arrived in the United States from Mexico in the 1980s. The following decade, this number jumped to 4.9 million, despite the increased militarization of the US-Mexico border and the passing of the most severe anti-immigrant legislation to date. In the five years that followed, from 2000 to 2005 alone, there were another 4.4 million undocumented migrants.[48]

In the wake of 9/11, there was a temporary drop in migrant trips across the border, due to heightened security. In 2008, there was also a decline in unauthorized entries. While the cause of this decline remains debatable, it could be due to the rapid drop in US employment (particularly in sectors like construction) or the delayed effects of heightened border enforcement and a decline in back-and-forth migration.[49] In the valley, migrants are indeed extending their stays on either side of the border, but many young residents either continue to journey across the border or are in the process of planning and preparing for such journeys.

Unlike their predecessors, who worked in Californian agriculture, young migrants from San José find work largely in the US food industry as dishwashers and bus boys in restaurants and fast food chains, in food processing and packing plants, and on fishing boats that leave from the northwest coast. Most of the young interviewees reported sending money home to help their parents. Generally, they earmark money for building their own cement block house or opening a small business, like a store. While some migrants were successful in saving for the completion of their houses, starting up a business, or purchasing agricultural inputs (a tractor, irrigation water, etc.) others were not. In other words, the economic benefits of migration are not uniform, which helps to widen class differences among residents.

Young migrants report little knowledge about agriculture: they cannot identify or describe the traits of local varieties, soil qualities, or other aspects of agriculture. This can be seen as a generational interruption in the transmission of agricultural knowledge. When I asked interviewees why they thought their older relatives or townspeople grew corn, I was told that maize was grown as

48   Gomberg-Muñoz, *Labor and Legality*, 33-35.
49   Josiah Heyman, "Constructing a 'Perfect' Wall: Race, Class, and Citizenship in US-Mexico Border Policing," in Migration in the 21st Century: *Political Economy and Ethnography*, ed. Pauline Gardiner Barber and Winnie Lem (New York: Routlege, 2012), 153-74.

a custom or tradition and to produce food, but that it was not a means to make money: "People grow corn here to eat, so they don't lose the custom, or to get out of the house. They don't grow corn to make money. It's not a business."[50] The value of growing maize is not only economic but also has to do with the flexibility of the crop's uses, the older generation's contribution to the household, the widespread preference for the taste of local varieties, and the sense of autonomy that such agriculture brings to farmers, at least in theory if not in practice.

In addition to wages, migrants and maquila workers bring home ideas about agriculture, how to earn a living, and even about indigeneity and gender. As in other regions, migrants and maquila workers enjoy new social status in their hometowns. The money that migrants earn abroad enables them to build and improve homes in Mexico, buy consumer goods, and participate in local celebrations.[51] Richard C. Jones suggests that migrant income and purchasing power translate into a new "migrant elite" whose prestige comes from "wage labor earnings rather than from land, commerce, social status, and political pull."[52] To an extent, this is also evident in San José, where younger returned migrants gain social prestige from their purchasing power and experience abroad rather than from their control of irrigation water, participation in ritual kinship and celebrations, or affiliation with political factions, as was true of older Sanjosepeños and even older migrants who are also farmers.

Young women see maquila work as an economic necessity, and residents often say they are glad to have it. It is repetitive and low-paid work, and some women endure harassment in the factories as well as face local disdain about their unaccompanied travel and interaction with nonrelated men at work. Yet, at the same time, the experience and income provides young women with a sense of independence and freedom from some of the social constraints that their mothers or grandmothers faced. Several young women mentioned to me that they felt their income gave them more respect in the home. Their journey to work challenges ideas about gender on the one hand, while the industry depends on normative ideas about gender on the other: the ideas that women are more subservient, have nimble fingers, and are supplemental earners who therefore can be paid less than men.[53]

---

50   Interview with twenty-nine-year-old male migrant, June 8, 2005.
51   Luin Goldring, "Power and Status in Transnational Social Spaces," in Migration and Transnational Spaces, ed. Ludger Prier (Aldershot, UK: Ashgate, 1999), 162-86; María Leticia Rivermar Pérs, "La reconstrucción de las identidades sociales en e context de las migraviones," in Conflictos migratorios transnacionales y respuestas communitarias, ed. Leigh Binford and Maria Eugenia D'Aubeterre (Puebla: Instituto de Ciencias Sociales y Humanidades, BUAP, 2000), 81-96.
52   Richard C. Jones, "US Migration: An Alternative Economic Mobility Ladder for Rural Central Mexico," Social Science Quarterly 73, no. 3 (1992): 496-510, 507. (check pg. nos. 496-510, 507 looks strange)
53   Flores Morales, "No me gustaba."

In the United States, Mexican workers are inserted into the racial hierarchy as inexpensive, disposable, and deportable labor.[54] Despite harsh anti-immigration policies, there is tacit if not explicit acceptance of the employment of undocumented Mexicans, especially in the food system. Ruth Gomberg-Muñoz provides an excellent summary of the myths and realities of undocumented workers in the United States, pointing out that while hard work contributes to a sense of self-worth among migrants, it is also used as a cultural trope about Mexican workers. Undocumented Mexicans are particularly vulnerable because they are unable to complain or report unfair wages, dangerous working conditions, and abuse, or they might face enormous risks if they do so. Moreover, Mexicans, and other Latin Americans, are often assumed to be undocumented workers, regardless of their citizenship or immigration status. As Gomberg-Muñoz explains in her study of Mexican restaurant staff in Chicago, "[T]he desirability of low-end service workers is often evaluated on subjective criteria such as their 'work ethic' and 'good attitude,' conditions that are promoted by workers' powerlessness."[55]

Yet migrants from San José also experience working abroad, as an improvement in their social status and self-perception—in the United States they are seen as Mexicans and not *indigenas* (indigenous)—despite the exploitation and racism. Additionally, this experience, along with wages, work experience, consumer goods, and the ability to speak English, are steps toward assimilation—though not necessarily complete or successful—when back in Mexico. According to accounts by returned migrants, in the United States employers, customers, and residents tend to view Sanjosepeños as homogeneously Mexican. A group of teenage migrants told me that in the restaurant kitchen where they worked in Las Vegas, even though they often spoke Nahuatl to each other, their employers referred to them as *Mexicans*. Contrastingly, when they were in Tehuacán—historically known as the City of Indians—they avoid speaking Nahuatl because they do not want people to think that they are "indios" (Indians). It is just "too embarrassing," I was told.[56] Ironically, these young migrants felt more a part of a larger Mexican society based on their work experience in the United States.

Studies of migrants from other indigenous regions of Puebla have also found that their experience in the United States provides a path toward assimilation when back home,[57] but that assimilation often is not successful or complete. Ideas about, and experiences of, being campesino and indígena—not to mention male or female, young, middle-aged, or old—change over time and place, as well as in different social spaces and encounters.

---

54   Nicholas De Genova, *Working the Boundaries: Race, Space, and "Illegality" in Mexican Chicago* (Durham, NC: Duke University Press, 2005).
55   Gomberg-Muñoz, *Labor and Legality*, 37.
56   Interview, November 12, 2001.
57   Rivermar Pérez, *La reconstrucción*.

Labor migration to the United States builds the confidence of some Sanjosepeños. But for those who do not learn English, their experiences abroad may confirm their insecurities about traveling and interacting with people outside the valley. Several migrants reported that if you do not speak English in the United States, your capacity to earn and save will be more difficult, as will be your overall experience. Not all male migrants preferred working in the United States over staying in San José, and many were not successful in saving part of their income. However, without other remunerative employment options, many are compelled to return to the United States regardless of whether or not they had a positive experience there.

Their income, travel experience, English-language ability, and greater access to consumer goods enable some migrants to cast off the negative associations of being indigenous or to redeploy them.[58] For others, their experience abroad as Mexicans and exposure to other, more positive ideas about Mesoamerican Indians contribute to their rethinking the meaning of being an indigenous. In contrast to their parents and grandparents, migrants and maquila workers have access to social prestige through their income and travel experience rather than via more traditional avenues such as patron-client relationships or ritual kinship. In this way the experience of working in the United States and in the valley maquilas is transforming some notions about rural life and identity, while simultaneously reproducing others.

I also found that in interviews with migrants who had worked in the US food sector, although they discussed low pay, the hardship of being away from family, and exploitative work conditions, they also reported feeling a certain amount of freedom from what they saw as the outdated agricultural livelihoods of their elders, as well as from parental and, in the case of women, gender expectations. A few migrants also mentioned that, back in the valley, they were "free" from the fear of *la migra* (US border and immigration enforcement agents) and from the exploitation of food service work in the United States.

Although a sense of freedom most often came up as a point of discussion among returned migrants, I interviewed one young mother in her early twenties who described living in San José as freedom. She sold lunch foods outside of a school in the valley when I first interviewed her. She lived with her campesino parents who grew maize for household consumption and sale. She told me that residents were "free [here in the valley], but there is almost no food or work."[59]

---

58   Similarly, anthropologist Judith Friedlander found, in her study on indigenous ethnicity in Morelos forty years ago, that residents felt to a certain degree that "the more material symbols of Hispanic [mestizo] culture they obtain [ed], the less Indian they will become." Judith Friedlander, *Being Indian in Hueyapan: A Study of Forced Identity in Contemporary Mexico* (New York: St. Martin's Press, 1975), 131.
59   Interview, May 31, 2001.

She was referring to the freedom (*"somos libres"*) of being able to go to one's own land to pick fruit or grow maize and, perhaps, as in her case, start a small business instead of working for someone else. Several years later, this young mother moved to the city of Tehuacán for work, telling me she hoped the move was temporary. Unlike the other residents and migrants I had interviewed in their teens and twenties, she had discussed rural life as a kind of freedom.

Accumulation by dispossession in the valley is a process that works over generations transforming increasing numbers of rural residents into disposable surplus labor. This also has paradoxical effects. Marx described "primitive accumulation" as the process that affected the European countryside starting in the sixteenth century, but that also characterizes capitalism in other places and times as "freedom."[60] Rural peoples were "freed" of their access, control, or ownership of resources (their means of production), and this "freed" them to search for work. The process generates an abundance of potential workers and consumers for market goods. However, this process cannot simply be reduced to a mechanism to generate inexpensive or reserve labor forces for capitalists. There are many instances when a living wage is beyond reach. Sometimes this process can also be experienced as a freedom from inherited social relations and cultural norms, as is certainly the case with a younger generation from the valley.

At this point, it appears that young migrants and maquila workers face conditions distinct from previous generations and also express new identities and ideas about agriculture. However, the question remains whether younger migrants will take up maize agriculture as they age. Older residents rely on maize agriculture as a social safety net. Yet, we have also seen that in a neoliberal food system, the processes that push young migrants off farms also undermine the next generation's ability to remain on the land, if they so choose, as agricultural producers. The ability to maintain an agricultural livelihood is undermined by increasing production costs, declining levels of spring water, changes to rural subsidies, counter-agrarian policies (which enable communal landholders to sell land), and other factors like home construction on arable land.[61]

Conclusion

I began this chapter with a quote about Latin American immigrants to the United States being out-of-work farmers, followed by my question about whether these rural migrants would prefer returning home in order to farm. My case study from the Tehuasán Valley complicates this further, compelling us to

---

60   Marx, *Capital*, part 26.
61   Fitting, *The Struggle for Maize*.

consider whether all of the immigrants looking for work on street corners were in fact farmers back home or children and grandchildren of farmers. Juan's story about being a returned migrant with little knowledge or interest in agriculture, for instance, is typical among my interviewees in their teens, twenties, and early thirties. Older migrants in their thirties and forties were more likely to farm when in the valley or to send home remittances to be spent on agricultural inputs.

What does it mean for food activism when rural youth no longer want to farm food crops for their own communities or others? Food activism and scholarship importantly criticizes how neoliberal capitalism and the modern food system contribute to rural displacement and "accumulation by dispossession." Food sovereignty, advanced by Via Campesina, the international peasant rights group, promotes the ability of each community and nation to "maintain and develop its own capacity to produce its basic foods respecting cultural and productive diversity."[62] This concept and platform has gained considerable traction as a critique of, and alternative to, the current food system. My point is that in our support of alternatives to conventional farming and the idea that small-scale food producers should be self-sufficient, we—as food activists and scholars— need to be careful not to romanticize rural life in a way that overlooks the desire among younger residents to escape the farming life of their elders.

What larger lessons or questions for future research does this chapter raise? Learning from rural Mexicans about their livelihood strategies provides a window into the food system in North America, particularly the motivations, concerns, and cross-border familial and economic ties of workers and food producers. Such case studies are important because they can help challenge discourses about peasant inefficiency, romanticizations of rural life, and debunk culturalist arguments that justify the exploitation of food workers. They help us better understand how contemporary capitalism and the food system work "on the ground" in specific locales, while also portraying residents as agents who engage, negotiate, criticize and may even help transform the system. The intergenerational livelihood strategy found in the valley—which combines migrant and maquila labor with small scale maize production—has had paradoxical effects, particularly when we compare the experiences of residents of different resources, generations, and genders. This case study helps unsettle the idea of a homogenous rural community and illustrates the importance of taking the "intersectionality" of experience seriously, or how gender, age, class, and ethnicity shape an individual's experience.

---

62   Delphine Thivet, "Peasants' Transnational Mobilization for Food Sovereignty in La Via Campesina," in *Food Activism: Agency, Democracy and Economy*, ed. Carole M. Counihan and Valeria Siniscalchi (London: Bloomsbury Publishing, 2014), 193-210, 193. (check pg. nos.: 193-210, 193 seems strange)

Finally, does information about who produces and prepares our food help transform the food system? If consumers (and producers) translate such knowledge into political action, it certainly can make a difference. I think this is particularly the case if we examine the larger political economic context in which food producers live and work, the reasons rural peoples migrate, and how food producers and workers experience the food system, perhaps differently, over the course of their lives. At the same time, because nativism and racism against undocumented (or perceived to be undocumented) migrants is a powerful discourse in North America, and particularly against Mexicans and Central Americans in the United States, knowing *who* produces and prepares food, might not always generate change in and of itself. In our efforts to change the food system, we also need to strive to create policies that support those campesinos who want to stay home and work the land, improve food workers' rights, reform immigration policies, and challenge sexism and racism. Like all complex problems, real transformation of the food system requires multidimensional solutions at home and abroad.

Questions for Discussion

1. Fitting focuses on a single case study, that of the Heuacan Valley, also known as the "cradle of maize." What happened there? Why did it happen? What is your sense of what's meant by "case study"?

2. Fitting argues that economic pressures have displaced traditional rural food producers from Mexico into the migrant sector, victimizing them twice—first through displacement and second through attitudinal shifts, especially among young people. She quotes a young migrant who says, "There is no money in the milpa." (79). How does this quote contribute to her argument?

3. Perhaps you have heard of Barbara Kingsolver's best-selling nonfiction book, *Animal, Vegetable, Miracle: A Year of Food Life* which describes her (white, suburban) family's decision to subsist for one year on only the food they could produce or find locally. (If you haven't heard of this book, take a look at this link: (See http://www.animalvegetablemiracle.com/Mineral, Animal, Vegetable for an excerpt.) In what ways might Kingsolver's experience with subsistence food production be different from the experiences of subsistence food production among Mexican rural peoples, as described by Fitting?

Pig Out

Nicolette Hahn Niman

The New York Times, March 2007

> This *New York Times* article from 2007 was authored by an environmental lawyer and cattle rancher who provides consultation services on the environmental effects of farming operations. In this article Nicolette Hahn Niman argues that there should be stronger laws regulating the use of crates in the raising of pigs intended for slaughter. She states that a policy that eliminated gestation cages (for pregnant pigs) was a start but did not go far enough. An indicator of the argument she uses is contained in her observation that crated pigs don't act like normal pigs, which are inquisitive and active while crated pigs are sullen and nearly immobile. Niman conveys her disapproval not only with crating itself but with the fact that crate facility conditions persist despite laws passed in the late 1950s requiring humane treatment of livestock.

With some fanfare, the world's largest pork producer, Smithfield Foods, recently announced that it intended to phase out certain cages for its breeding females. Called gestation crates, the cages virtually immobilize pigs during their pregnancies in metal stalls so narrow they are unable to turn around.

Numerous studies have documented crated sows exhibiting behavior characteristic of humans with severe depression and mental illness. Getting rid of gestation crates (already on their way out in the European Union) is welcome and long overdue, but more action is needed to end inhumane conditions at America's hog farms.

Of the 60 million pigs in the United States, over 95 percent are continuously confined in metal buildings, including the almost five million sows in crates. In such setups, feed is automatically delivered to animals who are forced to urinate and defecate where they eat and sleep. Their waste festers in large pits a few feet below their hooves. Intense ammonia and hydrogen sulfide fumes from these pits fill pigs' lungs and sensitive nostrils. No straw is provided to the animals because that would gum up the works (as it would if you tossed straw into your toilet).

In my work as an environmental lawyer, I've toured a dozen hog confinement operations and seen hundreds from the outside. My task was to evaluate their polluting potential, which was considerable. But what haunted me was the miserable creatures inside.

They were crowded into pens and cages, never allowed outdoors, and never even provided a soft place to lie down. Their tails had been cut off without anesthetic. Regardless of how well the operations are managed, the pigs subsist in inherently hostile settings. (Disclosure: my husband founded a network of farms that raise pigs using traditional, non-confinement methods.)

The stress, crowding and contamination inside confinement buildings foster disease, especially respiratory illnesses. In addition to toxic fumes, bacteria, yeast, and molds have been recorded in swine buildings at a level more than 1,000 times higher than in normal air. To prevent disease outbreaks (and to stimulate faster growth), the hog industry adds more than 10 million pounds of antibiotics to its feed, the Union of Concerned Scientists estimates. This mountain of drugs—a staggering three times more than all antibiotics used to treat human illnesses—is a grim yardstick of the wretchedness of these facilities.

There are other reasons that merely phasing out gestation crates does not go nearly far enough. Keeping animals in such barren environments is a serious deprivation. Pigs in nature are active, curious creatures that typically spend 10 hours a day foraging, rooting, and roaming.

Veterinarians consider pigs as smart as dogs. Imagine keeping a dog in a tight cage or crowded pen day after day with absolutely nothing to chew on, play with or otherwise occupy its mind. Americans would universally denounce that as inhumane. Extreme boredom is considered the main reason pigs in confinement are prone to biting one another's tails and engaging in other aggressive behavior.

Finally, even if the gestation crate is abandoned, pork producers will still keep a sow in a narrow metal cage once she gives birth to her piglets. This slightly larger cage, called a farrowing crate, severely restricts a sow's movements and makes normal interactions between mother and piglets impossible.

Because confinement buildings are far from cities and lack windows, all of this is shielded from public view. But such treatment of pigs contrasts sharply with what people say they want for farm animals. Surveys consistently find that

Americans believe all animals, including those raised for food, deserve humane treatment. A 2004 survey by Ohio State University found that 81 percent of respondents felt that the well-being of livestock is as important as that of pets.

Such sentiment was behind the widely supported Humane Slaughter Act of 1958, which sought to improve treatment of cattle and hogs at slaughterhouses. But it's clear that Americans expect more—they want animals to be humanely treated throughout their lives, not just at slaughter. To ensure this, Congress should ban gestation crates altogether and mandate that animal anti-cruelty laws be applied to farm animals.

As a cattle rancher, I am comfortable raising animals for human consumption, but they should not be made to suffer. Because we ask the ultimate sacrifice of these creatures, it is incumbent on us to ensure that they have decent lives. Let us view the elimination of gestation crates as just a small first step in the right direction.

Questions for Discussion

1. Hahn Niman makes a disclosure about her own relationship to farming practices that may be important to her position. What does she reveal and why might this matter?

2. Hahn Niman points out that pigs are considered as intelligent as dogs. Explain the type of appeal that Hahn Niman is using in the paragraph in which she questions whether we would tolerate the treatment of dogs that was similar to that of crated pigs.

3. Consider Hahn Niman's argument alongside the argument of Temple Grandin who argues for the humane slaughter of cows. Where would these two agree? Where would they disagree?

Consumption

"The act of using, eating, or drinking something."

– Cambridge English Dictionary

Listening to the Conversation

"There's so much misinformation floating around about G.M.O.'s that is taken as fact by people."

– Michael D. Purugganan, Professor of Genomics & Biology,
Dean of Science at New York University

"There is a deep irony in the fact that many dieticians are advocating [traditional and indigenous foods and diets] and yet [the] modern [western] diet is what is being pushed on tribal peoples around the world, with devastating results"

– Jo Woodman, Senior Research & Campaigner
for Survival International, an indigenous advocacy group

"Very simply, we subsidize high-fructose corn syrup in this country, but not carrots. While the surgeon general is raising alarms over the epidemic of obesity, the president is signing farm bills designed to keep the river of cheap corn flowing, guaranteeing that the cheapest calories in the supermarket will continue to be the unhealthiest."

– Michael Pollan, author

"The rise of the industrial model of agriculture has contributed greatly to people being disconnected from the food on their plates."

– Sarah Somian, nutritionist.

"I have discovered that the relationship to food for Native communities has been ruptured, making food central to the question of empowerment and power...food cannot be disentangled from people and relationships; consuming, producing, and foraging for food all have meaning because they facilitate the strengthening of community bonds."

– Rachel Vernon, staff member at Cooperative Food Empowerment Directive (CoFED) and Colorado State University alumni

"When it comes to junk food, we seem to follow an implicit script that powerfully biases the way we feel about food. We like fries not in spite of the fact that they're unhealthy but because of it."

– Malcolm Gladwell, author & reporter

Golden Rice: Lifesaver?

Amy Harmon

The New York Times, August 2013

> Golden rice is a GMO that was created in response to severe vitamin A deficiencies in many developing countries. However, as this article finds, the responses in those countries has been largely negative and kept golden rice out of people's diets. The *New York Times* website shows that Amy Harmon is a national science correspondent for their publication and has won two Pulitzer Prizes. She has written several pieces on GMOs which include the development of GMO rice and oranges, as well as the ensuing bans on GMO foods.

One bright morning this month, 400 protesters smashed down the high fences surrounding a field in the Bicol region of the Philippines and uprooted the genetically modified rice plants growing inside.

Had the plants survived long enough to flower, they would have betrayed a distinctly yellow tint in the otherwise white part of the grain. That is because the rice is endowed with a gene from corn and another from a bacterium, making it the only variety in existence to produce beta carotene, the source of vitamin A. Its developers call it "Golden Rice."

The concerns voiced by the participants in the Aug. 8 act of vandalism—that Golden Rice could pose unforeseen risks to human health and the environment, that it would ultimately profit big agrochemical companies—are a familiar refrain in the long-running controversy over the merits of genetically engineered crops. They are driving the desire among some Americans for mandatory "G.M.O." labels on food with ingredients made from crops whose DNA has been altered in a laboratory. And they have motivated similar attacks on trials of other genetically modified crops in recent years: grapes designed to fight off a deadly virus in France, wheat designed to have a lower glycemic index in Australia, sugar beets in Oregon designed to tolerate a herbicide, to name a few.

"We do not want our people, especially our children, to be used in these experiments," a farmer who was a leader of the protest told the Philippine newspaper *Remate*.

But Golden Rice, which appeared on the cover of *Time Magazine* in 2000 before it was quite ready for prime time, is unlike any of the genetically engineered crops in wide use today, designed to either withstand herbicides sold by Monsanto and other chemical companies or resist insect attacks, with benefits for farmers but not directly for consumers.

And a looming decision by the Philippine government about whether to allow Golden Rice to be grown beyond its four remaining field trials has added a new dimension to the debate over the technology's merits.

Genetically engineered Golden Rice grown in a facility in Los Baños, Laguna Province, in the Philippines. Credit Jes Aznar for *The New York Times*

Not owned by any company, Golden Rice is being developed by a nonprofit group called the International Rice Research Institute with the aim of providing a new source of vitamin A to people both in the Philippines, where most households get most of their calories from rice, and eventually in many other places in a world where rice is eaten every day by half the population. Lack of the vital nutrient causes blindness in a quarter-million to a half-million children each year. It affects millions of people in Asia and Africa and so weakens the immune system that some two million die each year of diseases they would otherwise survive.

The destruction of the field trial, and the reasons given for it, touched a nerve among scientists around the world, spurring them to counter assertions of the technology's health and environmental risks. On a petition supporting Golden Rice circulated among scientists and signed by several thousand, many vented a simmering frustration with activist organizations like Greenpeace, which they see as playing on misplaced fears of genetic engineering in both the developing and the developed worlds. Some took to other channels to convey to American foodies and Filipino farmers alike the broad scientific consensus that G.M.O.'s are not intrinsically more risky than other crops and can be reliably tested.

At stake, they say, is not just the future of biofortified rice but also a rational means to evaluate a technology whose potential to improve nutrition in developing countries, and developed ones, may otherwise go unrealized.

"There's so much misinformation floating around about G.M.O.'s that is taken as fact by people," said Michael D. Purugganan, a professor of genomics and biology and the dean for science at New York University, who sought to calm health-risk concerns in a primer on GMA News Online, a media outlet in the Philippines: "The genes they inserted to make the vitamin are not some weird manufactured material," he wrote, "but are also found in squash, carrots and melons."

Mr. Purugganan, who studies plant evolution, does not work on genetically engineered crops, and until recently had not participated in the public debates over the risks and benefits of G.M.O.'s. But having been raised in a middle-class family in Manila, he felt compelled to weigh in on Golden Rice. "A lot of the criticism of G.M.O.'s in the Western world suffers from a lack of understanding of how really dire the situation is in developing countries," he said.

Some proponents of G.M.O.'s say that more critical questions, like where biotechnology should fall as a priority in the efforts to address the root causes of hunger and malnutrition and how to prevent a few companies from controlling it, would be easier to address were they not lumped together with unfounded fears by those who oppose G.M.O.'s.

"It is long past time for scientists to stand up and shout, 'No more lies—no more fear-mongering,' " said Nina V. Fedoroff, a professor at the King Abdullah University of Science and Technology in Saudi Arabia and a former science adviser to the American secretary of state, who helped spearhead the petition. "We're talking about saving millions of lives here."

Precisely because of its seemingly high-minded purpose, Golden Rice has drawn suspicion from biotechnology skeptics beyond the demonstrators who forced their way into the field trial. Many countries ban the cultivation of all genetically modified crops, and after the rice's media debut early in the last decade, Vandana Shiva, an Indian environmentalist, called it a "Trojan horse" whose purpose was to gain public support for all manner of genetically modified crops that would benefit multinational corporations at the expense of poor farmers and consumers.

In a 2001 article, "The Great Yellow Hype," the author Michael Pollan, a critic of industrial agriculture, suggested that it might have been developed to "win an argument rather than solve a public-health problem." He cited biotechnology industry advertisements that featured the virtues of the rice, which at the time had to be ingested in large quantities to deliver a meaningful dose of vitamin A.

Mothers with masks made from baby bathtubs protested Golden Rice in Quezon City, the Philippines, in June. CreditErik De Castro/Reuters

But the rice has since been retooled: a bowl now provides 60 percent of the daily requirement of vitamin A for healthy children. And Gerard Barry, the Golden Rice project leader at the International Rice Research Institute—and, it must be said, a former senior scientist and executive at Monsanto—suggests that attempts to discredit Golden Rice discount the suffering it could alleviate if successful. He said, too, that critics who suggest encouraging poor families to simply eat fruits and vegetables that contain beta carotene disregard the expense and logistical difficulties that would thwart such efforts.

Identified in the infancy of genetic engineering as having the potential for the biggest impact for the world's poor, beta-carotene-producing rice was initially funded by the Rockefeller Foundation and the European Union. In a decade of work culminating in 1999, two academic scientists, Ingo Potrykus and Peter Beyer, finally switched on the production of beta carotene by adding daffodil and bacteria DNA to the rice's genome. They licensed their patent rights to the agribusiness company that later became Syngenta, on the condition that the technology and any improvements to it would be made freely available to poor farmers in the developing world. With the company retaining the right to use it in developed countries, potentially as an alternative to vitamin supplements, Syngenta scientists later improved the amount of beta carotene produced by substituting a gene from corn for the one from daffodil.

If the rice gains the Philippine government's approval, it will cost no more than other rice for poor farmers, who will be free to save seeds and replant them, Dr. Barry said. It has no known allergens or toxins, and the new proteins produced by the rice have been shown to break down quickly in simulated gastric fluid, as required by World Health Organization guidelines. A mouse feeding study is under way in a laboratory in the United States. The potential that the Golden Rice would cross-pollinate with other varieties, sometimes called "genetic contamination," has been studied and found to be limited, because rice is typically self-pollinated. And its production of beta carotene does not appear to provide a competitive advantage—or disadvantage—that could affect the survival of wild varieties with which it might mix.

If Golden Rice is a Trojan horse, it now has some company. The Bill and Melinda Gates Foundation, which is supporting the final testing of Golden Rice, is also underwriting the development of crops tailored for sub-Saharan Africa, like cassava that can resist the viruses that routinely wipe out a third of the harvest, bananas that contain higher levels of iron and corn that uses nitrogen more efficiently. Other groups are developing a pest-resistant black-eyed pea and a "Golden Banana" that would also deliver vitamin A.

Beyond the fear of corporate control of agriculture, perhaps the most cited objection to G.M.O.'s is that they may hold risks that may not be understood. The decision to grow or eat them relies, like many other decisions, on a cost-benefit analysis.

How food consumers around the world weigh that calculation will probably have far-reaching consequences. Such crops, *Scientific American* declared in an editorial last week, will make it to people's plates "only with public support."

Greenpeace, for one, dismisses the benefits of vitamin supplementation through G.M.O.'s and has said it will continue to oppose all uses of biotechnology in agriculture. As Daniel Ocampo, a campaigner for the organization in the Philippines, put it, "We would rather err on the side of caution."

For others, the potential of crops like Golden Rice to alleviate suffering is all that matters. "This technology can save lives," one of the petition's signers, Javier Delgado of Mexico, wrote. "But false fears can destroy it."

Questions for Discussion

1. How is golden rice different from other GMOs?

2. What perspectives do the various stakeholders have on golden rice? How are contextual factors affecting these perspectives?

3. How do you think golden rice could better be introduced to developing countries, assuming that it is in fact healthy?

Food Choices and Store Proximity

Ilya Rahkovsky and Samantha Snyder

USDA Economic Research Service, 2015

> The USDA's mission is "to provide economic opportunity through innovation, helping rural America to thrive; to promote agriculture production that better nourishes Americans while also helping feed others throughout the world; and to preserve our Nation's natural resources." They publish their research through various reports each year like the one you're about to read. This particular report was conducted by the Economic Research Service, a group within the USDA focused on analyzing agriculture and food through an economic lens to inform public and private choices about production and consumption. The study is in response to concerns about food deserts, or areas without easy access to fresh produce and healthy food.

Introduction

Much research in recent years has investigated the links between household access—specifically in low-income low-access (LILA) areas—to food stores and subsequent purchases, consumption patterns, and health outcomes. There has been extensive investigation into the presence of LILA areas and their characteristics. Wilde and colleagues (2014) find a negative correlation between an area's average income and store density, while Dutko and colleagues (2012) find that, among low- income areas, there were fewer stores in areas with very poor or minority consumers.

Store density is primarily determined by population density, which varies in both high- and low- income areas. Moore and Diez Roux (2006) studied census tracts in Maryland, New York, and North Carolina and found that large supermarkets were more likely to be located in low-income than high-income tracts and less likely to be in tracts with large minority populations. Morland and colleagues (2002)—using data from Mississippi, North Carolina, Maryland, and Minnesota—found fewer stores in poor and minority areas.

Cummins and colleagues (2014) found no increase in the consumption of fruits and vegetables after a new grocery opened in a low-access area of Philadelphia. This suggests that exact store location may be inconsequential to consumers in the habit of shopping at favored stores. Edin and colleagues (2013) found that poor consumers are quite aware of food prices in different stores and are willing to travel far to access the lower prices, a finding corroborated by studies in Minneapolis, New York City, and Chicago (Chung and Myers, 1999; Horowitz et al., 2004; Block and Kouba, 2006).

Studies have linked a poor food environment to negative health outcomes, such as the prevalence of overweight/obesity and associated diseases. Most have used rates of overweight and obesity as indicators of health and pointed to higher prevalence of these as proof that the food environ-

ment impacts residents' health outcomes. Holsten (2009), in reviewing a number of these studies, contends that the food environment-obesity relationship found is often undermined by inadequate data or research design. Ford and Dzewaltowski (2008) focus on disadvantaged populations and find that the disparities in the food environment along socioeconomic and demographic lines coincide with the gradient in obesity prevalence along the same factors. Morland and colleagues (2006) find a negative relationship between the presence of supermarkets and rates of obesity/overweight and a positive relationship between access to convenience stores and the same health indicators. However, significant links between store access and diabetes, cholesterol levels, and high blood pressure were not observed. Chen and colleagues (2010, 2013) show that the presence of nearby grocery stores is associated with lower body mass index (BMI) and the presence of fast-food restaurants with higher BMI. The second Chen study exploits detailed data and econometric techniques to identify a causal relationship between fast-food restaurants and BMI.

To reasonably connect food environment with obesity and overweight, researchers must assume the existence of an intermediate step, specifically differences in *behavior* resulting from food- access disparities that ultimately result in observable health outcomes. It is within this body of literature that the research presented here best fits. Rose and Richards (2004), using 1996-97 National Food Stamp Program Survey data, found that access to supermarkets among low- income consumers increased their consumption of fruits and vegetables (only fruit consumption was significantly higher, however). Using the same data, Lin and colleagues (2014) found store access to have a very small effect on purchases, though households with very limited store access spent more on canned meats and less on beverages. Morland and colleagues (2002) also noted negative and significant effects of low food access on the purchases of fruits and vegetables for both Black and White residents. Notably, the increase in purchases for Blacks was triple the increase for Whites.

Focusing specifically on rural seniors, Sharkey and colleagues (2010) found that both objective and perceived low access to food stores were correlated with poorer diets in terms of fruits and vegetables consumed. Using two separate composite measures of diet quality, Moore and colleagues (2008) confirmed that good access to grocery stores (measured in three ways) exhibited a strong relationship with healthy dietary patterns. However, these results are not universal across studies.

Examining the components of LILA areas (low access, low incomes, and high food prices) both separately and together, Pearson and colleagues (2005) found no relationship between diet quality (specifically fruit and vegetable consumption) and living in or near a LILA area.

The challenges of limited access to healthful food and the consequences of poor food choices—both social and physical—have led some to press for governments subsidizing the entry of grocery retailers into underserved areas. The Food, Conservation, and Energy Act of 2008 authorized a Federal study (by USDA) of food desert areas (Ver Ploeg et al., 2009). The Agricultural Act of 2014 introduced $125 million in spending over 5 years for the Healthy Food Financing Initiative to promote healthy food access in underserved communities (Aussenberg, 2014). In addition, many States introduced separate programs to support food access. These attempts to attract supermarkets to the underserved areas generally were part of larger community revitalization schemes. From 2001 to 2011, 11 States enacted legislation to address these issues and 7 States attempted legisla- tion (CDC, 2012). And in 2014, Maryland passed legislation to provide $1 million in assistance— including State loans and grants—to food desert areas (Maryland House Bill 451, 2014).

This report investigates the correlation between living in low-access, low-income areas and food purchases made for at-home consumption. We are able to trace the effect of food environment on consumer purchases due to the unique datasets used. With information on household and shop- ping locations, we calculate the distance traveled by each household on each shopping trip and the items purchased on that trip. To our knowledge, previous studies have looked only at the avail- ability of shopping outlets at the household level. For the most part, this characteristic may be quantified by the number of grocery/ convenience stores or restaurants in a household's ZIP Code, census tract, or defined radius. Attempts are then made to relate either purchasing decisions or health outcomes to these measures of access.

With information on both residential location and shopping outlet location, we are able to determine whether there is a relationship between distance traveled for shopping and the healthfulness of the items purchased on that trip. This examination is different in a few very important ways. First, we are not concerned with characterizing the food environment for each household, per se. While we do use information on whether a household is located in a LILA area to refine our model, we allow for the fact that households likely travel outside of their immediate surroundings to shop for food. Second, because we observe households over an entire year (2010) and for multiple shopping trips, our model captures how households vary their purchases over distance. Since we observe a household's purchasing decisions and the distance it travels to its chosen retail food store, we are better able to predict whether improved access to supermarkets would, in fact, improve the nutritional profile of low-income households. Because of these differences, our results may be more policy relevant.

Data

The study of food demand by level of food access in LILA areas requires information on consumer purchases, the local food environment, and shopping behavior. Our information on consumer purchases is from the 2010 Nielsen Homescan Survey, the largest nationwide survey of food purchases. Households are asked to record all food purchases from all outlets

for in-home consumption. (Food purchased in restaurants and fast-food places for consumption outside the home does not appear in the survey.) Nielsen households are recruited via mail and Internet ads and are awarded with points for prizes and sweepstakes. Low-income consumers are underrepresented in the survey (Einav et al., 2008 and 2010).

The Homescan purchase record provides information on date, price, quantity, product, and store, as well as whether the product was purchased at a discount. For most products, consumers need to scan the Universal Product Code (UPC), enter a date, and provide information about the place of purchase and any discounts using a special hand-held device given for this purpose. If Nielsen collects sales information from the store where a product was purchased, the price of the product from the store record and detailed product information (size, product type) from a UPC dictionary is matched to the household's reported purchase in Homescan. If Nielsen does not have price information about a product, then a Homescan panelist is asked to manually enter the price. For random-weight items without a UPC code, such as fresh tomatoes, consumers identify the product from a catalog, enter its code, weight, and expenditures.

Households are sampled from 52 markets in the 48 contiguous States.[1] A random-weight panel (27,418 households in 2010) records all food purchases, including items without UPC codes that are priced per unit of weight. A second panel (33,217 households) records just UPC purchases. Prior to 2007, Homescan participants recorded detailed information, such as weight and expen- ditures, for a finely differentiated category (e.g., tomatoes). After 2007, to reduce participant burden, Nielsen stopped recording the weight of random-weight items and aggregated product categories (e.g., from tomatoes to vegetables). Participants must provide consistent information on their purchases for at least 9 months to appear in the final dataset, after which they can stay in the survey as long as they want, and some do for many years.

The Homescan survey also includes detailed demographic information on the panelists, which is updated once a year. Projection weights, based on participants' demographics, are also provided by Nielsen to mimic demographics across the U.S. population. The survey provides census tract information for participating households, from which we extrapolate latitude and longitude of the household residence.

Underreporting of food purchases is a serious problem in many household studies. To alleviate this problem, we dropped households that spent less than $250 on groceries per quarter. This can alter the sample's composition by dropping not only the underreporting panelists but also panelists who mostly eat away from home, which is less of an issue in our at-home food investigation.

We started with 27,418 households in the Homescan random-weight panel, but dropped households for 3 reasons. First, we dropped 28 households with missing random-weight prices and purchase dates, leaving 27,390 households in the sample. Then, as this study requires matching food purchases with food environment data, we dropped from the sample 906 households that we were unable to match to the census. (The dropped households have similar characteristics to the households remaining in the sample.) Finally, we dropped 737 households that purchased less than $250 of groceries per quarter, leaving 25,747 households in our analysis sample.

Food Prices

Estimation of the demand models requires aggregating thousands of food products into a small number of food groups,[14] here characterized by descriptive similarity (grains vs. meat) and by nutritional similarity (low-fat meats vs. regular

---

1   The 52 Nielsen market areas mostly correspond to metropolitan areas. Some market areas are rural and can span several States.

meats): fruits, vegetables, sweets, oil and nuts, eggs, regular meats, low-fat meats, fish and poultry, processed foods, grains, regular milk products, low-fat milk products, diet drinks, and nondiet drinks. This classification helps to assess the healthfulness of consumer choices while maintaining food groups that align with consumer perceptions (see table 2).

For random-weight items such as fresh produce and refrigerated meats, 2010 Homescan data provide only total expenditures, not prices and quantities. However, in the 2005 and 2006 Homescan data, consumers provided this information. We use these 2 years (with prices converted to 2010 dollars using the Food at Home Consumer Price Index) as a base to impute prices and quantities for random-weight items purchased in 2010. This imputation introduces a measurement error in the price data, but avoids the more troublesome bias in prices from omitting the random-weight products.

Many household demand studies face problems related to omitted price information (if the consumer did not purchase a particular product) and aggregation of food groups, which can mask substantial differences across consumers in the quality purchased within food groupings. Some consumers may choose to buy higher quality products at higher prices and using unit values for these consumers fails to capture average prices of all product offerings. Also, some consumers may be better at finding lower prices and this aptitude may be correlated with their preferences for particular food products.

To address this "selectivity" problem, we use the superlative Fisher ideal price index based on UPC-level prices and quantities, which alleviates the missing quality information as suggested by Diewert (1976):

$$p_{hjt} = \sqrt{\frac{\sum p_{kht} q_{k0} \sum p_{kht} q_{kht}}{\sum p_{k0} q_{k0} \sum p_{k0} q_{kht}}},$$

where p_{kht} and q_{kht} are prices and quantities in household h in time t for UPC k, q_{k0} is the national average for the quantity of UPC k, and p_{k0} is the average price of UPC k.

As some Nielsen households did not purchase a single product in a food group that quarter, we need a price measure based on the prices paid by other consumers. To do this, we calculated consumer-specific market-area prices based on all consumer purchases made in a Nielsen market.

In the index, we weighted the prices other Nielsen consumers paid by the inverse Euclidian distance between them and the (nonpurchasing) consumer for whom we calculate the prices. When a consumer has no purchases of a particular food group, we assign a consumer-specific area price to this consumer for the missing food group prices.

Store Data

For store locations, we used TDLinx, a dataset of food retailers collected by Nielsen with information on retailer location, size, and characteristics. We matched TDLinx with Nielsen Household data using a key provided by Nielsen. Homescan surveys provide the census tract of each house- hold, so we assigned household location to the population-weighted centroid of the census tract.

Using the key, we were able to link most but not all of the stores. When Homescan provided ZIP Codes of the missing stores, we assigned store locations to the centroids of these ZIP Codes. In addition, we searched TDLinx data for stores with the same name as the stores in Homescan and assigned a location to the store (with the same name) nearest the consumer residence. A few

recorded distances were very far, possibly because panelists were traveling that far, were living in another home at the time of the survey, or because of a simple panelist-store mismatch. To reduce the bias from implausibly long distances, we dropped all distances greater than 40 miles.

Food Environment

We use the USDA definition of low-income low-access (LILA) area as a census tract identified in the Food Access Research Atlas. The tract is classified as low access if at least 500 people or 30 percent of residents live more than 1 mile from a supermarket in urban areas (10 miles in rural areas). We used the census classification of rural and urban tracts to determine the relevant distance. A tract is classified as low-income using the U.S. Department of Treasury's New Markets Credit program, which applies to any tract where the poverty rate is above 20 percent or median family income is less than 80 percent of the statewide (or metropolitan area) median.

The 2010 Nielsen Homescan data provide information on consumer food purchases. The survey records home locations based on census tract definitions from 2000. To match these tracts to food environment information, we used access measures defined in the Food Desert Locator created by USDA's Economic Research Service, which is also based on 2000 census tracts.[2] We used Food Desert Locator data for the disaggregated measures of food environment (i.e., both the low-income and low-access criteria for LILA areas). The information on distance to stores is provided by USDA's Economic Research Service, which compiled a supermarket directory in 2006.

According to 2010 census numbers, an estimated 32 percent of urban and 42 percent of rural resi- dents lived in low-income areas, although they are not necessarily poor themselves. In our Nielsen data, 25 percent of urban and 39 percent of rural consumers lived in low-income areas. So the Homescan survey may undersample consumers in poor areas, but these differences are small.

Descriptive Statistics

Household quarterly purchases are the unit of observation. Lower levels of aggregation such as individual shopping trips or even household-store combinations did not work because many shop- ping trips were inconsequential and the food spending of households was highly concentrated in one or two favorite stores. Therefore, we collapsed all shopping trips in a quarter to one observation and all shopping trip information was aggregated to the quarterly level. In particular, we created an expenditure-weighted average distance measure, which averaged the distances from a panelist's home to various stores visited during the quarter. Similarly, we created indicators for store formats/ channels—such as groceries, supercenters, or convenience stores—that reflect the share of quarterly food expenditures in these channels. Just a few stores dominated food expenditure for both LILA and non-LILA consumers. The most frequented store, for example, accounts for 58 percent of food expenditure (fig. 1).

In our sample, 7.8 percent of households lived in the areas designated as LILA in 2010. These consumers have lower income and education and are more likely to be Black. LILA households also tend to travel slightly farther to purchase food. The average expenditure-weighted trip of LILA households was 7.5 miles, versus 5.6 miles for non-LILA households (table 1).

---

2   The current version of this Food Access Research Atlas (USDA, 2015) is impossible to match precisely with 2000 Census tracts as it is based on 2010 Census tracts.

Figure 1
Share of food expenditures in top 5 stores

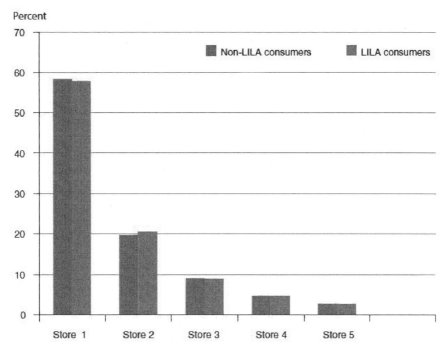

LILA = Low-income, low-access.
Source: USDA, Economic Research Service.

Table 1
Descriptive statistics for LILA and non-LILA households (percent)

	Non-LILA area		LILA area	
Variable	Mean	S.D.	Mean	S.D.
Household size	2.66	1.44	2.63	1.64
Age female head	**41.8**	15.34	42.25	16.65
Age male head	**39.65**	16.59	38.6	18.66
Household income ($)	**65,534**	50,017	47,574	40,883
Children 0-6 years old	**0.13**	0.34	0.12	0.35
Children 7-12 years old	0.20	0.40	0.21	0.43
Children 13-17 years old	**0.16**	0.37	0.18	0.41
No children	0.64	0.48	0.65	0.51
Black	**0.11**	0.31	0.18	0.41

White	**0.86**	0.35	0.81	0.42
Asian	**0.031**	0.172	0.018	0.142
Hispanic	0.12	0.32	0.11	0.34
Less than high school education	**0.045**	0.208	0.080	0.292
High school graduate	**0.73**	0.44	0.78	0.45
College graduate	**0.22**	0.42	0.14	0.37
Share of supermarkets	**0.63**	0.2989	0.57	0.3266
Share of drug and convenience stores	0.020	0.0529	0.021	0.0593
Share of mass merchandise stores	**0.026**	0.0699	0.023	0.0854
Share of club stores	**0.086**	0.1624	0.070	0.1644
Share of supercenters	**0.159**	0.2512	0.221	0.2909
Share of other stores	**0.080**	0.1572	0.091	0.1776
Average distance to store weighted by the purchase	**5.62**	4.81	7.45	7.23
Live in census tract >1 mile from a supermarket	**0.42**	0.39	0.62	0.34
Live in census tract >10 mile from a supermarket	**0.009**	0.059	0.085	0.220
Low-income tract	**0.22**	0.41	1	0
Urban	**0.82**	0.38	0.68	0.50
Number of households	23,890		1,857	

Bold denotes statistical significant difference at 5% level. LILA = Low-income, low-access.
Source: Nielsen Homescan, 2010; Nielsen TDLinx, 2010; U.S. Census, 2000.

We used the Nielsen Homescan classification of food retailers to divide all stores into five groups. *Supermarkets*—including natural and health food stores, warehouse stores, and military commis- saries—accounted for about 57 percent of the food dollars spent by LILA and 63 percent by non- LILA households. *Supercenters* were the second most popular retail channel, with 15.9 percent of non-LILA food spending and 22.1 percent of LILA spending. A supercenter (for example, Walmart supercenter, Super Target, and Meijer) is usually more than 50,000 square feet, and sells both food and nonfood products. Volpe and colleagues (2013) found that consumers tend to purchase less healthy products from supercenters. *Club stores*, such as Costco and Sam's, were the third most popular channel with 8.6 of non-LILA food expenditures and 7.0 percent of LILA spending. Stores not classified by Nielsen, mostly small independent stores, are responsible for 8.0 percent of food spending among non-LILA consumers and 9.1 percent among LILA consumers. *Mass merchandise stores* and *convenience stores* were responsible for less than 3 percent of food spending in 2010.

LILA and non-LILA consumers exhibit no difference in the number of stores they visit; on average, a LILA consumer visits 10.9 stores a year and a non-LILA consumer visits 11 stores per year.

Consumers who lived in LILA and non-LILA areas faced similar food prices in 2010, with prices in non-LILA areas about 1 percent higher. LILA consumers, on average, spent $698 per quarter on food, while non-LILA consumers spent $730 (table 2).[3] By category, LILA consumers spent 29 percent less on low-fat milk products, 13 percent less on fruits, 8 percent less on vegetables, 13 percent more on red meats, and 5 percent more on nondiet drinks.

LILA consumers purchase *more* food, despite spending less on it and facing similar prices. Thus, LILA consumers were purchasing more low-price food products in almost every food category than non-LILA consumers. Measured by weight, LILA consumers purchased 21 percent more red meats (regular and low-fat), 13 percent more nondiet drinks, and 9 percent more fish and poultry. Only in three categories—fruits, sweets, and low-fat milk products—did non-LILA consumers purchase significantly more food than LILA consumers.

Regional studies on whether the poor face higher food costs are inconclusive (Beaulac et al., 2009; Ver Ploeg et al., 2009) Kristjansson et al., 2009; USDA, Ver Ploeg et al., 2009. Even less evidence exists on the prices faced by consumers in LILA areas. The poor tend to purchase similar products at lower prices than other consumers (Broda et al., 2009). So prices in the immediate neighborhood may not provide useful information if consumers are willing to travel for lower prices. Our results suggest that LILA consumers face similar prices, but choose to buy cheaper products (within a food group) than non-LILA consumers.

---

3   This is lower than the $906 quarterly expenditures estimated by the Consumer Expenditure Survey in 2010. The difference is probably due to the differences in sample composition and participants' reporting practices in the two surveys (U.S. Department of Labor, 2011).

Table 2
Descriptive statistics for food purchases in LILA and non-LILA markets

	Non-LILA area		LILA area	
Variable name	Mean	S.D.	Mean	S.D.
Price of (percent)				
Fruits	1.00	0.14	1.00	0.15
Vegetables	**1.00**	0.13	1.00	0.13
Sweets	**1.01**	0.11	1.00	0.11
Oils, nuts	**1.01**	0.15	1.00	0.14
Eggs	1.01	0.17	1.01	0.17
Regular meats	**1.01**	0.15	1.00	0.15
Low-fat meats	1.01	0.16	1.01	0.17
Fish, poultry	**1.01**	0.17	1.00	0.18
Processed foods	**1.01**	0.10	1.00	0.10
Grains	**1.01**	0.11	1.00	0.13
Regular milk products	**1.01**	0.11	1.00	0.11
Low-fat milk products	1.01	0.16	1.01	0.17
Diet drinks	1.01	0.14	1.00	0.16
Nondiet drinks	1.01	0.18	1.00	0.20
Quantity of (oz)				
Fruits	**897**	873	825	871
Vegetables	788	680	789	723
Sweets	**883**	1594	848	951
Oils, nuts	**128**	158	134	185
Eggs	**108**	119	112	132
Regular meats	**165**	192	210	299
Low-fat meats	**30**	53	32	62
Fish, poultry	**67**	102	73	117
Processed foods	**2,353**	2,320	2,414	2,297
Grains	454	335	456	390
Regular milk products	**806**	896	866	1019
Low-fat milk products	**483**	787	389	794
Diet drinks	1,462	2,095	1,447	2,288
Nondiet drinks	**1,560**	1,918	1,802	2,505

Fruits	**53.6**	52.7	47.4	48.2
Vegetables	**53.4**	48.1	49.3	41.5
Sweets	**88.7**	88.1	84.0	71.4
Oils, nuts	**18.9**	22.7	17.9	22.4
Eggs	**6.7**	7.3	6.9	8.2
Regular meats	**29.1**	29.2	33.3	36.0
Low-fat meats	7.1	12.2	7.1	12.3
Fish, poultry	13.5	19.9	13.5	21.1
Processed foods	**257.9**	183.8	247.1	178.3
Grains	51.6	36.9	48.4	40.7
Regular milk products	**59.0**	44.7	56.6	48.2
Low-fat milk products	**19.4**	25.7	15.1	23.3
Diet drinks	**35.7**	42.1	33.5	42.0
Nondiet drinks	**34.9**	42.8	37.3	47.6
Total expenditures	**729.6**	397.1	697.5	396.6

The leftmost two groups are labeled *Expenditures on ($)* and *Expenditures on ($)*.

Bold indicates statistically significant difference at 5% level. LILA = Low-income, low-access. Source: Nielsen Homescan Data 2010.

Exact Affine Stone Index Demand Model

We estimate demand using the censored Exact Affine Stone Index (EASI) Implicit Marshallian Demand system (Lewbel and Pendakur 2009; Zhen et al., 2013). The EASI model is an improvement over traditional demand models like the Almost Ideal Demand model as it allows easy incorporation of demographic variables in the demand system, accounting for unobserved preference heterogeneity, and highly nonlinear Engel curves. The original EASI model was modified by Zhen and colleagues (2013) to allow for censoring of households with zero consumption of some products.

Let a consumer maximize his/her utility by choosing over a vector of J-products that results in the budget shares $\boldsymbol{w} = [w^1,...,w^J]$. The choice is constrained by the vector of prices $\boldsymbol{p} = [p^1,...,p^J]$ and by the total amount of nominal expenditures x. The consumer minimizes a cost function $C(\boldsymbol{p},u) = x$ to reach a target utility level u. From this minimization

of cost, we can derive a Hicksian budget share demand function that depends on utility and prices: $w^j = w^j(\boldsymbol{p},u)$. Hicksian demand is useful in measuring welfare changes as it allows the measurement of utility. However, the utility is difficult to observe in reality where we usually observe paired quantities and prices. The relationship between the prices and quan- tities is described by a Marshallian demand function where the consumer maximizes utility while being constrained by prices and expenditures $w^j = w^j(\boldsymbol{p},x)$. The Implicit Marshallian demand proposed by Lewbel and Pendakur (2009) depends not only on prices and expendi- tures, but also on budget shares: $w^j = w^j(\boldsymbol{p},x,\boldsymbol{w})$. The implicit Marshallian demand function is flexible enough to allow for nonlinear Engel curves and random utility parameters, which account for preference heterogeneity. The price of this flexibility is that there are budget shares on both sides of the demand function. This introduces endogeneity in the model, which requires instruments to address. (Susan: should all variables in parens be bold?)

The Hicksian demand $w^j = w^j(\boldsymbol{p},u)$ is derived from Shephard's Lemma $w^j(\boldsymbol{p},u)=\partial C(\boldsymbol{p},u)/\partial p^j$. We can preserve the general structure of the Hicksian demand, while substi- tuting a function of prices, expenditures, and budget shares for the generally unobserved utility. Lewbel and Pendakur (2009) propose a simple and flexible Hicksian budget share demand function that is unrelated to goods: $w^j(\boldsymbol{p},u) = m^j(u)$. Then the cost function should be $\ln C(\boldsymbol{p},u) = u + \sum_{j=1}^J m^j(u) \ln p^j$. Knowing the budget shares, we can present utility as $u = \ln x - \sum_{j=1}^J w^j \ln p^j$. If we substitute this utility function back into the Hicksian budget share demand, we get an implicit Marshallian demand $w^j = m^j(\ln x - \sum_{j=1}^J w^j \ln p^j)$. This demand uses the Hicksian demand structure with variables from the Marshallian demand. To differen- tiate this unobserved explicit utility, we denote implicit utility as $y = \ln x - \sum_{j=1}^J w^j \ln p^j$.

After enhancing the model with flexible Engel curves, we need to add unobserved preference heterogeneity $\varepsilon = [\varepsilon^1,...,\varepsilon^J]$, where ε has a mean of zero. We want ε to enter the budget share equation as an additive element: $w^j(\boldsymbol{p},u,\varepsilon)= m^j(u) + \varepsilon^j$. Hence, the error term in the model can be interpreted as an unobserved taste heterogeneity parameter. To comply with Shephard's Lemma, ε should enter the cost function as $C(\boldsymbol{p},u,\varepsilon)= u + \sum_{j=1}^J m^j(u) \ln p^j + \varepsilon^j \ln p^j$, where we substitute explicit utility, u, with implicit utility, y.

Next, we need to incorporate prices, p, and the demographic characteristics of the consumers, $\mathbf{z} = [z_1,\ldots,z_T]$ (in our specification, living in a LILA area will be one of the z's), where $z_1 = 1$ serving as a constant term. This exercise produces an Exact Affine Store Index with a cost function:

$$\ln C(p,y,z,\varepsilon) = y + \sum_{j=1}^{J} m^j(y,z)\ln p^j + \tfrac{1}{2}\sum_{j=1}^{J}\sum_{k=1}^{J}a^{jk}\ln p^j \ln p^k + \sum_{t=1}^{T} g^j_{\,t}\, z_t \ln p^j + \sum_{j=1}^{J}\varepsilon^j \ln p^j$$

and a Hicksian budget share equation:

$$w_{hjt}^{*} = \Sigma a_{ij}\ln p_{hjt} + \Sigma b^i y^r_{ht} + \Sigma g_{ik}\, z_{hkt} + u_{hit}$$

$$h=1,\ldots,H; j=1,\ldots,J; t=1,\ldots,T$$

where w_{hjt}^{*} is the latent budget share, which is related to the observed share as $w_{hjt} = \max(w_{hit}^{*},0)$, and p_{hjt} is the the price index of product j for household h in time period t. H is the total number of households, J is the number of food groups, and the Jth good is used as a numeraire. y_{ht} is a Stone price index of food expenditures $y_{ht} = \ln x_{ht} - \Sigma^J_{j=1}w_{hjt} \ln p_{hjt}$. The model allows for non-linear Engel curves by choosing $L > 1$. After a few tries, we chose L=3; for values of L>3, the estimation failed because of nonpositive definite variance-covariance matrix. We believe that a cubic polynomial is sufficiently flexible to measure the Engel curve. z_{hkt} is a set of household characteristics k for household h in time period t. z_{hkt} is a demand shifter such as demographics or food environment; one of the demand shifters is a constant term. We follow Zhen et al. (2010) by using Amemiya's generalized least squares, AGLS estimator for censored equation (Amemiya, 1979; Newey, 1987). We choose L=3 since any higher order utility polynomial introduces multi-collinearity. The formulas to calculate demand elasticities are presented in the appendix.

Results

In table 3, we present results of the estimated elasticities of the baseline model. All own-price elas- ticities are negative, validating the demand estimation. The own-price elasticities ranged from -0.46 for grains to -0.76 for nondiet drinks. Own-price elasticities for LILA and non-LILA consumers, estimated separately, were very similar and not presented here.

Low-Income, Low-Access Areas and Distance to Retail Foodstores

In table 4, we present our baseline model of the demand elasticities with respect to unit changes in the explanatory variables. All coefficients in the model are statistically significant, so we will discuss magnitudes only. Given the structure of the z-variables, our baseline household is non-Hispanic White or Asian, lives in a rural non-LILA area, has no children, and has a high school education.

Living in a LILA area is associated with a less healthy diet. Consumers who lived in these areas purchased 4.3 percent fewer fruits, 2.4 percent fewer vegetables, 8.6 percent more red meat, 10.4 percent less low-fat milk products, 5.2 percent more diet drinks, and 2.6 percent more nondiet drinks in 2010. While statistically significant, the magnitudes of the differences between LILA and non- LILA consumers are modest.

Other demographic variables have much larger effects on food purchases than LILA residence. For example, consumers with children under age 7 purchased 23 percent more fruits than consumers with no children. Black consumers bought 31 percent more red meat and 35 percent more nondiet drinks than White/ Asian consumers. College-educated consumers purchased 19 percent more fruit than consumers who only graduated from high school; urban consumers purchased 17 percent less red meat than rural consumers.

Table 5 presents the effect of expenditure-weighted average shopping trip distance on food purchases. Specification 1 presents results from the baseline model discussed earlier. Specification 2 adds average distance traveled to the store, with a column showing the effect on food purchases of increasing the average distance traveled in the (reporting) quarter by 1 mile. Traveling farther has only a modest effect on purchases, the largest being an increase in purchases of oils/nuts by 0.77 percent/mile traveled and a decrease in purchases of low-fat red meats by 0.77 percent per mile.

In the third specification, we interact the LILA indicator with the distance variable to test whether the diet of LILA consumers improves (more than the diet of non-LILA consumers would) by trav- elling farther from home. This hypothesis is weakly supported by the results. If LILA households travel 1 extra mile to the store, they tend to increase purchases of fruits (0.42 percent/mile), vege- tables (0.55 percent/mile), low-fat milk products (0.61 percent/mile) and fish/poultry (0.67 percent/ mile). At the same time, LILA consumers reduce their purchases of diet drinks (-0.56 percent/mile), nondiet drinks (-0.33 percent) and low-fat red meats (-0.40 percent/mile). We conclude that LILA consumers improve their diet modestly as they travel farther from home, and the magnitude of the effect is small. Given that LILA consumers, on average, travel 7.5 miles to a foodstore, it may be difficult for an average LILA consumer to travel even farther.

Table 3
Estimated elasticities of demand across 14 food groups (percent)

	Fruits	Vegetables	Sweets	Oils, nuts	Eggs	Red meats	Low fat red meats	Fish, poultry	Processed foods	Grains	Milk products	Low-fat milk products	Diet drinks	Non-diet drinks
Fruits	-0.61 (0.07)	-0.01 (0.01)	-0.03 (0.01)	0.01 (0.01)	0.00 (0.00)	-0.06 (0.01)	0.00 (0.01)	-0.01 (0.01)	-0.14 (0.03)	-0.01 (0.01)	-0.06 (0.01)	0.04 (0.01)	-0.04 (0.00)	-0.03 (0.00)
Vegetables	-0.01 (0.01)	-0.89 (0.05)	-0.04 (0.05)	-0.05 (0.03)	0.00 (0.00)	-0.04 (0.01)	-0.02 (0.00)	-0.01 (0.00)	-0.09 (0.03)	0.00 (0.01)	-0.02 (0.01)	0.00 (0.02)	0.00 (0.01)	-0.01 (0.02)
Sweets	-0.02 (0.01)	-0.02 (0.03)	-0.59 (0.03)	0.00 (0.01)	-0.01 (0.00)	-0.01 (0.01)	-0.01 (0.00)	-0.01 (0.00)	-0.10 (0.03)	-0.07 (0.01)	-0.03 (0.01)	0.00 (0.00)	-0.07 (0.01)	-0.03 (0.01)
Oils, nuts	0.03 (0.02)	-0.10 (0.07)	-0.01 (0.02)	-0.59 (0.08)	-0.02 (0.00)	-0.01 (0.01)	0.00 (0.00)	-0.03 (0.01)	-0.20 (0.03)	-0.05 (0.01)	-0.01 (0.01)	0.00 (0.01)	0.02 (0.01)	0.01 (0.01)
Eggs	0.00 (0.03)	0.02 (0.03)	-0.06 (0.05)	-0.06 (0.02)	-0.57 (0.08)	-0.03 (0.02)	0.03 (0.01)	-0.01 (0.01)	-0.19 (0.07)	0.01 (0.06)	0.02 (0.03)	0.01 (0.02)	0.04 (0.04)	-0.05 (0.01)
Red meats	-0.10 (0.01)	-0.07 (0.03)	-0.03 (0.02)	-0.01 (0.01)	-0.01 (0.00)	-0.54 (0.07)	0.00 (0.02)	0.00 (0.00)	-0.08 (0.08)	-0.05 (0.01)	-0.03 (0.02)	-0.06 (0.01)	0.03 (0.01)	0.00 (0.01)
Low-fat red meats	-0.02 (0.06)	-0.06 (0.02)	-0.04 (0.02)	0.01 (0.01)	0.02 (0.00)	0.00 (0.05)	-0.63 (0.09)	-0.01 (0.01)	-0.26 (0.06)	-0.03 (0.02)	0.01 (0.01)	-0.01 (0.01)	0.09 (0.03)	-0.04 (0.04)
Fish, poultry	-0.04 (0.02)	-0.04 (0.01)	-0.05 (0.02)	-0.03 (0.01)	-0.01 (0.00)	0.00 (0.01)	-0.01 (0.01)	-0.65 (0.05)	-0.08 (0.06)	-0.04 (0.03)	-0.10 (0.04)	0.02 (0.02)	0.02 (0.01)	-0.02 (0.02)
Processed foods	-0.04 (0.01)	-0.03 (0.01)	-0.05 (0.00)	-0.03 (0.00)	-0.01 (0.00)	-0.02 (0.01)	-0.02 (0.00)	-0.01 (0.00)	-0.71 (0.04)	-0.05 (0.00)	-0.05 (0.01)	-0.03 (0.00)	-0.03 (0.01)	-0.01 (0.00)
Grains	0.00 (0.02)	0.01 (0.01)	-0.11 (0.01)	-0.02 (0.00)	0.00 (0.01)	-0.03 (0.01)	-0.01 (0.00)	-0.01 (0.01)	-0.16 (0.04)	-0.46 (0.09)	0.00 (0.04)	-0.02 (0.00)	-0.02 (0.01)	-0.03 (0.00)
Milk products	-0.05 (0.01)	-0.02 (0.01)	-0.04 (0.01)	0.00 (0.00)	0.00 (0.00)	-0.02 (0.01)	0.00 (0.00)	-0.03 (0.01)	-0.16 (0.04)	0.00 (0.03)	-0.53 (0.07)	-0.04 (0.01)	-0.01 (0.00)	0.00 (0.02)
Low-fat milk products	0.08 (0.02)	0.02 (0.04)	0.02 (0.01)	0.00 (0.01)	0.00 (0.01)	-0.06 (0.02)	0.00 (0.00)	0.02 (0.01)	-0.16 (0.04)	-0.03 (0.01)	-0.08 (0.01)	-0.64 (0.07)	-0.02 (0.00)	0.00 (0.01)
Diet drinks	-0.06 (0.01)	0.00 (0.02)	-0.15 (0.02)	0.01 (0.00)	0.01 (0.01)	0.02 (0.01)	0.03 (0.01)	0.01 (0.00)	-0.16 (0.05)	-0.03 (0.01)	-0.02 (0.00)	-0.02 (0.00)	-0.65 (0.05)	0.01 (0.02)
Non-diet drinks	0.00 (0.03)	0.03 (0.03)	0.02 (0.05)	0.02 (0.01)	0.00 (0.01)	0.02 (0.01)	0.00 (0.01)	0.00 (0.02)	0.18 (0.10)	0.00 (0.03)	0.03 (0.04)	0.01 (0.01)	0.04 (0.03)	-0.76 (0.03)

Coefficients statistically significant at 1% level are marked bold. Source: Computed by USDA, Economic Research Service.

The EASI model is relatively complicated, so to show its robustness, we present a simple OLS (Ordinary Least Squares) regression of the budget shares for fruits and vegetables. Appendix table 1 presents estimated changes to fruit and vegetable purchases (in percent) associated with living in LILA areas. The estimated coefficients are similar to the ones presented in table 4.

Table 4
The effect of demographic factors on food purchases

	LILA	Household size	Children 0-6 years old	Children 7-12 years old	Children 13-17 years old	Black	Hispanic	Less than high school	College graduate	Urban	Household income ($)
Fruits	-4.34	-7.92	22.65	7.14	-2.42	11.27	9.27	-13.67	19.45	7.77	1.32
	(0.0017)	(0.0031)	(0.0088)	(0.0028)	(0.0009)	(0.0044)	(0.0036)	(0.0053)	(0.0075)	(0.0030)	(0.2448)
Vegetables	-2.43	-2.01	-4.58	-8.43	-11.01	-5.82	3.16	-5.81	5.10	3.70	0.78
	(0.0017)	(0.0014)	(0.0033)	(0.0061)	(0.0079)	(0.0042)	(0.0023)	(0.0042)	(0.0037)	(0.0027)	(0.1972)
Sweets	0.02	-1.63	-6.03	0.33	-0.22	-3.79	-6.38	2.23	-6.21	-1.06	-0.88
	(0.0000)	(0.0013)	(0.0049)	(0.0003)	(0.0002)	(0.0031)	(0.0052)	(0.0018)	(0.0051)	(0.0009)	(0.1076)
Oils, nuts	0.21	-5.74	-11.97	-11.55	-11.33	7.31	2.44	-14.48	15.02	-3.64	0.46
	(0.0002)	(0.0049)	(0.0103)	(0.0099)	(0.0097)	(0.0063)	(0.0021)	(0.0124)	(0.0129)	(0.0031)	(0.3085)
Eggs	3.37	5.24	-0.45	-7.15	-9.34	16.41	16.11	11.05	0.90	-3.76	-1.01
	(0.0011)	(0.0016)	(0.0001)	(0.0022)	(0.0029)	(0.0051)	(0.0050)	(0.0035)	(0.0003)	(0.0012)	(0.3819)
Red meats	8.55	8.46	-2.92	-1.44	-2.61	31.03	-1.61	19.27	-9.96	-16.97	-1.42
	(0.0089)	(0.0089)	(0.0031)	(0.0015)	(0.0027)	(0.0325)	(0.0017)	(0.0202)	(0.0104)	(0.0178)	(0.2356)
Low-fat red meats	4.01	2.84	13.80	19.08	8.49	-20.29	26.15	3.66	7.73	-6.26	-0.81
	(0.0103)	(0.0073)	(0.0356)	(0.0492)	(0.0219)	(0.0523)	(0.0674)	(0.0094)	(0.0199)	(0.0162)	(0.6247)
Fish, poultry	1.25	3.15	-13.78	-12.45	-5.36	60.46	7.79	-11.86	7.33	-0.25	-0.19
	(0.0029)	(0.0073)	(0.0318)	(0.0287)	(0.0124)	(0.1395)	(0.0180)	(0.0274)	(0.0169)	(0.0006)	(0.2397)
Processed foods	0.18	-0.11	-3.23	0.83	2.96	6.66	0.63	1.19	-4.04	3.50	0.11
	(0.0005)	(0.0003)	(0.0095)	(0.0024)	(0.0087)	(0.0196)	(0.0019)	(0.0035)	(0.0119)	(0.0103)	(0.0592)
Grains	-2.71	5.62	1.66	6.46	3.98	-8.28	0.03	-0.17	3.93	-2.64	-0.25
	(0.0030)	(0.0061)	(0.0018)	(0.0071)	(0.0043)	(0.0090)	(0.0000)	(0.0002)	(0.0043)	(0.0029)	(0.1459)
Milk products	0.97	3.84	17.91	-2.01	0.65	-28.12	-0.08	-4.89	0.35	-7.29	-0.35
	(0.0008)	(0.0033)	(0.0156)	(0.0017)	(0.0006)	(0.0244)	(0.0001)	(0.0042)	(0.0003)	(0.0063)	(0.1150)
Low-fat milk products	-10.37	-5.44	30.46	22.76	9.15	-66.73	-18.27	-28.50	27.88	8.22	1.72
	(0.0089)	(0.0047)	(0.0262)	(0.0195)	(0.0079)	(0.0573)	(0.0157)	(0.0245)	(0.0239)	(0.0071)	(0.3184)

Diet drinks	5.23	-4.49	-21.30	-10.40	-12.52	-36.59	-8.57	8.87	-5.25	-3.74	1.03
	(0.0065)	(0.0056)	(0.0264)	(0.0129)	(0.0155)	(0.0453)	(0.0106)	(0.0110)	(0.0065)	(0.0046)	(0.1456)
Nondiet drinks	2.61	6.24	-5.92	-3.44	10.99	35.25	0.07	24.74	-14.19	-6.36	-1.46
	(0.0284)	(0.0679)	(0.0643)	(0.0374)	(0.1194)	(0.3832)	(0.0007)	(0.2689)	(0.1543)	(0.0691)	(0.1488)

All coefficients are statistically significant at 5% level, except the underlined coefficients.
LILA - Low-income, low-access. Source: Computed by USDA, Economic Research Service.

Table 5
Effect on food purchases of distance traveled to stores

(1)	(2)		(3) (what does asterisk indicate?)		
LILA	LILA	distance	LILA	distance	LILA* distance
Fruits	-4.34 (0.0017)	-4.08 (0.0016)	-0.21 (0.0001)	-7.26 (0.0028)	-0.26 (0.0001)	0.42 (0.0002)
Vegetables	-2.43 (0.0017)	-2.54 (0.0018)	0.09 (0.0001)	-6.71 (0.0048)	0.02 (0.0000)	0.55 (0.0004)
Sweets	0.02 (0.0000)	0.13 (0.0001)	-0.10 (0.0001)	1.64 (0.0013)	-0.07 (0.0001)	-0.20 (0.0002)
Oils, nuts	0.21 (0.0002)	-0.72 (0.0006)	0.77 (0.0006)	-3.05 (0.0026)	0.73 (0.0006)	0.30 (0.0003)
Eggs	3.37 (0.0011)	3.44 (0.0011)	-0.05 (0.0000)	5.95 (0.0019)	-0.01 (0.0000)	-0.33 (0.0001)
Red meats	8.55 (0.0089)	8.33 (0.0087)	0.19 (0.0002)	10.63 (0.0111)	0.23 (0.0002)	-0.30 (0.0003)
Low-fat red meats	4.01 (0.0103)	4.92 (0.0127)	-0.77 (0.0020)	7.90 (0.0204)	-0.72 (0.0018)	-0.40 (0.0010)
Fish, poultry	1.25 (0.0029)	0.69 (0.0016)	0.44 (0.0010)	-4.40 (0.0101)	0.36 (0.0008)	0.67 (0.0015)
Processed foods	0.18 (0.0005)	0.24 (0.0007)	-0.05 (0.0001)	0.97 (0.0029)	-0.04 (0.0001)	-0.10 (0.0003)
Grains	-2.71 (0.0030)	-2.65 (0.0029)	-0.06 (0.0001)	-2.49 (0.0027)	-0.05 (0.0001)	-0.02 (0.0000)
Milk products	0.97 (0.0008)	0.74 (0.0006)	0.18 (0.0002)	-0.46 (0.0004)	0.16 (0.0001)	0.16 (0.0001)

Low-fat milk products	-10.37 (0.0089)	-9.90 (0.0086)	-0.37 (0.0003)	-14.53 (0.0126)	-0.44 (0.0004)	0.61 (0.0005)
Diet drinks	5.23 (0.0065)	4.99 (0.0061)	0.22 (0.0003)	9.19 (0.0113)	0.29 (0.0004)	-0.56 (0.0007)
Nondiet drinks	2.61 (0.0284)	2.66 (0.0289)	-0.04 (0.0004)	5.19 (0.0564)	0.00 (0.0000)	-0.33 (0.0036)

All coefficients are statistically significant at 1%. LILA - Low-income, low-access. Source: Computed by USDA, Economic Research Service.

Urban and Rural LILA Areas

Rural and urban areas need to pass different distance thresholds to be classified as LILA areas (10 miles and 1 mile, respectively). The effect of traveling an extra mile to the store may be more modest for rural residents who typically have to travel longer distances for services and shopping. The effect on food purchases of living in a rural LILA area is much weaker than the effect of living in an urban one (table 6). Living in an urban LILA area is associated with fewer purchases of fruits (-6.7 percent), vegetables (-4.9 percent), and low-fat milk products (-14.6 percent) and greater purchases of red meats (10.1 percent) and nondiet drinks (5.4 percent). (The urban column shows the average difference in purchases between urban and rural consumers.) We find that urban consumers have more healthful diets, purchasing more fruits, vegetables, and low-fat milk products and fewer red meats and nondiet drinks. This general difference makes the diet of urban LILA and rural non-LILA consumers roughly similar.

Next, we interact average shopping distance traveled with the indicators for rural and urban LILA areas. For consumers living in urban LILA areas, traveling 1 more mile to the store is associated with increased purchases of vegetables (0.79 percent), fruits (0.55 percent), oils/nuts (0.89 percent), low-fat red meats (1.33 percent), and fish/poultry (0.56 percent), and reduced purchases of nondiet drinks (-0.32 percent) (table 7). For rural LILA consumers, a 1-mile increase in distance traveled is associated with an increase in purchases of milk products (0.29 percent) and a decrease in the purchase of oils/nuts (-0.69 percent) and sweets (-0.54 percent).

Poverty or Low Access as Greater Factor in Food Purchases: Disaggregation of LILA

For a census tract to be classified as LILA, it needs to have both low-income households and limited access to retail foodstores. In this section, we consider these criteria separately to assess their relative importance.

Depth of poverty and urban residence have larger impacts on consumers' diets than the distance to supermarkets. Consumers living in poor areas purchase less fruit (-5.7 percent), fewer vegetables (-2.7 percent), more sweets (2.6 percent), more red meats (6 percent), fewer low-fat milk products (-15.1 percent), and more nondiet drinks (9.9 percent) than consumers in rural non-LILA areas (table 8). On the other hand, living in an urban census tract that is not a LILA area is associated with a healthier diet. Consumers in urban tracts buy 11.3 percent more fruits, 4.4 percent more vegetables, 21.6 percent less red meats, and 9.7 percent more low-fat milk products.

Curiously, residents of rural areas more than 10 miles from a supermarket and residents of rural LILA areas have healthier diets than rural residents closer to supermarkets. Seemingly, the benchmark of 10-mile distance from a supermarket does not equate to a disadvantaged rural population.

Longer distance in an urban context has a stronger effect on diet. Urban consumers who are more than 1 mile from a supermarket purchase 7.3 percent fewer fruit and 11.1 percent more red meats (table 8). On the positive side, they purchase 6.8 percent fewer nondiet drinks and 5.1 percent more fish and poultry. The joint effect of low income and low access in urban areas (Urban LILA indicator) is associated with the purchase of 2.7 percent fewer vegetables, 3.6 percent more red meats, and 5.5 percent less fish and poultry.

Table 6

Effect on food purchases of living in rural and urban low-income, low-access areas 1

	Rural LILA	Urban LILA	Urban
Fruits	0.62	-6.69	8.49
	(0.0002)	(0.0026)	(0.0033)
Vegetables	2.83	-4.92	4.47
	(0.0020)	(0.0035)	(0.0032)
Sweets	0.72	-0.32	-0.95
	(0.0006)	(0.0003)	(0.0008)
Oils, nuts	8.05	-3.51	-2.52
	(0.0069)	(0.0030)	(0.0022)
Eggs	-0.09	5.00	-4.26
	(0.0000)	(0.0016)	(0.0013)
Red meats	5.25	10.12	-17.45
	(0.0055)	(0.0106)	(0.0183)

Low-fat red meats	-1.45	6.62	-7.05
	(0.0037)	(0.0171)	(0.0182)
Fish, poultry	8.62	-2.26	0.82
	(0.0199)	(0.0052)	(0.0019)
Processed foods	-1.90	1.18	3.19
	(0.0056)	(0.0035)	(0.0094)
Grains	-1.39	-3.34	-2.45
	(0.0015)	(0.0036)	(0.0027)
Milk products	2.10	0.42	-7.13
	(0.0018)	(0.0004)	(0.0062)
Low-fat milk products	-1.50	-14.56	9.49
	(0.0013)	(0.0125)	(0.0082)
Diet drinks	-2.59	8.94	-4.88
	(0.0032)	(0.0110)	(0.0060)
Nondiet drinks	-3.31	5.40	-7.17
	(0.0360)	(0.0587)	(0.0779)

All coefficients are statistically significant at 1% level. LILA - Low-income, low-access.
Source: Computed by USDA, Economic Research Service.

Table 7
Effect on food purchases of living in rural and urban low-income, low-access areas 2

	Urban	Rural LILA	Urban LILA	Rural LILA *distance	Urban LILA* distance	distance	Urban * distance
Fruits	12.37	4.01	-9.52	-0.30	0.55	0.16	-0.62
	(0.0049)	(0.0016)	(0.0037)	(0.0001)	(0.0002)	(0.0001)	(0.0002)
Vegetables	3.71	0.43	-9.14	0.20	0.79	-0.04	0.11
	(0.0027)	(0.0003)	(0.0066)	(0.0001)	(0.0006)	(0.0000)	(0.0001)
Sweets	-0.01	7.47	0.20	-0.54	-0.09	0.04	-0.15
	(0.0000)	(0.0061)	(0.0002)	(0.0004)	(0.0001)	(0.0000)	(0.0001)
Oils, nuts	3.24	13.59	-8.28	-0.69	0.89	0.96	-0.32
	(0.0027)	(0.0115)	(0.0070)	(0.0006)	(0.0008)	(0.0008)	(0.0003)
Eggs	-5.71	-0.18	7.73	0.04	-0.52	-0.13	0.18
	(0.0018)	(0.0001)	(0.0024)	(0.0000)	(0.0002)	(0.0000)	(0.0001)
Red meats	-22.47	5.94	9.22	0.02	0.16	-0.27	0.74
	(0.0234)	(0.0062)	(0.0096)	(0.0000)	(0.0002)	(0.0003)	(0.0008)

Low-fat red meats	-22.17 (0.0573)	10.89 (0.0281)	-0.38 (0.0010)	-0.50 (0.0013)	1.33 (0.0034)	-1.70 (0.0044)	1.51 (0.0039)
Fish, poultry	5.42 (0.0125)	3.46 (0.0080)	-5.23 (0.0120)	0.23 (0.0005)	0.56 (0.0013)	0.62 (0.0014)	-0.38 (0.0009)
Processed foods	2.11 (0.0062)	-4.34 (0.0128)	2.62 (0.0077)	0.22 (0.0007)	-0.27 (0.0008)	-0.12 (0.0003)	0.11 (0.0003)
Grains	-4.34 (0.0047)	-1.79 (0.0020)	-1.59 (0.0017)	0.08 (0.0001)	-0.33 (0.0004)	-0.18 (0.0002)	0.21 (0.0002)
Milk products	-7.30 (0.0064)	-1.91 (0.0017)	0.24 (0.0002)	0.29 (0.0002)	0.03 (0.0000)	0.09 (0.0001)	0.11 (0.0001)
Low-fat milk products	8.20 (0.0071)	-2.91 (0.0025)	-14.18 (0.0123)	0.21 (0.0002)	-0.06 (0.0001)	-0.38 (0.0003)	-0.06 (0.0001)
Diet drinks	-1.22 (0.0015)	0.56 (0.0007)	9.20 (0.0113)	-0.37 (0.0005)	-0.05 (0.0001)	0.47 (0.0006)	-0.32 (0.0004)
Nondiet drinks	-3.82 (0.0415)	-3.51 (0.0382)	7.14 (0.0776)	-0.06 (0.0006)	-0.32 (0.0035)	0.26 (0.0029)	-0.43 (0.0047)

All coefficients are statistically significant at 1% level. LILA - Low-income, low-access.
Source: Computed by USDA, Economic Research Service.

Table 8
Effect of distance and low income on food purchases

	Urban	Poor	Mile 1/urban	Mile 10/rural	LILA/urban	LILA/rural
Fruits	11.28 (0.0045)	-5.72 (0.0023)	-7.25 (0.0029)	6.21 (0.0025)	-0.96 (0.0004)	3.42 (0.0014)
Vegetables	4.40 (0.0032)	-2.71 (0.0019)	-0.45 (0.0003)	0.25 (0.0002)	-2.69 (0.0019)	4.73 (0.0034)
Sweets	-1.28 (0.0010)	2.59 (0.0021)	0.14 (0.0001)	-12.89 (0.0104)	-2.41 (0.0020)	1.72 (0.0014)
Oils, nuts	-2.26 (0.0019)	-1.58 (0.0013)	1.09 (0.0009)	21.90 (0.0187)	-2.40 (0.0021)	4.30 (0.0037)
Eggs	-4.85 (0.0015)	0.37 (0.0001)	0.87 (0.0003)	-6.46 (0.0020)	4.59 (0.0014)	1.05 (0.0003)
Red meats	-21.61 (0.0223)	5.99 (0.0062)	11.09 (0.0114)	0.77 (0.0008)	3.63 (0.0037)	0.67 (0.0007)
Low-fat red meats	-12.50 (0.0321)	0.97 (0.0025)	12.14 (0.0312)	-6.19 (0.0159)	4.10 (0.0105)	-0.87 (0.0022)

Fish, poultry	0.24	3.10	5.05	31.83	-5.54	-0.77
	(0.0005)	(0.0071)	(0.0116)	(0.0733)	(0.0127)	(0.0018)
Processed foods	3.60	-0.09	-1.14	-1.73	1.42	-1.44
	(0.0106)	(0.0003)	(0.0034)	(0.0051)	(0.0042)	(0.0042)
Grains	-4.47	-2.90	3.91	-1.20	-1.59	0.95
	(0.0049)	(0.0032)	(0.0043)	(0.0013)	(0.0017)	(0.0010)
Milk products	-7.49	1.07	2.54	15.19	-0.82	-2.06
	(0.0065)	(0.0009)	(0.0022)	(0.0132)	(0.0007)	(0.0018)
Low-fat milk products	9.68	-15.07	-4.23	-3.09	-1.66	10.13
	(0.0083)	(0.0129)	(0.0036)	(0.0026)	(0.0014)	(0.0087)
Diet drinks	-6.60	2.42	4.23	-3.53	6.37	-3.60
	(0.0081)	(0.0030)	(0.0052)	(0.0043)	(0.0078)	(0.0044)
Nondiet drinks	-3.39	9.93	-6.83	-5.96	-1.69	-9.08
	(0.0368)	(0.1075)	(0.0740)	(0.0645)	(0.0183)	(0.0984)

All coefficients are statistically significant at 1% level. LILA - Low-income, low-access.
Source: Computed by USDA, Economic Research Service.

Store Channels and Their Effect on Food Purchases

There is little difference in the retail channels patronized by LILA and non-LILA consumers (LILA consumers purchase more from supercenters and non-LILA consumers purchase more from super- markets), but it is possible that the same retail channels offer different products in LILA areas. In this section, we investigate whether LILA and non-LILA consumers buy similar products in the same retail channels. We include five retail channel indicators in the estimation, with grocery stores (the most popular channel) the omitted category.

Retail channel or format has a large effect on food purchases. Purchases in supercenters were associated with less healthful purchases. When consumers increase the share of expenditures in supercenter stores by 10 percentage points, this change is associated with an increase in purchases of low-fat meats (16 percent) and red meats (4.4 percent) and a decrease in purchases of fruits (2.5 percent) and vegetables (2.6 percent). Other store channels have average expendi- ture shares less than 10 percent, so we can reliably estimate only small changes to the expenditure share of these channels.

Explaining Food Disparities: Access or Preferences?

LILA consumers living far from supermarkets with limited means of transportation may face a food environment that makes it difficult to purchase healthy foods. In this report, we measured the effect of living in LILA areas on consumer food purchases. Consumers living in LILA areas consume fewer fruits, vegetables, and low-fat milk products and more red meats and drinks (diet and nondiet). The magnitudes of the differences are small and, even if eliminated, would not translate into signifi- cant dietary or health improvements. The effects of demographic variables—such as race, education, and income—on food purchases are much larger than the effect from living in a LILA area.

LILA consumers travel slightly farther from home to purchase their food. Almost all LILA house- holds travel to stores more than 1 mile from their home, the distance commonly used to delineate low food access. Thus, of the 7.7 percent of households in the Homescan sample who lived in LILA areas, very few limited their food purchases to the LILA areas.

LILA consumers who travel farther to buy food purchase more fruits, vegetables, fish, and poultry and fewer drinks (diet and nondiet). Perhaps, stores close to LILA consumers sell a variety of prod- ucts similar to those offered at convenience stores, such as drinks, milk, sweets, and limited meats and produce. When LILA consumers travel farther to retail stores that offer a greater variety of foods and they are unconstrained in their choices, LILA consumers exhibit stronger preferences for fish, poultry, and produce, but the magnitudes of these effects are small and they cannot explain large nutritional disparities observed in the population.

The LILA definition requires that a rural area be at least 10 miles from the nearest supermarket to be classified as a low food-access area. However, even with this generous parameter, food demand in rural LILA areas is hardly different from other rural areas. Rural residents generally tend to buy fewer healthy food products than urban consumers.

For an area to classify as LILA, it must have both limited access to supermarkets and low income levels. The poverty level of a census tract, we find, is a more important factor for unhealthy food purchases than is access to stores. Distance to retail foodstores has almost no effect on purchases in rural areas, but a small negative effect in urban areas.

If LILA consumers are restricted in their choice of stores and are compelled to shop in stores with high prices and a scarcity of healthy food, we would expect to see differences in the retail channels where LILA and non-LILA consumers shop. However, our results do not bear this out. Instead, the descriptive statistics of retail channels (table 1) show that the difference in retail channels patron- ized by LILA and non-LILA households is small. Thus, if we assume that stores in the same retail channel offer a similar variety of healthy foods, then there is little difference in the availability of healthy foods to LILA and non-LILA consumers. Nor do we find that LILA consumers are facing higher prices; in fact, they are facing slightly lower prices for most food products (see table 2).

After controlling for the retail channel where consumers shop (table 9), the baseline difference in food purchases between LILA and non-LILA households decreases by half. LILA consumers purchased less healthful food in all retail channels except supercenters compared to non-LILA

consumers. On the other hand, LILA consumers purchased less healthful products in supermarkets and club stores, which tend to have the most healthful product offerings, suggesting lower prefer- ences for these products among LILA consumers.

The relatively poor diet of LILA consumers cannot be explained by their inability to reach super- markets or by different relative prices in supermarkets where they shop. Two likely explanations are that LILA consumers have different preferences than non-LILA consumers, or that LILA consumers shop in stores that offer a different variety of products than the stores where non-LILA consumers shop, even if these stores belong to the same retail channel. Future research examining the variety of products offered in the stores where LILA consumers shop may illuminate this issue.

Conclusion

Our results begin to shed light on whether the quality of food choices in low-access areas is a demand or supply problem. Do consumers in LILA areas value supermarkets less or do those   retail outlets, for some reason, avoid these areas? We find that LILA area consumers purchase unhealthier food products than consumers living elsewhere. The difference in the healthfulness of their purchases, however, is quite small. Also, LILA area consumers tend not to purchase much healthier items farther from home, suggesting that these consumers exhibit less demand for such items. Households in LILA areas must travel unrealistically long distances to erase even the small disparity with non-LILA households in healthfulness of food purchases. Thus, as the effect of living in LILA areas on diets is modest, the dietary effect of a policy attracting supermarkets to these areas will be similarly modest.

There are three important caveats to our results. First, Nielsen HomeScan data underrepresent poor consumers. We correct this problem somewhat by using population weights, but this remedy cannot help if the poor in Homescan are systematically different from the poor not sampled by it. We suspect that the coverage of the very poor may be particularly lacking. Second, our match of store locations to consumers is imperfect, which introduces a measurement error to our distance variable for the unmatched stores. Finally, we observe the food purchased in stores only to the extent that participants correctly report it, and we don't have information on food consumed away from home in restaurants, schools, and other places, which are important components of overall food consumption.

While these caveats may be daunting, this is the best data available at the moment that links food purchases with consumer and store locations. In addition, this study benefits from a large consumer panel with frequent and detailed information on food purchases. The fact that this is the first large national study of food purchases in LILA areas illustrates the data difficulties faced by researchers. Future research might combine a better measurement of food consumed away from home with better coverage of poor consumers. USDA's National Household Food Acquisition and Purchase Survey (FoodAPS), recently available, combines both and is an attractive avenue for future research on food access and food purchases.

Our results show that living in LILA areas does not have major adverse effects on the food purchases for most residents of these areas. At the same time, given our data limitations, it is possible that living in LILA areas is a large problem for a small minority of particularly disad- vantaged consumers. Future research with a better coverage of the very poor consumers can shed light on this question.

Appendix

Calculating Elasticity: Price Elasticity of Demand

In the fully interactive EASI model we estimate

$$w^j = \sum_{r=1}^{R} b_r^j y^r + \sum_{t=1}^{T} g_t^j z_t + \sum_{k=1}^{J} a_n^{jk} \ln p^k + \sum_{t=1}^{T} \sum_{k=1}^{J} c^{jkt} z_t \ln p^k +$$
$$\sum_{k=1}^{J} d_n^{jk} \ln p^k y + \sum_{t=1}^{T} h_t^j z_t y + \varepsilon^j \qquad (2)$$

Hicksian price semi-elasticity

$$\frac{\partial w_j}{\partial \ln p_k} = a_n^{jk} + \sum_{t=1}^{T} z_t c^{jkt} + \sum_{l=0}^{L} A_{lji} z_t + d_n^{jk} y \qquad (3)$$

From Hicksian semi-elasticity we can calculate Hicksian elasticity:

$$\frac{\partial w_i}{\partial \ln p_j} = \frac{\partial \left[\frac{q_i^h p_i}{x^h}\right]}{\partial \ln p_i} = \frac{\partial q_i^h}{\partial \ln p_j}\frac{p_i}{x^h} + \frac{\partial p_i}{\partial \ln p_j}\frac{q_i^h}{x^h} - \frac{q_i^h p_i}{\left(x^h\right)^2}\frac{\partial x^h}{\partial \ln p_j}$$

$$= \frac{\partial q_i^h}{\partial \ln p_j}\frac{q_i^h}{q_i^h}\frac{p_i}{x^h} + \frac{\partial p_i}{\partial \ln p_j}\frac{p_i}{p_i}\frac{q_i^h}{x^h} - \frac{q_i^h p_i}{\left(x^h\right)^2}\frac{\partial x^h}{\partial p_j}\frac{p_j}{1}$$

$$= \frac{\partial \ln q_i^h}{\partial \ln p_j}w_i^h + \frac{\partial \ln p_i}{\partial \ln p_j}\frac{q_i^h p_i}{x^h} - \frac{q_i^h p_i}{x^h}\frac{q_j^h p_j}{x^h}$$

$$= \frac{\partial \ln q_i^h}{\partial \ln p_j}w_i^h + 1_{ij}w_i^h - w_i^h w_j^h$$

Then the Hicksian elasticity is

$$h_{ij} = \frac{\partial \ln q_i^h}{\partial \ln p_j} = \frac{\partial w_i}{w_i^h \partial \ln p_j} + w_j^h - 1_{ij}$$

Where $1_{ij} = 1$ if $i = j$ and $1_{ij} = 0$ if $i \neq j$.

Where $1_{ij} = 1$ if $i = j$ and $1_{ij} = 0$ if $i \neq j$.

From equation (2) we can derive Marshallian expenditure semi-elasticity (see details in the Appendix of Lewbel and Pendakur (2009)) where x^m x^m is the Marshallian expenditures.

From the semi-elasticity we can derive elasticity:

$$\frac{\partial w_i}{\partial \ln x^m} = \frac{\partial \left[\frac{q_i^m p_j}{x^m} \right]}{\partial \ln x^m} = \frac{\partial q_i^m}{\partial x} \frac{x^m}{x^m} \frac{p_i}{x^m} + \frac{\partial \left(\frac{1}{x^m} \right)}{\partial x^m} \frac{p_i q_i^m x^m}{1}$$

$$\frac{\partial w_i}{\partial \ln x^m} = \frac{\partial q_i^m}{\partial x} \frac{x^m}{q_i^m} \frac{p_i q_i^m}{x_m} + \frac{p_i q_i^m x^m}{\left(x^m \right)^2}$$

$$e_i = \frac{\partial q_i^m}{\partial x} \frac{x^m}{q_i^m} = \frac{\partial w_i}{w_i \partial \ln x^m} + 1$$

From Slutsky's equation for elasticities

$$e_{ij} = h_{ij} - w_j e_i$$

we can derive Marshallian price elasticities:

$$e_{ij} = \frac{\partial w_i}{w_i^h \partial \ln p_j} + w_j^h - 1_{ij} - w_j \left(\frac{\partial w_i}{w_i \partial \ln x^m} + 1 \right)$$

Elasticity with respect to Z's

Lewbel and Pendakur (2009) present a general formula for budget semi-elasticity:

$$\nabla_z w \left(p, x, z, \varepsilon \right) = \left[I_J + \nabla_y w \left(p, y, z, \varepsilon \right) P' \right]^{-1} \left[\nabla_z w \left(p, y, z, \varepsilon \right) \right]$$

From (2) we know that:

$$\nabla_z w(p,y,z,\varepsilon) = \frac{\partial w_j}{\partial z_t} = g_t^j + \sum_{k=1}^J c^{jkt} \ln p^k + h_t^j y \quad and \quad \nabla_y w(p,y,z,\varepsilon) = \frac{\partial w_j}{\partial y} =$$

$$r \sum_{r=1}^R b_r^j y^{r-1} + \sum_{k=1}^J d_n^{jk} \ln p^k y + \sum_{t=1}^T h_t^j z_t$$

and

Then a budget semi-elasticity with respect to z's is:

$$\frac{\partial w_j(p,x,z,\varepsilon)}{\partial z_t} = \frac{r \sum_{r=1}^R b_r^j y^{r-1} + \sum_{k=1}^J d_n^{jk} \ln p^k y + \sum_{t=1}^T h_t^j z_t}{1 + g_t^j + \sum_{k=1}^J c^{jkt} \ln p^k + h_t^j y}$$

Next we find the quantity elasticity of demand with respect to z's:

$$\frac{\partial \ln q_j}{\partial z_t} = \frac{\partial q_j}{\partial z_t} \frac{1}{q_j} = \frac{\partial \frac{w_j x}{p_j}}{\partial z_t} \frac{1}{\frac{w_j x}{p_j}}$$

As total spending and market prices do not depend on z variables:

$$\frac{\partial x}{\partial z_t} = 0 \,, \frac{\partial p_j}{\partial z_t} = 0$$

Then the quantity elasticity of demand with respect to z's is:

$$\frac{\partial \ln q_j}{\partial z_t} = \frac{\partial w_j}{\partial z_t} \frac{x}{p_j} \frac{p_j}{w_j x} = \frac{1}{w_j} \frac{\partial w_j}{\partial z_t}$$

Appendix table 1

Robustness check: OLS estimated expenditures (percent)

	Budget share of fruits	Budget share of vegetables
LILA	-2.93***	-5.31*** (0.93)
	(0.77)	
LILA	-5.92***	-7.36*** (1.41)
	(1.17)	
Dist_w	-0.012	-0.34***
	(0.042)	(0.051)
LILA * distance	0.39	0.34**
	(0.18)	(0.15)

Coefficients statistically significant at 1% level are marked bold. LILA = Low-income, low-access. OLS = Ordinary Least Squares.
Source: Computed by USDA, Economic Research Service.

References

Amemiya, T. (1979). "The estimation of a simultaneous-equation Tobit model," *International Economic Review*: 169-181.

Anderson, M. L., and D. A. Matsa (2011). "Are restaurants really supersizing America?" *American Economic Journal: Applied Economics* 152-188.

Aussenberg, R. A. (2014). *SNAP and Related Nutrition Provisions of the 2014 Farm Bill* (P.L. 113-79), Congressional Research Service Report.

Beaulac, J., E. Kristjansson, and S. Cummins (2009). "Peer Reviewed: A Systematic Review of Food Deserts, 1966-2007," *Preventing Chronic Disease* 6(3).

Block, D., and J. Kouba (2006). "A comparison of the availability and affordability of a market basket in two communities in the Chicago area," *Public Health Nutrition* 9(07): 837-845.

Broda, C., E. Leibtag, and D. E. Weinstein (2009). "The role of prices in measuring the poor's living standards," *The Journal of Economic Perspectives* 23(2): 77-97.

Chen, S., R. J. Florax, S. Snyder, and C. C. Miller (2010). "Obesity and access to chain grocers," *Economic Geography* 86(4): 431-452.

Chen, S.E., R.J. Florax, and S.D. Snyder (2013). "Obesity and fast food in urban markets: a new approach using geo-referenced micro data," *Health Economics* 22(7): 835-856.

Chung, C., and S.L. Myers (1999). "Do the poor pay more for food? An analysis of grocery store availability and food price disparities," *Journal of Consumer Affairs* 33(2):276-296.

Cummins, S., F. Flint, and S.A. Matthews (2014). "New neighborhood grocery store increased awareness of food access but did not alter dietary habits or obesity,." *Health Affairs* 33(2): 283-291.

Diewert, W. E. (1976). "Exact and superlative index numbers," *Journal of Econometrics* 4(2): 115-145.

Dutko, Paula, Michele Ver Ploeg, and Tracey Farrigan. *Characteristics and Influential Factors of Food Deserts*, ERR-140, U.S. Department of Agriculture, Economic Research Service, August 2012.

Edin, K., M. Boyd, J. Mabli, J. Ohls, J. Worthington, S. Greene, N. Redel, and S. Sridharan (2013). SNAP Food Security In-Depth Interview Study, Mathematica Policy Research.

Einav, L., E. Leibtag, and A. Nevo (2008). *On the Accuracy of Nielsen Homescan Data*. U.S. Department of Agriculture, Economic Research Service. ERR-69.

Einav, L., E. Leibtag, and A. Nevo (2010). "Recording discrepancies in Nielsen Homescan data: Are they present and do they matter?" Quant Marc Econ 8(2): 207-239.

Ford, P.B., and D. A. Dzewaltowski (2008). "Disparities in obesity prevalence due to variation in the retail food environment: three testable hypotheses,." *Nutrition Reviews* 66(4): 216-228.

Holsten, J. E. (2009). "Obesity and the community food environment: a systematic review," *Public Health Nutrition* 12(03): 397-405.

Horowitz, C. R., K. A. Colson, P.L. Hebert, and K. Lancaster (2004). "Barriers to buying healthy foods for people with diabetes: evidence of environmental disparities," *American Journal of Public Health* 94(9).

Lewbel, A., and K. Pendakur (2009). "Tricks with Hicks: The EASI demand system," *The American Economic Review*: 827-863.

Lin, B.-H., M. Ver Ploeg, P. Kasteridis, and S. T. Yen (2014). "The roles of food prices and food access in determining food purchases of low-income households," *Journal of Policy Modeling* 36(5): 938-952.

Maryland House Bill 451 (2014). Neighborhood Business Development Program - Financial Assistance for Food Deserts. HB 451. Maryland General Assembly, Department of Legislative Services: 1-7.

Moore, L. V., and A. V. Diez Roux (2006). "Associations of neighborhood characteristics with the location and type of food stores," *American Journal of Public Health* 96(2): 325-331.

Moore, L. V., A. V. D. Roux, J. A. Nettleton, and D. R. Jacobs (2008). "Associations of the Local Food Environment with Diet Quality—A Comparison of Assessments Based on Surveys and Geographic Information Systems: The Multi-Ethnic Study of Atherosclerosis." *American Journal of Epidemiology* 167(8): 917-924.

Morland, K., A. V. Diez Roux, and S. Wing (2006). "Supermarkets, other food stores, and obesity: the atherosclerosis risk in communities study," *American Journal of Preventive Medicine* 30(4): 333-339.

Morland, K., S. Wing, A. Diez Roux, and C. Poole (2002). "Neighborhood characteristics associated with the location of food stores and food service places," *American Journal of Preventive Medicine* 22(1): 23-29.

Newey, W. K. (1987). "Efficient estimation of limited dependent variable models with endogenous explanatory variables," *Journal of Econometrics* 36(3): 231-250.

Park, C. W., E. S. Iyer, and D. C. Smith (1989). "The effects of situational factors on in-store grocery shopping behavior: the role of store environment and time available for shopping," *Journal of Consumer Research*: 422-433.

Pearson, T., J. Russell, M. J. Campbell, and M. E. Barker (2005). "Do 'food deserts' influence fruit and vegetable consumption?—A cross-sectional study," *Appetite* 45(2): 195-197.

Rose, D., and R. Richards (2004). "Food store access and household fruit and vegetable use among participants in the US Food Stamp Program," *Public Health Nutrition* 7(08): 1081-1088.

Sharkey, J. R., C. M. Johnson, and W. R. Dean (2010). "Food access and perceptions of the community and household food environment as correlates of fruit and vegetable intake among rural seniors," *BMC Geriatrics* 10(1): 32.

U.S. Centers for Disease Control and Prevention (2012). *State Initiatives Supporting Healthier Food Retail: An Overview of the National Landscape*, National Center for Chronic Disease Prevention and Health Promotion: 1-10. U.S. Department of Agriculture (2015). "Food Access Research Atlas."

U.S. Department of Labor, Bureau of Labor Statistics (2011). *Consumer Expenditures - 2010*. USDL-11-1395.

Ver Ploeg, V. Breneman, T. Farrigan, K. Hamrick, D. Hopkins, P. Kaufman, B.-H. Lin, M. Nord, T. Smith, and R. Williams (2009). "Access to affordable and nutritious food: measuring and under- standing food deserts and their consequences." Report to Congress. USDA, Economic Research Service.

Ver Ploeg, Michele, Vince Breneman, Paula Dutko, Ryan Williams, Samantha Snyder, Chris Dicken, and Phil Kaufman (2012). *Access to Affordable and Nutritious Food: Updated Estimates of Distance to Supermarkets Using 2010 Data*, ERR-143, U.S. Department of Agriculture, Economic Research Service, Nov.

Volpe, R., A. Okrent, and E. Leibtag (2013). "The effect of supercenter-format stores on the healthfulness of consumers' grocery purchases," *American Journal of Agricultural Economics* 95(3).

Wilde, P., J. Llobrera, and M. Ver Ploeg (2014). "Population Density, Poverty, and Food Retail Access in the United States: An Empirical Approach," *International Food and Agribusiness Management Review*, Volume 17, Special Issue A.

Zhen, C., E. A. Finkelstein, J. M. Nonnemaker, S. A. Karns, and J. E. Todd (2013). "Predicting the effects of sugar-sweetened beverage taxes on food and beverage demand in a large demand system," *American Journal of Agricultural Economics* 96(1).

Zhen, C., M. K. Wohlgenant, S. Karns, and P. Kaufman (2010). "Habit formation and demand for sugar-sweetened beverages," *American Journal of Agricultural Economics* 93(1).

Questions for Discussion

1. What was the exigence for this study? In other words, why did the USDA conduct this research?

2. How does the authoring organization, the USDA, affect the ethos of this text?

3. What did you think about the results of this study? Are they surprising? Expected? What follow-up study would you want to do if you were on the research team?

Fighting Food Insecurity on Campus

Christopher Nellum

Higher Education Today, June 2015

Christopher Nellum is a senior policy analyst for the American Council of Education's (ACE) Center for Policy and Research Strategy. According to their website, *Higher Education Today* is a blog published by ACE which is perhaps the most well-known higher education association in the U.S. and is supported by the presidents of more than 1800 higher education institutions in the United States. This article addresses the issue of college students' food insecurity, meaning students who have little or no access to food due to economic circumstances. According to the USDA, college students must be a U.S. citizen and be in a work-study program, work at least 20 hours a week, or have a dependent to qualify for SNAP (formerly known as food stamps). Therefore, many students are ineligible for this aid and have limited food resources. Nellum addresses these challenges and suggests methods for improvement.

College and university administrators and leaders around the country increasingly are realizing that undergraduate students are among the millions of Americans who experience food insecurity, or a lack of resources to obtain nutritional food.

The numbers are striking. *Feeding America*, a national nonprofit network of food banks that provides food assistance to 46.5 million individuals and 15.5 million households, estimates that nearly half (49.3 percent) of its clients in college must choose between educational expenses (i.e., tuition, books and supplies, rent) and food annually, and that 21 percent did so for a full 12 months.

While we lack national data on all college students, these data provide insight on the extent of the problem.

Many college students who experience food insecurity struggle to reach milestones such as year-to-year persistence and certificate or degree completion and need additional institutional support to continue their studies.

In response, some of the country's largest systems of higher education have conducted or are planning studies to better understand food insecurity and poverty among its students:

The City University of New York found that about two in five (40 percent) of its 274,000 students experienced food insecurity in the past 12 months; notably those numbers were higher among students who worked at least 20 hours per week and for Black and Latino students (2010).

The University of California (UC) found that roughly one in four (25 percent) of the approximately 150,000 undergraduate students at the nine campuses skipped meals to save money (2014). UC President Janet Napolitano recently allocated $75,000 to each campus to improve food security efforts.

The California State University (CSU), the largest four-year public university system in the country, earlier this year funded a $100,000 research project that will assess the number of undergraduates across all 23 CSU campuses who experience food insecurity. The system serves about 390,000 undergraduates, many of whom are low income and students of color.

To suggest that an undergraduate student is unable to access nutritional food likely conjures up our own memories of occasionally eating ramen noodles for dinner before studying at the library or joining friends at a party. The profile of college students today, however, is much different than that of undergraduates from previous generations.

More of today's college students are non-traditional: they tend to be older, first generation, from lower-income and communities of color, and attend community colleges. Growing numbers of undergraduates are also post-traditional students who juggle family responsibilities

Increase in CUFBA Alliance Food Banks & Pantries, 1993-2015

	No. of Food Banks & Pantries
1993-2007	1
2008	4
2009	9
2010	35
2011	64
2012	88
2013	117
2014	121
2015	184

Source: CUFBA/MSU Food Bank

and part- or full-time work while they pursue a college-level certification or degree. These students also face other circumstances that make paying for a college education more challenging, including a decade of state retrenchment from funding public higher education and a significant rise in the cost of tuition, coupled with a general increase in the cost of goods and services.

In addition to shifting student demographics and decreased state funding, another sign of the changing times is the growth in the number of campus-based food pantries that are members of the College and University Food Bank Alliance (CUFBA). The Alliance provides support, training and resources to the almost 200 food banks and pantries that primarily serve college students across the nation.

The rise in food pantries at colleges and universities seems appropriate since the increased presence of post-traditional students on college campuses also means that our notions of postsecondary opportunity, access, and equity should be interrogated and expanded to be inclusive of these students and their needs. Ensuring college affordability broadly is essential so that low-income and students of color have access to affordable, quality options for an undergraduate degree, won't be inequitably saddled with debt, and once enrolled, do not have to choose between pursuing that education and meeting basic needs.

The upcoming reauthorization of the Higher Education Act (HEA) presents an opportunity to rethink not only issues related to college financing and affordability, but financial aid and its ability to adequately cover cost of living expenses. The Senate Health, Education, Labor, and Pensions (HELP) Committee hearing held earlier this month is early evidence that college affordability will be an issue at the center of HEA debates.

While food insecurity issues might not be central to HEA reauthorization hearings, postsecondary leaders, researchers and policymakers can take this opportunity to consider how to improve institutional responses to food insecurity and our understanding of the students who make decisions between food and educational expenses, and how to advocate for making college affordable for post-traditional students.

References

Cady, Clare L. (2014). *Food insecurity as a student issue.* Journal of College & Character, 15(4), 265-272.

Feeding America, *Hunger in America 2014*, National Report. August 2014.

The Campaign for a Healthy CUNY. *Food insecurity at CUNY: Results from a survey of CUNY undergraduate students.* Retrieved from www.gc.cuny.edu

Uhlenjamp, M. (2015). *CSULB Awarded $100,000 Grant to Study Homelessness, Food Instability Among Students in the CSU.* Retrieved from www.csulb.edu

Rosenberg, A. (2015). *UC focuses on student food security.* Retrieved from www.universityofcalifornia.edu

Soares, L. (2013). Post-traditional leaders and the transformation of postsecondary education: A manifesto for college leaders. Retrieved from www.acenet.edu

Westat. (2014). "*Hunger in America 2014: Household Educational Spending Tradeoffs by Adult Student.*" Unpublished data from WesDaX (Westat's intranet-based data analysis system) for Feeding America. Rockville, MD: Author.

Questions for Discussion

1. What are some of the main effects of food insecurity on college students?

2. Who is Nellum's audience, and what suggestions does he provide to help alleviate the problem?

3. What do you know about access to food pantries and/or other resources on your campus? What do you think your university could do to improve access to food on campus?

Excerpt from *The Omnivore's Dilemma*

Michael Pollan

The Omnivore's Dilemma: A Natural History of Four Meals, 2006

Michael Pollan is an acclaimed, best-selling author of *In Defense of Food: An Eater's Manifesto* (2008) and *The Omnivore's Dilemma: A Natural History of Four Meals* (2006). He is featured in the controversial documentary, *Food, Inc.* (2010), which catalogs the negative impacts of modern day industrial agriculture on the environment, domestic animals, and humans. This article is an excerpt from *The New York Times* bestseller, *The Omnivore's Dilemma*, which is often credited with changing the way readers view the ecology of eating. He asks the seemingly simple question: What should we have for dinner? Tracing from source to table each of the food chains that sustain us—whether industrial or organic, alternative or processed—he develops a portrait of the American way of eating. The result is a sweeping, surprising exploration of the hungers that have shaped our evolution, and of the profound implications our food choices have for the health of our species and the future of the planet.

The Consumer: A Republic of Fat

In the early years of the nineteenth century, Americans began drinking more than they ever had before or since, embarking on a collective bender that confronted the young republic with its first major public health crisis—the obesity epidemic of its day. Corn whiskey, suddenly superabundant and cheap, became the drink of choice, and in 1820 the typical American was putting away half a pint of the stuff every day. That comes to more than five gallons of spirits a year for every man, woman, and child in America. The figure today is less than one.

As the historian W. J. Rorabaugh tells the story in *The Alcoholic Republic*, we drank the hard stuff at breakfast, lunch, and dinner, before work and after and very often during. Employers were expected to supply spirits over the course of the workday; in fact, the modern coffee break began as a late-morning whiskey break called "the elevenses." (Just to pronounce it makes you sound tipsy.) Except for a brief respite Sunday morning in church, Americans simply did not gather—whether for a barn raising or quilting bee, corn husking or political rally—without passing the whiskey jug. Visitors from Europe—hardly models of sobriety themselves—marveled at the free flow of American spirits. "Come on then, if you love toping," the journalist William Cobbett wrote his fellow Englishmen in a dispatch from America."For here you may drink yourself blind at the price of sixpence."

The results of all this toping were entirely predictable: a rising tide of public drunkenness, violence, and family abandonment, and a spike in alcohol-related diseases. Several of the Founding Fathers—including George Washington, Thomas Jefferson, and John Adams—denounced the excesses of "the Alcoholic Republic," inaugurating an American quarrel over drinking that would culminate a century later in Prohibition.

But the outcome of our national drinking binge is not nearly as relevant to our own situation as its underlying cause. Which, put simply, was this: American farmers were producing far too much corn. This was particularly true in the newly settled regions west of the Appalachians, where fertile, virgin soils yielded one bumper crop after another. A mountain of surplus corn piled up in the Ohio River Valley. Much as today, the astounding productivity of American farmers proved to be their own worst enemy, as well as a threat to public health. For when yields rise, the market is flooded with grain, and its price collapses. What happens next? The excess biomass works like a vacuum in reverse: Sooner or later, clever marketers will figure out a way to induce the human omnivore to consume the surfeit of cheap calories.

As it is today, the clever thing to do with all that cheap corn was to process it—specifically, to distill it into alcohol. The Appalachian range made it difficult and expensive to transport surplus corn from the lightly settled Ohio River Valley to the more populous markets of the East, so farmers turned their corn into whiskey—a more compact and portable, and less perishable, value-added commodity. Before long the price of whiskey plummeted to the point that people could afford to drink it by the pint. Which is precisely what they did.

The Alcoholic Republic has long since given way to the Republic of Fat; we're eating today much the way we drank then, and for some of the same reasons. According to the surgeon general, obesity today is officially an epidemic; it is arguably the most pressing public health problem we face, costing the health care system an estimated $90 billion a year. Three of every five Americans are overweight; one of every five is obese. The disease formerly known as adult-onset diabetes has had to be renamed Type II diabetes since it now occurs so frequently in children. A recent study in the *Journal of the American Medical Association* predicts that a child born in 2000 has a one-in-three chance of developing diabetes. (An African American child's chances are two in five.) Because of diabetes and all the other health problems that accompany obesity, today's children may turn out to be the first generation of Americans whose life expectancy will actually be shorter than that of their parents. The problem is not limited to America: The United Nations reported that in 2000 the number of people suffering from overnutrition—a billion—had officially surpassed the number suffering from malnutrition—800 million.

You hear plenty of explanations for humanity's expanding waistline, all of them plausible. Changes in lifestyle (we're more sedentary; we eat out more). Affluence (more people can afford a high-fat Western diet). Poverty (healthier whole foods cost more). Technology (fewer of us use our bodies in our work; at home, the remote control keeps us pinned to the couch). Clever marketing (supersized portions; advertising to children). Changes in diet (more fats; more carbohydrates; more processed foods).

All these explanations are true, as far as they go. But it pays to go a little further, to search for the cause behind the causes. Which, very simply, is this: When food is abundant and cheap, people will eat more of it and get fat. Since 1977 an American's average daily intake of calories has jumped by more than 10 percent. Those two hundred calories have to go somewhere, and absent an increase in physical activity (which hasn't happened), they end up being stored away in fat cells in our bodies. But the important question is, Where, exactly, did all those extra calories come from in the first place? And the answer to that question takes us back to the source of almost all calories: the farm.

Most researchers trace America's rising rates of obesity to the 1970s. This was, of course, the same decade that America embraced a cheap food farm policy and began dismantling forty years of programs designed to prevent overproduction. Earl Butz, you'll recall, sought to drive up agricultural yields in order to drive down the price of the industrial food chain's raw materials, particularly corn and soybeans. It worked: The price of food is no longer a political issue. Since the Nixon administration, farmers in the United States have managed to produce 500 additional calories per person every day (up from 3, 300, already substantially more than we need); each of us is, heroically, managing to put away 200 of those surplus calories at the end of their trip up the food chain. Presumably the other 300 are being dumped overseas, or turned (once again!) into ethyl alcohol: ethanol for our cars.

The parallels with the alcoholic republic of two hundred years ago are hard to miss. Before the changes in lifestyle, before the clever marketing, comes the mountain of cheap corn. Corn accounts for most of the surplus calories we're growing and most of the surplus calories we're eating. As then, the smart thing to do with all that surplus grain is to process it, transform the cheap commodity into a value-added consumer product—a denser and more durable package of calories. In the 1820s the processing options were basically two: You could turn your corn into pork or alcohol. Today there are hundreds of things a processor can do with corn: They can use it to make everything from chicken nuggets and Big Macs to emulsifiers and nutraceuticals. Yet since the human desire for sweetness surpasses even our desire for intoxication, the cleverest thing to do with a bushel of corn is to refine it into thirty three pounds of high-fructose corn syrup.

That at least is what we're doing with about 530 million bushels of the annual corn harvest—turning it into 17.5 billion pounds of high-fructose corn syrup. Considering that the human animal did not taste this particular food until 1980, for HFCS to have become the leading source of sweetness in our diet stands as a notable achievement on the part of the corn-refining industry, not to mention this remarkable plant. (But then, plants have always known that one of the surest paths to evolutionary success is by gratifying the mammalian omnivore's innate desire for sweetness.) Since 1985, an American's annual consumption of HFCS has gone from forty-five pounds to sixty-six pounds. You might think that this growth would have been offset by a decline in sugar consumption, since HFCS often replaces sugar, but that didn't happen: During the same period our consumption of refined sugar actually went up by five pounds. What this means is that we're eating and drinking all that high-fructose corn syrup *on top* of the sugars we were already consuming. In fact, since 1985 our consumption of all added sugars—cane, beet, HFCS, glucose, honey, maple syrup, whatever—has climbed from 128 pounds to 158 pounds per person.

This is what makes high-fructose corn syrup such a clever thing to do with a bushel of corn: By inducing people to consume more calories than they otherwise might, it gets them to really chomp through the corn surplus. Corn sweetener is to the republic of fat what corn whiskey was to the alcoholic republic. Read the food labels in your kitchen and you'll find that HFCS has insinuated itself into every corner of the pantry: not just into our soft drinks and snack foods, where you would expect to find it, but into the ketchup and mustard, the breads and cereals, the relishes and crackers, the hot dogs and hams.

But it is in soft drinks that we consume most of our sixty-six pounds of high-fructose corn syrup, and to the red-letter dates in the natural history of *Zea mays*—right up there with teosinte's catastrophic sexual mutation, Columbus's introduction of maize to the court of Queen Isabella in 1493, and Henry Wallace's first F-1 hybrid seed in 1927—we must now add the year 1980. That was the year corn first became an ingredient in Coca-Cola. By 1984, Coca-Cola and Pepsi had switched over entirely from sugar to high-fructose corn syrup. Why? Because HFCS was a few cents cheaper than sugar (thanks in part to tariffs on imported sugarcane secured by the corn refiners) and consumers didn't seem to notice the substitution.

The soft drink makers' switch should have been a straightforward, zero-sum trade-off between corn and sugarcane (both, incidentally, C-4 grasses), but it wasn't: We soon began swilling a lot more soda and therefore corn sweetener. The reason isn't far to seek: Like corn whiskey in the 1820s, the price of soft drinks plummeted. Note, however, that Coca-Cola and Pepsi did not simply cut the price of a bottle of cola. That would only have hurt profit margins, for how many people are going to buy a second soda just because it cost a few cents less? The companies had a much better idea: They would supersize their sodas. Since a soft drink's main raw material —corn sweetener—was now so cheap, why not get people to pay just a few pennies more for a substantially bigger bottle? Drop the price per ounce, but sell a lot more ounces. So began the transformation of the svelte eight-ounce Coke bottle into the chubby twenty-ouncer dispensed by most soda machines today.

But the soda makers don't deserve credit for the invention of supersizing. That distinction belongs to a man named David Wallerstein. Until his death in 1993, Wallerstein served on the board of directors at McDonald's, but in the fifties and sixties he worked for a chain of movie theaters in Texas, where he labored to expand sales of soda and popcorn—the high-markup items that theaters depend on for their profitability. As the story is told in John Love's official history of McDonald's, Wallerstein tried everything he could think of to goose up sales—two-for-one deals, matinee specials—but found he simply could not induce customers to buy more than one soda and one bag of popcorn. He thought he knew why: Going for seconds makes people feel piggish.

Wallerstein discovered that people *would* spring for more popcorn and soda—a lot more—as long as it came in a single gigantic serving. Thus was born the two-quart bucket of popcorn, the sixty-four-ounce Big Gulp, and, in time, the Big Mac and the jumbo fries, though Ray Kroc himself took some convincing. In 1968, Wallerstein went to work for McDonald's, but try as he might, he couldn't convince Kroc, the company's founder, of supersizing's magic powers.

"If people want more fries," Kroc told him, "they can buy two bags." Wallerstein patiently explained that McDonald's customers did want more but were reluctant to buy a second bag. "They don't want to look like gluttons."

Kroc remained skeptical, so Wallerstein went looking for proof. He began staking out McDonald's outlets in and around Chicago, observing how people ate. He saw customers noisily draining their sodas, and digging infinitesimal bits of salt and burnt spud out of their little bags of French fries. After Wallerstein presented his findings, Kroc relented, approved supersized portions, and the dramatic spike in sales confirmed the marketer's hunch. Deep cultural taboos against gluttony—one of the seven deadly sins, after all—had been holding us back.

Wallerstein's dubious achievement was to devise the dietary equivalent of a papal dispensation: Supersize it! He had discovered the secret to expanding the (supposedly) fixed human stomach.

One might think that people would stop eating and drinking these gargantuan portions as soon as they felt full, but it turns out hunger doesn't work that way. Researchers have found that people (and animals) presented with large portions will eat up to 30 percent more than they would otherwise. Human appetite, it turns out, is surprisingly elastic, which makes excellent evolutionary sense: It behooved our hunter-gatherer ancestors to feast whenever the opportunity presented itself, allowing them to build up reserves of fat against future famine. Obesity researchers call this trait the "thrifty gene." And while the gene represents a useful adaptation in an environment of food scarcity and unpredictability, it's a disaster in an environment of fast food abundance, when the opportunity to feast presents itself 24/7. Our bodies are storing reserves of fat against a famine that never comes.

But if evolution has left the modern omnivore vulnerable to the blandishments of supersizing, the particular nutrients he's most likely to encounter in those supersized portions—lots of added sugar and fat—make the problem that much worse. Like most other warm-blooded creatures, humans have inherited a preference for energy-dense foods, a preference reflected in the sweet tooth shared by most mammals. Natural selection predisposed us to the taste of sugar and fat (its texture as well as taste) because sugars and fats offer the most energy (which is what a calorie is) per bite. Yet in nature—in whole foods—we seldom encounter these nutrients in the concentrations we now find them in in processed foods: You won't find a fruit with anywhere near the amount of fructose in a soda, or a piece of animal flesh with quite as much fat as a chicken nugget.

You begin to see why processing foods is such a good strategy for getting people to eat more of them. The power of food science lies in its ability to break foods down into their nutrient parts and then reassemble them in specific ways that, in effect, push our evolutionary buttons, fooling the omnivore's inherited food selection system. Add fat or sugar to anything and it's going to taste better on the tongue of an animal that natural selection has wired to seek out energy-dense foods. Animal studies prove the point: Rats presented with solutions of pure sucrose or tubs of pure lard—goodies they seldom encounter in nature—will gorge themselves sick. Whatever nutritional wisdom the rats are born with breaks down when faced with sugars and fats in unnatural concentrations—nutrients ripped from their natural context, which is to say, from those things we call foods. Food systems can cheat by exaggerating their energy density, tricking a sensory apparatus that evolved to deal with markedly less dense whole foods.

It is the amped-up energy density of processed foods that gets omnivores like us into trouble. Type II diabetes typically occurs when the body's mechanism for managing glucose simply wears out from overuse. Just about everything we eat sooner or later winds up in the blood as molecules of glucose, but sugars and simple starches turn to glucose faster than anything else. Type II diabetes and obesity are exactly what you would expect to see in a mammal whose environment has overwhelmed its metabolism with energy-dense foods.

This begs the question of why the problem has gotten so much worse in recent years. It turns out the price of a calorie of sugar or fat has plummeted since the 1970s. One reason that obesity and diabetes become more prevalent the further down the socioeconomic scale you look is that the industrial food chain has made energy-dense foods the cheapest foods in the market, when measured in terms of cost per calorie. A recent study in the *American Journal of Clinical Nutrition* compared the "energy cost" of different foods in the supermarket. The researchers found that a dollar could buy 1,200 calories of potato chips and cookies; spent on a whole food like carrots, the same dollar buys only 250 calories. On the beverage aisle, you can buy 875 calories of soda for a dollar, or 170 calories of fruit juice from concentrate. It makes good economic sense that people with limited money to spend on food would spend it on the cheapest calories they can find, especially when the cheapest calories—fats and sugars—are precisely the ones offering the biggest neurobiological rewards.

Corn is not the only source of cheap energy in the supermarket—much of the fat added to processed foods comes from soybeans—but it is by far the most important. As George Naylor said, growing corn is the most efficient way to get energy—calories—from an acre of Iowa farmland. That corn-made calorie can find its way into our bodies in the form of an animal fat, a sugar, or a starch, such is the protean nature of the carbon in that big kernel. But as productive and protean as the corn plant is, finally it is a set of human choices that have made these molecules quite as cheap as they have become: a quarter century of farm policies designed to encourage the overproduction of this crop and hardly any other. Very simply, we subsidize high-fructose corn syrup in this country, but not carrots. While the surgeon general is raising alarms over the epidemic of obesity, the president is signing farm bills designed to keep the river of cheap corn flowing, guaranteeing that the cheapest calories in the supermarket will continue to be the unhealthiest.

Questions for Discussion

1. The sub-title for this excerpt from Michael Pollan's book is entitled The Consumer: A Republic of Fat. In the excerpt he states that "Corn sweetener is to the republic of fat what corn whiskey was to the alcoholic republic." Explain the historical context and significance of this statement.

2. In this excerpt Pollan expresses a "tongue in cheek" mocking admiration for the seemingly endless ways in which the American farmer and the agricultural industry, supported and subsidized by government, have been able to increase corn production to excess, and found innovative ways to incorporate the excess product into the American diet. What effect does this rhetorical style of sarcasm have on readers? Is it effective?

3. If you consider Pollan's argument about ecologies of eating alongside McLean-Meyinsse' et al.'s examination of college students' eating habits, what connections can you make between food choices in young adulthood and lasting effects in terms of habits and health?

More Hospitals Are Ditching Antibiotics In The Meat They Serve

Eliza Barclay

National Public Radio, January 2016

> Eliza Barclay is a correspondent for National Public Radio who works primarily with issues relating to food. Her article examines hospitals' reactions to the growing problem with superbugs (antibiotic resistant bacteria). According to the CDC, roughly two million people contract a superbug annually and nearly 23,000 of those people die. The CDC reports that using antibiotics unnecessarily is the leading cause of superbugs, and so our exposure to antibiotics through the meat we eat is the exigence for hospitals' action against buying meat which contain antibiotics. Farmers and ranchers feed their animals antibiotics to make them gain more weight, and *Frontline* found that roughly 15-17 million pounds of antibiotics are used annually by both people and animals. The current debate concerns the impact of this consumption on human health.

Every year some 2 million Americans get infections from antibiotic-resistant bacteria, and 23,000 of them die from these superbugs.

Superbugs are mostly a hospital problem: They're where these pathogens are often born and spread, and where the infected come for help. But hospitals are not where the majority of antibiotics sold in the U.S. are used.

Food and Drug Administration data show that 62 percent of antibiotics important for human health are sold to food animal producers and used on farms. And in December, the agency noted that antibiotics for use on the farm increased in 2014, including antibiotics important in human medicine.

Concern about the livestock industry's overuse of antibiotics has led a number of health care institutions to start choosing meat from animals raised without antibiotics whenever they can. According to Practice Greenhealth, a nonprofit that's helping the health care industry on this issue, more than 400 U.S. hospitals are working toward a goal of making 20 percent of their meat purchases "antibiotic-free." And around a dozen hospitals have already switched the majority of their chicken purchases to antibiotic-free.

"Health care is really voicing their demand for [antibiotic-free meat] products," says Hillary Bisnett, a food expert for Practice Greenhealth and Health Care Without Harm. "Hospitals understand antibiotic resistance, and they're being asked to steward their own use of antibiotics. So it's very easy for them to say, 'Livestock producers need to be doing their part, too.'"

Is meat from animals raised without antibiotics really better? Public health groups who follow this issue, like the Pew Charitable Trusts, say it can be safer. Of greatest concern is that when chicken, hog, or cattle farmers use drugs to promote growth or prevent disease in their animals, they'll overuse the drugs and create resistant bacteria, like *Salmonella* and *Campylobacter*, that could make people sick.

Various studies, including ones by George Washington University microbiologist Lance Price and advocacy groups like *Consumer Reports* and the Environmental Working Group, have found resistant bacteria on samples of beef, pork, turkey and chicken from supermarkets. If meat contaminated this way isn't cooked properly, the resistant bacteria can infect humans. And if the pathogens are resistant to antibiotics designed to kill them, then doctors may have few tools to treat the infections.

Among the hospitals that have made antibiotic-free meat a priority for their food services is Hackensack University Medical Center in New Jersey. But according to Kyle Tafuri, senior sustainability adviser at the hospital, it wasn›t easy to figure out how to switch 100 percent of their chicken purchases to antibiotic-free.

At first, the hospital's distributor said it didn't have enough antibiotic-free chicken to sell the hospital. But over the course of a few years, and after several meetings with the distributor and a group purchasing organization, they were able to find a way to make it work.

Eventually, Tafuri says, the supplier, Perdue, agreed to specially ship the chicken up to the distributor's warehouse just for the hospital. "It took a lot of work to make this happen and a lot of pushing, but hospitals should be inclined to push the industry to make a change," he says.

His hospital pays 30 percent more for Perdue's antibiotic-free chicken under its Harvestland brand, but Tafuri says it's worth it to his institution to be able to offer a "higher quality and healthier product." He's now working on sourcing more antibiotic-free pork and beef, but he says they're dramatically more expensive, and more difficult to source.

Chris Linamen, executive chef at Overlake Medical Center in Bellevue, Wash., says he's managed to find antibiotic-free sources for 79 percent of his total meat purchases. (next 2 sentences s/b in this graf)"The biggest challenge is budget," says Linamen. He's also struggled to find antibiotic-free sources for specific items, like chicken strips, sausage patties, duck, and lamb.

Part of what explains Linamen and Tafuri's success in getting more antibiotic-free meat on the plates they serve is the fact that neither of their institutions is locked into a contract with a big food service management company, like Aramark, Sodexo or Compass, says Bisnett of Practice Greenhealth. Many other hospitals tell her they would like to source more antibiotic-free meat but can't, because their contracts do not allow them to.

The biggest food-service management companies have very limited supply of these items. And the hospitals "don't have flexibility in changing vendors or supply," says Bisnett.

"That's why it's really important that the food service sector get more involved with this issue, too, since one third of hospitals in the U.S. have food service managed by Sodexo, Compass or Aramark," she says.

Hospitals are far from the only big buyers to get interested in sourcing antibiotic-free meat and apply pressure to biggest meat producers, like Perdue, Tyson, JBS, and Smithfield, to make more of it available. Several restaurant and retail chains in 2015 committed to sourcing more antibiotic-free meat, including McDonalds, Subway, Panera, CostCo, and Chick-fil-A. Some have committed to sourcing antibiotic-free poultry, while others have also given suppliers of beef and pork a mandatory timetable to go antibiotic-free as well.

Questions for Discussion

1. Why do livestock producers use antibiotics, and what are the effects of overusing antibiotics in livestock?

2. How is the increased cost and limited supply of antibiotic-free meat a social issue as well as an economic issue?

3. How might hospitals' involvement in purchasing antibiotic-free meat affect the industry?

The Trouble with Fries

Malcolm Gladwell

The New Yorker, March 2001

Malcolm Gladwell has been a staff writer at *The New Yorker* since 1996, before which he was a reporter at the *Washington Post*, according to his profile on *The New Yorker* website. He is an award winning author and speaker, and has published five books. These include *The Tipping Point, Blink, Outliers, David and Goliath,* and *What the Dog Saw,* which is a compilation of his *New Yorker* articles. According to the website famousauthors.org, all of his books have appeared on *The New York Times* bestsellers list. His works address research in the topics of sociology and psychology. Additionally, the author has been awarded honors such as the American Sociological Associations' first Award for Excellence in the Reporting of Social Issues as well as honorary degrees from both the University of Waterloo and the University of Toronto. Critics often offer mixed reviews on Gladwell's work. He has been criticized for his reliance on anecdotal evidence and his tendency to make broad claims. For instance, the *New Republic* writes that Gladwell believes that, "a perfect anecdote proves a fatuous rule." Meanwhile a *New York Times* book review of *Blink* by David Leonardt claims that, "in the vast world of nonfiction writing, Malcolm Gladwell is as close to a singular talent as exists today."

Fast food is killing us. Can it be fixed?

In 1954, a man named Ray Kroc, who made his living selling the five-spindle Multimixer milkshake machine, began hearing about a hamburger stand in San Bernardino, California. This particular restaurant, he was told, had no fewer than eight of his machines in operation, meaning that it could make forty shakes simultaneously. Kroc was astounded. He flew from Chicago to Los Angeles, and drove to San Bernardino, sixty miles away, where he found a small octagonal building on a corner lot. He sat in his car and watched as the workers showed up for the morning shift. They were in starched white shirts and paper hats, and moved with a purposeful discipline. As lunchtime approached, customers began streaming into the parking lot, lining up for bags of hamburgers. Kroc approached a strawberry blonde in a yellow convertible.

"How often do you come here?" he asked.

"Anytime I am in the neighborhood," she replied, and, Kroc would say later, "it was not her sex appeal but the obvious relish with which she devoured the hamburger that made my pulse begin to hammer with excitement." He came back the next morning, and this time set up inside the kitchen, watching the griddle man, the food preparers, and, above all, the French-fry operation, because it was the French fries that truly captured his imagination. They were made from top-quality oblong Idaho russets, eight ounces apiece, deep-fried to a golden brown, and salted with a shaker that, as he put it, kept going like a Salvation Army girl's tambourine. They were crispy on the outside and buttery soft on the inside, and that day Kroc had a vision of a chain of restaurants, just like the one in San Bernardino, selling golden fries from one end of the country to the other. He asked the two brothers who owned the hamburger stand if he could buy their franchise rights. They said yes. Their names were Mac and Dick McDonald.

Ray Kroc was the great visionary of American fast food, the one who brought the lessons of the manufacturing world to the restaurant business. Before the fifties, it was impossible, in most American towns, to buy fries of consistent quality. Ray Kroc was the man who changed that. "The french fry," he once wrote, "would become almost sacrosanct for me, its preparation a ritual to be followed religiously." A potato that has too great a percentage of water—and potatoes, even the standard Idaho russet burbank, vary widely in their water content—will come out soggy at the end of the frying process. It was Kroc, back in the fifties, who sent out field men, armed with hydrometers, to make sure that all his suppliers were producing potatoes in the optimal solids range of twenty to twenty-three per cent. Freshly harvested potatoes, furthermore, are rich in sugars, and if you slice them up and deep-fry them the sugars will caramelize and brown the outside of the fry long before the inside is cooked. To make a crisp French fry, a potato has to be stored at a warm temperature for several weeks in order to convert those sugars to starch. Here Kroc led the way as well, mastering the art of "curing" potatoes by storing them under a giant fan in the basement of his first restaurant, outside Chicago.

Perhaps his most enduring achievement, though, was the so-called potato computer—developed for McDonald's by a former electrical engineer for Motorola named Louis Martino—which precisely calibrated the optimal cooking time for a batch of fries. (The key: when a batch of cold raw potatoes is dumped into a vat of cooking oil, the temperature of the fat will drop and then slowly rise. Once the oil has risen three degrees, the fries are ready.) Previously, making high-quality French fries had been an art. The potato computer, the hydrometer, and the curing bins made it a science. By the time Kroc was finished, he had figured out how to turn potatoes into an inexpensive snack that would always be hot, salty, flavorful, and crisp, no matter where or when you bought it.

This was the first fast-food revolution—the mass production of food that had reliable mass appeal. But today, as the McDonald's franchise approaches its fiftieth anniversary, it is clear that fast food needs a second revolution. As many Americans now die every year from obesity-related illnesses—heart disease and complications of diabetes—as from smoking, and the fast-food toll grows heavier every year. In the fine new book *Fast Food Nation*, the journalist Eric Schlosser writes of McDonald's and Burger King in the tone usually reserved for chemical companies, sweatshops, and arms dealers, and, as shocking as that seems at first, it is perfectly appropriate. Ray Kroc's French fries are killing us. Can fast food be fixed?

Fast-food French fries are made from a baking potato like an Idaho russet, or any other variety that is mealy, or starchy, rather than waxy. The potatoes are harvested, cured, washed, peeled, sliced, and then blanched—cooked enough so that the insides have a fluffy texture but not so much that the fry gets soft and breaks. Blanching is followed by drying, and drying by a thirty-second deep fry, to give the potatoes a crisp shell. Then the fries are frozen until the moment of service, when they are deep-fried again, this time for somewhere around three minutes. Depending on the fast-food chain involved, there are other steps interspersed in this process. McDonald's fries, for example, are briefly dipped in a sugar solution, which gives them their golden-brown color; Burger King fries are dipped in a starch batter, which is what gives those fries their distinctive hard shell and audible crunch. But the result is similar. The potato that is first harvested in the field is roughly eighty per cent water. The process of creating a French fry consists, essentially, of removing as much of that water as possible—through blanching, drying, and deep-frying—and replacing it with fat.

Elisabeth Rozin, in her book *The Primal Cheeseburger*, points out that the idea of enriching carbohydrates with fat is nothing new. It's a standard part of the cuisine of almost every culture. Bread is buttered; macaroni comes with cheese; dumplings are fried; potatoes are scalloped, baked with milk and cheese, cooked in the dripping of roasting meat, mixed with mayonnaise in a salad, or pan-fried in butterfat as latkes. But, as Rozin argues, deep-frying is in many ways the ideal method of adding fat to carbohydrates. If you put butter on a mashed potato, for instance, the result is texturally unexciting: it simply creates a mush. Pan-frying results in uneven browning and crispness. But when a potato is deep-fried the heat of the oil turns the water inside the potato into steam, which causes the hard granules of starch inside the potato to swell and soften: that's why the inside of the fry is fluffy and light. At the same time, the outward migration of the steam limits the amount of oil that seeps into the interior, preventing the fry from getting greasy and concentrating the oil on the surface, where it turns the outer layer of the potato brown and crisp. "What we have with the french fry," Rozin writes, "is a near perfect enactment of the enriching of a starch food with oil or fat."

This is the trouble with the French fry. The fact that it is cooked in fat makes it unhealthy. But the contrast that deep-frying creates between its interior and its exterior—between the golden shell and the pillowy whiteness beneath—is what makes it so irresistible. The average American now eats a staggering thirty pounds of French fries a year, up from four pounds when Ray Kroc was first figuring out how to mass-produce a crisp fry. Meanwhile, fries themselves have become less healthful. Ray Kroc, in the early days of McDonald's, was a fan of a hot-dog stand on the North Side of Chicago called Sam's, which used what was then called the Chicago method of cooking fries. Sam's cooked its fries in animal fat, and Kroc followed suit, prescribing for his franchises a specially formulated beef tallow called Formula 47 (in reference to the forty-seven-cent McDonald's "All-American meal" of the era: fifteen-cent hamburger, twelve-cent fries, twenty-cent shake). Among aficionados, there is general agreement that those early McDonald's fries were the finest mass-market fries ever made: the beef tallow gave them an unsurpassed rich, buttery taste. But in 1990, in the face of public concern about the health risks of cholesterol in animal-based cooking oil, McDonald's and the other major fast-food houses switched to vegetable oil. That wasn't an improvement, however. In the course of making vegetable oil suitable for deep frying, it is subjected to a chemical process called hydrogenation, which creates a new substance called a trans unsaturated fat. In the hierarchy of fats, polyunsaturated fats—the kind found in regular vegetable oils—are the good kind; they lower your cholesterol. Saturated fats are the bad kind. But trans fats are worse: they wreak havoc with the body's ability to regulate cholesterol. According to a recent study involving some eighty thousand women, for every five-per-cent increase in the amount of saturated fats that a woman consumes, her risk of heart disease increases by seventeen per cent. But only a two-per-cent increase in trans fats will increase her heart-disease risk by ninety-three per cent. Walter Willett, an epidemiologist at Harvard—who helped design the study—estimates that the consumption of trans fats in the United States probably causes about thirty thousand premature deaths a year.

McDonald's and the other fast-food houses aren't the only purveyors of trans fats, of course; trans fats are in crackers and potato chips and cookies and any number of other processed foods. Still, a lot of us get a great deal of our trans fats from French fries, and to read the medical evidence on trans fats is to wonder at the odd selectivity of the outrage that consumers and the legal profession direct at corporate behavior. McDonald's and Burger King and Wendy's have switched to a product, without disclosing its risks, that may cost human lives. What is the difference between this and the kind of thing over which consumers sue companies every day?

The French-fry problem ought to have a simple solution: cook fries in oil that isn't so dangerous. Oils that are rich in monounsaturated fats, like canola oil, aren't nearly as bad for you as saturated fats, and are generally stable enough for deep-frying. It's also possible to "fix" animal fats so that they aren't so problematic. For example, K. C. Hayes, a nutritionist at Brandeis University, has helped develop an oil called Appetize. It's largely beef tallow, which gives it a big taste advantage over vegetable shortening, and makes it stable enough for deep-frying. But it has been processed to remove the cholesterol, and has been blended with pure corn oil, in a combination that Hayes says removes much of the heart-disease risk.

Perhaps the most elegant solution would be for McDonald's and the other chains to cook their fries in something like Olestra, a fat substitute developed by Procter & Gamble. Ordinary fats are built out of a molecular structure known as a triglyceride: it's a microscopic tree, with a trunk made of glycerol and three branches made of fatty acids. Our bodies can't absorb triglycerides, so in the digestive process each of the branches is broken off by enzymes and absorbed separately. In the production of Olestra, the glycerol trunk of a fat is replaced with a sugar, which has room for not three but eight fatty acids. And our enzymes are unable to break down a fat tree with eight branches— so the Olestra molecule can't be absorbed by the body at all. "Olestra" is as much a process as a compound: you can create an "Olestra" version of any given fat. Potato chips, for instance, tend to be fried in cottonseed oil, because of its distinctively clean taste. Frito-Lay's no-fat Wow! chips are made with an Olestra version of cottonseed oil, which behaves just like regular cottonseed oil except that it's never digested. A regular serving of potato chips has a hundred and fifty calories, ninety of which are fat calories from the cooking oil. A serving of Wow! chips has seventy-five calories and no fat. If Procter & Gamble were to seek F.D.A. approval for the use of Olestra in commercial deep-frying (which it has not yet done), it could make an Olestra version of the old McDonald's

Formula 47, which would deliver every nuance of the old buttery, meaty tallow at a fraction of the calories.

Olestra, it must be said, does have some drawbacks—in particular, a reputation for what is delicately called "gastrointestinal distress." The F.D.A. has required all Olestra products to carry a somewhat daunting label saying that they may cause "cramping and loose stools." Not surprisingly, sales have been disappointing, and Olestra has never won the full acceptance of the nutrition community. Most of this concern, however, appears to be overstated. Procter & Gamble has done randomized, double-blind studies—one of which involved more than three thousand people over six weeks—and found that people eating typical amounts of Olestra-based chips don't have significantly more gastrointestinal problems than people eating normal chips. Diarrhea is such a common problem in America—nearly a third of adults have at least one episode each month—that even F.D.A. regulators now appear to be convinced that in many of the complaints they received Olestra was unfairly blamed for a problem that was probably caused by something else. The agency has promised Procter & Gamble that the warning label will be reviewed.

Perhaps the best way to put the Olestra controversy into perspective is to compare it to fibre. Fibre is vegetable matter that goes right through you: it's not absorbed by the gastrointestinal tract. Nutritionists tell us to eat it because it helps us lose weight and it lowers cholesterol—even though if you eat too many baked beans or too many bowls of oat bran you will suffer the consequences. Do we put warning labels on boxes of oat bran? No, because the benefits of fibre clearly outweigh its drawbacks. Research has suggested that Olestra, like fibre, helps people lose weight and lowers cholesterol; too much Olestra, like too much fibre, may cause problems. (Actually, too much Olestra may not be as troublesome as too much bran. According to Procter & Gamble, eating a large amount of Olestra—forty grams—causes no more problems than eating a small bowl—twenty grams—of wheat bran.) If we had Olestra fries, then, they shouldn't be eaten for breakfast, lunch, and dinner. In fact, fast-food houses probably shouldn't use hundred-per-cent Olestra; they should cook their fries in a blend, using the Olestra to displace the most dangerous trans and saturated fats. But these are minor details. The point is that it is entirely possible, right now, to make a delicious French fry that does not carry with it a death sentence. A French fry can be much more than a delivery vehicle for fat.

Is it really that simple, though? Consider the cautionary tale of the efforts of a group of food scientists at Auburn University, in Alabama, more than a decade ago to come up with a better hamburger. The Auburn team wanted to create a leaner beef that tasted as good as regular ground beef. They couldn't just remove the fat, because that would leave the meat dry and mealy. They wanted to replace the fat. "If you look at ground beef, it contains moisture, fat, and protein," says Dale Huffman, one of the scientists who spearheaded the Auburn project. "Protein is relatively constant in all beef, at about twenty per cent. The traditional McDonald's ground beef is around twenty per cent fat. The remainder is water. So you have an inverse ratio of water and fat. If you reduce fat, you need to increase water." The goal of the Auburn scientists was to cut about two-thirds of the fat from normal ground beef, which meant that they needed to find something to add to the beef that would hold an equivalent amount of water—and continue to retain that water even as the beef was being grilled. Their choice? Seaweed, or, more precisely, carrageenan. "It's been in use for centuries," Huffman explains. "It's the stuff that keeps the suspension in chocolate milk—otherwise the chocolate would settle at the bottom. It has tremendous water-holding ability. There's a loose bond between the carrageenan and the moisture." They also selected some basic flavor enhancers, designed to make up for the lost fat "taste." The result was a beef patty that was roughly three-quarters water, twenty per cent protein, five per cent or so fat, and a quarter of a per cent seaweed. They called it AU Lean.

It didn't take the Auburn scientists long to realize that they had created something special. They installed a test kitchen in their laboratory, got hold of a McDonald's grill, and began doing blind taste comparisons of AU Lean burgers and traditional twenty-per-cent-fat burgers. Time after time, the AU Lean burgers won. Next, they took their invention into the field. They recruited a hundred families and supplied them with three kinds of ground beef for home cooking over consecutive three-week intervals—regular "market" ground beef with twenty per cent fat, ground beef with five per cent fat, and AU Lean. The families were asked to rate the different kinds of beef, without knowing which was which. Again, the AU Lean won hands down—trumping the other two on "likability," "tenderness," "flavorfulness," and "juiciness."

What the Auburn team showed was that, even though people love the taste and feel of fat—and naturally gravitate toward high-fat food—they can be fooled into thinking that there is a lot of fat in something when there isn't. Adam Drewnowski, a nutritionist at the University of Washington, has found a similar effect with cookies. He did blind taste tests of normal and reduced-calorie brownies, biscotti, and chocolate-chip, oatmeal, and peanut-butter cookies. If you cut the sugar content of any of those cookies by twenty-five per cent, he found, people like the cookies much less. But if you cut the fat by twenty-five per cent they barely notice. "People are very finely attuned to how much sugar there is in a liquid or a solid," Drewnowski says. "For fat, there's no sensory break point. Fat comes in so many guises and so many textures it is very difficult to perceive how much is there."This doesn't mean we are oblivious of fat levels, of course. Huffman says that when his group tried to lower the fat in AU Lean below five per cent, people didn't like it anymore. But, within the relatively broad range of between five and twenty-five per cent, you can add water and some flavoring and most people can't tell the difference.

What's more, people appear to be more sensitive to the volume of food they consume than to its calorie content. Barbara Rolls, a nutritionist at Penn State, has demonstrated this principle with satiety studies. She feeds one group of people a high-volume snack and another group a low-volume snack. Even though the two snacks have the same calorie count, she finds that people who eat the high-volume snack feel more satisfied. "People tend to eat a constant weight or volume of food in a given day, not a constant portion of calories," she says. Eating AU Lean, in short, isn't going to leave you with a craving for more calories; you'll feel just as full.

For anyone looking to improve the quality of fast food, all this is heartening news. It means that you should be able to put low-fat cheese and low-fat mayonnaise in a Big Mac without anyone's complaining. It also means that there's no particular reason to use twenty-per-cent-fat ground beef in a fast-food burger. In 1990, using just this argument, the Auburn team suggested to McDonald's that it make a Big Mac out of AU Lean. Shortly thereafter, McDonald's came out with the McLean Deluxe. Other fast-food houses scrambled to follow suit. Nutritionists were delighted. And fast food appeared on the verge of a revolution.

Only, it wasn't. The McLean was a flop, and four years later it was off the market. What happened? Part of the problem appears to have been that McDonald's rushed the burger to market before many of the production kinks had been worked out. More important, though, was the psychological handicap the burger faced. People liked AU Lean in blind taste tests because they didn't know it was AU Lean; they were fooled into thinking it was regular ground beef. But nobody was fooled when it came to the McLean Deluxe. It was sold as the healthy choice—and who goes to McDonald's for health food?

Leann Birch, a developmental psychologist at Penn State, has looked at the impact of these sorts of expectations on children. In one experiment, she took a large group of kids and fed them a big lunch. Then she turned them loose in a room with lots of junk food. "What we see is that some kids eat almost nothing," she says. "But other kids really chow down, and one of the things that predicts how much they eat is the extent to which parents have restricted their access to high-fat, high-sugar food in the past: the more the kids have been restricted, the more they eat." Birch explains the results two ways. First, restricting food makes kids think not in terms of their own hunger but in terms of the presence and absence of food. As she puts it, "The kid is essentially saying, 'If the food's here I better get it while I can, whether or not I'm hungry.' We see these five-year-old kids eating as much as four hundred calories." Birch's second finding, though, is more important. Because the children on restricted diets had been told that junk food was bad for them, they clearly thought that it had to taste good. When it comes to junk food, we seem to follow an implicit script that powerfully biases the way we feel about food. We like fries not in spite of the fact that they're unhealthy but because of it.

That is sobering news for those interested in improving the American diet. For years, the nutrition movement in this country has made transparency one of its principal goals: it has assumed that the best way to help people improve their diets is to tell them precisely what's in their food, to label certain foods good and certain foods bad. But transparency can backfire, because sometimes nothing is more deadly for our taste buds than the knowledge that what we are eating is good for us. McDonald's should never have called its new offering the McLean Deluxe, in other words. They should have called it the Burger Supreme or the Monster Burger, and then buried the news about reduced calories and fat in the tiniest type on the remotest corner of their Web site. And if we were to cook fries in some high-tech, healthful cooking oil—whether Olestrized beef tallow or something else with a minimum of trans and saturated fats—the worst thing we could do would be to market them as healthy fries. They will not taste nearly as good if we do. They have to be marketed as better fries, as Classic Fries, as fries that bring back the rich tallowy taste of the original McDonald's.

What, after all, was Ray Kroc's biggest triumph? A case could be made for the field men with their hydrometers, or the potato-curing techniques, or the potato computer, which turned the making of French fries from an art into a science. But we should not forget Ronald McDonald, the clown who made the McDonald's name irresistible to legions of small children. Kroc understood that taste comprises not merely the food on our plate but also the associations and assumptions and prejudices we bring to the table—that half the battle in making kids happy with their meal was calling what they were eating a Happy Meal. The marketing of healthful fast food will require the same degree of subtlety and sophistication. The nutrition movement keeps looking for a crusader—someone who will bring about better public education and tougher government regulations. But we need much more than that. We need another Ray Kroc.

Questions for Discussion

1. What challenges does Malcolm Gladwell point out in regards to the marketing of healthy fast food?

2. Why does Gladwell choose to begin his essay with the story of Ray Kroc? How does this story help support and shape the author's final point?

3. Gladwell writes that, "taste comprises not merely the food on our plate, but also the associations, assumptions, and prejudices we bring to the table." What kind of assumptions and prejudices do you think inform the way that we understand food today?

Indigenous Diets Can Help Fight Modern Illnesses, Health Experts Say

The Guardian

The Guardian, February 2014

> *The Guardian* is a weekly British-based publication. It was originally founded directly after the signing of the Treaty of Versaille in 1919, according to the publication's website. The paper pulls from various editorial sources such as *The Washington Post, Le Monde,* and the *Observer.* This newspaper's online publication was the fifth most widely read in the world, as of 2014. It won the newspaper of the year at the 2014 British Press Awards for its reporting on government surveillance. This article was published in February of 2014 and responds to the growing concerns raised by Indigenous Food organizations. One of these organizations is the Working Group on Indigenous Food Sovereignty, based in Canada, whose mission statement establishes their exigence as a "recognized need to carry the Indigenous voice in the various meetings, conferences and discussions that have taken place within the food security movement."

Traditional food consumed by rural communities contain nutrients that are lacking in high- and middle-income countries

Unprecedented levels of chronic non-communicable diseases are prompting calls to revert to the diets of our ancestors to regain lost nutrients.

It is believed that such a shift would help to improve society's relationship with the Earth and restore human and environmental health.

"The rise of the industrial model of agriculture has contributed greatly to people being disconnected from the food on their plates," says Sarah Somian, a France-based nutritionist.

Many traditional and non-processed foods consumed by rural communities, such as millet and caribou, are nutrient-dense and offer healthy fatty acids, micronutrients and cleansing properties widely lacking in diets popular in high- and middle-income countries, say experts.

Indigenous diets worldwide—from forest foods such as roots and tubers in regions of eastern India to coldwater fish, caribou, and seals in northern Canada—are varied, suited to local environments, and can counter malnutrition and disease.

"For many tribal and indigenous peoples, their food systems are complex, self-sufficient and deliver a very broad-based, nutritionally diverse diet," says Jo Woodman, a senior researcher and campaigner at Survival International, a UK-based indigenous advocacy organisation.

But the disruption of traditional lifestyles due to environmental degradation, and the introduction of processed foods, refined fats and oils, and simple carbohydrates, contributes to worsening health in indigenous populations, and a decline in the production of nutrient-rich foodstuffs that could benefit all communities.

"Traditional food systems need to be documented so that policymakers know what is at stake by ruining an ecosystem, not only for the indigenous peoples living there, but for everyone," Harriet Kuhnlein, founding director of the Centre of Indigenous Peoples' Nutrition and Environment at McGill University, Canada.

Since the early 1960s, economic growth, urbanisation and a global population increase to more than 7 billion have multiplied the consumption of animal-sourced foods—including meat, eggs and dairy products—which comprised 13% of the energy in the world's diet in 2013, according to the International Livestock Research Institute (ILRI) in Nairobi, Kenya. Farm-raised livestock consumes up to a third of the world's grains, the institute notes.

Agricultural expansion, some of it to cultivate more grains, accounts for 80% of the world's deforestation, says the UN Environmental Programme.

With the global population expected to rise to some 9 billion by 2050, 50% more food must be produced to feed these people, depending on whether there is a healthy ecosystem. "When environments are destroyed or contaminated, this affects the food they can provide," Kuhnlein says.

Indigenous food systems—gathering and preparing food to maximise the nutrients an environment can provide—range from nomadic hunter-gatherers such as the Aché in eastern Paraguay, the Massai pastoralists in northern Kenya, and herding and fishing groups including the Inuit in northern Canada, to the Saami of Scandinavia and the millet-farming Kondh agriculturalists in eastern India.

But the trait these groups share is a keen knowledge of how to eat nutritiously without damaging the ecosystem. "Indigenous peoples' food systems contain treasures of knowledge from long-evolved cultures and patterns of living in local ecosystems," says an FAO-supported study on indigenous food systems, nutrition, and health co-authored by Kuhnlein in 2009.

In recent years, grains such as quinoa, fonio and millet—long harvested by indigenous and rural communities in developing countries but increasingly overlooked by a younger, richer generation that prefers imported foods—have instead grown in popularity in developed countries.

Research, marketing and donor-funded financing have helped raise awareness of the ability of these high-protein grains to reduce cholesterol, provide micronutrients and lower the risk of diabetes. "Because of the many health benefits of these forgotten, or until [recently] unknown foods, valuing the wisdom of indigenous cultures [and] earlier generations is vital for reducing disease and inflammation," Somian says.

Marginalised farmers

The Kondh community in Odisha state traditionally grows up to 16 varieties of millet, according to Debjeet Sarangi, head of Living Farms, a local NGO that has worked with marginalised indigenous farmers since 2005.

But millet-growing among the roughly 100,000 Kondh, who are spread over about 15,000 villages, has dropped by nearly 63% from an estimated 500,000 hectares in 1975 to more than 200,000 hectares in 2008. This is because land is being converted to paddy in exchange for government-subsidised rice programmes offering refined white rice, even though it carries health risks.

"When there is so much malnutrition existing in the area, why do you replace land which has been growing nutritious food [with rice paddies]?" says Sarangi, whose NGO reported in 2011 that 75% of under-fives in Kondh weighed too little for their age, and 55% were too short for their height group, a sign of chronic malnutrition.

Another so-called superfood declining in popularity is spirulina, a type of cyanobacteria that grows in ponds and is a staple in many traditional food systems, such as among the Kanembu in Chad.

Spirulina has the potential to boost immunity, reduce inflammation, decrease allergic reactions, and provide a healthy source of protein, according to the Langone Medical Centre of New York University in the US.

"There is a deep irony in the fact that many dieticians are advocating [traditional and indigenous foods and diets] and yet [the] modern [western] diet is what is being pushed on tribal peoples around the world, with devastating results," Woodman says.

"We have lost our primary relationship with our world around us," says Dr Martin Reinhardt, assistant professor of Native American studies at Northern Michigan University.

Native American elders historically planned seven generations ahead when creating food systems, teaching each generation that it was their responsibility to ensure the survival of the seventh, says Reinhardt, an Anishinaabe Ojibway citizen of the Sault Ste. Marie Chippewa Native American people in Michigan state. They did this by hunting and gathering only what they needed, conserving resources such as wood and water, and protecting food biodiversity.

But when Native Americans were forced to assimilate, historical access to this nutritional knowledge was lost, Reinhardt points out. According to the special diabetes programme for Indians, run by the US federal government's Indian health service, the 566 registered indigenous peoples in the US have a diabetes rate nine times higher than the national average.

Similarly, rates of the disease among First Nations and Inuit groups in Canada are up to five times higher than the countrywide average, according to the government's federal health department.

In Laos, northern highland minorities such as the Yawa, Htin and Khmu traditionally eat forest-based diets, including wild pigs, birds, bamboo shoots, banana flowers, and yams rich in vitamin C. But in recent decades the Laos government has moved thousands of people from the highlands to towns for economic reasons, documented in a 2012 report by the International Fund for Agricultural Development.

"Communities [have less access] to natural resources than before," says Jim Chamberlain, an anthropologist and former World Bank consultant based in the capital, Vientiane. He says their traditional diet relies on forests and the move has led to a decline in nutritional status. Malnutrition rates in Laotian under-fives are among the highest in southeast Asia.

While reinstating traditional food systems is key for everyone's health, as well as for the environment, the lack of a market to support superfoods poses serious challenges, advocates say.

In northern Canada, many of the fishes rich in omega-3 fatty acids—a staple in the traditional diets of Arctic tribes—spawn and live in waters increasingly tainted with mercury, according to the government.

Deforestation worldwide, often to make way for large-scale agricultural production, curtails the nutrients that can be gathered from forests.

Much environmental destruction is a consequence of modern society's detachment from its food systems, says Reinhardt, who coordinated a UNM project called decolonise your diet, which ran from 2010-12 and aimed to teach people the link between food, culture, health, and the environment.

"Humans can, and need to, reconnect with nature in such an intimate way as to depend on it for survival," he says. "I hope we have not yet passed the thresholds [of what the earth can tolerate]."

Questions for Discussion

1. This article quotes Harriet Kuhnlein who writes that, "Traditional food systems need to be documented so that policymakers know what is at stake by ruining an ecosystem, not only for the indigenous peoples living there, but for everyone." What specifically does the article claim is at stake?

2. How would you characterize the author's tone in this article? Based on this, what can we assume about the author's intended audience? What kind of audience might respond positively to the tone of this article?

3. What kind of evidence does the author use in this source? How is it relayed? How do these specific rhetorical choices help to shape the author's message?

4. In what way does the article's concern over resources compare to the Wang piece? In what way do these two stories address a similar problem?

The Marvels in Your Mouth

Mary Roach

The New York Times, March 2013

> Mary Roach is a science writer and the author of eight books including her newest which was released in June 2016 called *Grunt: The Curious Science of Humans at War*. The article included here was published in *The New York Times*, which runs an entire section focusing on science every Tuesday. If you enjoy Roach's article, try picking up the free *New York Times* that is available every day in locations across the Colorado State University campus. This chapter is taken from her book *Gulp: Adventures on the Alimentary Canal*, which explores chewing and swallowing. Her style has been described as taking complex ideas, particularly from science, and making them accessible. Known also for her use of humor, Roach helps us in this article to appreciate one of the wonders of our biological being—i.e., our sophisticated machinery for eating (teeth, tongue, esophagus, etc.)!

When I told people I was traveling to Food Valley, I described it as the Silicon Valley of eating. At this cluster of universities and research facilities, nearly 15,000 scientists are dedicated to improving—or, depending on your sentiments about processed food, compromising—the quality of our meals.

At the time I made the Silicon Valley comparison, I did not expect to be served actual silicon.

But here I am, in the restaurant of the future, a cafeteria at Wageningen University where hidden cameras record diners as they make decisions about what to eat. And here it is, a bowl of rubbery white cubes the size of salad croutons. Andries van der Bilt has brought them from his lab in the brusquely named Department of Head and Neck, at the nearby University Medical Center Utrecht.

"You chew them," he said.

The cubes are made of a trademarked product called Comfort Putty, more typically used in its unhardened form for taking dental impressions. Dr. Van der Bilt isn't a dentist, however. He is an oral physiologist, and he likely knows more about chewing than anyone else in the world. He uses the cubes to quantify "masticatory performance"—how effectively a person chews. I take a cube from the bowl. If you ever, as a child, chewed on a whimsical pencil eraser in the shape of, say, an animal or a piece of fruit, then you have tasted this dish.

"I'm sorry." Dr. Van der Bilt winces. "It's quite off." As though fresh silicone might be better.

Dr. Van der Bilt and his colleagues have laid claim to a strange, occasionally repugnant patch of scientific ground. They study the mouth—more specifically, its role as the human food processor. Their findings have opened up new insights into quite a few things that most of us do every day but would rather not think about.

The way you chew, for example, is as unique and consistent as the way you walk or fold your shirts. There are fast chewers and slow chewers, long chewers and short chewers, right-chewing people and left-chewing people. Some of us chew straight up and down, and others chew side-to-side, like cows. Your oral processing habits are a physiological fingerprint.

Dr. Van der Bilt studies the neuromuscular elements of chewing. You often hear about the impressive power of the jaw muscles. In terms of pressure per single burst of activity, these are the strongest muscles we have. But it is not the jaw's power to destroy that fascinates Dr. Van der Bilt; it is its nuanced ability to protect.

Think of a peanut between two molars, about to be crushed. At the precise millisecond the nut succumbs, the jaw muscles sense the yielding and reflexively let up. Without that reflex, the molars would continue to hurtle recklessly toward one another, now with no intact nut between.

To keep your he-man jaw muscles from smashing your precious teeth, the only set you have, the body evolved an automated braking system faster and more sophisticated than anything on a Lexus. The jaw knows its own strength. The faster and more recklessly you close your mouth, the less force the muscles are willing to apply. Without your giving it conscious thought.

Teeth and jaws are impressive not for their strength but for their sensitivity, Dr. Van der Bilt has found. Chew on this: Human teeth can detect a grain of sand or grit 10 microns in diameter. A micron is 1/25,000 of an inch. If you shrank a Coke can until it was the diameter of a human hair, the letter O in the product name would be about 10 microns across.

As it happens, my masticatory performance is "just fine," Dr. Van der Bilt said. But the study of oral processing is not just about teeth. It's about the entire "oral device"—teeth, tongue, lips, cheeks, saliva, all working together toward a singular revolting goal, bolus formation.

The word "bolus" has many applications, but we are speaking of this one: a mass of chewed, saliva-moistened food particles. Food that is in, as one researcher has put it, sounding like a license plate, "the swallowable state."

In Dr. Van der Bilt's line of work, on any given day you may find yourself documenting "intraoral bolus rolling" or shooting magnified close-ups of "retained custard" with the Wageningen University tongue-camera. Should you need to employ, say, the Lucas formula for bolus cohesiveness, you will need to figure out the viscosity and surface tension of the moistening saliva as well as the average radius of the chewed food particles and the average distance between them.

To do that, you'll need a bolus. You'll need to stop your subject on the brink of swallowing and have him, like a Siamese with a hairball, relinquish the mass. If the bolus in question is a semisolid—yogurt and custard are not chewed but "orally manipulated" and mixed with saliva—the work is yet less beautiful.

Bolus formation and swallowing depend on a highly coordinated sequence of neuromuscular events and reflexes, researchers here and elsewhere have found. Disable any one of these—via stroke, degenerative neurological condition, tumor irradiation—and the seamless, moist ballet begins to fall apart. The umbrella term is dysphagia (from the Greek for "disordered eating," which may or may not explain flaming Greek cheese appetizers).

Most of the time, while you're just breathing and not swallowing, the larynx (voice box) blocks the entrance to the esophagus. When a mouthful of food or drink is ready to be swallowed, the larynx has to rise out of the way, both to allow access to the esophagus and to close off the windpipe and prevent the food from "going down the wrong way."

To allow this to happen, the bolus is held momentarily at the back of the tongue, a sort of anatomical metering light. If, as a result of dysphagia, the larynx doesn't move quickly enough, the food can head down the windpipe instead. This is, obviously, a choking hazard. More sinisterly, inhaled food and drink can deliver a troublesome load of bacteria. Infection can set in and progress to pneumonia.

A less lethal and more entertaining swallowing misstep is nasal regurgitation. Here the soft palate—home turf of the uvula, that queer little oral stalactite—fails to seal the opening to the nasal cavity. This leaves milk, say, or chewed peas in peril of being horked out the nostrils. Nasal regurgitation is more common with children, because they are often laughing while eating and because their swallowing mechanism isn't fully developed.

"Immature swallowing coordination" is the reason 90 percent of food-related choking deaths befall children under 5. Also contributing: immature dentition. Children grow incisors before they have molars; for a brief span of time they can bite off pieces of food but cannot chew them.

Round foods are particularly treacherous because they match the shape of the trachea. If a grape goes down the wrong way, it blocks the tube so completely that no breath can be drawn around it. Hot dogs, grapes, and round candies take the top three slots in a list of killer foods published in the July 2008 issue of *The International Journal of Pediatric Otorhinolaryngology* (itself a calamitous mouthful). A candy called Lychee Mini Fruity Gels has killed enough times for the Food and Drug Administration to have banned its import.

The safest foods, of course, are those that arrive on the plate pre-moistened and machine-masticated, leaving little for your own built-in processor to do. They are also, generally speaking, the least popular. Mushy food is a form of sensory deprivation. In the same way that a dark, silent room will eventually drive you to hallucinate, the mind rebels against bland, single-texture foods, edibles that do not engage the oral device.

Those who can chew want to chew. We especially enjoy crunch. A colleague of Dr. Van der Bilt, Ton van Vliet, has spent the past seven years figuring out just how crunch works.

Back at the restaurant of the Future, he stops by to instruct me in the basics of crispy-crunchy. We begin with nature's version, a fresh apple or carrot.

"It's all bubbles and beams," he said, sketching networks of water-filled cells and cell walls on a sheet of my notepad paper. When you bite into an apple, the flesh deforms and at a certain moment the cell walls burst. And there is your crunch. (Ditto crispy snack foods, but there the bubbles are filled with air.)

As a piece of produce begins to decay, the cell walls break down and water leaks out. Now nothing bursts. Your fruit is no longer crisp. It is mealy or limp or mushy. The same thing happens with a snack food degraded by moisture: Cell walls dissolve, air leaks out. The staler the chip, the quieter.

For food to make an audible noise when it breaks, there must be what's called a brittle facture: a sudden, high-speed crack. Dr. Van Vliet takes a puffed cassava chip from a bag and snaps it in two.

"To get this noise, you need crack speeds of 300 meters per second," he said. The speed of sound. The crunch of a chip is a tiny sonic boom inside your mouth.

Crispiness and crunchiness appeal to us because they signal freshness, Dr. Van Vliet said. Old, rotting, mushy produce can make you ill. At the very least, it has lost much of its nutritional vim. To a certain extent, we eat with our ears.

"People eat physics," said Dr. Van Vliet. "You eat physical properties with a little bit of taste and aroma. And if the physics is not good, then you don't eat it." During this discussion, I have been working my way through our props. I tilt a bag of cassava chips toward Dr. Van Vliet, who waves it off.

"I don't like chips and things."

In his eight years at Wageningen University, in fact, he has never tried any of the food in the Restaurant of the Future.

Sidebar:

The Mouth's Guard

Humans secrete two kinds of saliva, stimulated and unstimulated, no more alike than most siblings. The prettier child is stimulated saliva. It comes from the parotid glands, between cheek and ear. When a plate of spaghetti carbonara makes your mouth water, that's stimulated saliva. It makes up 70 to 90 percent of the two to three pints of saliva each of us generates daily. Stimulated saliva looks, tastes and flows like water—it is, in fact, 99 percent water with some proteins and minerals. Each person's saliva contains minerals in unique proportions.

The main digestive enzyme in stimulated saliva is amylase, which breaks starches down into simple sugars that the body can make use of. You can taste this happening when you chew bread. A sweet taste materializes as your saliva mixes with the starch. Add a few drops of saliva to a spoonful of custard, and within seconds it's much more like water.

Allowing you to eat is the most obvious, but far from the only, favor granted by saliva. Vinegar, cola, citrus juice, wine—all are in the acid range of the pH scale: from around pH 2 to 3. Anything under pH 4 will dissolve calcium phosphate, a key component of tooth enamel.

Take a drink of anything acid, and if you are paying attention, you will notice a sudden warm slosh: parotid saliva arriving like the cavalry to bring the pH back up to the safe zone. Sugar—all carbohydrates, really—contributes to tooth decay only indirectly; it's the acidic metabolites of the bacteria that feed on the sugar. As with acidic foods, saliva dilutes the acid and brings the mouth back to a neutral pH.

Relatively little is known about unstimulated saliva. This is background saliva, the kind that's always flowing, though much more slowly. Unstimulated saliva's trademark ropiness is due to mucins, long chains of amino acids repeating to form vast webs. Mucins are responsible for saliva's least endearing traits: its viscosity, elasticity, stickiness. They also account for some of its more heroic attributes.

Unstimulated saliva forms a protective film that clings to the surfaces of the teeth. Proteins in this film bind to calcium and phosphate and serve to remineralize the enamel. Webs of mucins trap bacteria, which are then swallowed and destroyed by stomach acids.

As a germ killer itself, salvia has few rivals. Its anti-clumping properties, keep bacteria from forming colonies on the teeth and gums. And it contains histatins, which not only kill bacteria but have been shown to speed wound closure independent of antibacterial action.

"It is a known observation among the vulgar that the saliva is efficacious in cleansing foul wounds, and cicatrizing recent ones," wrote the 18th-century physician Herman Boerhaave. He was correct. Wounds that would take several weeks to heal on one's skin disappear in a week inside the mouth.

Questions for Discussion

1. Explain what Roach is talking about when she refers to the automated braking system of the human mouth as a hereditary adaptation of great importance.

2. Roach takes a decidedly informal approach in this article. Find three examples of locations where she takes liberties with writing "rules" that you have learned or are familiar with. What is the effect of her informal style? Why does she write the way that she does? Does she ever make you laugh, or at least smile? How do you explain the fact that an article with "grammatical errors" was published in *The New York Times*?

3. Refer to the extensive explanation of the bolus, or the glob or digestible goo that's created when we chew and swallow. Read this section closely and with great care. Take notes in the margin and then write a summary of the complex process Roach describes. Think of a complex procedure that you're familiar with and sketch out in bullet points what might be involved in describing it fully and in terms that a non-expert (lay) audience would understand.

Desde el Corazón

Josie Méndez-Negrete

Latin@'s Presence in the Food Industry: Changing How We Think About Food, 2016

> Published by the University of Arkansas Press, an academic press whose mission is to publish books that serve the broad academic community, *Latin@s Presence in the Food Industry,* of which this essay by Méndez-Negrete is part, offers, according to the University Press's website "a vibrant new collection that acknowledges issues of labor conditions, economic politics, and immigration laws—structural vulnerabilities...—and strives to understand more fully the active and conscious ways in Latin@s create spaces to maneuver global and local food systems." Josephine Méndez-Negrete, her professional website reports, is an associate professor of Mexican American studies at the University of Texas at San Antonio, earned her PhD at the University of California, Santa Cruz, and is the author of *Las Hijas de Juan: Daughters Betrayed,* Duke University Press, 2006. She is a community activist who works on behalf of women and children. In this chapter, Méndez-Negrete provides what she describes in her essay as a "reflexive autoethnography" which is research that involves self-interrogation of experiences that resonate with cultural implications. This examination of her experience in a household where both violence and love involved food ultimately focuses on the relationships of the women in the household and the building of strength and solidarity through food preparation.

Nourishing Bodies, Feeding Souls

> *Cocinar era algo muy especial...me sentaba a mirar a Chenda...ella cocinaba con mucha autoridad—todo tenia su ritmo, las brasas, el tiempo, la comida, y el orden del sazón. Cocinar, para mi, era el modo de enseñarles que los quería...lo hacia con much cariño y amor—el cocinar me daba fuerza—al darles sustento, yo me animaba.*
>
> *(Cooking has always been something special...I would sit to look at Chenda... she cooked with much authority—everything had its rhythm, the embers, the*

*timing, the food, and the sequences in her use of spices. Cooking, for me,
was a way to show you that I loved you…I did it with much care and
love—cooking gave me strength—nourishing you, enlivened me.)*

—*Amá*

Daily Life and Its Complexities

Framed inside the emotions of everyday life is the love of making food. The
cooking practices and philosophies I learned from women ancestors still guide
my cooking, as well as the ways in which I express love. Their voices and sage
advice still resonate deep inside me, beginning with the warming of the power
of emotions: "Don't cook when you're mad because anger disconnects you from
the portions and taints you ability to salt the food"; and, "Be careful, rage does
not allow you to detect the fire in the chile pods and your salsa will be too
hot to enjoy." Other voices spoke to the process of preparation: "Distractions
distort timing. When making tortillas, pay attention, otherwise when you cook
them they will come out raw or burnt and won't even be good enough for the
chuchos"—what we called dogs. Still, others' messages of food as nurturance
come through in connection to love. "It's through the belly that you find love,"
Doña Cata, our neighbor, would often chime in when talking about the value
of food preparation.

Founded in the collectivity of women's practices of the everyday, our oral
cooking tradition relied on storytelling, or *pláticas*, where *comadres*, blood
related, or social kinswomen, traded recipes in conversation with each other.
Their talk about food and cooking framed the *recetarios* of our lives—where
they detailed *recetas* (recipes) and cooking technique but also focused on the
travails of the daily lives with which we contended. Patience and the willingness
to share what was produced became central to our understanding that cocineras
who made the food had the authority. As such, I honored their admonitions:
"No se meta en mi cocina…Si menea el mole se hara ralo, ¡dejelo!" (Do not
enter my kitchen…If your stir the pot, the mole will thin out; leave it be!)

It was from these women that I learned one finds love through the belly and not
the heart because the passage to the heart is through the stomach, the source of
our emotional core. "The best way to snare a loved one," they would say, "is to
pay attention and imagine the best meal you could prepare for the intended."
From these women, Mague, Fela, my sisters, and I learned life lessons that defied
expectations of authority assigned by the rigid gender rules that see women
only in reproductive roles: reproducing workers and the food to maintain them.

My mother imparted lessons through her cooking. From her we learned
to navigate our everyday lives in a home where contradictions—physical,
psychological, emotional, and sexual violence—were perpetrated by Juan, our
father, who was later diagnosed as a sociopath and serial pedophile. In the

context of intense and varied types of pains, we found sentient connections to the delectable dishes prepared by our mother. The nourishing practices that mended our wounded hearts and bodies emerged in the special dishes Amá created. The dishes consoled us from the violent perpetrations no one within the house spoke about or those outside the house dared to imagine taking place in our so-called sacred space of the privacy of our home.[1] More often than not, her cooking was the only consolation we received from the physical psychological, emotional, and spiritual pain we confronted in our domestic lives. The food Amá prepared for us was always the bridge to our hearts as Amá made every effort to convey her unspoken actions of protection through her food.

Amá's Reimagined *Cocina:* Cooking Lessons in the Practices of the Everyday

Whether it be *con el casí nada*—just a few wild greens—*quelites, verdolagas u ostras yerbas comestibles*—tossed, cooked, or blanched, ordinary edible weeds in a salad, or broth made into a *caldo* or soup. Amá often reminded us to share what we had. *Con una estufa de brazas o Madera, o un fogón*—with a fire stove fueled by coals or twigs, or with a gas burner, Amá's delectable dishes took care of us. In food preparation she taught us to read the world. The connections she made through food deepened relationships with *comadres*, relatives, and neighbors. Literate in the ways in which food can strengthen connections, Amá recognized that allies are critical in contesting the boundaries of domestic containment.

Food, emotions, and nurturance are expressive aspects of reproductive responsibilities generally assigned to women. Meredith E. Abarca examines women's work in the kitchen as an act of agency that transforms that site from the "women's *place* into her *space*."[2] Through the voices of *mujeres* with whom she talked, we learn that not all women perceive their work as "socially mandated" labor but as a "celebration and affirmation of [their] talent, knowledge, and affection."[3] Abarca argues that it is women's labor in the kitchen that "sustains [their] sense of self by validating emotions and claiming the right to [their] sense of self by validating emotions and claiming the right to [their] own *sazón*, culinary knowledge and talent base on the epistemology of the senses."[4] Moreover, Abarca posits that women take charge of and transform their everyday cooking practices in their "culinary creations inspired by an array of

---

1   What my ancestral women and my mother's cooking taught me is a "food consciousness" that speaks to the power implicated in food practices. Meredith E. Abarca and Nieves Pascual Soler introduce "food consciousness" to capture the ways in which material and symbolic food meanings inform our knowledge of selves and the ways in which we are included or excluded citizens from a particular culture, social class, and a nation. See *Rethinking Chicana/o Literature through Food: Postnational Appetites*, ed. Nieves Pascual Soler and Meredith E. Abarca (New York: Palgrave Macmillian, 2013).
2   Meredith E. Abarca, Voices in the Kitchen: *Views of Food and the World from Working-Class Mexican and Mexican American Women* (College Station: Texas A&M University Press, 2006), 23
3   Ibid., 23.
4   Ibid.

emotions."[5] Such cultural practices can be witnessed in narrative films such as *Like Water for Chocolate* directed by Alfonso Arau.[6]

Emotions are central to women's work in the domestic sphere, including cooking and food preparation, and these acts are not limited to the socialization of emotions and feelings as gendered ways of interaction. I offer that culinary creations are possible because of women's abilities to listen, see, smell, and taste, as they "theorize about the aesthetic value" of their cooking.[7] Cooking and food preparation serve as ways of teaching and nurturing those who are the recipients of this gift and as a way to contest and resist the difficulties of patriarchy. Patriarchy is a rationalization under notions of the privacy of home where gender power distortions are enacted, especially when serving the so-called master of the house. The place and space of the kitchen provides a site for a consciousness of being that frames the experiences of those who cook as they learn to deal with distortions of power. Pérez and Abarca argue the "[f]ood is fundamental to the workings of identity and belonging, power, and social change."[8] As was the case for *Las hijas de Juan*,[9] we, the daughters, were carving out an identity in the context of oppositional and oppressive experiences—on the one hand, the silent love of Amá, and on the other, the vicious and depraved ways of Juan. It was in this space that I learned to use all of my senses to give meaning to my environment. I understood the value of food for us, as well as in the lives of those who lacked resources of every type. I amassed ways of negotiating the emotions and feelings of others, as well as my own.

When cooking occurs in the private realm of volatile homes, a mother's food can act as a revolutionary gesture that fights to soothe the consequences of trauma. Her cooking can convey the multidimensional, subtle, and not-so-subtle power food has to appease pain. In our home, while the brute physical force and authority might have been the venue of the patriarch, and the relegation to kitchen duty was construed as submission to patriarchy, Amá's food often served to counter, neutralize, and even equalize Juan's power. Amá turned her "submissive" role to one of strategic power by pacifying the beast with any one of his favorite dishes, thus taming him while freeing us from the abuse at least for one day. Because it is inside the domestic sphere that sociocultural messages and expectations are gendered, Amá used the kitchen as a powerful site to teach us how to reclaim our humanity through food practices that we now reproduce in our own kitchens.

Food as Voice against Cultural and Social Violence

5   Ibid., 79.
6   *Like Water for Chocolate*, directed by Alfonso Arau (1992; Mexico, Arau Films Internacional), DVD.
7   Abarca, *Voices in the Kitchen*, 79.
8   Ramona L. Pérez and Meredith E. Abarca, "*Cocinas Públicas*: Food and Border Consciousness in Greater Mexico," Food & Foodways 15 (2007): 137-51.
9   See Josie Méndez-Negrete, *Las hijas de Juan: Daughters Betrayed* (Durham, NC: Duke University Press, 2006) to place in context the relationship of control under which we lived as Juan's family. It is in the context of our lived experience that we learned to understand the meaning of nurturing and emotional care through culinary preparation practices.

Feminist food scholars present methodologies to explore the relationship between violence and food within the domestic sphere.[10] Carole M. Counihan displays "differential consciousness" through her methodology of food-centered life histories that reveals "women's voice, identity, and world view."[11] Similarly, in her *charlas culinarias*, Abarca theorizes on issues of agency and power of Mexican and Mexican American working-class women. She enacts a type of *testimoniando* to narrate the witnessing of the ways in which women engage in the everyday practices of preparing and eating the food they cook.[12] For Amá, it was her singing and whistling while cooking that let us know that she was connected to her self—an act of defiance to the messages we received about our gendered status through Juan's authority. The delectable morsels Amá so lovingly created for us became the unspoken signal to let us know that Juan's moments of violence would pass and that she would take care of us in the only way she could.

The common assumption about food is that its preparation is often associated with oppression rather than power and creativity. Counihan, relying on Chela Sandoval for the theoretical framing, argues for a differential consciousness through which "women can challenge subordination and strive for agency through food-centered life histories."[13] Furthermore, this method "is a key strategy used by dominated people to survive demeaning and disempowering structures and ideologies but at the same time to generate alternative beliefs and tactics that resist domination."[14] In the kitchen, Amá taught us about food practices as a way to resist, challenge, and contest the patriarchal imperative.[15] In a similar vein, Counihan speaks about spaces of reciprocity and mutuality, and Abarca examines "issues of subjectivity and acts of agency" to document women as "critical thinkers in their own rights who use the language of food to formulate their theories."[16] Abarca suggests that her research "offers the women...public recognition, acknowledgment, admiration, and respect for their lives, their struggles, their knowledge, and above all their *coraje* (courage) grounded in the mundane activities of everyday cooking."[17] Because it was in her kitchen that Amá dispensed her love for us, she taught us to see the kitchen as a space of power rather than a place designed to serve the man whom society perceives as the master of the home. In her everyday domestic practices, Amá

---

10   Carole M. Counihan and Penny Van Esterik, eds., *Food and Culture: A Reader*, 3rd ed. (London: Routledge, 2013).
11   Carole M. Counihan, "*Mexicanas'* Food Voice and Differential Consciousness in the San Luis Valley of Colorado," in *Food and Culture: A Reader*, ed. Carole M. Counihan and Penny Van Esterik (New York: Routledge, 2013). 173-86, 173.
12   For more on this form of testimonio (testimony), see Latina Feminist Group, *Telling to Live: Latina Feminist Testimonios* (Durham, NC: Duke University Press, 2001).
13   Counihan, "*Mexicanas'* Food Voice and Differential Consciousness in the San Luis Valley of Colorado," 175.
14   Ibid.
15   Chela Sandoval, *Methodology of the Oppressed* (Minneapolis: University of Minnesota Press, 2000), 183. Sandoval's work provides me with an understanding of love as a liberatory strategy in "food consciousness" and as a means of creating social change in the home. It is in the fluid space of the home that we gained an understanding that love becomes a strategy for creating alliances to contest patriarchal powers.
16   Abarca, *Voices in the Kitchen*, 12.
17   Ibid., 17.

contested power through the creation of nourishment. She showed us that even at the individual level of resistance love shapes an oppositional consciousness that carves the path to emancipation.

Reflexive autoethnography, a process of self-interrogation and the study of relationship in the context of shared memories, allowed me to query Amá, brothers and sisters, and others who lived within the vicinity of our lives about the recollections of memories we carried regarding the violence we survived. However, it was never my intention to document to foodstuff or culinary practices of those who loved me and protected me. Intertwined with the everyday experiences of what we lived, contended with, and survived, these narratives surfaced to the forefront in the telling of our story. We shared special meals and memories of food that marked our creative and resilient spirit as *las hija de Juan*.

Abarca's analysis of my book[18] inspired my return to Amá's kitchen to reflect on the culinary cartography she carved as we moved as (im)migrants from place to place: from Mexico to the United States and from rural to urban spaces. It was in Amá's kitchen where I learned that cooking takes place inside dialectics of nurturing, contestation, and resistance, a lesson marked with significant importance when there is active violence in the home. In Amá's kitchen we learn viscerally the meaning of "food consciousness." As Abarca and Pascual Soler argue, "food consciousness" allows us to "not only turn food into a means of thought but also align consciousness with a sense of taste."[19] My "food consciousness" helped me to enable my sense of taste as I was able simultaneously to recognize Juan's abuses so well that I could taste them, and just as powerfully, to savor the spiritual and emotional resistance to such abuse in Amá's cooking. In this essay, I speak about food memories and recollections that allow me to discuss the ways in which Amá enacted agency despite the confines of a domineering husband. I also focus on the way in which she expressed subjectivity by modeling for us a revolutionary spirit that keeps food as the central source of love and nourishment.

De allá Pá Acá: Learning about Foodways

For Amá, love and nourishment were a part of the many recipes she still carries in her *recetario*, which contains recipes filed in her memory, not written on lined paper. In her hands, common greens and other foodstuffs became gifts of the goddesses. With her special *sazón*, she kept her escuincles (children) salivating as we awaited her gifts. In her kitchen, foodstuff became food and medicine that would nourish our bodies and heal our soul and spirit. Amá cooked with produce and herbs that have a long ancestral history. Our food history and legacy long taught us that the *avocado* was not just about *guacamole*, a word that

---

18   Meredith E. Abarca, "Families Who Eat Together, Stay Together, But Should They?" in *Rethinking Chicana/o Literature through Food: Postnational Appetites*, ed. Nieves Pascual Soler and Meredith E. Abarca (New York: Palgrave Macmillan, 2013).
19   Abarca and Pascual Soler, Introduction in *Rethinking Chicanoa/o Literature through Food*, 8.

comes from the Nahuatl *ahuacamolli*, a sauce (molli), and avocado (*ahuaca*). Avocados have curative properties that placed the fruit in high esteem. Amá had many uses for this curative fruit: she took the leaves to spice up special dishes, especially *caldos* and *moles*; she used the bark to fight *torzones*, or stomach pains and diarrhea; and she used the outer skin to rid the children's stomachs of worms. She transmitted her knowledge not just of avocados but also other edible *yerbas*, wild greens, that we almost lost when we migrated north.[20]

Once in the United States, Amá crossed many culinary borders. For her, each new space provided cooking experiences to explore. She had no choice but to find new ways of doing old things, thus expanding her culinary repertoire. In Mexico and the United States, Amá adapted her cooking practices while gaining new ways of preparing food.[21] In the United States, she did not have to overcook the meat because there was refrigeration, a luxury that she had not always had. Refrigeration allowed us to keep goods that would normally spoil. However, it also took away the fresh taste of those meats and goods that were more delectable when freshly taken from the market or when fruits and vegetables were freshly picked. She learned to add more spices such as garlic, pepper, and salt. She adopted others such as cumin. Through her flexible and innovative ability to engage new spaces, Amá taught me to negotiate the locations and positionalities I encountered in unfamiliar and new environments. For example, once in the United States, I had to not only contend with gender discrimination, but also with race and class biases.

One of Amá's innovations was to use what was at her disposal to dress whatever she cooked. In Mexico, we dressed our tacos and tostadas with *pico de gallo de repoyo y queso* (freshly diced chile sauce with cabbage and cheese). In south Texas, although known as the Winter Garden, it was hard for Amá to find greens to feed us. Outside St. Patrick's Day when cabbage was harvested en masse, she had a hard time finding it for our tacos and tostadas. Since *Mexicano* products were no longer available to us, we learned to eat iceberg lettuce and yellow cheese, even though it was too greasy and rich for our bellies. We missed our *queso cotija, queso panela y queso de chiva*, especially *la rata de la familia*, Amá's nickname for me because I love cheese.[22] Of course, I complained the most and had the most difficulty adjusting to the changes, but Amá's revolutionary spirit to find moments of strength and joy regardless of all oppressive and limiting factors served as a model of thriving adaptation.

---

20   Migration or *migrante* not *inmigrante*—words I learned from Rosita, *mi supermaestra de elementaria*, who often clarified when we spoke about California or Texas. After all, she would often remind us that Mexico was taken right from under our feet. So, in our view, Amá's movement was a migratory one because of her back-and-forth life.

21   David Montejano, *Anglos and Mexicans in the Making of Texas, 1936-1986* (Austin: University of Texas Press, 1987). In his discussion about the organization of labor in south Texas, Montejano shows that while Mexicans worked the fields to produce varying agricultural products, the crops they harvested were not often consumed by the workers.

22   Various qualities of cheese: *queso cotija* or dried and salty cow-milk cheese; *queso panela*, also known as basket cheese, is similar to mozzarella; *y queso de chiva* or goat cheese.

Our tortillas reflected another adaptation. Despite the fact that corn is a staple for *Mexicanos del sur*, who cling to their Indian ways, she nonetheless learned to make *tortillas de harina* because corn was difficult to find. What was never difficult to create were metaphorical and symbolic associations with food. Even though we did not have much occasion to engage with "white" people, since we lived and shopped in areas that were predominantly Mexican, we created an imaginary, though racialized, relation with "whites" by calling flour tortillas *gringas* due to their white color. By the same token, the only time whites entered our personal spaces was through their own dispersion of racial food insults: "tío taco" and "taco bender" as a type of Mexican identity, to name but two. Food served as a way to teach us who we were in relationship to our cultural and social environments, in Mexico and the United States.

At times, Amá discovered Mexican culinary staples while working in the fields alongside her husband. Amá never got a penny for working *en el campo* because Juan kept the money; however, one day her "free" labor paid off. For the first time, she found those edible weeds she has long used as a part of our diet growing wild among the cotton bushes that she helped her husband tend to for *el patron*. It was just another ordinary workday when she found them. Double-checking and bending to see if the weed was really what she thought it was, her mind repeated a child's ditty to underscore her disbelief:

> *Verdolagas y quelites que deveras te creistes..*
>
> *(It'll be purslane and pigweed for you, if you believe that…)*
>
> *Verdolagas y quelites que deveras te creistes…*
>
> *(It'll be purslane and pigweed for you, if you believe that…)*

Swiftly, Amá snipped a handful of new growth and placed its leaves in her mouth to taste them. Her eyes had not deceived her. She was right. It was the precious weed she had savored in her village. It was the *verdolagas* (purslane) we longed to eat. That day she delighted in knowing that she would provide special food for us. She picked enough greens to add them raw to the *ensalada* (salad) and to fold them into those mouth-watering *carne de puerco* (pork dishes) that she so lovingly prepared for her children. In those fields she spied verdolagas, the magical weedy herb with bright yellow flowers, to make her special *guisos* (stews) and soups that protected our kidneys. Finally, something good had come out of working in the fields.

While working in the fields, she continued her search for edibles on her path. In time she found *quelites* (weeds) that she cooked with pork meat and nopales, or that she sautéed with onions, tomatoes, chiles, and other spices to add to the pot of beans. In Nahuatl, quilitl or quelites were vegetables or edible greenery. I had long learned from the elders in my family to identify weeds called *xihuitl*, distinguishing the edible ones from those used for grazing or as feed, *tzacatl*, now known as *zacate* (grass).

The vegetables she had the most difficulty finding were nopales, the emerald of vegetables, known for their healing properties. In those days in south Texas, these pads were not even available in Doña Maria cans or jars as we find them today. However, Amá learned from the locals of south Texas about *nopales de castilla* or wild cactus, and she soon incorporated the cacti baby leaves into our diet. At first, we did not like them that much, longing for the varieties we left behind in Zacatecas. Not having other options, we decided these slimy nopales were better than none at all. Soon, Texas nopales became part of our diet despite their almost invisible bristles that no one wanted to tangle with. Those near-see-through *espinas* or thorns on its pads were enough to keep people away from the staple, but Amá found a way. She built a broom with twigs from the Texas *ceniso* (sagebrush) to dust the pads off, ridding them of those pernicious thorns. That is the way nopales became a seasonal staple at our table for the duration of their harvest, especially during Lent.

As a result of Amá's culinary creativity, we became very happy with our nopales. It was almost like being back in Tabasco, Mexico, our hometown from where the family originates. Yet, our love for nopales was often a reason for others to deride us. We proudly wore our nopal, not just for our *frente* or forehead as they branded those of us who came from Mexico, but we also carried it snuggly inside our bellies. Still, there were those who thought us weird because for them nopales were feed for cattle and livestock roaming the ranges of south Texas and were not for human consumption. Later, I would appreciate these culinary practices through the work of Gloria E. Anzaldúa, who relied on nopales as metaphors for self-identity and protection. In her poem, "Nopales," they are both a lifeline and a threat because Anzaldúa has to "defang the cactus" to eat it.[23]

Food was not the only weapon Amá used to create a semblance of home, notwithstanding living in a place of violence. She dressed up the environments of our poor dwellings with plants of spices and flowers she grew and tended to. Her hand-embroidered tablecloths and napkins, *manteles y servilletas*, adorned our table. She made those manteles from cloth discards, *trocitos de material*, or cotton sacks of flour. Sometimes they had tiny flowers. Other times the cloth was lined in radiant greens, passionate purples, or ravishing reds, or in small plaids of pastel yellows or blues. She matched their lines just so, joining six or eight *bolsas de harina* to make the most elaborate tablecloths. With her sewing skills, one could not detect where a bag began and the other ended. When she pulled out a near-border design of threads, she reinforced it with hand stitches and fringed them with a crochet border or *deshilado*, making them look prettier

23   Gloria Anzaldúa, *Borderlands/La Frontera: The New Mestiza*, 1ˢᵗ ed. (San Francisco; aunt lute, 1987), 134.

than the ones sold at the store. Her décor helped buffer the fear and violence Juan's abusive authority created. Her décor gave us the feeling of home.

And...We Were not Dirty Mexicans

Home was sacrosanct to Amá. As an agricultural worker, she was fastidious about the way we looked. She often reminded us that we were "*pobrecitas, pobrecitas, pero siempre lavaditas, planchaditas y limpiecitas,*" really poor, but always washed, ironed, and very clean. Her effort was as if to reinscribe pride in our brown and Indian bodies when someone tried to imply otherwise. We were clean Mexicans. She did not want anybody to think we were any less worthy because we came from Mexico. For that reason, she always told us to mind our manners. Amá affirmed that we knew how to act and that we came from a proud people. Just because she came from a *rancho* did not mean she lacked the *cultura* to know how to act. Amá would tell us this as she gave us our lessons on proper behavior: "Pick up the cup with your thumb and the two nearest fingers. Lift out your pinkies just so, to show that you know how to act like the best mannered people in town."

Her recetarios of culinary knowledge were not just about cooking. They included lessons about social graces and ways to tend to home and children. Her life's recetarios reflected a "food consciousness" that guided our everyday interactions around and with food. Growing up, the social graces she taught us seemed paradoxical to me. They reflected contradictions to the violence, gender, and sexuality standards we navigated living inside a house of horrors and the racism and classism we often confronted outside the house. Growing up, it never made sense to me how etiquette of social graces would help, but I learned it anyway. In retrospect, what she taught me has given me the skills to negotiate identity and power in multisited spaces.

En Mexico: As If We Did not Leave

Amá traveled back and forth from Mexico to the United States, but in every space she would soon get into the local routine of life. In Mexico, Amá went to the garden to gather whatever greens were in season for our food. She walked over to the neighbors' *milpa*[24] to see what she could buy. She sent us to the corral to collect eggs or to milk the cows or goats that would yield the milk for our cream of oats or make the *atole* for our breakfast. What we did not gather from the garden, the field, or the barn, we got at the *mercado*, the food market, to complete the needed staples for the day. Our bread did not come from bakeries or grocery stores, but out of the open-air wood-fueled oven.

Amá always knew how to make use of leftovers, but nothing could compete with the corn tortillas she made while we were in Mexico. To make tortillas for the day, she began from scratch by grinding the *nixtamal* on the *metate*. When

---

24   While the meaning of the word *milpa* translates to cornfield, we easily bandied around to mean orchard and parcel.

she grinded the corn, her movement was a divine act; she became one with the *masa* as she put her entire self into making the dough. The work that she put into making her tortillas was so replete with soul that her perfectly shaped tortillas became a slice of love in our belly. I could feel my heart doing a jog with the clap, clap, clapping of her hands; it was music to my ears and nourishment for my *panza*. Her *tortilleo* made my stomach sing and dance with anticipation. Amá's tortillas, a few *frijoles*, and her best *chile salsa* became the perfect meal, especially when crowned with sprinkles of homemade cheese.

She often set aside some of the masa to use for our morning atole and as a condiment to other meals. Like other foods, atole is an ancestral gift from the Nahuas. It derives from the words *tlaolli*, for ground corn, and *atl*, for water. Amá knew how to make all kinds of atoles from many substances; *maizena* (cornstarch) and oats were but a few. Our favorites were *atole de avena, arroz*, and the chocolaty-rich *champurrado* she made for special occasions or when we wore her down with our requests. If we got sick, we did not even have to ask, as some atoles were medicine to her.

As the granddaughter of a *curandera*, Amá believed food was medicine and had many ways to cure. She used oats to stop loose bowels, or what we called *corridas*, a take off from the word *runs* in English. I remember she would soak a cup of oats in a pitcher with two cups of water, sometimes overnight, to use as needed for our stomachs. Before she gave it to us to drink, though, she separated the oats from the water, making sure that not a speck of the product filtered into the liquid. It only took one day for us to be okay. With her cures and her cooking, on this side of the border or *en el otro lado*, Amá forged heaven on earth with her creations. Her belief in the curative power of food, and the reality of the abusive environment affecting our lives, converted her cooking into a revolutionary act that aimed to heal bodies and souls.

Manjares del Pueblo

Recollections of Amá's culinary knowledge and the lessons imparted with it are not complete without mentioning the fruits and edible flowers of my childhood. Second only to Amá's food was the fruit of our childhood that was disappearing from our diet in el norte. While plentiful in our hometown of Tabasco, fruits were not easily accessible in the patrón's store.[25] My palate's memory, however, could easily help me imagine and taste the *xoconochtli*, a round and somewhat unappealing verdant fruit that hid inside its heart a pulpy sweet delight with the taste of *pitaya*, prickly pear, and *guayaba*, all in one. It made me dream. My palate's memory could so help me savor *piñas*, mangos, papayas, and *guayabas* that had the sweetest taste. Even though their cousins in the United States came from Mexico like us, they were no competition in terms of flavor. But then

---

25   As migrant fieldworkers, we were often limited to shop for basic provisions in the grocery store owned by the farm's owner, *el patron*.

again, I imagine my palate not being as receptive to fruits' natural sweetness while living under Juan's authority.

The *zapote* fruit taught us patience, as we contemplated the ripening of its deep green ovoid fruit it turned to yellow, a sign that it was ready. We left it alone because it tasted best when it fell from the tree. Its white mushy pulp inside, with one single deep brown seed, was heaven sent. The *cherimoya*, a green round fruit with snakeskin designs on its outer layer, had a pulpy off-white inside with round black seeds that perfected our target practice as we ate the fruit and spit out the seeds to see who could send them the farthest. *Chia*, small seeds used for *agua fresco*, along with *arroz, jamaica*, and other fruits that were a bit *pasadas*, or a tad too mature to eat, became *aguas frescas* fit for kings. Quenching our thirst, we did not even think to complain about overripeness and overlooked the presence of those rice grains that would sometimes end up trapped between our teeth.

Flower petals were also food for us. We used them for *aguas frescas*, as cooking ingredients, and as medicinal cures. Hibiscus, or jamaica, and *flores de calabaza* were the two I most loved. The deep magenta of the hibiscus got my mouth watering just thinking about its agua fresco taste, and Amá's *guiso* of pumpkin flowers sautéed with vegetables and spices, topped with my favorite cheese, was a meal to celebrate. We loved the pumpkin flowers when she melted them into our *quesadillas* with the just-off-the-*metate* corn she made into a turnover, which we later learned to call *tlacoyos*.

Transiciones de Amor

Counihan argues that food is a source of contesting gender power relations.[26] Certainly, this was the case in our home. It was through food and cooking that Amá aimed to protect us and create a home for us. But it was through food that Juan tried to diminish Amá's power as he tried to dictate what she could or should cook. For example, we found ourselves having to eat the heart of mature copal pads that I detested because it was Juan's favorite dish. I managed to avoid liver because its taste and texture were too weird for my palate. She tried to protect me from that awful liver by not cooking it or feeding me only arroz or *fideos* in a bowl with beans in its juice, flavored by chile salsa, and sprinkled with cheese. Thanks to our migration that availed goods previously unavailable, Amá gained the empowerment of selecting and experimenting with food items that resisted Juan's domination, as they were not part of his culinary demands; nevertheless, we could enjoy eating them. Amá knew how to reward and soothe us to make our lives emotionally bearable.

Once Amá was free from Juan,[27] who had believed he controlled her kitchen, she could prepare whatever dish she desired without having to use food as the

---

26 Carole M. Counihan, *The Anthropology of Food and Body: Gender, Meaning, and Power* (New York: Routledge, 1999).
27 In *Las hijas de Juan*, I address Juan's arrest for his abusive behavior. He was released after serving his prison sentence, and never returned to our family.

balm to tend to our broken hearts. While cooking still felt like a responsibility, there was no hierarchy or authority to control her love in the kitchen, Juan's absence did not change the connection she had carved into that language of food that gave her a voice when she had no tongue to speak. In her body and mind, she knew the kitchen was her dispensary of love where only she had control over its space. Still now, at the age of eighty-four, Amá continues to prepare *chilaquiles*, her famous enchiladas made with Salsa Las Palmas, the canned cause that substituted the *chiles cascabel*, *puya*, and *ancho*. Even with this canned product, her enchiladas are like no other. And her *picadilla de carne desebrada* and her *nopales con carne* and *chile colorado* are among those dishes often requested by visiting relatives.

Mague, Fela, and I treasure Amá and the ways in which she made a hostile home tolerable through cooking, as well as the ways in which she cared for and supported us through the food she prepared. Because of her and the care she exercised to impart silent messages of love, we have created our own sazón in the kitchen and have learned to identify emotions in others with an intuition bar none. In addition to learning to become creative with what was available to us, we learned to create community through food. During an adolescence that was framed in the poverty of being a charge on public assistance, *en la mesa de* Amá we ate what was available. We also opened up our home to others to create community in a culture of breaking bread, where there was always food to share—*donde come uno, comen todos*.

Amá's philosophy of food, inscribed in the words she uttered, gave us the freedom to open our home as a site for sharing love. She taught us to survive as we took in the environment and conditions under which we had to participate in the creation of the everyday. Regardless of what was happening around us, Amá never failed to nurture us with the love she could quietly give us as she prepared and placed our food on the table. Identifying each of the special meals we enjoyed, she doled out her love to the one she perceived was most in need of it, while continuing to create ways to let us know we mattered in her and one anothers' lives. Throughout our later upbringing with her alone, the anger, pain, and violence dissipated in the comfort of knowing that she would be there to love us in the best way she could. In her own way, she did what she could to nurture and take care of us, to the point of having taken abuses and mistreatment in our place.

Agency, Love, and Empowerment in Amá's Kitchen

I love to cook. Food making and preparation is an act of creation. I make art with my food because it is the glue that binds our communities, and I share my appreciation for others by cooking for them. The palette of colors, the flavors, and the aromas that merge when I practice the legacy I have inherited from the cooking *curanderas* with who I grew up inspire me. Like Amá in the early years, because my options have expanded with the global market I have at my disposal, I have made my own modifications. I add things I never would have imagined. I have also made changes for health reasons. Because I like to invent tastes, I mix ingredients or create new dishes. Moreover, I make conscious choices about the food I use by often avoiding the purchase of goods that rely on pesticides that harm workers and consumers alike. Even when costs are higher.

New options, new ingredients, and adventurous taste buds have pushed for modification and improvement of the dishes I love. Adding new spices and changing ingredients to the panoply of dishes I have inherited, I make new creations while still honoring those that have a special place in my life. Unlike Amá, I do not grind corn in the *metate*. The masa I use has been packaged as a dry good or I buy it at the *tortilleria* already prepared; although, I exercise care to stay away from genetically modified corn. Depending on need, I could use a coarse *masa harina* for *tamales* and fine masa for tortillas, *atoles*, or as a thickening agent. *Masa seca* has become a part of my cooking repertoire; my labor and my taste buds have adjusted yet again. Virgin and classic olive oils are central and main ingredients in my cooking. One dresses the salads I make, and the other is an integral part of the dough for my tamales. Classico is the oil with which I make sautés, and the oil signifies my commitment to preparing Mexican dishes that are already healthy and good. Regardless of cost, olive oil has long substituted the lard or Mazola in those dishes I learned from Amá.

Still, as it was for Amá, love is the main ingredient with which I cook. Love is the energy that guides the choice of dishes and the tastes I mix. Because I believe that our stomach is truly the heart of our emotions, my senses and my love for self and others serves me to tend to those for whom I care and who have become my social family. The division of labor in the kitchen also has changed. Children and men participate in the work that precedes and follows a meal, men and boys now do work they had not done in the past.

With few exceptions, I have reclaimed those fruits, products, spices, and ingredients that I ate in the Mexico of my childhood. The global market has erased inaccessibility to the products with which I grew up. These products are now at my disposal because I can order nopales and other foodstuff through the Internet. With these global linkages, the art of cooking acquires infinitesimal possibilities. Past practices I continue to use include the sprinkling of lemon and chile pepper in my cooking. My husband, who has been known to comment that Mexicans put *limón* and chile on everything, makes lip-smacking sounds to celebrate the condiments I use in my *picos de fruta*. He continues to delight in the food I prepare for us. If he comments as I prepare one or another of the foods with which I grew up, I retort with a word of caution, telling him to be careful or I will spice him up. My *picos* have become *nuevo-Chicano* dishes that now incorporate ingredients not previously available to Amá. In my kitchen, kiwi now substitutes for that chameleon *tuna* or prickly pear of yesteryear. In the context of the United States, these dishes become new ethnic expressions of food bridging the Mexican and Chicano experiences in which I interact. *Salsa de mango, guayaba, piña, o tamarindo* are the Mexican chutneys that flavor the tortillas or spice the fish that I prepare for our meals.

As resilient women who survived the emotional and psychological traumas of violence, in addition to reproducing the dishes of our legacy, *las hijas de Juan* now create our own recetarios as we modify the spaces we occupy to degenderize the kitchen. We incorporate the food tastes, recipes, and labor of those with whom we have made family and community. With our cooking practices we have created an equal and revolutionary environment where the men in our family participate in the creation and production of the dishes that make our household a home. In our respective homes, we rely on a family culinary consciousness to create a space where we can reclaim ourselves, as we tend to our loved ones, and as our loved ones also become an integral part in the preparation of food.

I must add that my now more than thirty-seven-year relationship to my husband was the product of the culinary sensibilities I learned from ancestral women sages. My intuition and ability to read the environment, as well as my husband's predilection for food, was the *anzuelo* with which I *fished* him or *cooked* him— words my friends are prone to use whenever they hear the story about how I caught him, even though I was not looking. Without asking or providing him notice, the first meal I prepared for him consisted of all his favorite dishes: *carne de puerco con espinacas,* nopales, and a *guiso de chile verde,* arroz, frijoles, and flour tortillas, as well as an apple pan pie and a sweet tea that connected him to my sazón for life. Despite the years, he continues to appreciate and value the meals I prepare, with comments such as, "You haven't made this," as he smacks his lips with pleasure. My cooking is a testament of love to those who are dear to me. It is a form of self-love that inspires me to create from *lo que tengo* for those I love.

Amá only assumed domestic responsibilities when she married because when she was a young woman her older sisters protected her from these chores. Later, she learned to cook by memory through her creativity and imagination and, thus, has given us a legacy. She called back the food of our ancestors and gave us the gift of cooking as a dispensary of power. She taught us to see food as love. Instead of raising us to think of cooking as a burden, Amá showed us food was nurturance and art-in-the-making. Most of all, for her, food was central to the relationships among those we love and with whom we were making community, as she tried to protect us as best she could in an unsafe home. Through her culinary actions, we learned lessons to deal with the violence surrounding us. We learned to fight it through her efforts to diffuse the power of the patriarch.

Mague, the sister after me, who cooks with knowledge gained from a home economics high school curriculum and the enfolding of Pilipino foods she adopted from her first husband, has created alternative food practices from other ethnic food expressions. Her chicken adobo has been adopted by all of us, making our kitchen a multicultural expression of love. Through Amá, she learned that the kitchen was a place of expression and one where all whom we love are nurtured in a space of care and love.

Fela, our younger sister, learned how to cook to feed her first husband, and has also incorporated the Cuban dishes of her second husband's family recipes of *Havana Vieja*. She creates such delectable fares such as *moros y cristianos* (black beans with rice) and *ropa vieja* (a type of beef stew) like no other in the California Bay Area. Fela cooked to mediate the volatility of her first marriage, while in the second marriage she relied on a "food consciousness" to reclaim her own self from a failed and violent first marriage. Like Amá, Fela tended to the needs of her children and made the kitchen her space of expression and self-nurturance.

Amá's hijas carry legacies carved out of revolutionary options of everyday life in the midst of turmoil and violence.

Questions for Discussion

1. Méndez-Negrete is very specific in her detailing of the cooking and food selections of her mother, Ama. How did those decisions change when the family moved to the U.S.? What was eventually salvaged from earlier practices?

2. Examine one example of food you are unfamiliar with that Méndez-Negrete describes. How does her careful description provide evidence of her overall argument/claim? What point is she making overall regarding the role of her mother in a home that might have been dominated by the abusive behavior of her father?

3. Like Cordain and Fitting, Méndez-Negrete elevates traditional food preparation practices. If these three scholars were in a room together, what might each contribute to a conversation on the value of particular kinds of food? In an imagined dialogue, provide one sentence for each writer that captures their fundamental agreement as well as the distinctions among their positions.

Excerpts from *The Paleo Diet*

Loren Cordain, Ph.D.

The Paleo Diet, 2011

According to his professional website, Dr. Loren Cordain is Professor Emeritus of the Department of Health and Exercise Science at Colorado State University where he directed the Human Performance Laboratory, is considered one of the foremost authorities on the human diet as a function of evolutionary science, and is the author of more than 100 articles and chapters. Originator of the Paleo Diet, he argues for a return to Stone Age practices in relation to eating. His goal, according to the publisher's information for his book *The Paleo Diet*, is to help the U.S. public understand what is wrong and might be fixed with regard to the standard American diet. In the following pages from his book *The Paleo Diet*, Dr. Cordain explains his theories about fats, carbohydrates, and their connections to preventable food-dependent conditions such as osteoporosis.

Lose Weight and Get Healthy by Eating the Foods You Were Designed to Eat

Introduction

This book represents the culmination of my lifelong interest in the link between diet and health, and of my fascination with anthropology and human origins. Although these scientific disciplines may at first appear to be unrelated, they are intimately connected. Our origins—the very beginnings of the human species— can be traced to pivotal changes in the diet of our early ancestors that made possible the evolution of our large, metabolically active brains. The Agricultural Revolution and the adoption of cereal grains as staple foods allowed us to abandon forever our previous hunter-gatherer lifestyle and caused the Earth's population to balloon and develop into the vast industrial-technological society in which we live today.

The problem, as you will see in this book, is that we are genetically adapted to eat what the hunter-gatherers ate. Many of our health problems today are the direct result of what we do—and do not—eat. This book will show you where we went wrong—how the standard American diet and even today's so-called healthy diets wreak havoc with our Paleolithic (Old Stone Age) constitutions. It will also show you how you can lose weight and regain health and well-being by eating the way our hunter-gatherer ancestors ate—the diet that nature intended.

The reason for this book is very simple: the Paleo Diet is the one and only diet that ideally fits our genetic makeup. Just 333 generations ago—and for 2.5 million years before that—every human being on Earth ate this way. It is the diet to which all of us are ideally suited and the lifetime nutritional plan that will normalize your weight and improve your health. I didn't design this diet—nature did. This diet has been built into our genes.

More than twenty years ago, I read a book that endorsed vegetarian dieting titles *Are You Confused?* I suspect that this title pretty much sums up how many of us feel about the conflicting breakthroughs and mixed messages we hear every day from scientific and medical authorities on what we should and shouldn't eat to lose weight and be healthy.

But here's the good news. Over the last twenty-five years, scientists and physicians worldwide have begun to agree on the fundamental principle underlying optimal nutrition—thanks in part to my colleague Dr. S. Boyd Eaton of Emory University in Atlanta. In 1985, Dr. Eaton published a revolutionary scientific paper called "Paleolithic Nutrition" in the prestigious *New England Journal of Medicine* suggesting that the ideal diet was to be found in the nutritional practices of our Stone Age ancestors. Although a few physicians, scientists, and anthropologists had been aware of this concept, it was Dr. Eaton's writings that brought this idea to center stage.

Dr. Eaton applied the most fundamental and pervasive idea of biology and medicine—the theory of evolution by natural selection—to diet and health. His premise was simple: our genes determine our nutritional needs. And our genes were shaped by the elective pressures of our Paleolithic environment, including the foods our ancient ancestors ate.

Many modern foods are at odds with our genetic makeup—which, as we'll discuss in the book, is basically the same as that of our Paleolithic ancestors—and this is the cause of many of our modern diseases. By restoring the food types that we are genetically programmed to eat, we can not only lose weight, but also restore our health and well-being.

I have studied diet and health for the past three decades and have devoted the last twenty years to studying the Paleo Diet concept. I have been fortunate enough to work with Dr. Eaton to define this groundbreaking idea and explore a wealth of new evidence. Together with many of the world's top nutritional scientists and anthropologists, I have been able to determine the dietary practices of our hunter-gatherer ancestors. Understanding what they ate is essential for understanding what we should eat today to improve our health and promote weight loss. Our research has been published in the top nutritional journals in the world.

It's all here for you in this book[1]—all the dietary knowledge and wisdom that my research team and I have gleaned from our distant ancestors who lived in the days before agriculture. Part One explains what our Paleolithic ancestors ate, the basics of the Paleo Diet, and how civilization has made us stray from our original diet, bringing us ill health and obesity. Part Two shows how you can lose weight and how much you can lose, and also how the Paleo Diet can prevent and heal disease. Part Three spells out everything you need to know to follow the Paleo Diet—including meal plans for the three levels of the diet and more than 100 delicious Paleo recipes. That's the best part of the Paleo Diet—you'll eat well, feel great, and lose weight! The book ends with a complete list of scientific references that back up all of this information.

How Our Healthy Way of Life Went Wrong

The Agricultural Revolution began 10,000 years ago—just a drop in the bucket compared to the 2.5 million years that human beings have lived on Earth. Until that time—just 333 generations ago—everyone on the planet ate lean meats, fresh fruits, and vegetables. For most of us, it's been fewer than 200 generations since our ancestors abandoned the old lifestyle and turned to agriculture. If you happen to be an Eskimo or a Native American, it's been barely four to six generations. Except for perhaps a half-dozen tiny tribes in South America and a few on the Andaman Islands in the Bay of Bengal, pure hunter-gatherers have vanished from the face of the Earth. When these few remaining tribes become Westernized during the next decade or so, this ancient way of life—which allowed our species to thrive, grow, and mature—will come to an end.

This loss of humanity's original way of life matters a great deal. Why? Look at us. We're a mess. We eat too much, we eat the wrong foods, and we're fat. Incredibly, more Americans are overweight than aren't: 68 percent of all American men over age twenty-five are either overweight or obese. And it's killing us. The leading cause of death in the United States—responsible for 35 percent of all deaths or 1 of every 2.8 deaths—is heart and blood vessel disease. Seventy-three million

---

1 *The Paleo Diet*

Americans have high blood pressure; 34 million have high cholesterol levels, and 17 million have type 2 diabetes. It's not a pretty picture.

Most people don't realize just how healthy our Paleolithic ancestors were. They were lean, fit, and generally free from heart disease and the other ailments that plague Western countries. Yet many people assume that Stone Age people had it rough, that their lives were "poor, nasty, brutish, and short," as Thomas Hobbes wrote in *The Leviathan*.

But the historical and anthropological record simply does not support this line of reasoning. Almost without exception, descriptions of hunter-gatherers by early European explorers and adventurers showed these people to be healthy, fit, strong, and vivacious. These same characteristics can be yours when you follow the dietary and exercise principles I have laid out in the Paleo Diet.

I have examined thousands of early-nineteenth and twentieth-century photographs of hunter-gatherers. They invariably show indigenous people to be lean, muscular, and fit. The few medical studies of hunter-gatherers who managed to survive into the twentieth century also confirm earlier written accounts by explorers and frontiersmen. No matter where they lived—in the polar regions of Canada, the deserts of Australia, or the rain forests of Brazil— the medical records were identical. These people were free from signs and symptoms of the chronic diseases that currently plague us. And they were lean and physically fit. The medical evidence shows that their body fat, aerobic fitness, blood cholesterol, blood pressure, and insulin metabolism were always superior to those of the average modern couch potato. In most cases, these values were equivalent to those of modern-day, healthy, trained athletes.

High blood pressure (hypertension) is the most prevalent risk factor for heart disease in the United States. It's almost unheard of in indigenous populations. The Yanomamo Indians of northern Brazil and southern Venezuela, to whom salt was unknown in the late 1960s and early 1970s, were absolutely free from hypertension. Their blood pressure didn't increase with age and remained remarkably low by today's standards. Amazingly, scientific studies of Greenland Eskimos by Drs. Hans Bang and Jørn Dyerberg from Aalborg Hospital in Aalborg, Denmark, showed that despite a diet containing more than 60 percent animal food, not one death from heart disease—or even a single heart attack—occurred in 2,600 Eskimos from 1968 to 1978. This death rate from heart disease is one of the lowest ever reported in the medical literature. For a similar group of 2,600 people in the United States during a ten-year period, the expected number of deaths from heart disease would be about twenty-five.

When you put into practice the nutritional guidelines of the Paleo Diet, you will be getting the same protection from heart disease that the Eskimos had. You will also become lean and fit, like your ancient ancestors. This is your birthright. By going backward in time with your diet, you will actually be moving forward. You'll be combining the ancient dietary wisdom with all of the health advantages that modern medicine has to offer. You will reap the best of both worlds.

Chapter 1

Not Just Another Low-Carb Diet

What's the diet craze this week? You name it, there's a book selling it—and people buying it, hoping for a "magic bullet" to help them shed excess pounds. But how can everybody be right? How can we lose weight, keep it off—and not feel hungry all the time? What's the best diet for our health and well-being?

For more than thirty years, as an avid researcher of health, nutrition, and fitness, I have been working to answer these questions. I started this quest because I wanted to get past all the hype, confusion, and political posturing swirling around dietary opinion. I was looking for facts: the simple, unadulterated truth. The answer, I found, was hidden back in time—way back, with ancient humans who survived by hunting wild animals and fish and gathering wild fruits and vegetables. These people were known as "hunter-gatherers," and my research team and I published our analysis of what many of them (more than 200 separate societies) ate in *The American Journal of Clinical Nutrition*. We were astonished at the diversity of their diet. We were also amazed at what they did *not* eat—which we'll get to in a minute and which may surprise you.

Health Secrets of Our Ancestors

What do Paleolithic people have to do with us? Actually, quite a lot: DNA evidence shows that basic human physiology has changed little in 40,000 years. Literally, we are Stone Agers living in the Space Age; our dietary needs are the same as theirs. Our genes are well adapted to a world in which all the food eaten daily had to be hunted, fished, or gathered from the natural environment—a world that no longer exists. Nature determined what our bodies needed thousands of years before civilization developed, before people started farming and raising domesticated livestock.

In other words, built into our genes is a blueprint for optimal nutrition—a plan that spells out the foods that make us healthy, lean, and fit. Whether you believe the architect of that blueprint is God, or God acting through evolution by natural selection, or by evolution alone, the end result is still the same: We need to give our bodies the foods we were originally designed to eat.

Your car is designed to run on gasoline. When you put diesel fuel into its tank, the results are disastrous for the engine. The same principle is true for us: We are designed to run best on the wild plant and animal foods that all human beings gathered and hunted just 333 generations ago. The staples of today's diet—cereals, dairy products, refined sugars, fatty meats, and salted, processed foods—are like diesel fuel to our bodies' metabolic machinery. These foods clog our engines, make us fat, and cause disease and ill health.

Sadly, with all of our progress, we have strayed from the path designed for us by nature. For instance:

Paleolithic people ate no dairy food. Imagine how difficult it would be to milk a wild animal, even if you could somehow manage to catch one.

Paleolithic people hardly ever ate cereal grains. This sounds shocking to us today, but for most ancient people, grains were considered starvation food at best.

Paleolithic people didn't salt their food.

The only refined sugar Paleolithic people ate was honey, when they were lucky enough to find it.

Wild, lean animal foods dominated Paleolithic diets, so their protein intake was quite high by modern standards, while their carbohydrate consumption was much lower.

Virtually all of the carbohydrates Paleolithic people ate came from nonstarchy wild fruits and vegetables. Consequently, their carbohydrate intake was much lower and their fiber intake much higher than those obtained by eating the typical modern diet.

The main fats in the Paleolithic diets were healthful, monounsaturated, polyunsaturated, and omega 3 fats—not the trans fats and certain saturated fats that dominate modern diets.

With this book, we are returning to the diet we were genetically programmed to follow. The Paleo Diet is more than a blast from the past. It's the key to *speedy weight loss, effective weight control, and, above all, lifelong health*. The Paleo Diet enlists the body's own mechanisms, evolved over millions of years, to put the brakes on weight gain and the development of the chronic diseases of civilization. It is the closest approximation we can make, given the current scientific knowledge, to humanity's original, universal diet—the easy-to-follow, cravings-checking, satisfying program that nature itself has devised.

The Problems with Most Low-Carb Diets

The Paleo Diet is a low-carbohydrate diet—but that's where any resemblance to the glut of low-carbohydrate fad diets ends. Remember, the Paleo Diet is the only diet based on millions of years of nutritional facts—the one ideally suited to our biological needs and makeup and the one that most closely resembles hunter-gatherer diets. How does the Paleo Diet compare with the law-carb fad diets and the average U.S. diet?

Diet	Protein	Carbohydrate	Fat
The Paleo Diet	19-35%	22-40%	28-47%
Typical U.S. Diet	15.5%	49%	34%
Low-carb fad diets	18-23%	4-26%	51-78%

Modern low-carbohydrate weight-loss diets are really high-fat diets that contain moderate levels of protein. They don't have the high levels of protein that our ancestors ate—the levels found in the Paleo Diet. Actually, compared with what our ancestors ate, the carbohydrate content of these modern weight-loss diets is far too low. Even worse, almost all of these low-carbohydrate diets permit unlimited consumption of fatty, salty processed meats (such as bacon, sausage, hot dogs, and lunch meats) and dairy products (cheeses, cream, and butter) while restricting the consumption of fruits and vegetables. Cancer-fighting fruits and vegetables! This dietary pattern is drastically different from that of our ancestors.

And although low-carbohydrate diets may be successful in promoting weight loss, many dieters are achieving short-term weight loss at the expense of long-term health and well-being. Here's what the sellers of these diet plans don't want you to know: when low-carbohydrate diets cause weight loss in the short term, it's because they deplete the body's reserves of muscle and liver glycogen (carbohydrate), and the weight you're losing rapidly is mostly water weight.

When low-carbohydrate diets cause weight loss in the long run (weeks or months), it's because more calories are being burned than consumed, plain and simple. Low-carbohydrate diets tend to normalize insulin metabolism in many people, particularly in those who are seriously overweight. This normalization prevents swings in blood sugar that, in turn, may cause some people to eat less and lose weight. It is the cutback in total calories that lowers total cholesterol and low-density lipoprotein (LDL) cholesterol (the bad cholesterol) levels. Also, reductions in dietary carbohydrates (whether calories are cut or not) almost always cause a decline in blood triglycerides and an increase in blood high-density lipoprotein (HDL) cholesterol (the good cholesterol).

So, if low-carbohydrate diets cause someone to consume fewer calories, they may help produce weight loss and improvements in blood chemistry, at least over the short haul. However, dieters beware: when low-carbohydrate, high-fat diets are followed *without* a decrease in the daily consumption of calories, they are, according to the American Dietetic Association, "a nightmare." Let's see why.

Low Carb Doesn't Mean Low Cholesterol

Despite what anybody tells you—despite the outrageous claims of the low-carbohydrate, high-fat diet doctors—if you eat a lot of the saturated fats found in cheeses, butter, and bacon and don't cut your overall calorie intake, your cholesterol will go up. The medical community has known this for more than fifty years. It's been demonstrated in metabolic ward studies, in which people are locked into a hospital wing and only allowed to eat foods that have been carefully weighed and analyzed. Many of the low-carbohydrate diet doctors claim that these clinical trials are invalid because none of them reduced the carbohydrate content sufficiently. These doctors should know better; low carbohydrates don't guarantee low cholesterol.

Dr. Stephen Phinney and colleagues from the Massachusetts Institute of Technology conducted a normal caloric intake metabolic ward trial involving nine healthy, lean men. These men consumed nothing but meat, fish, eggs, cheese, and cream for thirty-five days. They had a low carbohydrate intake—less than 20 grams a day—but it didn't matter. Their blood cholesterol levels still went up, from 159 to 208 on average in just thirty-five days. This study indicates that diets high in a specific saturated fat called palmitic acid tends to raise blood cholesterol levels when caloric intake levels are normal.

So, at best, low-carbohydrate, high-fat diets are a temporary fix. At worst, they can cause big trouble in the long run by elevating LDL cholesterol levels, which increases the risk for heart and cardiovascular disease.

Healthy Fats, Not Lethal Fats

One major difference between the Paleo Diet and the low-carbohydrate, high-fat diets we just talked about is the fats. In most modern low-carbohydrate weight-loss diets, no distinction is made between good fats and bad fats. All fats are generally lumped together; the goal is simply to reduce carbohydrates and not worry about fats.

But you *should* worry about fats. Not all fats are created equal, and the impact of fat on blood cholesterol—and the odds of developing heart disease—can't be ignored. The problem is, fats are confusing for many people trying to make good dietary decisions. For one thing, many of them sound alike. How are saturated fats different from monounsaturated—or even polyunsaturated—fats? How are omega 6 fats different from the omega 3 variety?

Monounsaturated fats are good. They're found in olive oil, nuts, and avocados; are known to lower blood cholesterol; and help prevent artery clogging or atherosclerosis.

Saturated fats are mostly bad. They're found in processed meats, whole dairy products, and many bakery items; most of them are known to raise cholesterol. A key exception is a saturated fat called stearic acid, which, like monounsaturated fats, lowers blood cholesterol levels.

Polyunsaturated fats are a mixed bag—some are more beneficial than others. For example, omega 3 polyunsaturated fats (the kind found in fish oils) are healthy fats, which can improve blood chemistry and reduce your risk of many chronic diseases. But omega 6 polyunsaturated fats (found in vegetable oils, many baked goods, and snack foods) are not good when you eat too much of them at the expense of omega 3 fats.

People in the Paleolithic Age ate a lot of monounsaturated fats; they had saturated and polyunsaturated fats in moderation—but when they did have polyunsaturated fats, they had a proper balance of the omega 3 and omega 6 fats. They consumed far fewer omega 6 polyunsaturated fats than we do today. In addition, the main saturated fat in wild animals was healthful stearic acid, not the cholesterol-raising palmitic acid, which dominates the fat of feedlot cattle.

How important are fats in the diet? Here's a modern example: People who live in Mediterranean countries, who consume lots of olive oil, are much less likely to die of heart disease than Americans or northern Europeans, who don't consume as much olive oil. Instead, our Western diet is burdened by high levels of certain saturated fats, omega 6 fats, and trans fats and sadly lacking in heart-healthy, artery-protecting omega 3 fats.

Our studies of hunter-gatherers suggest that they had low blood cholesterol and relatively little heart disease. Our research team believes that dietary fats were a major reason for their freedom from heart disease.

Saturated Fats, Reconsidered

In the first edition of *The Paleo Diet*, I was adamant that you should avoid fatty processed meats such as bacon, hot dogs, lunch meats, salami, bologna, and sausages because they contained excessive saturated fats, which raise your blood cholesterol levels. That message still holds true today, but new information subtly alters this fundamental point of Paleo Dieting, and, as always, the devil lies in the details. Should you now go out and eat bacon and processed meats to your heart's desire? Absolutely not! Processed meats are synthetic mixtures of meat (muscle) and fat combined artificially at the meatpacker's or butcher's whim, with no regard for the true fatty acid profile of wild animal carcasses that our hunter-gatherer ancestors ate. In addition to their unnatural fatty acid profiles (high in omega 6 fatty acids, low in omega 3 fatty acids, and high in saturated fatty acids), processed fatty meats are full of preservatives such as nitrites, which are converted into potent cancer-causing nitrosamines in our guts. To make a bad situation worse, these unnatural meats are typically full of salt, high-fructose corn syrup, wheat, grains, and other additives that have multiple adverse health effects.

So, artificially produced, synthetic, factory meats have little or nothing to do with the wild animal foods our hunter-gatherer ancestors ate, and they should be avoided. But how about the unprocessed fatty meats that we routinely eat, day in and day out, that are produced in feedlots and butchered without adding fats or preservatives? These are meats such as T-bone steaks, spareribs, lamb chops, and chicken legs and thighs, as well as fatty cuts of pork and other fatty domestic meats. Are they a problem?

I realize that many, perhaps most, readers are not hunters and have never seen carcasses of wild animals, such as deer, elk, or antelope. Nor have you had the opportunity to visually contrast the carcasses of feedlot-produced animals to wild animals. I can tell you that there is no comparison. My research group and I have taken the time to do the chemical analyses between wild and feedlot-produced animals, and we have published our results in some of the top nutritional journals in the world.

Wild animal carcasses are lean, have little external fat, and exhibit virtually no fat between the muscles (marbling). In contrast, feedlot-produced cattle maintain a four-to-six inch layer of white fat covering the animal's entire body. These artificial products of modern agriculture are overweight, obese, and sick. Their muscles are infiltrated with that fat that we call marbling, a trait that improves flavor but makes the cattle insulin resistant and in poor health, just like us. Wild animals rarely or never exhibit marbling.

Because feedlot-raised animals are exclusively fed grains (corn and sorghum) in the last half of their lives, their meat has high concentrations of mega 6 fatty acids at the expense of health-promoting omega 3 fatty acids. The meat of a grain-fed livestock is vastly at odds with that of wild animals. A 100 gram (~1/4lb.) serving of T-bone beefsteak gives you a walloping 9.1 grams of saturated fat, whereas a comparable piece of bison roast yields only 0.9 grams of saturated fat. You would have to eat ten times more bison meat to get a similar amount of saturated fat than the amount in a single serving of T-bone steak.

It would be difficult for our hunter-gatherer ancestors to eat anywhere near the amount of saturated fat that we get on a yearly basis in the typical Western diet. So, does dietary saturated fat promote heart disease? Should Paleo Dieters try to limit the fatty domesticated meats in their diet in order to reduce saturated fat? This question is not as clear-cut as it seemed twenty-five years ago, when Drs. Michael Brown and Joseph Goldstein of the University of Texas Southwest Medical Center were awarded the Nobel Prize in medicine for discovering that saturated fats down-regulated the LDL receptor. Their discovery and subsequent randomized, controlled human trials have unequivocally shown that certain saturated fats (lauric acid [12:0], myristic acid [14:0], and palmitic acid [16:0]) but not all (stearic acid [18:0]), elevate blood cholesterol levels in humans, all other factors being equal. These facts are undeniable. Yet the next question is contentious and has divided the nutritional and medical community in recent years: do increased blood cholesterol levels necessarily predispose all people to an increased risk for cardiovascular disease?

As the scientific community has struggled with this question during the last few years, we should remember that the evolutionary template will almost always guide us to the correct answer. The clogging of arteries that eventually results in fatal heart attacks comes about through a process called atherosclerosis, in which plaque (cholesterol and calcium) builds up in the arteries that supply the heart itself with blood. It was originally thought that this buildup gradually narrowed and finally closed the arteries supplying the heart, thereby causing a heart attack. We now know that this model is inaccurate and too simple.

In the last ten to fifteen years, it has become apparent that inflammation is involved at every step of the way when arteries become clogged with plaque. In fact, the fatal event causing a heart attack is not the gradual narrowing of arteries supplying the heart but rather the rupturing of the fibrous cap that surrounds and walls off plaque that forms in the heart's arteries. Chronic low-level inflammation triggers the fibrous cap to rupture, which in turn causes a clot to form in the arteries that supply the heart, resulting in a heart attack. Without chronic, low-level inflammation, heart attacks probably would rarely or never occur.

So, do dietary saturated fats from fatty meats cause the artery-clogging process known as atherosclerosis? If we look at the evolutionary evidence, the answer is a resounding yes. Dr. Michael Zimmerman, a pathologist at Hahnemann University in Pennsylvania, had the rare opportunity to perform autopsies on a number of Eskimo mummies that had been frozen in Alaska's permafrost for hundreds of years. The first mummy was that of a fifty-three-year-old woman whose body washed out of the frozen banks of Saint Lawrence Island in October 1972. Radiocarbon dating indicated that she had died in 400 A.D. from a landslide that had completely buried her. Dr. Zimmerman's autopsy revealed moderate atherosclerosis in the arteries supplying her heart but no evidence of a heart attack. The second frozen mummy was also a female, forty to forty-five years of age, who had also been engulfed in an ice-and-mud-slide in

1520 A.D. near Barrow, Alaska. Similarly, the autopsy showed atherosclerotic plaques lining the arteries of her heart.

From my prior studies of worldwide hunter-gatherers, we know that these Eskimo women had a diet that consisted almost entirely (97 percent) of wild animal foods, including whales, walruses, seals, salmon, muskoxen, and caribou. Because they lived so far north (63 to 71 degrees north latitude), plant foods simply were unavailable; consequently their carbohydrate intake was virtually zero. Yet they still developed atherosclerosis. Perhaps Drs. Brown and Goldstein were right, after all: high dietary intakes of saturated fats do promote atherosclerosis. Despite these facts, the best archaeological and medical evidence shows that Eskimos living and eating in their traditional ways rarely or never died from heart attacks or strokes.

So, now we have the facts we need to come to closure with the saturated fat-heart disease issue. Dietary saturated fats from excessive consumption of processed fatty meats and feedlot-produced meats increase our blood cholesterol concentrations, but unless our immune systems are chronically inflamed, atherosclerosis likely will not kill us from either heart attacks or strokes.

The new advice I can give you is this: If you are faithful to the basic principles of the Paleo Diet, consumption of fatty meats will probably have a minimal outcome on your health and well-being—as it did for our hunter-gatherer ancestors. Consumption of fatty meats and organs had survival value in an earlier time when humans didn't eat grains, legumes, dairy products, refined sugars, and salty processed foods, the foods that produce chronic low-level inflammation in our bodies through a variety of physiological mechanisms. I will explain this in more depth in my next book, *Living the Paleo Diet*.

Disease-Fighting Fruits and Vegetables

A big problem with low-carbohydrate weight-loss diets is what they do to health-promoting fruits and vegetables—they nearly eliminate them. Because of a technicality—a blanket restriction on all types of carbohydrates, even beneficial ones, to between 30 and 100 grams per day—fruits and veggies are largely off-limits. This is a mistake. Fruits and vegetables—with their antioxidants, phytochemicals, and fiber—are some of our most powerful allies in the war against heart disease, cancer, and osteoporosis. Yet just one papaya (59 grams of carbohydrate) would blow the daily limit for two of the most popular low-carbohydrate diets. Eating an orange, an apple, and a cup of broccoli and carrots (73 grams of carbohydrate)—just a drop in the bucket to hunter-gatherers, whose diets were rich in fruits and vegetables—would wreck all but the most liberal low-carbohydrate diets.

Humanity's original carbohydrate sources—the foods we survived on for millions of years—didn't come from starchy grains and potatoes, which have high glycemic indices that can rapidly cause blood sugar to spike. Instead, they came from wild fruits and vegetables with low glycemic indices that produced *minimal*, gradual rises in blood sugar. These are the carbohydrates that you'll be eating on the Paleo Diet. These nonstarchy carbohydrates normalize your blood glucose and insulin levels, promote weight loss, and make you feel energized all day long.

The Osteoporosis Connection

One of the greatest—and least recognized—benefits of fruits and vegetables is their ability to slow or prevent the loss of bone density, called "osteoporosis," that so often comes with aging. As far back as 1999, Dr. Katherine Tucker and colleagues at Tufts University examined the bone mineral status of a large group of elderly men and women. These scientists found that the people who ate the most fruits and vegetable had the greatest bone mineral densities and the strongest bones. In the ensuring ten years, more than 100 scientific studies have confirmed this concept.

But what about calcium? Surely, eating a lot of cheese can help prevent osteoporosis? The answer is a bit more complicated. One of the great ironies of the low-carbohydrate, high-fat diets is that even though they allow unlimited consumption of high-calcium cheeses, they almost certainly will be found to promote bone loss and osteoporosis in the long run. How can this be? Because getting a lot of dietary calcium from cheese, by itself, isn't enough to offset the lack of fruits and vegetables.

Nutrition scientists use the term "calcium balance" to describe this process. It's the difference between how much calcium you take in and how much you excrete. Most of us have gotten the message about consuming calcium. But the other part of the equation—*how much calcium you excrete*—is just as important. It is quite possible for you to be in calcium balance on a low calcium intake if your calcium excretion is also low. On the other hand, it's easy for you to fall out of calcium balance even if you load up on cheese at every meal—if you lose more calcium than you take in.

The main factor that determines calcium loss is yet another kind of balance—the *acid-base balance*. If your diet has high levels of acid, you'll lose more calcium in your urine, if you eat more alkaline foods, you'll retain more calcium. A study in the *New England Journal of Medicine* by my colleague Dr. Anthony Sebastian and his research group at the University of California at San Francisco showed that simply taking potassium bicarbonate (an alkaline base) neutralized the body's internal acid production, reduced urinary calcium losses, and increased the rate of bone formation. In a follow-up report in the *New England Journal of Medicine*, Dr. Lawrence Appel at Johns Hopkins University reported that diets rich in fruits and vegetable (these are alkaline foods) significantly reduced urinary calcium loss in 459 men and women.

Cereals, most dairy products, legumes, meat, fish, salty processed foods, and eggs produce net acid loads in the body. By far the worst offenders on this list are the hard cheeses, which are rich sources of calcium. Again, unless you get enough fruits and vegetables, eating these acid-rich foods will actually promote bone loss and osteoporosis.

Virtually all fruits and vegetables produce alkaline loads in the body. When you adopt the Paleo Diet, you won't have to worry about excessive dietary acid causing bone loss—because you'll be getting 35 percent or more of your daily calories as healthful alkaline fruits and vegetable that will neutralize the dietary acid you get when you eat meat and seafood.

Toxic Salt

Most low-carbohydrate, high-fat diets don't address the dangers of salt; some even encourage its use. And yet there is a ton of medical evidence linking salt to high blood pressure, stroke, osteoporosis, kidney stones, asthma, and even certain forms of cancer. Salt is also implicated as a factor in insomnia, air and motion sickness, Ménière's syndrome (an agonizing ear ringing), and the preeclampsia of pregnancy.

Salt is made up of sodium and chloride. Although most people think that the sodium portion of salt is entirely responsible for most of its unhealthful effects, chloride is just as guilty, if not more so. The average American eats about 10 grams of salt a day (this turns out to be about 4 grams of sodium and 6 grams of chloride). Chloride, like cereals, dairy products, legumes, and meats, yields a net acid load to the kidneys after it is digested. Because of its high chloride content, salt is one of the worst offenders in making your diet more acid.

Paleolithic people hardly ever used salt and never ate anything like today's salty cheeses, processed meats, and canned fish advocated by most of the low-carbohydrate weight-loss diets. Do your body a favor and throw out your saltshaker along with all of the highly salted, processed, packaged, and canned foods in your pantry.

Lean Meat Helps You Lose Weight

It's taken half a century, but scientists have finally realized that when they stigmatized red meat, they threw out the proverbial baby with the bathwater. Meat is a mixture of fat and protein. Lean meat—such as that found in wild game and seafood—is about 80 percent protein and about 20 percent fat. But fatty processed meats like bacon and hot dogs can pack a whopping 75 percent of their calories as fat and only 25 percent or less as protein. What should have been obvious—that it was the high level of a certain saturated fat, palmitic acid, not the protein, that caused health problems—was essentially ignored. Meat protein had unfairly become a villain.

Here again, there's a major lesson to be learned from looking at the distant past: for more than 2 million years, our ancestors had a diet rich in lean protein and healthful fats. It gave them energy and, combined with fruits and vegetables, helped them stay healthy.

Protein Increases Your Metabolism and Slows Your Appetite

When scientists actually studied how lean protein influences health, well-being, and body-weight regulation—and this has occurred only in the last two decades—they found that our ancestors were right all along. It turns out that *lean protein is perhaps our most powerful ally in the battle of the bulge*. It has twice the "thermic effect" of either fats or carbohydrates, which means it revs up your metabolism. In other words, protein's thermic effect increases our metabolism and causes us to burn more calories than if we ate an equal caloric serving of either fat or carbohydrate. Also, more than fats, more than carbohydrates, protein has the highest "satiating value"—that is, it does the best job of making us feel full.

The principles I have laid out in the Paleo Diet—all based on decades of scientific research and proved over millions of years by our ancestors—will make your metabolism soar, your appetite shrink, and extra pounds begin to melt away as you include more and more lean protein in your meals.

Lean Protein and Heart Disease

But this diet gives you much more than a slimmer figure. Unlike other low-carbohydrate diets, it's good for your heart. High-protein diets have been shown by Dr. Bernard Wolfe at the University of Western Ontario in Canada to be more effective than low-fat, high-carbohydrate diets in lowering total and bad LDL cholesterol and triglycerides while simultaneously increasing the good HDL cholesterol. My colleague Neil Mann at the Royal Melbourne Institute of Technology in Melbourne, Australia, has demonstrated that people who eat a lot of lean meats have lower blood levels of homocysteine (a toxic substance in the blood that damages the arteries and predisposes them to atherosclerosis) than do vegan vegetarians. The new result is that high-protein diets produce beneficial changes in your blood chemistry that, in turn, reduce your overall risk of heart disease.

High-protein diets have been shown to improve insulin metabolism, help lower blood pressure, and reduce the risk of stroke. They have even prolonged survival in women with breast cancer.

Some people have been told that high-protein diets damage the kidneys. They don't. Scientists at the Royal Veterinary and Agricultural University in Copenhagen effectively put this myth to rest. Dr. Arne Astrup and colleague put sixty-five overweight people on a high-protein diet for six months and found that their kidneys easily adapted to increased protein levels. Furthermore, kidney function remained perfect at the end of the experiment.

Isn't it time you got protein on your side? Eating lean meat and fish at every meal, just as your Paleolithic ancestors did, could be the healthiest decision you ever made.

Compared to the faddish low-carbohydrate weight-loss diets, the Paleo Diet includes all the nutritional elements needed to encourage weight loss while promoting health and well-being. The Paleo Diet is designed to imitate the healthful diets of our pre-agricultural ancestors. It contains the proper balance of plant and animal foods—and the correct ratios of protein, fat, and carbohydrate required for weight loss and excellent health.

So, don't be fooled by the low-carbohydrate fad diets. The Paleo Diet gives you the same weight-loss benefits, but it's also a delicious, healthy diet you can maintain for a lifetime.

Questions for Discussion

1. What does Cordain say is the difference between feedlot—produced meat and the carcasses of wild animals such as deer, elk, and antelope?

2. In the section called "The Problems with Most Low-Carb Diets" Cordain uses a sentence fragment, saying, "Cancer-fighting fruits and vegetables!" Why does he use this fragment and what is its effect? Does his use of a sentence fragment reduce your respect for Cordain or cause you to reconsider any "rules" you have learned about grammar?

3. Both Cordain and Fitting seem to hold traditional forms of food consumption in high esteem, and they also both suggest that food preferences are culture bound. What criticisms do they separately level against current American food systems?

A Native Perspective: Food is More than Consumption

Rachel V. Vernon

Journal of Agriculture, Food Systems, and Community Development,
September 2015

Author and scholar Rachel Vernon, who earned her master's
degree from Colorado State University in 2014, works with the
Cooperative Food Empowerment Directive in Oakland, California,
which endeavors to assist Native communities in developing
revenue and self-sufficiency through food cooperatives. Vernon
argues that food security for Native peoples can only be obtained
through an understanding and respect for cultural values around
community and relationship. In this article, Vernon situates a case
study within the long history of Native land and food disruption
as a result of colonization, the legacy of which is chronic illness
among today's Native peoples.

Cooperative Food Empowerment Directive (CoFED)

As a person of Yaqui and Mescalero Apache descent, I have a long history of
personal engagement with Native people within the context of community
as well as working for Native organizations that work on Native issues. My
educational journey has also focused on Native people and their relationship
to food within the context of food justice. I currently work at the Cooperative
Food Empowerment Directive, where we hope to encourage a world where
food cooperatives build community wealth. My experiences working on
food issues with Native people have led me to the question: How do we
build resilient Native communities that are empowering *and* powerful? In
attempting to answer this question I have discovered that the relationship to
food for Native communities has been ruptured, making food central to the
question of empowerment and power. For many Native people a ruptured
relationship to food resulting from colonization has had profound effects
beyond nutrition and health. These effects must be examined in more detail
to develop a better understanding of food's power in community building

given historical realties that have informed current relationship to food for all Native communities in this country.

According to the 2010 census there are over 566 federally recognized tribes, 2.9 million people who identify as Native only, and 5.2 million who claim Native identity in combination with another race (Centers for Disease Control and Prevention [CDC], n.d.). As one works with Native people it is important to acknowledge that we are *not* one people. Although our experiences with U.S. society have helped to create a pan-Native identity, we are not one. Each tribe has its own language, customs, beliefs, and histories. However, there are many commonalities found among these diverse populations, commonalities such as Native philosophies of interconnectedness, obligations, and responsibilities between people, animals, land, water, and air.

The current perspective, drawn from research for my master's thesis at Colorado State University (Vernon, 2014), uses a qualitative Photo Voice project with participants from the Intertribal Friendship House (IFH) in Oakland, California. The goal of the project was to further the understanding of contemporary relationship to food for Native people, while also highlighting some of the tremendous work of Native organizations and people within their communities. Among the 11 tribal identities represented, some individuals had a history of occupation of their ancestral/reservation homelands and others did not have much connection to their homelands.[1] The majority of participants were women ranging in age from their late 20s to 60s. This project illuminated the ways that Native people challenged the myths of individual choices and consumption around food. To expand the narrative around health and food, I have chosen one story to share that I believe informs us about how we can work in solidarity to solve the food issues that Native people encounter.

What my research found was that food cannot be disentangled from people and relationship; consuming, producing, and foraging for food all have meaning because they facilitate the strengthening of community bonds. Some participants believed that eating "well" is not always about the nutrition of the food, that it has more meaning. Photo 1 highlights this idea. A quick or cursory look would suggest that this food means the person is not eating well, due to both the quality of the food and its potential effects on health and well-being.

This photo could be treated as evidence of the "problems" with food consumption among Native people, and this food—the McDonald's coffee and a sweet pastry—could easily be transformed into a warning poster of what not to do. It

---

1   The tribes represented were Zapotec, Ohlone, Chumash, Hopi, Tewa, Navajo, Yurok, Seminole, Stockbridge Munsee-Mohican, Sioux, and Shoshone.

confirms the dilemma nutritionists have identified with the diet of marginalized people, a diet that includes too much sugar and fast food and illuminates the unhealthy choices of an entire community. Too easily this image could be used to fuel a narrative of what is wrong with the food choices of Native people, placing the blame for health problems upon this community. However, there is an alternative reading of this image, one that tells a story of nourishment, relationships, and safety.

The hand in the photo belongs to the 82-year-old aunt of Ana, a participant who shared this picture during a focus group at the Intertribal Friendship House (IFH). Ana shared at that meeting how this picture was taken after she had endured a long day of arranging for the secure and affordable parking of her car, which required both negotiating informal arrangements at IFH and dedicating precious time to traveling on public transportation. Exhausted by the process, Ana still found a sense of happiness, love, and community as her aunt presented her with some food.

> I had to bring my car to IFH and leave it in the parking lot, and Carol was nice enough to let me do that because I don't have secure parking. And then, taking the BART to the San Francisco Airport and then getting a red eye—it was just really exhausting and such a long journey. It felt so good to get to that airport and my aunt that I'm really close, she's 82. So that's her there in the car and so she picked me up and she had brought me a sweet roll that another aunt had packed for me, that she had driven. So I just thought it was so sweet that my aunty making it the day before or something, and my other one [auntie] packing it and driving it about an hour to the airport and so it was already ready for me all packaged in the car. Then a senior priced coffee from McDonalds. You know she got her discount or whatever and got it for me. So, I know it's not healthy or something but it was, you know, just a meaningful moment and I really felt like I could totally relax at that moment.

This strikingly beautiful story illuminates the healing nature that food and connection have on people's lives. It illuminates deeper notions of nourishment, situating the relationships of the producers of the food as sacred, while also demonstrating how this food, this experience, is tied to home, to being on or near her reservation. This moment also signals satisfied emotional health. In sum, what this story teaches is that the meaning of food among Native people must be discussed with more depth. Food means more that simply personal responsibilities about food choices and includes a more complex understanding of how food invokes community, well-being, and connectedness. The key point in the interaction is not the food itself, or the act of consuming the food and the resultant health factors, but instead the role the food has in community and individual well-being.

Photo 1. Ana receives a sweet bun and coffee upon her arrival home.

The severe disruption of Native communities and lives extends to the altering of their relationship to food, and is deeply tied to racism, colonialism, and the loss of autonomy and power. Stripping Native communities of their food sovereignty and traditional diets increased nutritional deficiencies and starvation for Native people and contributed to current health disparities in obesity, heart disease, and diabetes. (First Nations Development Institute, 2014). Destruction that began at contact become apparent when the Native population dropped from over 5 million to 250,000 in 1900 (Thornton, 1987, p. 133), a decrease resulting from disease and war that had a dire impact on the ability of Native people to hunt, gather, grow, cure, and cook food. Many Native people were also relocated off their traditional lands onto bounded reservations. The policy to limit land access affected their hunting and gathering since they were no longer allowed to hunt in traditional places, and much of the reservation lands were not the best for planting. Some relocated tribes were also unfamiliar with the land they were relocated to, thus limiting their ability to find or produce traditional food.

Eventually, the U.S. government launched the Food Distribution Program on Indian Reservations, which is still currently available to "low-income households, including the elderly, living on Indian reservations, and to Native American families residing in designated areas near reservations and in the State of Oklahoma" (U.S. Department of Agriculture, 2015, para. 1). This program provides canned goods, powdered milk, white sugar, and commodity cheese. According to food sovereignty activist Winona LaDuke, "these highly processed, high sugar, high fat, and packaged foods" (LaDuke, 2005, p. 194) provided by the government have contributed to the high rates of diabetes rates found in Native communities and are a direct impact of the "loss of access to traditional foods" (LaDuke, 2005, p. 194). This loss affects the practice of consuming traditional foods and the teaching of food preparation and foodways across generations, between genders, and within families. This loss of traditional food practices is connected to a loss of human connection, a loss of community strength.

Both reservation and urban Natives have encountered a loss of control over the food they interact with through consumption, production, and distribution. Contrary to the common belief that Natives live on reservations, approximately 78 percent of Native peoples live off-reservation, which may further affect their ability to access traditional foods and knowledge (Norris, Vines, & Hoeffel, 2012). Urban Native communities have struggled to have access to quality food since moving to urban areas.[2] The Governmental Relocation Program in the 1950s moved thousands of Native people into urban areas with the hope of assimilating them into modern American society (Fixico, 1986). These programs have generally failed since Native people have been integrated into mostly poor urban areas and have been subject to the food deserts of the already existing marginalized communities of color.

This historical context helped shape Native communities' current relationship to food and should be central to addressing food related concerns within these communities. Too often, those involved in food justice work see the lack of consumption of healthy foods as an issue of personal choice rather than one resulting from a deeply traumatic history of food relations in Native communities. The common U.S. narrative about Native people is that we do not care about our health and subsequently make poor eating decisions. In her chapter in *Cultivating Food Justice* (2011), Guthman explores how universalism and colorblind logic inform the assumptions of white communities regarding "why" people of color do not frequent places such as farmers markets in the same numbers as white communities. Guthman's ethnographic study on farmers markets found that many white vendors relied on evaluative statements about whites having higher education levels and exhibiting greater interest in health as factors that lead to primarily white patronage of farmers markets. Guthman's study argues that farmers market vendors believe that low education levels lead to a disinvestment in health, participation, and education about food. Such ideologies and discourses around race, health, and food for Native and marginalized communities oversimplifies the relationship to food and denies the systemic way colonial oppression works.

There is no doubt that, given the limited scholarship, further research on food (in)security among Native people is needed. This exploration must include a

---

2   Some of these individuals have moved willingly, while others moved due to forced removal from their tribal communities by the U.S. government.

cultural understanding about food and its importance for community well-being. There is a dire need to connect food to community well-being rather than just individual health. Since some research finds that many "Native American communities experience a lack of access to high-quality and culturally appropriate foods" (Jernigan, 2012, p. 113) and these communities have "higher rates of chronic-disease-related outcomes, including obesity, diabetes, and cardiovascular diseases" (Jernigan, 2012, p. 113), more research on foodways is vital for understanding how these poor health outcomes and lack of access have affected communities' functioning and well-being. Those interested in working with Native people must develop a deeper, historically grounded understanding of Native food consumption, including knowledge about their specific food histories and elaborate foodways.

For many Native communities, including the participants of my study, food is the sinew that holds communities together. Food helps build cultural knowledge and practice, satisfies health holistically by satisfying emotional and physical needs, and brings people together through the act of producing, consuming, and distributing foods. This was evident in my work with the IFH and its food programs.

While food brings people together, it can also be a source of great pain, shame, loss, and disconnection. This was most evident through the story of a participant who lamented that her daughter did not like salmon, a traditional and sacred food of her tribe. Those devising strategies to build food sovereignty must have a deep historical understanding of how food has been lost, how people have been moved or constrained, and how food acts as a community-bonding factor. The narrow focus on food consumption and access as they relate to physical health limits Native attempts to achieve food justice for our communities.

To address the food needs and well-being of Native peoples, we must expand the contemporary scholarship and policy efforts addressing health disparities that focus only on personal accountability and personal choice in eating and exercising. While it is important to address access, accountability, and choice, these approaches are not a holistic solution for Native well-being. Mainstream attempts to address issues involving food among Native people are singular in analysis and deny the complex effects of colonialism. These attempts also deny the function and role that many "unhealthy" foods have in Native communities. Changing diets means creating new meaning and integrating new foods into old practices. In the case of Native people living near their homelands, it might also mean integrating old foods into current practices.

The food movement must support Native people in their work toward rebuilding tribal food systems. In Oakland, Native people have created a community garden, cooking classes, community dinners, a food pantry, and a cookbook in an effort to build their own urban food system. Several tribes are utilizing food as a means to change the economy, revitalize traditions, and provide more food security. Examples of this work can be seen among the traditional foods programs supported by the CDC among the Mohegan, Muscogee (Creek) Nation, Oneida, Laguna Pueblo, and Suquamish tribes (CDC, 2013). These projects share similar themes found in my own work (Vernon, 2014) that include strengthening cultural identity, sharing knowledge, and fostering intergenerational knowledge. Programs across the country in both urban spaces and on reservation lands are improving health and building community through engaging in food sovereignty. We must support these projects and help build leadership among Native people by providing them with resources and greater visibility for their projects. Those people interested in assisting these efforts must develop cultural competencies within the communities where projects are located that include historical and contemporary understandings of power relations that support rebuilding Native food systems in culturally relevant and meaningful ways.

References

Centers for Disease Control and Prevention [CDC]. (2013). Traditional *foods in Native America: A compendium of stories from the Indigenous food sovereignty movement in American Indian and Alaska Native communities – Part 1*. Atlanta: Native Diabetes Wellness Program, Centers for Disease Control and Prevention.

CDC. (N.D.). American Indian & Alaska Native population. Retrieved June 14, 2015, from http://www.cdc.gov/minorityhealth/populations/REMP/aian.html

First Nations Development Institute. (2014). Native food and health fact sheets (Nos. 1, 4-7). Longmont, Colorado: Author (should the publisher be here instead of Author?). Retrieved from http://firstnations.org/knowledge-center/foods-health/resources/fact-sheets.

Fixico, D.L. (1986). *Termination and relocation: Federal Indian policy, 1945-1960*. Albuquerque: University of New Mexico Press.

Guthman, J. (2011). "If they only knew": The unbearable whiteness of alternative food. In A.H. Alkin & J. Agyeman (Eds.), *Cultivating food justice: Race, class, and sustainability* (pp. 263-282).

Jernigan, V. B. B. (2012). Addressing food security and food sovereignty in Native American communities. In J.R. Joe & F.C. Gachupin (eds.), Health and social issues of Native American women (pp.113-152). Denver, Colorado: Praeger.

LaDuke, W. (2005*). Recovering the sacred: The power of naming and claiming*. Boston: South End Press.

Norris, T., Vines, P.L., & Hoeffel, E.M. (2012). *The American Indian and Alaska Native Population: 2010* (2010 Census Briefs No. C2010BR-10). Washington, D.C.: U.S. Department of

Commerce, U.S. Census Bureau. Retrieved from https://www.census.gov/prod/cen2010/briefs/c2010br-10.pdf

Thornton, R. (1987). *American Indian holocaust and survival: A population history since 1492.* Norman: University of Oklahoma Press.

United States Department of Agriculture [USDA]. (2015). *Food Distribution Program on Indian Reservations (FDPIR).* Retrieved June 11, 2015, from http://www.fns.usda/gov/fdpir/food-distribution-program-indian-reservations-fdpir

Vernon, R. V. (2014). *Food systems among Native American peoples in Oakland, California: An examination of connection* (Master's thesis). Colorado State University, Fort Collins, Colorado.

Questions for Discussion

1. Explain the food that is provided by the U.S. government through the effort known as the "Food Distribution Program on Indian Reservations." Why does Vernon say that such efforts actually undermine "the practice of consuming traditional food and the teaching of food preparation ...between genders and within families" (140)?

2. Consider the way that Vernon uses the photo in her essay. She reports that her research involved the use of a particular technology called PhotoVoice. How does she use the image to enhance her argument? Why does she frame the photo as she does, leaving out the subject's face?

3. Compare Vernon's discussion of the importance of relationship to food with Méndez-Negrete's recounting of her mother's efforts to establish a loving home through food and its preparation despite the abuse of her father.

Distribution

Listening to the Conversation

"Food justice activists employ many of the same strategies that have come to characterize the broader food movement—they build gardens, offer nutrition education, and develop local food markets. But in the food justice approach, cooking and eating are never simply about improving nutrition alone. Food is also a strategic organizing tool and a critical conversation starter, all in support of a multi-ethnic movement for social and environmental justice."

– Garrett Broad, Assistant Professor of Communication and Media Studies

"Those who believe food-stamp spending is too high sometimes argue that, if the government were to spend less on the program, people would simply work harder so they could buy their own food, or else they would get food from food pantries and other charities. That's not true in many cases... millions of others are trying to find work without success—or have jobs but are paid such low wages that they still qualify for public assistance."

– Sasha Abramsky, freelance journalist

"While heterogeneity among consumers does exist, animal welfare is identified as the most preferred CSR [Corporate Social Responsibility] activity by the great majority of study participants and a top priority for dairy farms."

– McFadden (Professor of Agricultural and Resource Economics, Colorado State University), Deselnicu (Market Analyst and Oracle), and Costanigro (Assistant Professor of Agricultural and Resource Economics, Colorado State University)

"Work changes lives, food creates jobs and passion inspires food and work. The youth that work on the truck are real, warm and inspiring. The food is amazing—probably the finest maple grilled cheese you will ever taste. But what is truly breathtaking is thinking about the Vendys and the street vendor universe as a pathway for change."

— Liz Neumark, CEO of Great Performances

"Three years into an economic recovery, this is the lasting scar of collapse: a federal program that began as a last resort for a few million hungry people has grown into an economic lifeline for entire towns. Spending on SNAP has doubled in the past four years and tripled in the past decade, surpassing $78 billion last year. A record 47 million Americans receive the benefit—including 13,752 in Woonsocket, one-third of the town's population, where the first of each month now reveals twin shortcomings of the U.S. economy: So many people are forced to rely on government support. The government is forced to support so many people."

— Eli Saslow, journalist for the Washington Post

"Economic status dictates class and diet. We arrange food in a hierarchy based on who originally ate it until we reach mullet, gar, possum, and squirrel—the diet of the poor. The food is called trash, and then the people are."

— Chris Offutt, memoirist, novelist, and screenwriter

The Black Panther Party: A Food Justice Story

Garrett Broad

The Huffington Post, February 2016

> Garrett Broad is an Assistant Professor of Communication and Media Studies and has authored books on food justice. The Black Panther Party was founded in 1966 in Oakland, California in response to police brutality and the Civil Rights Movement. They did not follow the nonviolent protest movement also prevalent at the time, instead believing in the philosophy of Malcolm X and using armed resistance to create change. The group is less known for their social programs in which they worked to feed impoverished communities, and this work toward food justice is the focus of Broad's article. According to justfood.org, food justice "is communities exercising their right to grow, sell, and eat healthy food. Healthy food is fresh, nutritious, affordable, culturally-appropriate, and grown locally with care for the well-being of the land, workers, and animals."

For most of my life, I didn't know much about the Black Panther Party.

As a white kid born the same year that Martin Luther King, Jr. became the name of a national holiday, the stories I *did* hear about the Panthers weren't very inspiring. Sure, I knew things were bad for Black folks back in the 1960s, but it was clear that the "drug-addicted, violent misogynists" of the BPP did more to prevent racial progress than to promote it.

Then I got involved in the "good food movement"—and the story I thought I knew began to change.

What does the Black Panther Party have to do with the food movement?

A lot, actually, even if it's a story that often goes untold, both in media narratives about the Panthers and throughout the food movement itself.

Setting the BPP's flaws aside—the truth is that at a moment when Black Americans were suffering from widespread hunger, sickness, unemployment, and police violence, the Black Panther Party was there to try to fill the gaps that institutional racism and government negligence had created. The late 1960s saw the Panthers develop a host of community-based initiatives, with chapters across the country shifting their focus away from armed militancy and toward the development of "survival programs"—survival pending revolution, of course.

Perhaps you learned a bit about this history while watching Stanley Nelson's recent documentary - *The Black Panthers: Vanguard of the Revolution*—or maybe you took a look at the BPP's Wikipedia page after Beyoncé's Super Bowl™ performance caught your eye. But these sources only scratch the surface of the BPP's innovative community-based activism.

Dig deep and you will see that food was central to the entire survival program strategy, serving two basic functions.

First, Black hunger in 1960s America was a reality, and the government showed little interest in fixing the problem. With no National School Lunch Program in place, this was particularly true among youth of color. In response, the Black Panther Party developed Free Breakfast for Children programs in cities across the nation, feeding at least twenty thousand schoolchildren in the 1968-1969 school year alone.

Food's second role, however, wasn't related to nutrition at all—it served as an organizing tool and a conversation starter. Throughout Black Panther Party history, cooking and eating provided strategic entry points into discussions about racism, capitalism, and the possibility of revolutionary change.

With power like that, is it any wonder that COINTELPRO—J. Edgar Hoover's covert FBI operation that surveilled and infiltrated "subversive" political groups during that era—saw the Panthers' survival programs as even more dangerous than armed insurrection?

Ultimately, it's not surprising that this counter-story of the Panthers' legacy wasn't told in the textbooks I read or the TV I watched. What is surprising, though, is that mainstream food activists have been mostly silent on this history too.

Indeed, in the urban farms, farmers' markets, and documentary films of the food movement, I've heard unending talk about the need to get people in low-income communities of color to eat better food. They're the ones, of course, who live in food deserts and suffer disproportionately from food insecurity, obesity, and other diet-related disease.

Why, then, does the food movement barely even mention the nation's largest grassroots food access initiative, the one developed in those very same communities decades before by the BPP?

It wasn't until I began to collaborate directly with urban food justice activists—a people-of-color-led subset of the food movement—that I heard any real discussion of the Panthers at all. Food justice activists employ many of the same strategies that have come to characterize the broader food movement—they build gardens, offer nutrition education, and develop local food markets. But in the food justice approach, cooking and eating are never simply about improving nutrition alone. Food is also a strategic organizing tool and a critical conversation starter, all in support of a multi-ethnic movement for social and environmental justice.

If that narrative sounds familiar, it's because the legacy of the Black Panther Party looms large in the work of the food justice movement. Several former Black Panthers have remained committed to developing food-related programs, while many young food justice activists have taken the Panthers' revolutionary message to heart. At least one active food justice group—Community Services Unlimited, Inc. in South Los Angeles—was actually founded in the mid-1970s as the non-profit arm of a reformulated BPP chapter.

Operating in a vastly different historical and economic moment, today's food justice groups echo many of the Black Panther Party's fundamental critiques of racism and capitalism, although they do tend to emphasize the BPP's commitment to grassroots community action over and above its armed militancy.

They also face a number of similar strategic and economic challenges—finding a sustainable economic model to fund a radical social movement is no easier now than it was then. And while the Panthers had to fight back against government repression in their time, today's food justice activists struggle to navigate the demands of the "nonprofit industrial complex."

Ultimately, as former Panther Chief of Staff David Hilliard described at a food justice event in 2011, "We've always been involved in food, because food is a very basic necessity, and it's the stuff that revolutions are made of."

For a better understanding of the Black Panther Party, and for a more just food system, it's a story we should tell more often.

Questions for Discussion

1. According to the author, what were the two major roles that food played for the Black Panther Party's (BPP) survival program strategy?

2. How are the current food justice movements influenced by the BPP's food justice activism?

3. What are the various contexts which food justice spans? How did the BPP's approach to food justice address some of these contexts?

Breaking the Food Chains: An Investigation of Food Justice Activism

Alison H. Alkon and Kari Marie Norgaard

Sociological Inquiry, 2009

Alison H. Alkon is an Assistant Professor in Sociology at the University of the Pacific, and Kari Marie Norgaard is currently an Associate Professor in Sociology at the University of Oregon. This scholarly article uses an ethnographic case study methodology to gather qualitative data about food justice. A case study is the in-depth investigation of a person or group to observe and analyze the phenomenon occurring, and ethnography is the study of cultural phenomenon through observation. *Sociological Inquiry* is published by Alpha Kappa Delta, the International Sociological Honor Society, and, according to their website, they are "committed to the exploration of the human condition in all of its social and cultural complexity."

Abstract

This article develops the concept of food justice, which places access to healthy, affordable, culturally appropriate food in the contexts of institutional racism, racial formation, and racialized geographies. Through comparative ethnographic case studies, we analyze the demands for food justice articulated by the Karuk Tribe of California and the West Oakland Food Collaborative. Activists in these communities use an environmental justice frame to address access to healthy food, advocating for a local food system in West Oakland, and for the demolition of Klamath River dams that prevent subsistence fishing. Food justice serves as a theoretical and political bridge between scholarship and activism on sustainable agriculture, food insecurity, and environmental justice. This concept brings the environmental justice emphasis on racially stratified access to environmental benefits to bear on the sustainable agriculture movement's attention to the processes of food production and consumption. Furthermore, we argue that the concept of food justice can help the environmental justice movement move beyond several limitations of their frequent place-based approach and the sustainable agriculture movement to more meaningfully incorporate issues of equity and social justice. Additionally, food justice may help activists and policymakers working on food security to understand the institutionalized nature of denied access to healthy food.

This article examines the concept of food justice through comparative case studies of two racially and spatially distinct Northern California communities. Food justice places the need for food security—access to healthy, affordable, culturally appropriate food—in the contexts of institutional racism, racial formation, and racialized geographies. Our analysis highlights the ability of food justice to serve as a theoretical and political bridge between existing work on sustainable agriculture, food insecurity, and environmental justice.

The West Oakland Food Collaborative[1] and the Karuk Tribe of California frame their food insecurity and high rates of diet-related diseases not as the result of poor individual food choices, but from institutionalized racism. We follow how each community highlights the political and economic histories through which their key food producers, African American farmers and Native American fishermen, were denied the land and water necessary for food production. In addition to poverty, the contemporary racialized geographies (Kobayashi and Peake 2000) through which institutional racism shapes the physical landscape prevent many black and indigenous communities from purchasing the quality of food they once produced. Lack of geographic and economic access confines their choices to processed, fast, and commodity foods. Additionally, black and Native American communities suffer from elevated rates of diet-related illnesses such as diabetes. Activists in the communities we study pursue food justice through a diverse array of strategies including challenging state policy and the creation of alternative food systems.

From these case studies, we demonstrate that the concept of food justice allows sustainable agriculture scholars to better contend with institutional racism and environmental justice theorists to connect disproportionate access to environmental benefits to social science analyses of race (Pulido 2000). Moreover, it is our hope that the concept of food justice may create political alliances between proponents of the environmental justice and sustainable agriculture movements through an understanding of food access as a product of institutionalized racism.

Ecology and Equity: Building Theoretical Bridges

While environmental justice advocates have long argued that low-income people and people of color suffer disproportionately from the burdens of environmental degradation, recent scholarship has also begun to emphasize the problem of disproportionate access to environmental benefits. Attention to environmental benefits helps the environmental justice movement to solidify its connection to larger democratic projects such as eco-populism (Szasz 1994), ecological democracy (Faber 1998), and just sustainability (Agyeman 2005). The sustainable agriculture movement, on the other hand, focusing primarily on the environmental benefits of fertile soil, clean water, and pesticide-free food, has often ignored the role of race in structuring agriculture in the United States (Allen 2004). Although the term sustainability includes both ecological protection and social justice by definition, sustainable agriculture activists have primarily aligned themselves with the environmental rather than environmental justice movement (Alkon 2008). Following a brief review of existing literature within sustainable agriculture and environmental justice, we offer two case studies in which activists situate their own lack of food access within historical processes of institutional racism, racial identity formation, and racialized geographies.

Bringing Social Justice Back into Sustainability

The sustainable agriculture movement has traditionally focused on technical solutions to problems of ecologically devastating food production, making use of the work of university extension agents and agroecologists. Social scientists, however, have portrayed an agriculture system embedded in specific, historically produced social relations as responsible for social and environmental problems. Foster and Magdoff (2000) trace social scientists' interest in sustainable agriculture to Marx's use of soil science in illustrating the environmental consequences of agriculture embedded in a capitalist economic system. The increased industrialization and consolidation of agricultural firms occurring since Marx's observations have held dire consequences for the soil and water on which food production depends (Buttel, Larson, and Gillespie 1990).

Social scientists have also examined the effects of farm consolidation on rural communities. Goldschmidt ([1947] 1978) examined two paired California towns, one dominated by family and the other by corporately owned farms. He observed more stores, higher per capita income, and a greater diversity of social institutions in the former. Goldschmidt can be seen as a predecessor to the concept of civic agriculture, which links the agricultural and environmental to the "economic, social, cultural, and political dimensions of community life" and encourages community involvement in the creation of local food systems (Lyson 2004:28).

The sustainable agriculture movement consists of actors working through such diverse strategies as direct marketing initiatives (farmers markets and community-supported agriculture), urban and/or self-sufficient production (urban farms, community and backyard gardens), and policy work (food policy councils, attempts to influence the farm bill). The most prominent sectors of the movement aim to ensure the economic success of small, regional, organic farmers by encouraging consumer support for locally grown organic food.

Several scholars, however, critique the sustainable agriculture movement's ability to make sweeping social changes in the agricultural sector. While support for sustainable agriculture is largely based on broad social values consistent with Dunlap and Catton's (1979) New Environmental Paradigm (Beus and Dunlap 1990), the changes advocated by the movement come through specific techniques and practices that do not disrupt the agribusiness system (Buttel 1997). As organic farming has become more popular and profitable, it has adapted many characteristics of the industrial agriculture it once sought to replace, constraining the sustainable agriculture movement's ability to advocate for progressive change (Guthman 2004). Social justice issues are also marginalized because of the emphasis on the economic success of farmers (Allen 2004). The movement's imperative that consumers pay the "true" cost of food, rather than allowing environmental costs to be externalized, and its association with fine dining and European food traditions, demonstrate its association with white privilege and affluence (Alkon and McCullen forthcoming). Sustainable agriculture, at least as it is currently practiced, cannot transform the dominant agribusiness system.

While scholarly critiques of the sustainable agriculture movement call broadly for more attention to social justice issues, the concept of food justice contextualizes disparate access to healthy food within a broader and more historicized framework of institutional racism. Because of its focus on racialized access to the environmental benefit of healthy food, food justice can link sustainable agriculture to environmental justice theory and practice.

Theorizing Food in Environmental Justice Scholarship

In the last two decades, environmental justice scholars have successfully documented the unequal distribution of environmental toxics through which low-income people and people of color bear the health burdens of environmental degradation (United Church of Christ 1987). These communities have organized numerous campaigns against the companies responsible (Allen 2003; Brown and Mikkelsen 1997; Bullard 1990; Sze 2006). Similarities in these cases shed light on an environmental justice frame (Capek 1993) or paradigm (Taylor 1997, 2000), linking distribution of environmental toxins to a culturally resonant (Gamson and Modigliani 1989) civil rights rhetoric.

While the environmental justice movement is best known for protests against site discrimination, many activists adopt a much broader approach. Often grounded in their own experiences as victims of environmental racism, activists have worked toward pollution prevention (Szasz 1994) and the internalization of the costs of production by the companies responsible (Faber 1998) so that no community should suffer the health effects of environmental toxics. Constantly looking to broaden the environmental justice frame through the inclusion of issues generally ignored by what Brulle (2000) terms the "reform" environmental movement, activists have created a complex approach incorporating the many environmental and social justice factors affecting the places where low-income people and people of color live, work, and play (Alston 1991).

Despite the central importance of food to human and environmental health, and the broad-reaching frame of the environmental justice movement, the literature devotes limited attention to food access. While Gottlieb and Fisher (1996) first highlighted an environmental justice approach to food security more than a decade ago, few environmental justice scholars have incorporated food or nutrition in their analyses. Several works in Adamson and colleagues' (Adamson et al. 2002) *Environmental Justice Reader* examine agriculture, but maintain a traditional environmental justice focus on the toxic despoiling of land cultivated by communities of color. Although some work on environmental justice in Native American communities deals with access to and protection of wild salmon, it tends to focus on the salmon's importance for Native American culture rather than its significance as healthy food (see, for example, Dupris, Hill, and Rodgers 2006; House 1999; Wilkinson 2000, 2005). While the cultural significance of salmon is fundamental, these analyses ignore its consequences for Native American health. The concept of food justice, offered as a conceptual extension of the more inclusive idea of environmental justice and sheds light on how the food system has been shaped by institutionalized racism.

Research Approach

Data on the West Oakland Food Collaborative (WOFC) came from three primary sources: participant observation, semistructured interviews, and a survey of customers at the West Oakland Farmers Market.[2] During 18 months of participant observation, Alkon took on a variety of roles including regular customer, volunteer gardener, researcher, and observer at the farmers market, WOFC meetings, and events and activities organized by WOFC member organizations. Copious notes were taken and later coded, allowing patterns to emerge. Eighteen in-depth interviews were conducted with WOFC participants and farmers market vendors. Interviews lasting approximately 1 hour were recorded and transcribed. The survey was administered to 100 farmers market customers over the course of 3 weeks through a sample of convenience.

Norgaard began her research in 2003 at the request of the Karuk Tribe. Tribal members had been less than successful articulating their concerns through the Federal Energy Regulatory Commission process on the relicensing of the Klamath River Hydroproject. The tribe sought to seek greater scientific backing for their claims. Data on the Karuk case study are drawn from four main sources: archival material, in-depth interviews with Karuk tribal members, Karuk medical records, and the 2005 Karuk Health and Fish Consumption Survey. The 2005 Karuk Health and Fish Consumption Survey was distributed to adult tribal members within the ancestral territory in the spring of 2005. The survey had a response rate of 38 percent, a total of 90 individuals. Additional medical data has been obtained from relevant federal, state, and county records (Norgaard 2005). Both researchers recognize the particular tensions that can arise in relationships between white researchers and communities of color. Alkon worked diligently with several individuals active in the West Oakland Food Collaborative to ensure that the community would benefit from her research. To this end, she has edited grant applications for several WOFC member organizations and hired a research assistant who was raised in West Oakland to aid in the distribution of surveys. Research on the Karuk tribe sought to achieve goals specified by tribal members that would correspond to the tribe's existing political needs. All aspects of the research process (interviews, survey design, and implementation) were carried out under direction of or by tribal members themselves.

Culture and Agriculture: The West Oakland Food Collaborative

In an old, partially refurbished Victorian home in West Oakland, now home to the Prescott Joseph Community Center, a group of activists sit around a long wood table discussing projects and strategies for the procurement of food justice. While the group is by no means entirely African American, discussions of institutional racism and inequality pervade many aspects of their work. Among other projects, those attending WOFC meetings run school and community gardens, cooking programs, and food distribution efforts focused on supplying healthy food to this low-income, predominantly African American neighborhood. The most prominent example of the WOFC's work is a weekly farmers market through which African American farmers and home-based business people sell organic produce, flowers, homemade jams, sweets, and beauty products.[3] Farmers markets are most commonly associated with the sustainable agriculture movement's promotion of small, local farmers. This market, however, emphasizes antiracism. Indeed, one market vendor described the market's primary purpose as "empowering black people."

Although the produce featured at the market is much less expensive than in wealthier neighborhoods, it struggles to attract customers unaccustomed to this kind of shopping. While the market is extremely small, it is a lively place. Customers and vendors, the majority of whom know each other by name, catch up on the week's events while shopping for the week's provisions. The farmers market celebrates African American culture through the products featured (such as black-eyed peas, greens, and yams), the music played (mostly soul and funk) and the special events celebrated (such as Black History Month and Juneteenth). The radical potential of merging racial identity formation with sustainable agriculture is recognized by one market farmer, who claims "this market fights the systems that are in place to keep down sharecroppers like my father and grandfather." Like other environmental justice efforts, the WOFC emphasizes racism and inequality, connecting environmental issues to the lived experiences of low-income people and people of color (Bullard 1990; Novotny 2000).

One of the most egregious instances of racism highlighted by the farmers market is the discrimination experienced by African American farmers. In the words of one vendor, the West Oakland farmers market is different from others because "we have black farmers . . . you don't see a lot of black farmers." WOFC members attribute the historic decline of black farmers nationwide to the United States Department of Agriculture (USDA)'s denial of loans, subsidies, and other support that enabled white farmers to transition to mechanized agriculture (Gilbert, Sharp, and Felin 2002).[4] In 1997, the USDA settled a class-action lawsuit on this issue, though black farmers and their descendents have reported difficulties claiming their portion of the settlement (Wood and Gilbert 2000). Discrimination against black farmers created an agricultural sector dominated by whites and deprived African Americans of a source of wealth and access to economic and environmental benefits.

The goal of the West Oakland Farmers Market is, in the words of one prominent WOFC member, "to connect black farmers to the black community." This view is reflected by the market's customers; a majority of those surveyed (52%) claim that support for black farmers is their most important reason for market attendance.[5] Several surveys also included responses to open-ended requests for additional information with comments reflecting this theme, such as "my consciousness about the plight of black farmers has grown." These responses suggest that the concept of food justice might productively connect access to environmental benefits to theories of racial identity formation (Omi and Winant 1989). (indent for new graf)Not only have African Americans been stripped of their abilities to produce healthy, culturally appropriate food, they are also unable to purchase similar items. WOFC members, along with food justice activists in many parts of the United States, popularize the term "food desert" in order to describe the lack of locally available healthy food (Wrigley, Margetts, and Whelan 2002). Many scholars have observed a positive correlation between the existence of grocery stores and income (Chung and Meyers 1999) and a negative one between grocery stores and the percentage of African American residents (adjust margins, here and above)(Morland et al. 2002).

One WOFC participant, currently organizing to open a worker-owned grocery store, describes the obstacles residents face in obtaining fresh food:

> West Oakland has 40,000 people and only one grocery store. [The many] corner stores sell generic canned goods. You have that option and then the fast food chains is the other option. So what people have the option to buy is putting more and more chemicals and additives and hormones and all of these things into their bodies.

With nearly 1.5 times as many corner liquor stores as the city average (California Alcoholic Beverage Control [CABC] 2006) as well as an abundance of fast food establishments, West Oakland is typical of low-income, African American food deserts in other cities (Block, Scribner, and DeSalvo 2004; LaVeist and Wallace 2000). WOFC members describe the process through which large grocery stores closed urban locations in favor of suburban ones as "supermarket redlining," likening it to racist lending policies and further linking their own work to a broad and historicized antiracist resistance. Through food justice activism, WOFC members link their own food insecurity to institutional racism and its historic and present-day effects on the built environment (Kobayashi and Peake 2000; Massey and Denton 1998)

Not surprisingly, residents of this food desert experience high rates of diet-related health problems such as diabetes. WOFC members racialize and politicize diabetes in much the same way that environmental justice activists portray asthma (Sze 2006). In the words of one food justice activist, who recently relocated to Oakland and became involved in many of the WOFC's projects, "diabetes kills more people in our communities than crack!" (Lappe and Terry 2006). In Alameda County, African Americans, more than other racial groups,[6] are twice as likely to suffer from diabetes (CDC 2002).

WOFC members link these health disparities to the lack of locally available healthy food. According to one market farmer, a son of Arkansas sharecroppers who has extensive training in herbal and Chinese medicine: "I've seen the African American people's health declining. It's not having access to healthy food, to a good lifestyle." Another vendor describes how the WOFC's projects provide that access:

> It's the whole process of learning how to grow things and reclaim [public] space and to live sustainable and healthy [lives]. And what it means to understand that, okay, you're prone [to] diabetes. [How do you] counteract that? 'Cause that's a huge thing in West Oakland, and [the WOFC has] things that help you live a more sustainable life knowing that you're prone to diabetes.

The WOFC deploys an analysis that attributes high rates of diabetes to food insecurity, which in turn results from institutional racism.

Because this analysis ties a place-based instance of environmental injustice to a more systemic and historicized understanding of racism, the WOFC's solution focuses on local food and local economics rather than attempts to attract corporate economic development. In the words of one farmers market vendor: "I don't want Safeway or Albertsons. They abandoned the inner city. They sell poison. They pay crap wages. Independent business is the most important thing." Instead of chain grocery stores, the WOFC emphasizes "community self-sufficiency" and the ability of marginalized communities to provide, at least partially, for themselves. One WOFC participant describes the goal of her activism in the following way:

> [It's about] building a community that takes care of each other's needs. And we can self sustain outside of the dominant system. . . . We want to buy and sell from each other . . . in a way that helps us sustain our neighborhoods or our communities. That's different than consuming in a way that sustains a mega business that's separate and distinct from us.

The WOFC's projects aim to address the needs of low-income, predominantly African American, West Oakland residents through the development of local food and local economic systems.

The West Oakland Food Collaborative's food justice activism combines antiracism with the creation of a local food system. For this reason, their case offers important insights on the development of an environmental justice approach to food and its consequences for theorizing and achieving environmental justice and sustainable agriculture.

Battling Corporate River Management on the Klamath

In the Northern part of the state, the Karuk Tribe of California has mobilized its demand for food justice by lobbying the federal government to block the relicensing of four dams on the Klamath River. These dams prevent the Karuk tribe from sustaining themselves on their traditional foods, which include salmon, lamprey, steelhead, and sturgeon (Norgaard 2005). In addition to lobbying, tribal members have engaged in a variety of protest strategies including working with commercial fishermen and environmental organizations to achieve greater visibility; pleading their case at meetings of the dam's multi-national corporate owners, directors, and shareholders; and participating in numerous regional protest activities.

The Klamath River dams disconnect the Karuk from their food sources in several ways. The dams degrade water quality by creating standing water where blue green algae blooms deplete oxygen and create toxic conditions downstream. Levels of the liver toxin mycrocystin were the highest recorded of any water body in the United States and 4,000 times the World Health Organization (WHO) safety limit in 2005 (Karuk Tribe of California 2006). The dams lack fish ladders or other features that would allow the passage of native salmon. When the lowest dam was built, Spring Chinook Salmon lost access to 90 percent of their spawning habitat. Around this time, most Karuk families reported the loss of these fish as a significant food source.

One tribal member describes the devastating effect of the dams on the Karuk food system as follows:

> A healthy riverine system has a profound effect on the people on the river. I have six children. If every one of those kids went down and fished and caught a good healthy limit . . . you could pretty much fill a freezer and have nice good fish all the way through the year. But now, without a healthy riverine system, the economy down here on the lower river is pretty much devastated. All the fishing community is devastated by the unhealthy riverine system.
> —(Ron Reed, Traditional Karuk Fisherman)

The dams and their ensuing environmental degradation have wreaked havoc on the food needs of the tribe.

The Karuk tribe articulates their right to traditional foods not only as an issue of food insecurity but of food justice. They locate their current food needs in the history of genocide, lack of land rights, and forced assimilation that have so devastated this and other Native American communities. These processes have prevented tribal members from carrying out land management techniques necessary to food attainment.

This tragic history provides context to understand the ability of the federal government to license a dam to a multinational corporation within Karuk territory. It is the dams themselves, however, that have had the most sweeping and immediate effect on Karuk food access. Until recently, Karuk people have experienced relatively high rates of subsistence living. Elder tribal members recall their first visit to the grocery store:

> I can remember first going to the store with mom when I was about in the fifth and sixth grade and going in there and it was so strange to buy, you know, get stuff out of the store. Especially cans of vegetables, like green beans and stuff; Mom used to can all that. And bread. I was about 6 years old when I saw my first loaf of bread in the store. That was really quite a change, I'll tell you.
>
> —(Blanche Moore, Karuk Tribal Member)

Traditional fish consumption for Karuk people is estimated at 450 pounds per person per year, more than a pound per day (Hewes 1973). Up until the 1980s many Karuk people, especially those from traditional families, ate salmon up to three times per day when the fish were running. Karuk survival has been directly linked to this important environmental resource.

When the dams were built, the Karuk tribe was stripped of access to much of its traditional food as well as the ability to manage the river ecosystem. In contrast to the traditional diet, present-day Karuk people consume less than 5 pounds of salmon per person per year. Self-report data from the 2005 Karuk Health and Fish Consumption Survey indicate that over 80 percent of households were unable to gather adequate amounts of eel, salmon, or sturgeon to fulfill their family needs (Norgaard 2005). As of 2006, so few fish existed that even ceremonial salmon consumption is now limited.

Like West Oakland residents, members of the Karuk tribe cannot purchase the food they once procured through a direct relationship with the nonhuman environment. Most Karuk do not believe in buying or selling salmon. Even if tribal members were willing to buy salmon, replacing subsistence fishing with store-bought salmon would be prohibitively expensive. Replacement cost analysis conducted in the spring of 2005 puts the cost of purchasing salmon at over $4,000 per tribal member per year (Stercho 2005). In the communities within the ancestral territory, this amount would represent over half of the average per capita annual income. While the Karuk are denied access to an environmental benefit because of institutional racism, they cannot replace that benefit through purchase because of poverty.

As in West Oakland, healthy, culturally appropriate food is not available within a convenient distance to tribal members. Tribal members must drive up to 40 miles each way to acquire commodity foods and up to 80 miles each way to shop at supermarkets. According to a nutritional analysis of the local store, it is nearly impossible to access fresh, healthy food on a limited budget:

> The local grocery store in Orleans is lacking in variety and quality of fresh produce and other food products. . . . In addition, the prices are high, making it financially difficult for a family to get adequate nutrition. The yearly median Karuk tribal income is $13,000 or $270 per week. Yet the average cost for a two-person family to eat healthy foods, based on the prices of foods available at the local grocery store in Orleans, is estimated at approximately $150 per week. Note that this represents 55 percent of the income of an average family for the week!—(Jennifer Jackson, 2005, p. 11)

Tribal members link the lack of access to traditional foods to the need for government food assistance:

> Instead of having healthy food to eat—fish—we are relegated to eating commodity foods that the government gives out. That's our subsidy: high starch foods, things that aren't so healthy that the Karuk people are pretty much forced to eat.
> —(Ron Reed, Traditional Karuk Fisherman)

Self-report data from the Karuk Health and Fish Consumption Survey indicate that 20 percent of Karuk people consume commodity foods.[5] Commodity foods tend to be low in essential nutrients and high in complex carbohydrates and fat (Jackson 2005).

Because of the greatly reduced ability of tribal members to provide healthy food to their community, the Karuk experience extremely high rates of hunger and disease. Recent data from University of California at Los Angeles (UCLA)'s California Health Interview Survey (Diamant et al. 2005) show that Native people have the highest rates of both food insecurity (37.2%) and hunger (16.9%) in California (Harrison et al. 2002). The estimated diabetes rate for the Karuk Tribe is 21 percent, approximately four times the U.S. average of 4.9

percent. The estimated rate of heart disease for the Karuk Tribe is 39.6 percent, three times the U.S. average (Norgaard 2005).

Diabetes is described as a new disease among this population and is the consequence of drastic lifestyle and cultural changes (Joe and Young 1993). Tribal members account for both the severity and the sudden onset of diet-related health problems:

> Our people never used to be fat. Our people never used to have these health problems that we are encountering today. Diabetes is probably the biggest one but not the only one. The ramifications of the food that we eat and the lives that we live. High blood pressure is another one. I have high blood pressure. My mother had diabetes. I'm borderline, I'm pretty sure. You can certainly tell that our people never used to be fat. Now you can't hardly find a skinny person around.
>
> —(David Arwood, Traditional Karuk Fisherman)

Tribal members posit this dramatic shift as a consequence of their denied access to salmon and other traditional foods.

The Karuk tribe is the first in the nation to deploy the concept of food justice in order to link declining salmon populations caused by the dams with high incidences of diabetes and other diet-related diseases. The tribe frames declined river health and the ensuing loss of salmon as a direct result of institutional racism. The Karuk have been stripped of access to an important resource as well as the ability to manage their ancestral land. Because of cost and distance, the tribe cannot purchase what it once produced. Tribe members must rely on locally available unhealthy alternatives and commodity foods—or in too many cases, go without. Because of this process of denied access to traditional or replacement foods, diabetes researcher Kue Young (1997:164) writes that the "resolution of the major health problems of Native Americans requires redressing the underlying social, cultural and political causes of those problems." In other words, food access must be connected to the historical process of institutional racism that created food insecurity. Tribal activists make this connection through the concept of food justice.

Conclusion: Political Implications and Alliance Building

Members of the West Oakland Food Collaborative and the Karuk Tribe clearly share similar experiences. Through access to land and water, black farmers and Karuk fishermen once provided the bulk of their community's food needs. Today, West Oakland residents and Karuk tribal members live in food deserts.

They cannot purchase what they once produced on their own. Activists link this lack of food access to their community's elevated rates of diabetes and other diet-related illnesses. Furthermore, both groups frame their grassroots struggles for food justice as attempts to reclaim their ability to produce and consume food.

We use these case studies to demonstrate how the concept of food justice can help the sustainable agriculture movement to better attend to issues of equity, and the environmental justice movement to articulate sustainable alternatives. Moreover, it is our hope that the concept of food justice may create political alliances between the two movements. These theoretical and practical alliances depend on a broader understanding of how racial and economic inequality affect the production and consumption of food, a project we will continue to develop in a forthcoming anthology called *The Food Justice Reader*.

Theoretically, food justice links food insecurity to institutional racism and racialized geography, reshaping thinking within the fields of sustainable agriculture and environmental justice. Scholars and activists in the sustainable agriculture movement have done well to challenge the corporate control of food production systems and identify resulting impacts to the long-term viability of soils and surrounding ecosystems. As food is increasingly controlled by large corporations, ecosystems suffer and communities have less control over localfoods. Yet sustainable agriculture scholars and activists have not yet understood the ways that race shapes a community's ability to produce and consume food.

Moreover, a food justice framework links food access to broader questions of power and political efficacy. While many sustainable agriculture advocates and scholars implicitly assume that all communities have the ability to choose ecologically produced food, the concept of food justice can help to illuminate the race and class privilege masked by this approach. Access to healthy food is shaped not only by the economic ability to purchase it, but also by the historical processes through which race has come to affect who lives where and who has access to what kind of services. Because it highlights institutional racism and (align) racialized geographies, food justice may therefore encourage the sustainable agriculture movement to embrace a more meaningful approach to social justice. (new graf)Attempting to survive as both a movement and an industry, sustainable agriculture has formed alliances with the consumption of elite, gourmet food. This prevents activists from critiquing the capitalist system of food production responsible for environmental degradation. Through a food justice approach emphasizing race and power, there may be space for sustainable agriculture activists to build coalitions with proponents of environmental justice. This coalescence may allow food activists to engage in a more fundamental critique of the global food system and the local stratification that results from it.

Additionally, the concept of food justice may allow sustainable agriculture activists to access the discursive power of the environmental justice movement. An antiracist approach to agriculture can borrow from the civil rights rhetoric that has become a master frame in U.S. society. This may make the concept of sustainable agriculture more culturally resonant to the low-income people and people of color who lack access to healthy food. Therefore, deploying the concept of food justice may enable sustainable agriculture and environmental justice activists to form new alliances.

Beyond naming food access as a dimension of environmental inequality, we hope the concept of food justice will contribute to environmental justice work in the following ways. In articulating a demand for access to healthy food, these cases contribute to the developing focus on racially stratified access to environmental benefits within environmental justice. Unfortunately, it is not only the extent of environmental degradation that has intensified in the past half century, but also the degree of social inequality. For this reason it will become more and more important for the environmental justice movement to place attention on access to environmental benefits. Additionally, because food is often central to communities' collective cultural identities, the concept of food justice can illuminate links between environmental justice activism and the process of racial identity formation. These dimensions address both Pellow's (2004) call for scholarly attention to process and history and Pulido's (2000) injunction to connect environmental justice to social science analyses of race.

As an issue, food justice may help environmental justice activists to galvanize a more proactive, solution-oriented approach that can complement its political pressure for government and corporate responsibility for localized epidemics and toxic pollutants. While some environmental justice organizations have moved toward a "pollution prevention" perspective, they have only begun to envision alternatives to environmental injustice conversant with traditional notions of environmental sustainability (Agyeman 2005; Pellow and Brulle 2005; Peña 2003). Because the sustainable agriculture movement has historically privileged the construction of alternative food systems over other kinds of activism, this issue can add an additional strategy to the environmental justice lexicon. Finally, it is also our hope that through the use of these case studies, activists and policymakers working on food security will understand the institutionalized nature of denied access to healthy foods in these communities.

ENDNOTES

*This research was made possible by support from the Floyd and Mary Schwall Fellowship, the Poverty and Race Research Action Council, and the Department of Sociology at University of California at Davis. Many thanks to those who read earlier drafts of this piece, including many of our colleagues and two anonymous reviewers. Our deepest gratitude goes to the members of the West Oakland Food Collaborative and Karuk Tribe, who have graciously shared their insights and experiences with us.

[1] Although the WOFC ceased to operate formally in 2005, many member organizations continue to work toward its principles. The WOFC remains a useful framework for discussing the network of activists addressing food justice issues in West Oakland. (right justify above and below)

[2] During my fieldwork, the farmers market was run by the WOFC. It had originally been founded by David Roach, whose Mo'Better Foods was one of the WOFC's member organizations. After my fieldwork, Roach became the farmers market's sole manager.

[3] While the WOFC focuses on African American farmers, Mexican, Hmong, and more recently, white women farmers have also been included. Nonfarming vendors are overwhelmingly African American residents of either West Oakland, or nearby predominantly African American neighborhoods. The WOFC's promotional activities emphasize the African American farmers while treating nonblack farmers as allies. While produce sold at the farmers market and other WOFC projects need not be certified organic, recognizing that the cost of certification is often prohibitive, farmers use the phrase chemical-free to connote organic growing practices.

[4] Although the decline of African American farmers took place in the rural south, it has direct bearing on African Americans living in West Oakland. Each of the African American farmers, as well as many of the other vendors, is directly descended from southern sharecroppers.

[5] Other choices included good quality food, support for local farmers and small businesspeople, convenient location, and atmosphere.

[6] Native Americans were not included in this data.

REFERENCES

Adamson, Joni, Mei Mei Evans, and Rachel Stein. 2002. *The Environmental Justice Reader: Politics, Poetics and Pedagogy.* Tucson, AZ: University of Arizona Press.

Agyeman, Julian. 2005. *Sustainable Communities and the Challenge of Environmental Justice.* Cambridge, MA: MIT Press.

Alkon, Alison Hope. 2008. "Paradise or Pavement: The Social Construction of the Environment in Two Urban Farmers Markets." *Local Environment: The Journal of Justice and Sustainability* 13(3):271–89.

Alkon, Alison Hope and Christie Grace McCullen. Forthcoming. "Whiteness and Farmers Markets: Performances, Perpetuations . . . Contestations?" *Antipode.*

Allen, Barbara. 2003. *Uneasy Alchemy: Citizens and Experts in Louisiana's Chemical Corridor Disputes.* Cambridge, MA: MIT Press.

Allen, Patricia. 2004. *Together at the Table: Sustainability and Sustenance in the American AgriFoods Movement.* University Park, PA: Pennsylvania State University Press.

Alston, Dana. 1991. "*Taking Back Our Lives: A Report to the Panos Institute on Environment, Community Development and Race in the United States.*" Washington, DC: Panos Institute.

Beus, C. E. and R. E. Dunlap. 1990. "Conventional Versus Alternative Agriculture: The Paradigmatic Roots of the Debate." *Rural Sociology* 55(4):590–616.

Block, Jason P., Richard A. Scribner, and Karen B. DeSalvo. 2004. "Fast Food, Race/Ethnicity, and Income: A Geographic Analysis." *American Journal of Preventative Medicine* 27:211–17.

Brown, Phil and Edwin J. Mikkelsen. 1997. *No Safe Place.* Berkeley, CA: University of California Press.

Brulle, Robert J. 2000. *Agency, Democracy, and Nature: The U.S. Environmental Movement from a Critical Theory Perspective.* Cambridge, MA: MIT Press.

Bullard, Robert. 1990. *Dumping in Dixie.* Boulder, CO: Westview Press.

Buttel, Fred. 1997. "Some Observations on Agro-food Change and the Future of Agricultural Sustainability Movements." Pp. 344–65 in *Globalising Food: Agrarian Questions and Global Restructuring*, edited by David Goodman and Michael Watts. London, UK: Routledge.

Buttel, Fred, Olaf F. Larson, and Gilbert W. Gillespie, Jr. 1990. *The Sociology of Agriculture.* New York: Greenwood Press.

California Alcoholic Beverage Control (CABC). 2006. "Fact Sheet: Oakland Alcohol Retailers." Retrieved April 3, 2006 <http://Z;\Community Safety and Justice/Alcohol outlets\Website\ Factsheet_1.24.6.doc>.

Capek, Stella. 1993. "The 'Environmental Justice' Frame: A Conceptual Discussion and an Application." *Social Problems* 40:5–24.

Center for Disease Control (CDC). 2002. "National Diabetes Fact Sheet." Retrieved April 9, 2006 <http://www.cdc.gov/diabetes/pubs/figuretext.htm#fig2>.

Chung C. and S. L. Myers. 1999. "Do the Poor Pay More for Food? An Analysis of Grocery Store Availability and Food Price Disparities." *Journal of Consumer Affairs* 33:276–96.

Diamant, Alison L., Susan H. Babey, E. Richard Brown, and Theresa A. Hastert. 2005. "Diabetes on the Rise in California." UCLA Center for Health Policy Research. Retrieved March 31, 2008 <http://www.healthpolicy.ucla.edu/pubs/files/diabetes_pb_122005.pdf>.

Dunlap, Riley and William R. Catton. 1979. "Environmental Sociology." *Annual Review of Sociology* 5:243–73.

Dupris, Joseph, Kathleen S. Hill, and William H. Rodgers. 2006. *The Si'lailo Way: Indians, Salmon, and Law on the Columbia River* Durham, NC: Carolina Academic Press.

Faber, Daniel. 1998. *The Struggle for Ecological Democracy: Environmental Justice Movements in the United States*. New York: Guilford Press.

Foster, John Bellamy and Fred Magdoff. 2000. "Liebig, Marx and the Depletion of Soil Fertility: Relevance for Today's Agriculture." Pp. 43–60 in *Hungry for Profit: The Agribusiness Threat to Farmers, Food, and the Environment*, edited by Fred Magdoff, John Bellamy Foster, and Fred Buttel. New York: Monthly Review Press.

Gamson, William A. and Andre Modigliani. 1989. "Media Discourse and Public Opinion on Nuclear Power: A Constructionist Approach." *American Journal of Sociology* 95:1–37.

Gilbert, Jess, Gwen Sharp, and Sindy M. Felin. 2002. "The Loss and Persistence of Black-Owned Farms and Farmland: A Review of the Research Literature and Its Implications." *Southern Rural Sociology* 18:1–30.

Goldschmidt, Walter. [1947] 1978. *As You Sow*. Montclair, NJ: Allanheld, Osmun & Co.

Gottlieb, Robert and Andrew Fisher. 1996. "First Feed the Face: Environmental Justice and Community Food Security. *Antipode* 28:193–203.

Guthman, Julie. 2004. *Agrarian Dreams: The Paradox of Organic Farming in California*. Berkeley, CA: University of California Press.

Harrison, Gail, Charles A. DiSogra, George Manolo-LeClair, Jennifer Aguayo, and Wei Yen. 2002. "Over 2.2 Million Low Income Californian Adults are Food-Insecure, 658,000 Suffer Hunger." UCLA Center for Health Policy Research. Retrieved March 31, 2009 <http:// www.lafightshunger.org/images/hunger.pdf>.

Hewes, Gordon W. 1973. "Indian Fisheries Productivity in Pre-contact Times in the Pacific Salmon Area." *Northwest Anthropological Research Notes* 7(3):133–55.

House, Freeman. 1999. *Totem Salmon*. Boston, MA: Beacon Press.

Jackson, Jennifer. 2005. "Nutritional Analysis of Traditional and Present Foods of the Karuk People and Development of Public Outreach Materials." Orleans, CA: Karuk Tribe of California.

Joe, Jennie and Robert Young. 1993. *Diabetes as a Disease of Civilization: The Impact of Cultural Change on Indigenous People*. New York: Walter de Gruyter and Co.

Karuk Tribe of California. 2006. "Toxic Algae Threaten Human Health in PacifiCorp's Klamath Reservoirs Blooms Worse than Last Year, Little Response from Company or County." Retrieved March 31, 2009 <http://karuk.us/press/06-08-08%20toxic%20reservoirs.pdf>.

Kobayashi, Audrey and Linda Peake. 2000. "Racism Out of Place: Thoughts on Whiteness and Antiracist Geography for the New Millennium." *Annals of the Association of American Geographers* 90(2):392–403.

Lappe, Anna and Bryant Terry. 2006. *Grub: Ideas for an Urban Organic Kitchen*. New York: Tarcher. LaVeist T. and J. Wallace. 2000. "Health Risk and Inequitable Distribution of Liquor Stores in African American Neighborhoods." *Social Science and Medicine* 51:613–17.

Lyson, Thomas A. 2004. *Civic Agriculture: Reconnecting Farm, Food and Community*. Boston, MA: Tufts University Press.

Massey, Doreen and Nancy Denton. 1998. *American Apartheid: Segregation and the Making of the American Underclass*. Cambridge, MA: Harvard University Press.

Morland, Kimberly, S. Wing, A. Deiz Roux, and C. Poole. 2002. "Neighborhood Characteristics Associated with the Location of Food Stores and Food Service Places." *American Journal of Preventive Medicine* 22:23–29.

Norgaard, Kari Marie. (2005) "The Effects of Altered Diet on the Health of the Karuk People." Report submitted to the Federal Energy Regulatory Commission Docket #P-2082 on behalf of the Karuk Tribe of California.

Novotny, Patrick. 2000. *Where We Live, Work and Play: The Environmental Justice Movement and the Struggle for a New Environmentalism.* Westport, CT: Praeger.

Omi, Michael and Howard Winant. 1989. *Racial Formation in the United States: From the 1960s to the 1980s.* New York: Routledge.

Pellow, David N. 2004. "The Politics of Illegal Dumping: An Environmental Justice Framework." *Qualitative Sociology* 27:511–25.

Pellow, David N. and Robert J. Brulle. 2005. *Power, Justice and the Environment: A Critical Appraisal of the Environmental Justice Movement.* Boston, MA: MIT Press.

Peña, Devon. 2003. "Identity, Place and Communities of Resistance." Pp. 146–67 in *Just Sustainabilities: Development in an Unequal World*, edited by Julian Agyeman, Robert Bullard, and Bob Evans. London: Boston, MA: MIT Press.

Pulido, Laura. 2000. "Rethinking Environmental Racism: White Privilege and Urban Development in Southern California" *Annals of the Association of American Geographers* 90(1):12–40.

Stercho, Amy. 2005. "The Importance of Place-based Fisheries to the Karuk Tribe of California: A Socio-economic Study." Master's thesis, Humboldt State University, Arcata, CA.

Szasz, Andrew. 1994. *Ecopopulism: Toxic Waste and the Movement for Environmental Justice.* Minneapolis, MN: University of Minnesota Press.

Sze, Julie. 2006. *Noxious New York: The Racial Politics of Urban Health and Environmental Justice.* Boston, MA: MIT Press.

Taylor, D. 2000. "The Rise of the Environmental Justice Paradigm." *American Behavioral Scientist* 43:508–90.

———. 1997. "American Environmentalism: The Role of Race, Class, and Gender in Shaping Activism 1820–1995." *Race, Gender & Class* 5:16–62.

United Church of Christ. 1987. *Toxic Wastes and Race in the United States: A National Report on the Racial and Socio-economic Characteristics with Hazardous Waste Sites.* New York: United Church of Christ Commission for Racial Justice.

Wilkinson, Charles. 2005. *Blood Struggle: The Rise of Modern Indian Nations.* New York: W.W. Norton and Co.

———. 2000. *Messages from Frank's Landing: A Story of Salmon, Treaties, and the Indian Way.* Seattle, WA: University of Washington Press.

Wood, Spencer D. and Jess Gilbert. 2000. "Returning African American Farmers to the Land: Recent Trends and a Policy Rationale." *Review of Black Political Economy* 27(4):43–64.

Wrigley, Neil Ward, B. Margetts, and A. Whelan. 2002. "Assessing the Impact of Improved Retail Access on Diet in a 'Food Desert': A Preliminary Report." *Urban Studies* 39:2061–82.

Young, Kue. 1997. "Recent Health Trends in the Native American Population." *Population Research and Policy Review* 16:147–67.

Questions for Discussion

1. In what ways is access to food limited for residents of West Oakland and the Karuk Tribe?

2. Why did researchers decide to conduct case studies with African American and Native American groups rather than focus on one group?

3. How does this study relate to Broad's "The Black Panther Party: A Food Justice Story" in terms of the concept of food justice and how to approach it?

Trash Food

Chris Offutt

The Oxford American, April 2015

> Chris Offutt is an award-winning author and screenwriter. According to the *Oxford American* website, he has written for *True Blood, Weeds,* and *Treme,* as well as TV pilots for Fox, Lionsgate, and CBS. Additionally, he has published the novels *Kentucky Straight, Out of the Woods, The Same River Twice, No Heroes: A Memoir of Coming Home,* and *The Good Brother.* His most recent memoir, *My Father, the Pornographer* was published in March of 2015. Offutt currently teaches at the University of Mississippi. He has served as a visiting faculty member at the Iowa Writer's Workshop, the University of Montana, and the University of New Mexico. His non-fiction has been published in *The New York Times, Men's Journal,* and on *NPR.* A *New York Times* book review of the author's short stories says, "Offutt's obvious kin among contemporary American writers are Richard Ford and Tobias Wolff, and his great-granddaddy (like theirs) is Ernest Hemingway. His sentences are generally short and chiseled, with flashes of lyricism...Offutt's own sophistication and integrity are evident in the nuances he injects into his prose—all without a scrap of condescension." This article was published in *The Oxford American* in April 2015.

Over the years I've known many people with nicknames, including Lucky, Big O, Haywire, Turtle Eggs, Hercules, two guys named Hollywood, and three guys called Booger. I've had my own nicknames as well. In college people called me "Arf" because of a dog on a t-shirt. Back home a few of my best buddies call me "Shit-for-Brains," because our teachers thought I was smart.

Three years ago, shortly after moving to Oxford, someone introduced me to John T. Edge. He goes by his first name and middle initial, but I understood it as a nickname—Jaunty. The word "jaunty" means lively and cheerful, someone always merry and bright. The name seemed to suit him perfectly. Each time I called him Jaunty he gave me a quick sharp look of suspicion. He wondered if

I was making fun of his name—and of him. The matter was resolved when I suggested he call me "Chrissie O."

Last spring John T. asked me to join him at an Oxford restaurant. My wife dropped me off and drove to a nearby secondhand store. Our plan was for me to meet her later and find a couple of cheap lamps. During lunch John T. asked me to give a presentation at the Southern Foodways Alliance symposium over which he presided every fall.

I reminded him that I lacked the necessary qualifications. At the time I'd only published a few humorous essays that dealt with food. Other writers were more knowledgeable and wrote with a historical context, from a scholarly perspective. All I did was write personal essays inspired by old community cookbooks I found in secondhand stores. Strictly speaking, my food writing wasn't technically about food.

John T. said that didn't matter. He wanted me to explore "trash food," because, as he put it, "you write about class."

I sat without speaking, my food getting cold on my plate. Three thoughts ran through my mind fast as flipping an egg. First, I couldn't see the connection between social class and garbage. Second, I didn't like having my thirty-year career reduced to a single subject matter. Third, I'd never heard of anything called "trash food."

I write about my friends, my family, and my experiences, but never with a socio-political agenda such as class. My goal was always art first, combined with an attempt at rigorous self-examination. Facing John T., I found myself in a professional and social pickle, not unusual for a country boy who's clawed his way out of the hills of eastern Kentucky, one of the steepest social climbs in America. I've never mastered the high-born art of concealing my emotions. My feelings are always readily apparent.

Recognizing my turmoil, John T. asked if I was pissed off. I nodded and he apologized immediately. I told him I was overly sensitive to matters of social class. I explained that people from the hills of Appalachia have always had to fight to prove they were smart, diligent, and trustworthy. It's the same for people who grew up in the Mississippi Delta, the barrios of Los Angeles and Texas, or the black neighborhoods in New York, Chicago, and Memphis. His request reminded me that due to social class I'd been refused dates, bank loans, and even jobs. I've been called hillbilly, stumpjumper, cracker, weedsucker, redneck, and white trash—mean-spirited terms designed to hurt me and make me feel bad about myself.

As a young man, I used to laugh awkwardly at remarks about sex with my sister or the perceived novelty of my wearing shoes. As I got older I quit laughing. When strangers thought I was stupid because of where I grew up, I understood that they were granting me the high ground. I learned to patiently wait in ambush for the chance to utterly demolish them intellectually. Later I realized that this particular battle strategy was a waste of energy. It was easier to simply stop talking to that person—forever.

But I didn't want to do that with a guy whose name sounds like "jaunty." A guy who'd inadvertently triggered an old emotional response. A guy who liked my work well enough to pay me for it.

By this time our lunch had a tension to it that draped over us both like a lead vest for an X-ray. We just looked at each other, neither of us knowing what to do. John T. suggested I think about it, then graciously offered me a lift to meet my wife. But a funny thing had happened. Our conversation had left me inexplicably ashamed of shopping at a thrift store. I wanted to walk to hide my destination, but refusing a ride might make John T. think I was angry with him. I wasn't. I was upset. But not with him.

My solution was a verbal compromise, a term politicians use to mean a blatant lie. I told him to drop me at a restaurant where I was meeting my wife for cocktails. He did so and I waited until his red Italian sports car sped away. As soon as he was out of sight I walked to the junk store. I sat out front like a man with not a care in the world, ensconced in a battered patio chair staring at clouds above the parking lot. When I was a kid my mother bought baked goods at the day-old bread store and hoped no one would see her car. Now I was embarrassed for shopping secondhand.

My behavior was class-based twice over: buying used goods to save a buck and feeling ashamed of it. I'd behaved in strict accordance with my social station, then evaluated myself in a negative fashion. Even my anger was classic self-oppression, a learned behavior of lower-class people. I was transforming outward shame into inner fury. Without a clear target, I aimed that rage at myself.

My thoughts and feelings were completely irrational. I knew they made no sense. Most of what I owned had belonged to someone else—cars, clothes, shoes, furniture, dishware, cookbooks. I liked old and battered things. They reminded me of myself, still capable and functioning despite the wear and tear. I enjoyed the idea that my belongings had a previous history before coming my way. It was very satisfying to repair a broken lamp made of popsicle sticks and transform it to a lovely source of illumination. A writer's livelihood is weak at best, and I'd become adept at operating in a secondhand economy. I was comfortable with it.

Still, I sat in that chair getting madder and madder. After careful examination I concluded that the core of my anger was fear—in this case fear that John T. would judge me for shopping secondhand. I knew it was absurd since he is not judgmental in the least. Anyone can see that he's an open-hearted guy willing to embrace anything and everyone—even me.

Nevertheless I'd felt compelled to mislead him based on class stigma. I was ashamed—of my fifteen-year-old Mazda, my income, and my rented home. I felt ashamed of the very clothes I was wearing, the shoes on my feet. Abruptly, with the force of being struck in the face, I understood it wasn't his judgment I feared. It was my own. I'd judged myself and found failure. I wanted a car like his. I wanted to dress like him and have a house like his. I wanted to be in a position to offer other people jobs.

The flip side of shame is pride. All I had was the pride of refusal. I could say no to his offer. I did not have to write about trash food and class. No, I decided, no, no, no. Later, it occurred to me that my reluctance was evidence that maybe I should say yes. I resolved to do some research before refusing his offer.

John T. had been a little shaky on the label of "trash food," mentioning mullet and possum as examples. At one time this list included crawfish because Cajun people ate it, and catfish because it was favored by African Americans and poor Southern whites. As these cuisines gained popularity, the food itself became culturally upgraded. Crawfish and catfish stopped being "trash food" when the people eating it in restaurants were the same ones who felt superior to the lower classes. Elite white diners had to redefine the food to justify eating it. Otherwise they were voluntarily lowering their own social status—something nobody wants to do.

It should be noted that carp and gar still remain reputationally compromised. In other words—poor folks eat it and rich folks don't. I predict that one day wealthy white people will pay thirty-five dollars for a tiny portion of carp with a rich sauce—and congratulate themselves for doing so.

I ran a multitude of various searches on library databases and the Internet in general, typing in permutations of the words "trash" and "food." Surprisingly, every single reference was to "white trash food." Within certain communities, it's become popular to host "white trash parties" where people are urged to bring Cheetos, pork rinds, Vienna sausages, Jell-O with marshmallows, fried baloney, corndogs, RC cola, Slim Jims, Fritos, Twinkies, and cottage cheese with jelly. In short—the food I ate as a kid in the hills.

Participating in such a feast is considered proof of being very cool and very hip. But it's not. Implicit in the menu is a vicious ridicule of the people who eat such food on a regular basis. People who attend these "white trash parties" are cuisinally slumming, temporarily visiting a place they never want to live. They are the worst sort of tourists—they want to see the Mississippi Delta and the hills of Appalachia but are afraid to get off the bus.

The term "white trash" is an epithet of bigotry that equates human worth with garbage. It implies a dismissal of the group as stupid, violent, lazy, and untrustworthy—the same negative descriptors of racial minorities, of anyone outside of the mainstream. At every stage of American history, various groups of people have endured such personal attacks. Language is used as a weapon: divisive, cruel, enciphered. Today is no different. For example, here in Mississippi, the term "Democrats" is code for "African Americans." Throughout the U.S.A., "family values" is code for "no homosexuals." The term "trash food" is not about food, it's coded language for social class. It's about poor people and what they can afford to eat.

In America, class lines run parallel to racial lines. At the very bottom are people of color. The Caucasian equivalent is me—an Appalachian. As a male Caucasian in America, I am supposed to have an inherent advantage in every possible way. It's true. I can pass more easily in society. I have better access to education, health care, and employment. But if I insist on behaving like a poor white person—shopping at secondhand shops and eating mullet—I not only earn the epithet of "trash," I somehow deserve it.

The term "white trash" is class disparagement due to economics. Polite society regards me as stupid, lazy, ignorant, violent, and untrustworthy.

I am trash because of where I'm from.

I am trash because of where I shop.

I am trash because of what I eat.

But human beings are not trash. We are the civilizing force on the planet. We produce great art, great music, great food, and great technology. It's not the opposable thumb that separates us from the beasts, it's our facility with language. We are able to communicate with great precision. Nevertheless, history is fraught with the persistence of treating fellow humans as garbage, which means collection and transport for destruction. The most efficient management of humans as trash occurred when the Third Reich systematically murdered people by the millions. People they didn't like. People they were afraid of. Jews, Romanis, Catholics, gays and lesbians, Jehovah's Witnesses, and the disabled.

In World War II, my father-in-law was captured by the Nazis and placed on a train car so crammed with people that everyone had to stand for days. Arthur hadn't eaten in a week. He was close to starvation. A Romani man gave him half a turnip, which saved his life. That Romani man later died. Arthur survived the war. He had been raised to look down on Romani people as stupid, lazy, violent, and untrustworthy—the ubiquitous language of class discrimination. He subsequently revised his view of Romanis. For Arthur, the stakes of starvation were high enough that he changed his view of a group of people. But the wealthy elite in this country are not starving. When they changed their eating habits, they didn't change their view of people. They just upgraded crawfish and catfish.

Economic status dictates class and diet. We arrange food in a hierarchy based on who originally ate it until we reach mullet, gar, possum, and squirrel—the diet of the poor. The food is called trash, and then the people are.

When the white elite take an interest in the food poor people eat, the price goes up. The result is a cost that prohibits poor families from eating the very food they've been condemned for eating. It happened with salmon and tuna years ago. When I was a kid and money was tight, my mother mixed a can of tuna with pasta and vegetables. Our family of six ate it for two days. Gone are the days of subsisting on cheap fish patties at the end of the month. The status of the food rose but not the people. They just had less to eat.

What is trash food? I say all food is trash without human intervention. Cattle, sheep, hogs, and chickens would die unless slaughtered for the table. If humans didn't harvest vegetables, they would rot in the field. Food is a disposable commodity until we accumulate the raw material, blend ingredients, and apply heat, cold, and pressure. Then our bodies extract nutrients and convert it into waste, which must be disposed of. The act of eating produces trash.

In the hills of Kentucky we all looked alike—scruffy white people with squinty eyes and cowlicks. We shared the same economic class, the same religion, the same values and loyalties. Even our enemy was mutual: people who lived in town. Appalachians are suspicious of their neighbors, distrustful of strangers, and uncertain about third cousins. It's a culture that operates under a very simple principle: you leave me alone, and I'll leave you alone. After moving away from the hills I developed a different way of interacting with people. I still get cantankerous and defensive—ask John T.—but I'm better with human relations than I used to be. I've learned to observe and listen.

As an adult I have lived and worked in eleven different states—New York, Massachusetts, Florida, New Mexico, Montana, California, Tennessee, Georgia, Iowa, Arizona, and now Mississippi. These circumstances often placed me in contact with African Americans as neighbors, members of the same labor crew, working in restaurants, and now university colleagues. The first interaction between a black man and a white man is one of mutual evaluation: does the other guy hate my guts? The white guy—me—is worried that after generations of repression and mistreatment, will this black guy take his anger out on me because I'm white? And the black guy is wondering if I am one more racist asshole he can't turn his back on. This period of reconnaissance typically doesn't last long because both parties know the covert codes the other uses—the avoidance of touch, the averted eyes, a posture of hostility. Once each man is satisfied that the other guy is all right, connections begin to occur. Those connections are always based on class. And class translates to food.

Last year my mother and I were in the hardware store buying parts to fix a toilet. The first thing we learned was that the apparatus inside commodes has gotten pretty fancy over the years. Like breakfast cereal, there were dozens of types to choose from. Toilet parts were made of plastic, copper, and cheap metal. Some were silent and some saved water and some looked as if they came from an alien spacecraft.

A store clerk, an African-American man in his sixties, offered to help us. I told him I was overwhelmed, that plumbing had gotten too complicated. I tried to make a joke by saying it was a lot simpler when everyone used an outhouse. He gave me a quick sharp look of suspicion. I recognized his expression. It's the same one John T. gave me when I mispronounced his name, the same look I gave John T. when he mentioned "trash food" and social class. The same one I unleashed on people who called me a hillbilly or a redneck.

I understood the clerk's concern. He wondered if I was making a veiled comment about race, economics, and the lack of plumbing. I told him that back in Kentucky when the hole filled up with waste, we dug a new hole and moved the outhouse to it. Then we'd plant a fruit tree where the old outhouse had been.

"Man," I said, "that tree would bear. Big old peaches."

He looked at me differently then, a serious expression. His earlier suspicion was gone.

"You know some things," he said. "Yes you do."

"I know one thing," I said. "When I was a kid I wouldn't eat those peaches."

The two of us began laughing at the same time. We stood there and laughed until the mirth trailed away, reignited, and brought forth another bout of laughter. Eventually we wound down to a final chuckle. We stood in the aisle and studied the toilet repair kits on the pegboard wall. They were like books in a foreign language.

"Well," I said to him. "What do you think?"

"What do I think?" he said.

I nodded.

"I think I won't eat those peaches."

We started laughing again, this time longer, slapping each other's arms. Pretty soon one of us just had to mutter "peaches" to start all over again. Race was no more important to us than plumbing parts or shopping at a secondhand store. We were two Southern men laughing together in an easy way, linked by class and food.

On the surface, John T. and I should have been able to laugh in a similar way last spring. We have more in common than the store clerk and I do. John T. and I share race, status, and regional origin. We are close to the same age. We are sons of the South. We're both writers, married with families. John T. and I have cooked for each other, gotten drunk together, and told each other stories. We live in the same town, have the same friends.

But none of that mattered in the face of social class, an invisible and permanent division. It's the boundary John T. had the courage to ask me to write about. The boundary that made me lie about the secondhand store last spring. The boundary that still fills me with shame and anger. A boundary that only food can cross.

Questions for Discussion

1. What does Offut find problematic about the concept of "trash food"?

2. How would you characterize this author's style? How does this style impact his message as a whole?

3. Several of the readings in this book consider the relationship between class and food. In what ways do see you these two things intersecting in our society?

Why Food Stamps Matter

Sasha Abramsky

The New Yorker, September 2013

> According to his website, Sasha Abramsky is a freelance journalist who has published articles in *The Nation, The Atlantic Monthly, Slate,* and *Rolling Stone.* This article is adapted from his book, *The American Way of Poverty: How the Other Half Still Lives,* published in 2013, and named by *The New York Times* as one of the 100 Most Notable Books of the year. His website describes the book as one that, "brings the effects of economic inequality out of the shadows, and ultimately, suggests ways for moving toward a fairer and more equitable social contract." This adapted excerpt was published in *The New Yorker* magazine in 2013, a publication that, according to its mission statement, offers a mix of "reporting and commentary on politics, international affairs, popular culture and the arts, science and technology, and business, along with fiction, poetry, humor, and cartoons."

On Saturday mornings in North Philadelphia, hundreds of people can be found lining up along the sidewalks of West LeHigh Avenue and Sixth Street, near the basement entrance of a local public library. They aren't looking for books, they are looking to be fed, by a large community food center housed in the library's basement. Until recently, the fire-gutted, stone-and-brick shell of a huge high school down the street from the center dominated the landscape, looking more like a ruined medieval monastery than a modern-day American urban academy. The school ruins have now been torn down, but the side streets are still lined with boarded-up houses.

North Philadelphia is one of America's poorest urban neighborhoods. In 2011, researchers with Pew Charitable Trusts estimated that Philadelphia's poverty rate stood at twenty-five percent. But that number hid huge disparities. Some suburbs were as leafy and affluent as Westchester, New York. Meanwhile, in the eastern part of North Philadelphia, the city's poorest district, the poverty rate stood at about fifty-six per cent. In 2010, the median home price for a house in the area was ten thousand dollars.

I met Vicenta Delgado in the fall of 2011, while she was sitting on the curb waiting for the pantry on LeHigh Avenue to open. It was a chilly morning, and she was bundled up against the cold, her walker resting on the sidewalk beside her, wearing a dark headscarf over her bald head.

Delgado, a sixty-one-year-old immigrant from Puerto Rico, told me that she had been undergoing chemotherapy to treat a brain tumor. She also had diabetes and high blood pressure, and had suffered from depression ever since her oldest son was killed. The health problems had taken a financial toll on her: she paid a three-dollar co-pay each time she filled a prescription; Medicaid didn't cover the nutritional supplement shakes that she needed because of her cancer, so she bought them herself; she had to pay a neighbor to drive her to the hospital for her treatments. And it was out of the question to stop paying her electricity bill: if her electricity got cut off, the machine that helped her breathe at night—she suffered from sleep apnea—wouldn't work.

Each month, Delgado said, she and her husband together received a little more than a thousand dollars from Social Security and thirty-four dollars in food stamps. She also received disability benefits. But this income was not nearly enough to fill her fridge and pay the bills. "You go to the store with thirty-four dollars, you can't buy nothing," she told me.

So she spent each Saturday morning waiting in line for several hours until the pantry opened its doors; get there too late, and they'd be out of food. It was a demoralizing ritual, but at least it kept her fed. (I tried to reach Delgado this week to see how she was doing, but wasn't able to track her down. A worker at the food pantry told me that, after being a regular attendee for years, she had not come to the LeHigh Avenue site since the end of December, 2011.)

House Republicans last week pushed through a bill that would cut forty billion dollars from the food-stamp program over ten years, limiting how long able-bodied adults could access the assistance and linking that aid to their ability to get a job or enroll in a job-training program. The measure isn't likely to get traction in the Senate, but it has ignited a heated debate over the value of food stamps and the significance of the program's growth.

Last year, the food-stamp program cost the federal government eighty-one billion dollars. More than forty-seven million Americans rely on food stamps; for America's poor, it is the most successful and comprehensive part of the modern safety net, expanding automatically as need expands. Food stamps also help sustain the economies of low-income neighborhoods, since the money is often spent in those areas' local stores.

Those who believe food-stamp spending is too high sometimes argue that, if the government were to spend less on the program, people would simply work harder so they could buy their own food, or else they would get food from food pantries and other charities. That's not true in many cases. Delgado probably can't work, and millions of others are trying to find work without success—or have jobs but are paid such low wages that they still qualify for public assistance.

And while many who receive food stamps also fall back on the country's network of food pantries, the organizations behind the pantries have been massively overstretched in the wake of the 2008 economic collapse. They function as a supplemental source of food when people's food stamps run out—but they're far from having enough resources to make up for a big cut to the food-stamp program. Already, some pantries routinely run out of food; others have had to cut back on what they can offer.

For the past several years, I have reported on poverty in America, interviewing hundreds of people in dozens of states. On the day that I met Delgado, I also met Bill Clark, the executive director of a huge nonprofit food-distribution organization named PhilAbundance, who oversaw four hundred and fifty pantries that helped support six hundred and fifty thousand families per week. Some of the communities PhilAbundance served were among the very poorest in the country.

Clark explained that, after the economic collapse of 2008, PhilAbundance received less surplus food from the U.S.D.A. and less salvaged foods. Dented cans, for example, which in the recent past had been donated by food producers to the pantries, started winding up in dollar stores, where they were sold at a discount. The amount of salvaged food in PhilAbundance pantries plunged eighty-five per cent from 2008 to 2011. At the same time, the number of people attending the centers each Saturday morning skyrocketed, leaving pantry administrators scrambling to plug the gap—canvassing the community for food donations and launching frantic fund-raising drives to generate money that they could spend to buy food.

North Philadelphia in 2011 was hardly alone in its desolation. Areas of Baltimore, Detroit, Los Angeles, New Orleans, and many other cities also suffered from poverty and hunger crises. Suburbs, too, saw explosions in hunger, especially in communities wrecked by the bursting of the housing bubble. Nor were rural areas, or smaller cities in the American heartland, immune.

In Des Moines, Iowa, I met a fifty-nine-year-old woman named Sandy Struznick, whose husband lost his job during the recession. They ate lunch regularly at a senior citizens' center—their main meal of the day, Struznick told me. "I can't buy for our grandkids, I can't buy them any gifts," she confided. "I can't go to see them. We're living in a crunch, feel like we don't have any hope some days. For dinner, we eat cereal or something cheap. We have meat just if they have it at the seniors' center. No fresh vegetables, no fresh fruit."

Questions for Discussion

1. Abramsky addresses the counterargument that if the government were to spend less on food stamps, the poor would work harder. How does he refute this claim?

2. The author ends his article with an anecdote. Why do you think the author chose to structure his article this way? What effect might this have on his intended audience?

3. Compare Abramsky's piece to Saslow's. How do the author's approaches differ? How are they similar? Who do you think is more effective in achieving their purpose?

Food Stamps Put Rhode Island on Monthly Boom-and-Bust Cycle

Eli Saslow

The Washington Post, March 2013

> Eli Saslow is a reporter for *The Washington Post* and *ESPN*. According to the publication's website, in 2014 Saslow won the Pulizer Prize for Explanatory Reporting for his year-long series about food stamps in the United States. As a sportswriter for the *Post*, two of his stories appeared in *The Best American Sports Writing*. This article is part of a series by *The Washington Post* entitled American Hunger. Before writing the series, Saslow spent a year traveling around the United States examining, as stated on the website, "the personal and political implications and repercussions of America's growing food stamp program." During his travels, Saslow gathered stories from towns in Rhode Island, Florida, and Texas, as well as in Washington DC.

The economy of Woonsocket was about to stir to life. Delivery trucks were moving down river roads, and stores were extending their hours. The bus company was warning riders to anticipate "heavy traffic." A community bank, soon to experience a surge in deposits, was rolling a message across its electronic marquee on the night of Feb. 28: "Happy shopping! Enjoy the 1st."

In the heart of downtown, Miguel Pichardo, 53, watched three trucks jockey for position at the loading dock of his family-run International Meat Market. For most of the month, his business operated as a humble milk-and-eggs corner store, but now 3,000 pounds of product were scheduled for delivery in the next few hours. He wiped the front counter and smoothed the edges of a sign posted near his register. "Yes! We take Food Stamps, SNAP, EBT!"

"Today, we fill the store up with everything," he said. "Tomorrow, we sell it all."

At precisely one second after midnight, on March 1, Woonsocket would experience its monthly financial windfall—nearly $2 million from the Supplemental Nutrition Assistance Program (SNAP), formerly known as food stamps. Federal money would be electronically transferred to the broke

347

residents of a nearly bankrupt town, where it would flow first into grocery stores and then on to food companies, employees and banks, beginning the monthly cycle that has helped Woonsocket survive.

Three years into an economic recovery, this is the lasting scar of collapse: a federal program that began as a last resort for a few million hungry people has grown into an economic lifeline for entire towns. Spending on SNAP has doubled in the past four years and tripled in the past decade, surpassing $78 billion last year. A record 47 million Americans receive the benefit—including 13,752 in Woonsocket, one-third of the town's population, where the first of each month now reveals twin shortcomings of the U.S. economy:

So many people are forced to rely on government support.

The government is forced to support so many people.

The 1st is always circled on the office calendar at International Meat Market, where customers refer to the day in the familiar slang of a holiday. It is Check Day. Milk Day. Pay Day. Mother's Day.

"Uncle Sam Day," Pichardo said now, late on Feb. 28, as he watched new merchandise roll off the trucks. Out came 40 cases of Ramen Noodles. Out came 230 pounds of ground beef and 180 gallons of orange juice.

SNAP enrollment in Rhode Island had been rising for six years, up from 73,000 people to nearly 180,000, and now three-quarters of purchases at International Meat Market are paid for with Electronic Benefit Transfer (EBT) cards. Government money had in effect funded the truckloads of food at Pichardo's dock ... and the three part-time employees he had hired to unload it ... and the walk-in freezer he had installed to store surplus product ... and the electric bills he paid to run that freezer, at nearly $2,000 each month.

Pichardo's profits from SNAP had also helped pay for International Meat Market itself, a 10-aisle store in a yellow building that he had bought and refurbished in 2010, when the rise in government spending persuaded him to expand out of a smaller market down the block.

The son of a grocer in the Dominican Republic, Pichardo had immigrated to the United States in the 1980s because he expected everyone to have money— "a country of customers," he had thought. He settled in Rhode Island with his brother, and together they opened a series of small supermarkets. He framed his first three $5s, his first three $20s and his first three $100s, the green bills lining a wall behind his register. But now he rarely dealt in cash, and he had built a plexiglass partition in front of the register to discourage his most desperate customers from coming after those framed bills when their EBT cards ran dry. The local unemployment rate was 12 percent. The shuttered textile mills along the river had become Section 8 housing. The median income had dropped by $10,000 in the last decade.

Of the few jobs still available in Woonsocket, many were part-time positions at grocery stores like his, with hours clustered around the first of the month.

Pichardo catered his store to the unique shopping rhythms of Rhode Island, where so much about the food industry revolved around the 1st. Other states had passed legislation to distribute SNAP benefits more gradually across the month, believing a one-day blitz was taxing for both retailers and customers. Maryland and Washington, D.C., had begun depositing benefits evenly across the first 10 days; Virginia had started doing it over four. But Rhode Island and seven other states had stuck to the old method—a retail flashpoint that sent shoppers scrambling to stores en masse.

Pichardo had placed a $10,000 product order to satisfy his diverse customers, half of them white, a quarter Hispanic, 15 percent African American, plus a dozen immigrant populations drawn to Woonsocket by the promise of cheap housing. He had ordered 150 pounds of the tenderloin steak favored by the newly poor, still clinging to old habits; and 200 cases of chicken gizzards for the inter-generationally poor, savvy enough to spot a deal at less than $2 a pound. He had bought pizza pockets for the working poor and plantains for the immigrant poor. He had stocked up on East African marinades, Spanish rice, Cuban snacks, and Mexican fruit juice. The boxes piled up in the aisles and the whir of an electronic butcher's knife reverberated from the back of the store.

Late on the 28th, a boyfriend and girlfriend arrived at Pichardo's register with a small basket of food. "Finally! A customer," Pichardo said, turning away from a Dominican League baseball game streaming on his computer. The last day of the month was always his slowest. The 1st was always his best, when he sometimes made 25 percent of his profits for the month. Pichardo rang up his last transaction of February: a gallon of milk, a box of pasta, and a bag of discount cookies.

"That's $5.28," he said.

The boyfriend handed over his EBT card: "Sorry. Running low," he said. "I only got $1.07 on there."

The girlfriend handed over hers: "I got $3.20 on this one."

They paid the remainder of their balance with change, and Pichardo dropped it into his nearly empty register. Slow days reminded him of times when he had worked 14-hour days to avoid paying employees and once faced charges for selling stolen merchandise. But now, thanks to SNAP, he had scheduled four extra employees to work the next morning, when they would hand out free eggs to big spenders.

Pichardo closed the register and totaled his sales for Feb. 28. He had made $526.

"Tomorrow, we do 15 times more," he said.

****

The last meal of the month was almost always their worst.

Rebecka and Jourie Ortiz usually ran out of milk first, after about three weeks. Next went juice, fresh produce, cereal, meat and eggs. By the 27th or 28th, Rebecka, 21, was often making a dish she referred to in front of the kids as "rice-a-roni," even though she and Jourie called it "rice-a-whatever." It was boiled noodles with canned vegetables and beans. "Enough salt and hot sauce can make anything good," she said.

Late on Feb. 28, Rebecka came home to their two-bedroom apartment to make a snack for her daughters, ages 1 and 3. The kitchen was the biggest room in their apartment, with a stove that doubled as a heater and a floral wall hanging bought at the dollar store that read: "All things are possible if you believe!" She opened the refrigerator. Its top shelf had been duct-taped and its cracked bottom shelf had been covered with a towel. Only a few jars of jelly, iced tea, rotten vegetables, and some string cheese remained in between.

For the past three years, the Ortizes' lives had unfolded in a series of exhausting, fractional decisions. Was it better to eat the string cheese now or to save it? To buy milk for $3.80 nearby or for $3.10 across town? Was it better to pay down the $600 they owed the landlord, or the $110 they owed for their cellphones, or the $75 they owed the tattoo parlor, or the $840 they owed the electric company?

They had been living together since Rebecka became pregnant during their senior year of high school, long enough to experience Woonsocket's version of recession and recovery. Jourie had lost his job at a pharmacy late in 2010 because of downsizing, and Rebecka had lost hers in fast food for the same reason a few months later. They had filled out a one-page application for SNAP and been accepted on Oct. 11, 2011, awarded $518 for a family of four, to be delivered on the first of every month. "Check Day!" they had begun calling it. They had applied for jobs until finally, late in 2012, they had both been hired for the only work high school graduates were finding in a low-wage recovery: part time at a nearby supermarket, the nicest one in the area, a two-story Stop & Shop across the Massachusetts line.

She made $8 an hour, and he earned $9. She worked days in produce, and he worked nights as a stocker. Their combined monthly income of $1,700 was still near the poverty line, and they still qualified for SNAP.

Rebecka had read once that nobody starved to death in America, and she believed that was true. But she had also read that the average monthly SNAP benefit lasted a family 17 days, and she knew from personal experience the anxiety headaches that came at the end of every month, when their SNAP money had run out, their bank account was empty and she was left to ply Woonsocket's circuit of emergency church food pantries. Saint Agatha's on Mondays. All Saints's on Tuesdays. Saint Charles's on Thursdays, where the pantry opened at 10 a.m. but the line of regulars began forming at 6.

To steady her nerves and improve her mood near the end of the month, Rebecka had started making elaborate grocery lists to prepare for the 1st—"an OCD habit," she said. She sorted the items in order of importance and then rewrote the list again and again, until her handwriting looked perfect and the list became irrelevant, because she had memorized it all.

Now she reached into the refrigerator and grabbed two string cheeses for her daughters. Then she reached back for a third.

"Do you want a snack for work?" she asked Jourie, who was getting dressed for his midnight shift.

"Do we have enough?"

"I think so," she said, handing him the cheese. "But I'm shopping tomorrow."

"I'll wait," he said, handing it back. He stood up and hugged her goodbye. "They'll fire me if I'm late," he said.

He had neither a driver's license nor a car, so he always walked the mile to work. He headed out of their apartment building in a hooded sweatshirt and turned down Privilege Street. His feet crunched against the snow, and his head steamed in the cold air. He passed a U-Save Liquors, a Cheap-O Tires, and an

Instant Payday Loans. He passed four stores with signs advertising that they accepted SNAP.

The government had designated Woonsocket a "highly distressed community" in 2012, and at night Jourie thought it also seemed deserted, a town that disappeared into twisting two-lane roads, shadowy mills and abandoned smokestacks. He watched his reflection in the empty store windows as he walked, crossing the border into Massachusetts and cutting through a parking lot toward the Stop & Shop. Its lights glowed neon. Four trucks idled at the loading docks, the sign of an economy coming alive for the 1st.

Jourie had almost never shopped at the store himself; it was too expensive. His family would spend Check Day somewhere else. He punched his timecard at 10:57 p.m. and walked into the store, where he stocked the aisles with cat food as Feb. 28 ended and March 1 arrived.

****

The first five customers came to International Meat Market at 7 a.m., 30 minutes before the store opened. They leaned on shopping carts and smoked cigarettes, passing around a yellow flier that advertised the market's bulk deals for the 1st. The flier detailed eight "Meat Packs." Five pounds of deli cuts went for $12.99; 28 pounds of beef for $49.99; a 58-pound variety pack with pork, pig's feet, chicken wings, and London broil for $99.99.

Pichardo unlocked the store and led the customers to the meat counter, where both the butcher and his apron were already smeared with blood.

"Lucky. You get first pick," Pichardo told his customers, gesturing at the full meat counter. "Place your orders, and we'll fill them as fast as we can."

Every store had a gimmick for the 1st, and Pichardo's was the meat packs, which accounted for most of his sales. The idea was to sell merchandise in bulk when customers were hungry and most likely to splurge, hours after the government had deposited an average benefit payment of $265 onto their EBT cards. The nearby Shaw's Market had started a dollar aisle, and the dollar store had 50-cent specials. Wal-Mart stayed open 24 hours, and customers sometimes waited out the final minutes of the month with full carts near the registers, counting down to midnight.

Grocery store chains had started discount spinoffs. Farmers markets had incentivized SNAP shopping by rewarding customers with $2 extra for every $5 of government money spent. Restaurants, long forbidden from accepting

SNAP, had begun a major lobbying campaign in Washington, and now a handful of Subways in Rhode Island were accepting the benefit as part of a pilot program.

But SNAP recipients at International Meat Market were allowed to spend their money only on uncooked foods—nothing hot or pre-prepared, no paper products, pet food, alcohol, or cigarettes. A line formed at Pichardo's register, and he lifted one heavy cardboard box of meat after the next.

A part-time janitor came through with a meat pack, vegetable oil, and canned tomatoes. "That's $132.20," Pichardo said.

An unemployed welder with two meat packs and a 24-pack of Ramen. "One-hundred and-ten," Pichardo said.

A retired teacher. A single mother of three. A Salvadoran immigrant who wanted the meat pack flier translated into Spanish. A part-time employee at International Meat Market, hired for the day, buying $69.99 worth of meat with a SNAP card during his 20-minute break.

"Thank you," Pichardo told one customer.

"Gracias," he told the next.

"Okay, my friend."

"See you next month."

By noon his shirt was drenched and his feet were swollen. His thumb and index finger were stained brown after grabbing and sliding 120 EBT cards in the past four hours. The store smelled like meat and sweat, and the aisles were a trail of discarded items. The exhausted butcher behind the meat counter had started mumbling under his breath in Spanish: "No mas. No mas. No mas."

Pichardo noticed none of it. His store had already sold more than $5,000, with $4,700 paid for in SNAP.

****

Rebecka went shopping early that afternoon. Jourie was still sleeping off his midnight shift, so she decided to take the girls by herself. She wanted to visit at least two stores to capitalize on the best deals. She packed snacks and diaper bags and loaded the girls into the car, a 2004 Mitsubishi Galant leased on

18 percent interest for $90 a week. They drove across town to Price Rite, the cheapest chain in Woonsocket, and the town's epicenter of the SNAP economy.

Nearly 150 cars filled the lot, and stray shopping carts edged into the adjacent road. The sign in front of the store advertised "Impossibly, Incredibly, Inconceivably Low Prices." A city bus had stopped at the entrance a few minutes earlier to drop off 30 shoppers before turning back to pick up 30 more. The residents of Woonsocket had petitioned for the route in 2011, but now buses suffered from overcrowding on the 1st and drivers enforced a limit of seven grocery bags per person on the way home. A line of opportunistic cab drivers had begun waiting outside Price Rite on the 1st, ready for customers with more than seven bags and with $4.75 for the fare.

Rebecka moved quickly through the lot and lifted her 1-year-old, Jaeliece, and her 3-year-old, Sariah, into an empty shopping cart.

"Please keep your hands in the cart," she told them. "Only Mommy gets to do the shopping."

The first tantrum came before they reached the front door. Sariah wanted a balloon, and then a gum ball, and then a bag of oranges off a display near the entrance. That was the trouble with shopping on the 1st, after a week of skimping and rice-a-whatever: There were so many things to want, and stores designed themselves to maximize temptation. Juices were placed low within reach of the kids. Candy and Coke displays blocked the aisles. A six-foot-tall mountain of Oreos towered just inside the Price Rite entrance, a temporary display for the 1st that Sariah was reaching for now.

"No," Rebecka said. "That's not on the list."

"Mine," Sariah said, grabbing a bag of cookies.

"No."

"Mine!" Other customers turned to look. Rebecka still had two stores and 70 items left on her shopping list for the day.

"Fine," she said. "You can hold it." She moved past the cookies and hustled through the store, weaving between customers who were shopping with two carts and grabbing items by the cardboard crate. Little boys ran around retirees on their motorized scooters. Rebecka focused on the list and calculated prices in her head. She grabbed two boxes of Cinnamon Toast Crunch ($2.49), a four-gallon bottle of cooking oil ($5.99) and three gallons of milk ($3.10).

She pushed the kids toward checkout, where long lines snaked behind all 12 registers. Sariah started throwing items out of their cart. Jaeliece began to cry. "Damn it," Rebecka said. She pushed her cart into an express lane for 10 items or less and set her 22 items on the conveyer belt. "I'm sorry," she told the cashier. Then she handed over her EBT card, paid $49.20, and loaded the kids back into the car for Wal-Mart.

The crowds got bigger.

The prices got higher.

The tantrums got worse.

"Damn it!" Rebecka said again, racing around the store, oblivious to her own list, picking up anything that looked healthy or filling and dropping it into the cart. Sariah grabbed a box of Goldfish off the shelf and opened it. "I guess we have to buy that now," Rebecka said. Jaeliece opened a string cheese and threw it on the floor. "I guess we have to buy that, too," Rebecka said. Sariah ran away, and Rebecka ran after her. Sariah hid, and Rebecka searched for her in produce.

"I can't do this anymore," she said, after almost an hour in Wal-Mart. She pushed the kids toward the checkout line. Another SNAP shopper was already in front of her with $230 worth of food on the conveyer belt, so they had to wait. Sariah grabbed a package of Play-Doh off the shelf and ripped it open, throwing green putty on the floor. "Are you serious?" Rebecka said. "That's another $6.50 you just cost me."

"I've been there," said the shopper in front of her, turning to help clean up the Play-Doh.

"I'm flipping," Rebecka said.

"The best and the worst day of the month," the shopper said.

Rebecka paid $168 and returned to the parking lot. Sariah fell on the gravel and started to cry. "We'll stop at Burger King," Rebecka said, crying now, too, so tired she didn't care what lunch would cost. They went to the drive-through and continued home. She left the groceries in the car, and Jourie hauled them up to the apartment. They wedged the boxes into the fridge. "I couldn't get it all," she told Jourie, explaining that she had made it only halfway through her list. She had spent about two weeks of SNAP money on groceries that would last seven or eight days.

Later that night, as the kids went to bed and Jourie readied for another shift at work, Rebecka grabbed a calendar off the wall and turned the page to March. The 1st was almost over. Price Rite had closed. The buses had stopped running. Pichardo and his employees at International Meat Market had all gone home, after mopping meat from the aisles at the end of an $8,200 day.

Rebecka touched each empty box on the calendar with her finger and counted out loud, plotting the long decline before the cycle of a SNAP economy began again.

"Thirty more days," she said.

Questions for Discussion

1. At the end of the piece, a shopper characterizes the 1st of the month as "the best and worst day of the month? What does she mean by this?

2. In this article, Saslow moves back and forth between the narratives of Rebecka Ortiz and Miguel Picardo. What might have been his purpose in structuring his essay this way?

3. Additionally, Saslow relies wholly on these two narratives to achieve his purpose. Do you feel that this technique was effective?

4. Referring to the town of Woonsocket, the author reflects, "So many people are forced to rely on government support. The government is forced to support so many people." Seeing as how this is presented as a vicious cycle, what do you think is the most effective way for policy makers to address this problem?

Social Justice through Food Trucks

Liz Neumark

OurTownNY, September 2015

As stated in her *Huffington Post* biography, Liz Neumark is the founder of Great Performances, a waitress service, founded in 1979, which offers struggling artists jobs with the catering industry. Neumark has served on the board of several non-profits, and has received many awards such as the Food Arts Silver Spoon Award, Crain's 100 Most Influential Women, and Ernst & Young New York Entrepreneur of the Year Award. This article was posted on her online blog, which is featured on *The Huffington Post*, a politically liberal news aggregator and blog. One of the food trucks, featured in this article, is Snowaday Food Truck, from the social enterprise Drive Change. According to its website, this organization hires and trains formerly incarcerated youth to build and operate their food trucks. The site claims, "our trucks are vehicles for social justice—allowing young people to have hands on experience and develop transferable skills to become leaders in today's society."

Once again, New Yorkers flocked to Governors Island on September 12, for the Annual Vendy Awards to determine the Best Street Food Vendor of the year and to raise funds for the Street Vendor Project, a 14-year-old non-profit providing "advocacy and support for the thousands of people who sell food and merchandise on the street."

From ancient pushcarts to 21st century food trucks, street vending has a long and rich tradition of providing jobs and upward mobility for generations of immigrants and aspiring entrepreneurs. Typically a family affair, today's vendors include veterans (who received special privileges), an increasingly wider range of immigrants and a younger generation who opt out of conventional work life in pursuit of food dreams. Not simply a means to an end, food vending has become an end unto itself.

And you don't need to think about the social mission of the day to enjoy the amazing selection of food, drinks and sweets from the 25 vendors—you just need to come hungry, have a plan of attack, navigate lines (a strategic partner helps) and ditch the diet. I admit to never waiting on food lines, so I go for the premium VIP tickets, which allows early access. It is so worth it. And I give myself permission (this day only) to sample a meat sauce for the sake of judging justly.

The front line of the Vendys is the crew of volunteers—over 100—who check in, direct, facilitate etc. Whatever their day job, they are smart because with the gig comes the opportunity to sample all the offerings either before or after your shift. I talked with seasoned volunteers Ryan and Robert, Pace University students, who do breakdown on a very full stomach. (BTW, they have zero food business aspirations, just love to eat while studying finance.) And I was delighted to bump into a handful of my own GP colleagues directing traffic; smart kids!

If the day was purely epicurean, it would be easy. But there are so many stories to hear and questions to ask. What makes a trio of post-army service Israelis start a (Shakshuka) Shuka Truck in a city that has never heard the word? The answer: Chutzpah, I guess. They got my vote. Flavor and healthful in the same bite; maybe the only dish there that was actually good for you.

What sort of vision motivates someone to give up the day job to start (another) dessert company (witness Butter & Scotch with their signature maple bacon cupcake)—or build a business on a foundation of marshmallows? Only in NYC is there a market for multi-textured & flavored, dynamic marshmallows as Katherine Sprung of Squish Marshmallows explains—think Smore's or Rocky Road or even Peanut Butter and Jelly filled. (She is a tech start-up survivor, so I guess this is easy.) And its not like we need more doughnuts, but dessert category Doughnuttery 'took the cake' with their freshly fried mini gems. (What is it about fried food?!) My favorite was BOOQOO Beignets. In all fairness, I fell in love with Matt Pace, a NOLA native, at Vendy Plaza earlier this summer. He is as sweet as his pastry and doesn't break a sweat despite standing over a hot fryer for hours. Wicked good with killer dips of chicory coffee praline or creole vanilla, you can find him on Sundays at La Marqueta. PlayJScream served a J shaped cone filled on both sides. Without a flat bottom, where's the drip and the fun? "I borrowed the idea," said CK of this unpatented Korean invention.

Just because I tasted each dessert does not make me a sweets person. If there were veggies, you'd be hearing about it. The closest thing was the hand cut spud from Home Frite which I would gladly eat daily savoring each cheesy, French fried, salted, and dip drenched bite. Crazy good if only to try each amazing dip (think malt vinegar aioli, herbocado, jalapeno cilantro, curry ketchup—get my drift?) The Gumbo, empanadas, mole, albondiga, and palatas were creative, tempting, and worth the occasional nibble from this vegetarian. Thank you Gumbo Bros for the non-meat option. I was really longing for the Cinnamon Snail, a ground breaking, award winning, brilliant 100% vegan truck that fell victim this past year to the lack of availability of food truck licenses.

On the subject of licenses, I asked the newer vendors how they managed to get one. The answers were a blend of 'you know,' 'not easy,' a dip of the head, and the unspoken truth—that you finagled, found your way to the black market, and struggled to make it work. It is a tribute to this round up of vendors that despite the near impossibility of simple, legal options, they persevered and made their way to the street. It is also the proliferation of markets inspired by Smorgasbord, which provide welcome and legal outlets for new vendors. The City Council and Speaker are working to change this landscape. #liftthecaps—register your voice.

Back to food. Husbands & wives, moms & sons and other cheering relatives round out the truck teams and provided the support needed to feed the long lines. The Old Traditional Polish Cuisine truck served up tempting Kielbasa and pierogis—the wife of one of the owners does their marketing off hours from her job at Calvin Klein. Her husband and partner left construction in search of something different. Every ingredient (people included) comes from Poland and yes, they found their new calling.

Lil Zeus enlisted Mom to man the front line. I don't know what 'nachas' is in Greek, but she had it as she hawked wraps and salads as they were ready, belting out: "Who wants a sandwich?"

My other weakness is a good beverage. Renegade Lemonade, the category champ, was delicious and has morphed into a real business wholesaling to David Burke and BR Guest while planning large scale mass distribution. A good lemonade is an elixir and who could choose between Thai Chili Tart Cherry, Strawberry Basil, or Passion Hibiscus. So I had each one. Coco&Co had a sweet tale that started when a wedding trip to Sri Lanka morphed into living on coconuts when the money ran out, which in turn spawned a coconut water based bicycle-cart. Though in business only since April, Luke (a former News Corp journalist) and partner have 10 employees. Catalina's Champurrado and Best Juice Uptown represent the heart of Street Vendors Project, immigrant families who bring tastes of their countries to their new communities. Best Juice reminds me of an Orange Julius—the Dominican drink includes fresh OJ, milk, cane sugar plus a secret ingredient. I sampled Catalina's Oaxacan Champurrado, a warm drink incorporating chocolate and corn (masa de maiz) savoring the unique blend of flavors. These are flavors of home and their audience loves them.

The best for last. The Snowday Food Truck won 2014 Rookie of the Year and took the 2015 prize for Vendy Cup and People's Choice. Jordyn Lexton founded Drive Change to train, employ, and change the lives of formerly incarcerated young people utilizing food trucks as the nucleus of her program. Work changes lives, food creates jobs, and passion inspires food and work. The youth that work on the truck are real, warm, and inspiring. The food is amazing—probably the finest maple grilled cheese you will ever taste. But what is truly breathtaking is thinking about the Vendys and the street vendor universe as a pathway for change. From the struggling immigrants of 150 years or 150 days ago, street vendors work hard. I asked Crystal of Home Frite what her advice to the novice vendor would be. She said its all about hard work and taking the plunge. It's a long day, in a hot truck, on your feet, few breaks, getting hassled by cops or storekeepers, keeping up with the customers.

The very least I could do was to wait on line. So, uncharacteristically, I did. I thank the Vendy vendors for their delicious food and for sharing their stories with their words and in their flavors.

Questions for Discussion

1. What does the author mean when she says, "not simply a means to an end, food vending has become an end unto itself"?

2. What is Neumark's purpose? In shaping this text, what rhetorical choices does she employ in order to achieve her purpose?

3. Neumark ends her article by contemplating the way in which food trucks can be used as vehicals for positive social change. Based on other readings in this book, in what ways do you see a connection between food and fostering positive change within our society?

Excerpts from *The Real Cost of Cheap Food*: Introduction and Chapter 2

Michael Carolan

The Real Cost of Cheap Food, 2011

> Professor Michael Carolan is Associate Dean for Research, College of Liberal Arts, at Colorado State University and was formerly Chair of the Department of Sociology, also at CSU. The author of over 100 peer reviewed articles and chapters, Dr. Carolan studies environmental and agricultural law and policy and the sociology of food and food systems. He is the co-editor of the *Journal of Rural Studies* and is the author or co-author of 10 books, including the book the following excerpt is drawn from, *The Real Cost of Cheap Food* (2011). Throughout the following excerpt, we see Carolan's critical examination of mainstream approaches to food production and agriculture policy as undertaken in the U.S. Dr. Carolan questions the economic advantages that are claimed for mass agricultural production processes, particularly as they relate to corn and soybean production. Dr. Carolan writes in *The Real Cost of Cheap Food*: "The food system is more than markets. So when we talk about cheap food, it is important that we contextualize, *really* contextualize, the food system, not only in terms of its environmental additions (pollution) and withdrawals (resources extracted), but also in terms of what it affords physiologically, culturally, economically, and politically" (3). As a sociologist, Dr. Carolan helps us to understand that food is embedded in human dimensions of experience, spanning the physical, emotional, and spiritual and hence is irreducible to a "product" that is merely suitable for consumption for import or export.

Introduction

The 'cheap food argument': I hear it weekly. There was the instance, at a recent global food security conference, where an audience member was lambasted by someone on an expert panel for questioning the logic of the current food system: 'I'm interested in feeding the world, in producing as much food as cheaply and as efficiently as possible. What do you have against cheap food?' The audience member responded with a look of indignation but no words. Agricultural professionals, consumers, politicians and producers make the point repeatedly: if there was a more efficient (aka *cheaper*) way to produce, process and distribute food, we would be doing it. As evidenced by that silent rebuttal, the cheap food argument is quite powerful. It's an ace in the hole for proponents of the status quo. Whenever pressed into a corner, it can be pulled out at a moment's notice. Like at that global food security conference: "What do you have against cheap food?' Check and mate.

This book centers on something purportedly central to the cheap food argument: cost. Its conclusions will not please proponents of the current food system. The cheap food produced in today's food system, as I am about to detail, is actually quite expensive. Can we afford to stop producing cheap food? How can we afford not to?

I am employed by a Land Grant University (historically, a bastion of pro-industrial food production sentiments) (Beus and Dunlap, 1990): Colorado State University. Studying food and agricultural policy and its impacts routinely places me face-to-face with arguments as to why we cannot afford to shift the course of our food system juggernaut. Some of those faces are friends, such as colleagues in the College of Agriculture who tell me it is not the *spirit* of alternative food system visions that cause them concern, but rather their *impracticality*. They recognize the benefits of eating more whole foods and fewer of the highly processed artefacts that populate grocery stores, fast-food chain menus and kitchen cabinets. They question the long-term sustainability of a global food system heavily based upon corn (maize) and soybean production. And they admit that after decades of advancements in plant breeding, millions still starve. But, alas, in a case of failing to see the forest for the trees, they ultimately refuse to talk about systemic change. While well intentioned, they tell me, alternative food system visions cannot compete with the dominant food system in one important respect. The dominant system is our best chance at global food security because the one thing that it does better than all the alternative is supply us with the cheapest food possible.

We spend less on our annual incomes today on food than any previous generation. The percentage of disposable income spent on food within the US has steadily decreased since 1947 (Miller and Coble, 2007, p 98). Between 1970 and 2005, the percentage of disposable income spent on all food in the Us dropped from 13.9 to 9.8 per cent, a decrease all the more remarkable given that approximately half of what US consumers spend on food is spent eating away from home (up from 30 years ago when the figure was 34 per cent and 50 years ago when the figure was 25 per cent) (USDA, 2008). The same for Britons: in 1957 (three years after the end of rationing), the average household spent one third of its income on food; today the figure is 15 per cent (Wallop, 2008). And for many people, the most persuasive indicator is found no further than their local grocery store. Who hasn't noticed organic (insert your favorite fruit or vegetable here) commanding more per kilogram that the conventionally grown variety? And internationally: is not the growing global obesity epidemic (see, for example, James, 2008) proof that the food system is delivering on its promise of cheap, abundant food?

Yet, is *cheap* the same as *inexpensive*? Or to put it another way, can we afford this cheap food? I argue no, on both accounts. Using the concept of 'cost' against cheap food, this book attempts to change the parameters of the food debate. As long as 'cheapness'—a concept I define in a moment—remains something lauded and desired, the status quo is at an unfair advantage. This is because, for many critics of the status quo, cheap food is precisely what they *don't* want. Cheapness, rather, is part of the problem, not something to be praised and replicated around the world—an unsustainable example of market and social failures of the first order. We need inexpensive food, food we can afford, and food that affords us certain capabilities. Changing the debate over food from being about cheapness to about *affordability* allows us to seriously ask questions such as 'Can we afford cheap food?' and 'What exactly does cheap food afford us?'

So what do I mean by 'cheap' food? While standard uses of the term tend towards such meanings as 'inexpensive' (a favorite definition among cheap food proponents) and 'inferior' (a definition held by many cheap food critics), I have another designation in mind. Cheap food refers to the de-contextualization of food in its broadest sense (more about this in the next section). At one level, then, we can think about cheap food as a euphemism for myopic economic accounting practices, exemplified by the thinking that the price of a food item at the grocery store reflects its full cost. This is the most obvious angle from which to critique cheap food. Agro-food scholars, food and environmental activists, and ecological economists have been arguing for decades about how today's food system rests upon the market (and society) turning a blind eye to many of its costs (see, for example, Tegtmeier and Duffy, 2004; Carolan, 2006; Colman, 2008).

But the market does not a world make. To say that cheap food is only the effect of externalizing costs, minimizes—dare I say, cheapens—our understanding of the world. It assumes that there is a market solution to the problems that compel me to write this book. It assumes that if only we could assign the right value to those things currently externalized, we will have solved the problem of cheap food. If only it were that easy. The food system is more than markets. So when we talk about cheap food, it is important that we contextualize, really contextualize, the food system , not only in terms of its environment additions (pollution) and withdrawals (resources extracted), but also in terms of what it affords physiologically, culturally, economically and politically.

We need a system that produces food and feeds people, especially those who are starving. And, yes, this food—since the price of food at the grocery store matters—needs to be priced so that people can buy it. But let us also remember that price is a context-dependent concept. Slightly higher prices will not hurt someone's pocketbook if their pocketbook grows faster than the price of food. This gets at another understanding of the *afford-ability* of food. I am thinking here of the term's original meaning, which originates from the Old English word *geforthian*: to carry out. Affordability, following this usage, speaks to an artefact's *enabling* ability. Just like the sun affords plants the energy to grow, I want a food system that affords people and nations the capabilities to develop and enhance their overall well-being. Thinking of the food system in this manner, as something that affords society and individuals certain in/capabilities, allows for a more honest discussion to take place about what we want from food and whether the current system can achieve those desired ends. As discussed in later chapters, rather than affording those in the developing world the ability to obtain greater food (and economic, political, cultural, etc.) security, cheap food has had just the opposite effect. It creates disabilities.

Rethinking 'Food' Itself

Like so many of the things I write about, the idea for this book, was born in the classroom. We were discussing food security. It was a spirited discussion. Some students were critical of the current food system for reasons related to its long-term human and environment consequences. Expecting this to come up, since most have heard by now about how industrial food production externalizes certain costs, I had on hand calculations that attempt to give a value to these various impacts. One study, focusing on agricultural production in the US in the areas of natural resources, wildlife, biodiversity and human health, estimated these externalized costs to be between US \$5.7 to \$16.9 billion annually (Tegtmeier and Duffy, 2004, p 1).

A remarkable figure. Yet, such analyses sit uneasily with me for a number of reasons. To start with: how can one place a value on something like biodiversity or wildlife? I believe it was Einstein who said: 'Everything that can be counted does not necessarily count; everything that counts cannot necessarily be counted'—a useful quote to keep in mind when wading through these attempts to quantitatively internalize the costs of our food. Also, *who* makes these evaluative determinations? Extending upon a question posed by Robert Starr Allyn (1934, p 46), who asked: 'Pray tell me, what does an onion taste like?' to critique the idea that plant patents specify plants in their entirety, I might ask: 'What is the value of an onion's taste?' Focusing only on value that can be quantified is a slippery slope. As other less quantifiable aspects of food get pushed to the wayside through these internalization exercises, we risk sliding back to where we began: talking about cheap food (only now arrogantly thinking that all costs have been internalized).

I eventually asked my students the nebulous question: 'When is good?' As expected, I got a lot of confused looks (perhaps I am evoking such a look now). 'Don't you mean *what* is food?', someone asked. After explaining that I asked the question correctly, I waited, quietly, for about 30 seconds. Silence. I then told them the purpose of the question: of how it plays on something Yrjö Engeström (1990) asked over 20 years ago. In a paper entitled 'When is a tool?', Engeström illustrates how a tool is not a thing with fixed attributes, but an artifact that *becomes* a tool in practice. A tool, therefore, emerges *in situ*; it is an effect of practice, structures and cultural conventions (see also Star and Ruhleder, 1996). Asking '*what* is food?', I told my students, assumes too much. It presupposes a fixed essence of food; it views food as a thing, a noun. But, as Harris (1986, p 13) reminds us, 'We can eat and digest everything from rancid mammary gland secretions to fungi to rocks (or cheese, mushrooms, and salt if you prefer euphemisms).' The question '*when* is food?' situates food as part of—rather than apart from—this broader context.

This little exercise seemed to help my class better see the *system* part of the food system. I then proceeded to explain the various ways in which cheap food is really quite expensive. And it is not just expensive for those in developing countries, but to everyone, including those living in the US, a country which prides itself on having the cheapest food in the world. They appeared to get it. Instead of focusing on un-contextual factors, like yield per hectare or percentage of disposable income spent annually on food, the remainder of the class period was used discussing global food security in a more interconnected, complex and sophisticated way. We talked about the costs of the current food system to, among other things, the world's smallholder farmers, global equality, human health and well-being, the environment, taxpayers in developed nations, animal welfare, and cultural systems. I hope this book elicits a similar understanding of cheap food among readers.

The Audience

When I write I like to imagine who I am writing for. When putting together this book, I had in mind an international audience. For this reason, I tried not to limit its focus to any one country in order to increase its appeal to, and impact upon, the global community. That said, certain chapters take a long hard look at the US, in terms of its policies and practices. This simply cannot be avoided given its pivotal role in the world system. Thus, when focus is on the US, the intent is not to make the discussion only about the food policies and practices of this country, but to shine light on *why* today's food system looks like it does in terms of creating global winners and losers. The reader can be assured that the trip ahead will take them around the world.

I also imagined my students. The writing style, the content covered, the examples given, and the use of tables and figures—all have been informed by my years in the classroom. Since we're all students in some way, I hope the end product resonates both inside and outside the university.

I also hope that my vocabulary, by framing the argument around the *costs* and *affordability* of our food system, is something that proponents of today's food regime can relate to. When writing this book, I have tried to imagine how someone sympathetic to the current food system might be persuaded to revisit their convictions. Those already critical of how food is produced, traded, processed, transported and consumed will find in this book plenty more reasons to feel as they do. Yet, I am more interested in those who think, such as those friends of mine referenced earlier, that today's food system, warts and all, remains our best option because of its ability to produce copious amounts of cheap food. This book, I hope, will cause them to re-evaluate their mental ledger that tells them that cheap equals inexpensive. It most certainly does not. The dominant food system socializes many of its cots, while simultaneously privatizing the majority of its benefits. This is not only egregiously unjust, but makes for bad policy when the goal is affordable food.

Chapter Overview

Chapter 2 focuses upon the idea that affordable food is food that *affords* people the capabilities to pull themselves out of poverty and develop along trajectories of their own choosing—affordances that also produce 'savings' for the developed world. Specifically, the chapter examines cheap food through the lens of international development. In most developing countries, poverty is concentrated in rural areas (Pinstrup-Andersen, 2002). A popular argument among development scholars is that rural poverty in poorer nations can be alleviated by increasing the productivity—whether by traditional breeding methods or genetic engineering (GE) techniques—of the world's small-scale farmers (see, for example, Mellor, 1966; Pinstrup-Andersen, 2002; Paarlberg, 2008; Rao and Dev, 2009). The so-called Green Revolution, in fact, has been justified heavily by this logic. I discuss whether or not the Green Revolution actually delivered upon these promises. At the same time, I highlight how this attention to productivity has also acted as a smokescreen, directing energies away from other equally important problems that have plagued the world's smallholder farmers. Without access to markets, for example, yield increases benefit no one. The lack of markets for the world's smallholder farmers is a major problem—a problem that has only been exacerbated by policies promising cheap food. The ideology of cheap food seduces affluent nations to erect programmes that have crippled millions of farmers from less developed parts of the world. The latter half of the chapter discusses how (and why) free trade is rarely fair, especially when it comes to food, an argument that is bolstered by discussing the subjects of government subsidies, tariffs and food aid.

Chapter 3 examines the links between cheap food and conflict. To quote Susan Rice (2006, p 1), currently US Permanent Representative to the United Nations: 'global poverty is far more than solely a humanitarian concern. In real ways, over the long term, it can threaten US national security.' Among other things, poverty and food insecurity reduce the recruitment costs for extremists and 'non-friendly' militia groups. When facing a certain future of poverty for oneself and one's family, the promise of food and money, even a little, has been successfully used to enroll members, from foot soldiers to suicide bombers, into conflicts (UN Office for the Coordination of Humanitarian Affairs, 2008; al-Mukhtar, 2010). This gives a new meaning to the slogan 'food not bombs'. The relationship between food security and national security is only beginning to be explored, though we've known of this link for quite some time—after all, the theme of the 1999 World Food Prize was 'Food, agriculture, and national security in a globalized world'. Another timely example of cheap food-related conflict is that stirred up over immigration. Elaborating upon this link by looking at the current situation of the US, the chapter explains why comprehensive immigration legislation, to be truly *comprehensive*, needs to have a well thought-out food policy component. The chapter also looks at the phenomena of food riots as well as the recent rise of what has come to be known as the global land grab.

Chapter 4 explores the links between cheap food, health and obesity. Some figures to contextualize this discussion:

- The Food and Agriculture Organization of the United Nations (FAO) has calculated that world agriculture produces enough to provide everyone in the world with at least 2720 kilocalories (kcal) per person per day (FAO, 2002, p 9).

- A recent study estimates that over 23 percent of the world's population is overweight and an additional 10 percent obese (it was further calculated that by 2030, 58 percent of the world population will be obese) (Kelly et al, 2008).

- The number of 'undernourished' in the world rose to 1.02 billion people during 2009, even after food commodity prices declined from their earlier peak in 2008. This represents the highest level of chronically hungry people since 1970 (FAO, 2009, p11).

- We are witnessing the rise of the 'obesity-hunger paradox' in developed countries. In the words of a recent *New York Times* (Dolnick, 2010) article: 'the hungriest people in America today [those living with chronic food insecurity], statistically speaking, may well be not sickly skinny, but excessively fat'. That's right: we are now seeing obese individuals suffering from persistent malnutrition.

How could we let this happen, where one quarter of the world is at risk of dying from eating too much, another quarter at risk of dying from eating too little, and some at risk of dying from *both* obesity and malnourishment? The chapter attempts to provide some answers to this question. To provide the reader with a bit of a teaser (without spoiling anything): the chapter argues that cheap food policies rest upon a certain understanding of 'food'—namely, one that centres on elemental components such as calories, proteins, vitamins and the like: what has been called the ideology of nutritionism (Scrinis, 2008, p47). As long as nutritionism informs international food policy, we will never solve the problem of global malnourishment. The chapter concludes by listing some rather startling statistics about the costs to our health—being paid for by taxpayers—that come from eating all this cheap food. Reading these statistics, one can't help but wonder if the 'cheapness' of cheap food is not partially a product of cost shifting from the food sector to the healthcare sector.

Chapter 5 examines cheap meat. According to a recent article in the journal *Science*, animals currently utilize, either directly or indirectly, up to 80 per cent of the world's agricultural land (although, as discussed in greater length in Chapter 10, some of this land is only suitable for grazing). Yet they supply just 15 per cent of all calories produced (Stokstad, 2010, p810). Then there is the fact that livestock (some worse than others) poorly convert grain (e.g. corn) and plant proteins (e.g. soybeans) into animal proteins. This led Francis Moore Lappe (1971, p62) to famously quip decades ago that a concentrated animal feeding operation (CAFO) cow is a 'protein factory in reverse'. Cattle tend to receive the brunt of criticism because, in a CAFO environment, they are the least efficient of the lot. As Jeffrey Sachs, director of the Earth Institute at Columbia University, explained in a speech at the 1999 World Food Prize, in an attempt to summarize the various costs of cheap beef:

…a kilogram of final beef consumption requires up to 16 kilograms of grain input. The water use, the fertilizer use, the land used to produce that means the 49 percent of our grain production now is for animal feed.

The animal feed is soaring because meat production is rising. The United States stands way off the charts in this, of course. And the nutritionists tell us, persuasively, that our beef consumption is so high that it is highly deleterious to our human health at the same time. (Sachs, 1999)

To be sure, animal agriculture has its place in an affordable food system. Yet, I do not see how much longer we can afford the expense of meat that's produced as cheaply as we produce it today (see, for example, D'Silva and Webster, 2010). From its health effects to its impacts upon international food security, its environment footprint, and it s costs to animal welfare, the affordability of cheap meat is placed in serious doubt in this chapter.

Chapter 6 focuses on some of the ecological costs associated with producing, processing, shipping, packaging, marketing and consuming cheap food. The concept of 'food miles' is discussed (and extensively critiqued). A fair amount of time is also spent reviewing life-cycle analyses (LCAs) as they relate to components of our food system. This is followed by a thorough treatment of water as it relates to food, where concepts such as 'virtual water' and 'water footprint' are introduced and discussed, The subject of food waste is then reviewed, followed by a rather harrowing account of cheap food's addiction to (cheap) phosphorus.

Chapter 7 is, in many respects, a continuation of the previous chapter. Much of its focus remains on the cost of cheap food to the environment. The big difference is that discussion centres on the actual *pricing* of those costs. This chapter, more than any other, deals with more hardnosed economic assessments of the cost of cheap food. It begins by offering some brief economic explanations for why 20th-century agriculture built itself up around the substitution of external inputs for internal ecological controls. Discussion then moves to reviewing how some economists are now working to value ecological processes, such as ecosystem services, as they attempt to pain a more accurate picture of the real costs of our food. Other topics discussed in this chapter include the true costs of pesticides and attempts by economists to calculate the real price of meat.

Chapter 8 examines the costs of cheap food policies to communities and culture. I examine the negative impact that industrial large-scale farmers have had upon rural communities. Also discussed are the links between biological monocultures and cultural monocultures, and how cheap food policies increase the likelihood of both. The chapter then focuses on what I call monocultures of tastes, which allows me to talk about how today's food system narrows our collective understandings of 'food' itself—a trend with clear negative implication to both cultural and biological diversity. This brings me to a fourth monoculture brought about by today's food system: a monoculture of geopolitical space. This space is hinted at earlier in the chapter when noting that as communities become surrounded by industrial farms, there is a decline in local control over public decisions. This phenomenon is explored in greater detail through the empirical entry point of 'anti-GE' (genetically engineered) laws.

So: who actually benefits from cheap food? Having detailed the various ways in which cheap food is predicated upon a socialization of costs. Chapter 9 highlights the winners of these policies and practices. The real winners of cheap food lie in the 'middle' of the food system hourglass—the exclusive, but very profitable and influential, club. This represents one of those chapters where the US case dominates the discussion. My rationale for this is simple: in order to fully investigate this 'hourglass' structure, I needed to pick one from a single country and stick with it throughout the chapter. I do, however, regularly reference examples from other countries to highlight that the US case is representative of structural changes occurring throughout much of the world.

The chapter begins by sorting out the winners from the losers among producers, although, as we'll see, the category of 'farmer' has become terribly blurred thanks to contract farming, specifically, and vertical integration, more generally. Next I discuss food processors and manufacturers. This part of the hourglass has seen remarkable market concentration during recent decades, giving remaining large firms remarkable buyer power. The monopsony conditions—where buyers rather than the market set prices—that arise from this concentration are then discussed. The remainder of the chapter focuses on the retail sector, where large-scale supermarket firms such as Walmart are located. Of all 'links' connecting farm to fork, this is arguably the one where the biggest winners reside.

Chapter 10 lays out suggestions on how to make food more affordable. The reader will find the usual fare discussed towards this end. Farmers' markets, community-supported agriculture and community gardens are all pieces to the puzzle of affordable food. Yet, if I am to follow my own advice and contextualize, really contextualize, food, I must also recognize the need to go beyond the usual suggestions if we hope to ever turn the juggernaut of cheap food around. I therefore also discuss, for example, subsidies for consumers (particularly for the most food insecure), vertical agriculture, the need to adjust producer subsidies to better incentivize other forms of agriculture, the adoption of conservation practices among farmers, as well as polycultures and organic agriculture. Any serious discussion of affordable food also requires that we revisit how corporations do business and our complicity in letting those unaffordable practices continue. I therefore call for a re-examination of the concepts of 'free trade' and 'efficiency'. The goal: to make these terms more amenable to food systems that afford food security, sustainability and fairness, and that are just to all parties (human and non-human) involved. In addition, the chapter highlights cases where food is being kept sociologically and culturally relevant in an attempt to stave off those monocultures discussed in Chapter 8. Finally, in light of Chapter 5, I would be remiss if suggestions were not offered on how to make meat more affordable.

References

Allyn, R. S. (1934) *The First Plant Patents: A Discussion of the New Law and Patent Office Practice*, Educational Foundation, New York, NY

al-Mukhtar, U. (2010) 'Poor women in Iraq easily recruited by insurgents', *Statesmen.com*, 22February, www.statesman.com/opinion/al-mukhtar-poor-women-in-iraq-easily-recruited-268225.html, last accessed 2April2010

Beus, C. and R. Dunlap (1990) 'Conventional versus alternative agriculture: The paradigmatic roots of the debate', *Rural Sociology*, vol 55, no 4, pp 590-616

Bezemer, D. and D. Headey (2008) 'Agriculture, development, and the urban bias', *World Development*, vol 36, no 8, pp 1342-1364

Carolan, M. S. (2006) 'Do you see what I see? Examining the epistemic barriers to sustainable argiculture', *Rural Society*, vol 71, pp 232-260

Coleman, D. (2008) 'Ethics and externalities: Agricultural stewardship and other behavior, Presidential Address', *Journal of Agricultural Economics*, vol 45, no 3, pp 299-311

Dolnick, S. (2010) 'The obesity-hunger paradox', *The New York Times*, 12March, www.nytimes.com/2010/03/14/nyregion/14hunger.html?srx=me, last accessed 6 April 2010

D'Silvia, J. and J. Webster (eds) (2010) *The Meat Crisis: Developing More Sustainable Production and Consumption*, Earthscan, London

Engeström, Y. (1990) 'When is a tool? Multiple meanings of artifacts in human activity', in Y. Engeström (ed) *Learning, Working and Imagining: Twelve Studies in Activity Theory*, Orienta-Konsultit, Helsinki, pp 23-35

FAO (Food and Agriculture Organization) (2002) *Reducing Poverty and Hunger: The Critical Role of Financing for Food, Agriculture, and Rural Development*, FAO, International Fund for Agricultural Development, World Food Programme, www.fao.org/docrep/003/Y626e/y6265e00.hym, last accessed 6April2010

FAO (2009) *The State of Food Insecurity in the World, 2009*, FAO International Fund for Agricultural Development, World Food Programme, ftp:ftp.fao.org/docrep/fao/012/i0876e.pdf, last accessed 30September2010

Harris, M. (1986) *Good To Eat: Riddles of Food and Culture*, Allen and Unwin, London

James, W. P. T. (2008) 'WHO recognition of the global obesity epidemic: WHO and the obesity epidemic', *International Journal of Obesity*, vol 32, ppS120-S126

Kelly, T., W. Wang, C.S. Chen, K. Reynolds and J. He (2008) 'Global burden of obesity in 2005 and projections to 2030', *International Journal of Obesity*, vol 32, pp 1431-1437

Lappe, F. M. (1971) *Diet for a Small Planet*, Random House, New York, NY

Mellor, J. (1966) *The Economics of Agricultural Development*, Cornell University Press, Ithaca, NY

Miller, J. C. and K. Coble (2007) 'Cheap food policy: Fact or rhetoric', *Food Policy*, vol 32, pp 98-111

Paarlberg, R. (2008) *Starved for Science: How Biotechnology Is Being Kept Out of Africa*, Harvard University Press, Cambridge, MA

Pinstrup-Andersen, P. (2002) 'Food and agricultural policy for a globalizing world: Preparing for the future', *American Journal of Agricultural Economics*, vol 84, pp 1201-1214

Rao, N. C. and S. M. Dev (2009) 'Biotechnology and pro-poor agricultural development', *Economic and Political Weekly*, vol 44, no 52, pp 56-64

Rice, S. (2006) 'National security implications of global poverty', Lecture at University of Michigan Law School, 30January, www.brookings.edu/~/media/Files/rc/speeches/2006/0130globaleconomics_rice/20060130.pdf, last accessed 2April2010

Sachs, J. (1999) 'Food at the center of global crisis', The World Food Prize, 2009 Norman E. Borlaug International Symposium, Food, Agriculture, and National Security in a Globalized World, Des Moines, IA, 14-16 October, http://208.109.245.191/assets/Symposium/2009/transcripts/2009-Borlaug-Dialogue-Sachs.pdf, last accessed 8April2010

Scrinis, G. (2008) 'On the ideology of nutritionism', *Gastronomica*, vol 8, no 1, pp 38-48

Star, S. and K. Ruhleder (1996) 'Steps to an ecology of infrastructure: Complex problems in design and access for large-scale collaborative systems', *Information Systems Research*, vol 7, no 1, pp 111-134

Stokstad, E. (2010) 'Could less meat mean more food?', *Science*, vol 327, no 5967, pp 810-811

Tegtmeier, E. M. and M. D. Duffy (2004) 'External costs of agricultural productivity in the United States', *International Journal of Agricultural Sustainability*, vol 2, pp 1-20

UN Office for the Coordination of Humanitarian Affairs (2008) 'Afghanistan: Poverty pushing youth into arms of Taliban?', *IRINnews.com*, 27 February, www.irinnews.org/Report.aspx?ReportId=76986, last accessed 2April2010

USDA (US Department of Agriculture) (2008) *Total Expenditures*, Economic Research Service, www.ers.usda.gov/briefing/CPIFoodAndExpenditures/Data/, last accessed 27March2010

Wallop, H. (2008) 'Britons spend one-fifth of income on homes', *The Telegraph* 29 January, www.telegraph.co.uk/news/uknews/1576933/Britons-spend-one-fifth-of-income-on-homes.html, last accessed 28December2010

Chapter 2
Cheap Food, Globalization and Development

Once I went to a house where a farmer took his life by drinking a toxic chemical because of his uncontrollable debts. I could do nothing but listen to the howling of his wife. *If you were me how would you feel?*...I believe the situation of farmers in many other countries is similar. We have in common the problems of dumping, import surges, lack of government budgets...I have been so worried watching TV and hearing the news that starvation is prevalent in many less developed countries, although the international price of grain is so cheap. (cited in Rosset, 2006, pxiii; emphasis in original).

These words come from a pamphlet, distributed on 10 September 2003, at the World Trade Organization (WTO) Ministerial Meeting in Cancun, Mexico. Its author, Lee Kyung Hae—a South Korean farmer, founder of a South Korean farmers' association, ardent WTO critic, and inspiration to individuals around the world—is now dead. He killed himself later that day. A sign bearing the slogan 'WTO Kills Farmers' in one hand, Lee thrust a red penknife into his chest while standing on top of a police barricade. Within a matter of days tens of thousands of smallholder farmers from all around the world—from Bangladesh to Chile, South Africa and Mexico—marched in memory of Lee and in protest to the current food system. Heard among their chants of solidarity was once poignant phrase: 'We are Lee' (Patel, 2009, p35).

Any system that compels a farmer to take a penknife to his heart—an action in turn symbolically amplified by thousands of others in their taking to the streets—ought to be questioned. As Lee indicated in his pamphlet, cheap food does not equal development. Policies aimed at making the international prices of grains so cheap has hindered (and continues to hinder) progress for many nations and for most of the world's smallerholder farmers, as I'll now explain.

The War on Small Farms

Classical development theorists never looked too kindly on peasant agriculture. It's too labor intensive. Those bodies could be more efficiently utilized working in factories. Farmers need to be freed from an unproductive farm sector and put to work in the factory, where the real wealth is said to be generated. At the same time, the farmers who remain need to produce food more efficiently with the help of technology, inputs and advancements in seed breeding. Cheap food would not only help to feed a growing non-farming population, but would prevent rising food prices, which would in turn help to offset the initial low wages offered in cities. This act will redistribute wealth from the countryside to urban areas. And as more of a country's population moves to the city— why wouldn't they if that's where the jobs are?—more of the population will experience an increase in living standards (Lewis, 1954; Johnston and Mellor, 1961). Presto: cheap food offers a path to development.

Unfortunately, we have a case here of something that sounds good in theory but which has failed to deliver the fruits promised when put into practice. Why has cheap food been unsuccessful at best—and, arguable, disastrous in some cases—as a development tool? Let's look into this question.

The world's smallholder farmers are still under attack. As one economist recently quipped: as people are 'freed from the shackles of unremitting toil on the land...[t]owns and cities become teeming hives of small-scale activity' (Ellis, 2005, p144). Yet, the facts, for much of the world at least, say otherwise. The non-farming sectors of developing economies have rarely grown fast enough to absorb the surplus labor freed from the 'shackles' of farming. Building an industrial sector to absorb displaced farmers presupposes an already established infrastructure—among other things, roads, a steady and reliable supply of energy, and a water and waste disposal system. If an industry cannot supply its factors with, say, raw materials and electricity, or efficiently distribute products once manufactured, the depth of a country's surplus labor supply matters little. This strategy, of constantly squeezing the farming sector to build urban economic capacity (an act equivalent to robbing Peter to pay Paul), has made developing countries food insecure, economically fragile and heavily dependent upon major grain-exporting nations. Let's not forget: the small family farm in nations such as the US was not systematically wiped out in the name of 'development'. To be sure, their numbers have fallen dramatically over the last century. But this was a process decades in the making. In many developing nations, conversely, the structural adjustments that are said to represent the road to prosperity can (and have) put millions of smallholder farmers out of business within just a matter of years.

No longer a mere 'handmaiden of industrialization', greater attention needs to be placed on the role of 'agriculture *for* development rather than agriculture *in* development' (Byerlee et al, 2009, p17). With an estimated 2.5 billion people worldwide engaged in production agriculture—recognizing also, according to the World Bank (2007, p1), that 'three of every four poor people in developing countries live in rural areas'—it's hard to think of another developmental strategy that's more pro-poor and more interested in the needs of the developing world. Simply put: spending money on agriculture, even small-scale agriculture, is money well spent. Studies have consistently shown that public investments in agriculture in poor countries, in terms of research and extension, yield higher societal returns than, expenditures in other productive sectors (Fan et al, 2000; Bezemer and Headey, 2008). It is therefore quite disturbing to find that investment in agricultural development in developing nations is actually on the decline—for example, in real 2008 dollars, US investment in this area dropped from US$400 million a year during the 1980s to US$60 million in 2006 (Bertini and Glockman, 2009, p97).

The neglect of the rural poor in developing countries has been pointed to as evidence of what is called the 'urban bias' in international policy. Popularized by Michael Lupton (1977), the term refers to a tendency in developmental and international agricultural policy circles, dating back to World War II, to under-allocate resources to, and extract surplus from, the rural class of poor countries. The urban bias, in other words, is just as it suggests: a developmental bias towards urban areas and the sectors of the economy that tend to be located there. So why have these policies been allowed to continue even though they undermine the livelihoods of billions? If cheap food policies are so bad for the farmers in (and the countries of) the developing world, why do they persist? Many of those countries are democratic. Do not democratic nations have mechanisms—namely, *democracy*—to keep policies that harm major segments of the voting population from enduring?

The problem is that poor rural populations are perhaps the world's most politically disenfranchised group (Dasgupta, 1998; Grindle, 2004). This helps to explain why, for example, in India—the world's largest democratic state—80 per cent of the population live in rural areas but 80 per cent of government spending goes into urban areas (Patel, 2009, p241). Throughout much of Africa and Central and South America, rural populations are geographically isolated not only from centres of power, but also from each other, making collective mobilization difficult (Bezemer and Heady, 2008, p1348). The story in Asia is slightly different. Many Asian countries had, and still have, a high rural density, which greatly reduces the transaction costs of organizing rural pressure groups. The threat of a rural-based Communist insurgency—in countries such as South Korea, Taiwan, Malaysia and Indonesia—also made the political elite historically more sensitive to the interests of their country's small farmers (Bezemer and Headey, 29008, p1348).

But this book is not about international development. It is about cheap food and its costs and consequences to the world. Having provided a brief overview of some of the logics driving international development policy since World War II, which have been of enormous consequence to the world's smallholder farmers, I now return to the topic of cheap food. I have discussed some of the rationale lying behind why cheap food policy is viewed as good for the developing world (for a summary of these major points, see Table 2.1). Now let's see whether cheap food lives up the hype.

Table 2.1 Summary of some rationales for why cheap food benefits developing economies
Labour efficiency • A countryside populated by smallholders is an inefficient distribution of labour.
Production efficiency • Small farmers can't product food as cheaply in part because of their heavy reliance on labour (their own), whereas large farms, substituting capital for labour, can afford to make less per unit because they are producing many more units.
Redistribution of wealth from rural areas (and agriculture) to urban areas (and industry) • A surplus of cheap grain not only feeds the growing urban populations but also helps ensure that some of the wages earned there can be used to buy more than just food.

Free Trade is Rarely Fair

Equal rules for unequal players are unequal rules. No one would think it fair if two people played a game of basketball but one was forced to have their hands tied behind their back while they played. In many respects, this is what we are asking of the developing world: to play in the global food economy even though they lack the same capabilities as affluent nations.

Before a developing country can gain access to the international market, they have to first agree to abandon any and all policies that discourage, distort or in any way distract from free trade. I would say that they have to be more like the developed West except that countries such as the US and regions such as the European Union (EU) have very little interest in real (or perhaps I should say 'fair') free trade. Most developed nations so aggressively protect their domestic agricultural sectors that I do not know how anyone in good faith can say that their policies match their free market rhetoric.

The urban bias against agriculture in developing countries is, in part, the product of a bias in favour of agriculture in the developed world (Bezemer and Headey, 2008, p1350; Kay, 2009, p114), which can spend between US$6000 and $10,000 per farm labourer per year (Bezemer and Headey, 2008, p1350). For comparison, the typical African government spends less than US$10 per farm worker per year on agriculture (Bezemer and Headey, 2008, p1350). As agricultural economist E. Wesley Peterson (2009, pxv) notes in his book A Billion Dollars a Day, approximately US$1 billion are spent each day globally supporting agriculture, the vast majority of which is due to the spending priorities of wealthy nations. Take tariffs, which continue to hamper farmers in developing countries. While tariffs on industrial good coming from developing nations have slowly been on the decline since the 1970s, tariffs on many of their agricultural goods remain high. This not only perpetuates trade distortions in the short term, but erodes long-term investment in these countries as tariffs place them at a comparative disadvantage.

There's an interesting concept—comparative advantage. The idea assumes that countries are equal by being unequal; that all countries have something special about them—have some natural advantage—that allows them to do certain things better than others. Countries simply need to find out what that something is and do it. For centuries, comparative advantage referred to a 'natural' attribute, like annual rainfall patterns or soil type. More recently, comparative advantage refers to phenomena such as a country's cheap labor or lax environmental laws, making me wonder if comparative disadvantage might not be a more apt term. But with agricultural subsidies and tariffs, the levers that dictate who has a comparative advantage are being pulled by those who have already developed. In agriculture, it is becoming less important what advantageous internal attributes are held by a country (such as climate or cheap labor). More relevant is whether or not countries such as the US *choose* to give their farmers a comparative advantage over the rest of the world. Today, comparative advantages can be *produced* by using such things as direct payments, export subsidies and tariffs. In short, with affluence comes the ability as a nation to choose whether to have comparative advantage in the production of almost any agricultural commodity.

Why would a developing nation agree to open up its markets to cheap agricultural imports if doing so harms their farming sector? Before borders are opened to trade, agricultural exports typically account for approximately 10 per cent of the agricultural revenue generated in developing economies. The vast majority of this export revenue goes to a small handful of very large farmers. Conversely, most of the remaining 90 per cent of revenue finds its way into the hands of small-scale farmers (Rosset, 2006, p82). Becoming part of the global economy gives the country greater access to the affluent markets of wealthy nations. But this access really only benefits a small percentage of the country's farmers because only the largest grow for export.

What, then, are these nations giving up in exchange? They are giving up precisely what they are gaining from developed nations: market access. In exchange for giving their landed elite greater market access to wealthy nations, these governments are pitting the heavily subsidized, large-scale, technologically aided Western farmer in direct competition against the peasant. I don't need to tell you which of the two produces cheaper food. Many economists are okay with this, asking: 'Why should a farmer remain in agriculture if they cannot compete with other, more "efficient", producers?' Forcing peasants to compete in the open market will result in a redistribution of capital, resources and labor either within or across economic sectors, which, in the long run, will increase the overall efficiency and wealth of the economy—or, at least, so says the law of comparative advantage (Weis, 2007, p119).

There is also the belief that if the world's smallholder farmers were to become more market oriented, they could remain competitive–a point articulated recently, for example, by the World Bank (2007). The strategy is known as 'reconversion'. Smallholder farmers are told to shift from traditional forms of production to growing non-traditional crops aimed at the highly profitable export market (Kay, 2009, p126). Assuming that peasants are in a position to 'read' these market signals, which itself is a big assumption, resting the future of the world's smallholder farms on non-traditional export markets is a bad bet. It ignores the realities faced by most of the world's rural poor.

Take the experience of Mexican farmers following the signing of the North American Free Trade Agreement (NAFTA) and the structural adjustments that came with it. NAFTA is said to have displaced up to 15 million Mexican peasants (Bello, 2009, p49). As is too often the case, while neoliberal planners are happy to see the redundant labor force of peasant agriculture reduced, far less thought is given to what to do with this labor after it has been 'freed' from subsistence agriculture. Proponents of NAFTA recommended that small-scale Mexican farmers gen into non-traditional agricultural exports—namely, fruits, vegetables and cut flowers (Bello, 2009, p49). These recommendations, however, gloss over basic realities. First, there is the problem of finance. While corn requires an investment of approximately US$210 per hectare, non-traditional commodities typically come with a considerable higher per hectare investment: melons, US$500 to $700; cauliflower, US$971; broccoli, US$1096; and snow peas (mangetout), US$3145 (Bello, 2009, p49). Yet, as has happened in all developing countries, following structural adjustments, government credit evaporates, making the financing of such ventures impossible for the rural poor.

Then there are the barriers associated with international technological and production standards. All food coming into the US from Mexico must pass through United States Department of Agriculture (USDA)—certified packing stations—an additional link in the food chain that increases the costs of doing business in the export market (Bello, 2009, pp49–50). Smallholder farmers around the world are also finding new private standards—set in place by major supermarket firms—an additional expense that many can ill afford (Clapp and Fuchs, 2009). These standards can dictate any number of things, from how something is produced (the specific methods of production) to aesthetic standards telling producers how their commodities must look.

Most certifying organizations, which oversee the following of these standards, are located in affluent nations. Primus Labs in the US, for instance, certifies for 68 per cent of the fruit and vegetables firms in the northwest Mexico (Narrod et al, 2008, p361). This can add considerable expense for farmers in developing countries, who frequently need certain certifications to penetrate high-profit niche markets in countries and regions such as the4 US and the EU (Fuchs et al, 2009, p46). The costs to obtain certification can reach as high as US$850 per hour (Narrod et al, 2008, p361). Unable to afford necessary investments (e.g. equipment, buildings) that go along with satisfying production standards imposed upon them by organizations in other countries, hundreds of thousands of smallholders are expected to go out of business in Africa alone (Save for, perhaps, Kenyan farmers; see Box 2.1) (Fuchs et al, 2009, p46).

Box 2.1 The curious east of Kenya

Kenya's exports of approximately 450,000 tons of vegetables, fruit and cut flowers to UK and European markets have become the East African country's fastest growing economic sector. Generating US$1.3 billion a year, Kenyan horticulture brings in more revenue than banking, telecommunications and tourism (Manson, 2009), a remarkable fact given that the industry hardly existed just a couple of decades ago. The report *Kenya's Flying Vegetables*, published by the Africa Research Institute gives a first person account of this transformation. The report's author, James Gikunju Muuru (2009), tells of his experience as a smallholder farmer in central Kenya—one of 4.5 million in Kenya—who grows green beans, tomatoes, cabbage, sweet potato and baby corn on his 4 acres (1.6ha) and makes enough to support his wife and six children. Muuru claims to make seven times as much from growing green beans and other export crops as he would from growing a more traditional crop such as corn. It's a reasonable claim. A study from 2005 of smallholder farmers who produced for export found that net farm incomes were five times greater than smallholder farmers who did not grow horticultural products for export (Weinberger and Lumpkin, 2005, p10). Moreover, only 10 per cent of the total weight of food grown in Kenya is exported (yet this 10 percent represents 50 per cent of the industry's total value). The remaining 90 per cent remains within the region or country (Manson, 2009).

   Only time will tell if Kenya's farmers can sustain this success. While more than half the exports are produced by smallholders, the total number of smallholders producing for export is relatively small (Minor and Ngigl, 2004, p1). The benefits from export are therefore unevenly distributed. Moreover, recent research indicates that the fastest growing segment of Kenyan farmers growing for export is a new group of medium sized (and ready to expand further) commercial operations managed by well-educated farmers (see, for example, Neven et al, 2009)[1] What the case of Kenya *does* show us is the folly of the urban bias. A country can make significant developmental strides through agriculture. Indeed, in the case of Kenya, this development has largely occurred through agriculture alone.

Free market ideology expects all rational farmers to read market signals and invest in crops in which they have a comparative advantage. The realities on the ground, however, betray this philosophy—and not because most farmers are irrational (I am not about to disparage this hard-working segment of the population by calling them 'irrational'). For those already well-off farmers, perhaps such actions are possible. Yet 'development' should not just be able improving the quality of life of those least in need. As researchers for the United Nations (UN) have pointed out: 'free market rules in a context of highly concentrated property and imperfect and missing markets leads to the marginalization of otherwise perfectly viable enterprises' (David et al, 2000, p1685).

As for government subsidies and tariffs: how can these blatant trade-distorting practices continue even as institutions like the WTO are charged with reining in their use? Domestic supports are assigned to three 'boxes'—amber, blue and green (see Table 2.2). The amber box is reserved for those measures deemed trade distorting—namely, those that send signals to increase production (like an input subsidy). These are to be reduced, though not eliminated entirely. The blue box contains measures that limit production. Blue box measures are not restricted. Finally, there is the green box. This box is for measures *said* to have no effect on production. These too are not restricted by the WTO.

Table 2.2 *The WTO's colored boxes for domestic support in agriculture*

Amber box: Includes all domestic support measures believed to distort production and trade. These measures include policies to inflate commodity prices or subsidies that directly encourage production. Member states are required to reduce such support unless current levels fall below certain parameters. Developed countries can keep a total of amber box support that is equivalent to up to 5 per cent of total agricultural production, plus an additional 5 per cent on a per crop basis. In developing countries their amber box support can go up to an amount that is equivalent to 10 per cent of total agricultural production.

Blue box: Measures are directed at limiting production. There are currently no limits on spending on blue box subsidies.

Green box: Subsidies that do not distort trade or that at most cause a minimal distortion (like government monies for research and extension). Green box measures can provide support for things like environmentally sound farm management practices, policies defined as being for regional or rural development, pest and crop disease management, infrastructure, food storage, income insurance and even direct income support for farmers as long as that support is 'decoupled' from production. There are no limits on green box subsidies.

Compiled from World Bank (2005, p25) and Rosset (2006, pp84-86)

There is little to say about amber measures. Since they are frowned upon by the WTO, affluent nations—so they can proudly claim their policies are not trade distorting—have disguised any distorting policies in a rhetorical veil of green. Blue box measures are aimed at production reduction. The US abandoned production controls back in 1996, followed more recently by the EU. Other examples of blue box policies are conservation programmes, where farmers are paid to pull their land out of production for conservation purposes (Rosset, 2006, pp84-86). Green measures are the most interesting because this is the box where countries hide their trade-distorting subsidies.

The US, EU and Japan account for 87.5 per cent of the world's total green box expenditures (Maini and Lelchi, 2007, p176). These 'decoupled' payments (payments said to be independent of production levels and therefore non-trade distorting) can exist at unlimited levels. Yet, let there be no doubt: these payment affect production levels. Unlike production controls (also known as coupled payments), which provided payments to farmers who agreed to limit their production, green box measures pay farmers under the guise of something like 'income insurance'. The payment is *decoupled* because producers are assured to pay cheque regardless of how much they produce. Yet, in practice these payments still shield producers from low prices—prices that would otherwise, in a less distorted market, send signals to farmers to produce less or something else. Green box policies therefore *do* distort markets. They make farmers deaf to market signals, allowing them to continue to (over)produce and profit even when the costs of production exceed what the market is willing to bear. We should not be surprised, then, when farmers in the developing world fail to produce food as cheaply as US or European farmers. This is because farmers in developed countries cannot produce food that cheaply either, not without help from the government. And because these trade-distorting measures are disguised as green box measures, they are allowed to continue.

The costs of tariffs in developed nations, directed at agricultural commodities coming from the developing world, have been estimated at approximately US$11 billion per year (in 1995 US dollars) (Anderson et al, 2006, pp168-169). One study estimates that a 50 per cent reduction in agricultural tariffs would lead to a US$40 billion increase in the collective gross domestic product (GDP) of developing nations (ABARE, 2001). As an article in the influential journal *World Development* argues, 'conventional trade biases within OECD [Organization for Economic Co-operation and Development] countries are still a formidable source of underdevelopment in LDC [least developed countries] agriculture' (Bezemer and Headey, 2008, p1351).

Food Dependency Undermines Food Security

Cheap food has put tens, perhaps hundreds, of millions of small-scale farmers out of business. But we are assured that that's okay. Being food independent, you see, is unnecessary in a globalized world. Indeed, from the perspective of neoliberalism, food independence is the result of gross inefficiencies in terms of labor and resource allocation. Better to allocate resources according to the law of comparative advantage.[2] Find out what you do best as a nation and do it. For many developing countries, however, given the subsidy-dependent comparative advantage that affluent nations have in this sector, food production is probably not in the cards. Former US Secretary of Agriculture John Block made just this point in 1986: 'The idea that developing countries should feed themselves in an anachronism from a bygone era. They could better ensure their food security by relying on US agricultural products, which are available in most cases at lower cost' (cited in Bello, 2008, p452).

It's not like developing nations have much of a choice. Trade liberalization inevitably leads to a flood of cheap food imports. Farmers in the developing world are being asked to compete against farms in countries that spend billions propping up their agricultural sector. They are also competing against farms that benefit from living in nations with an extensive infrastructure (which reduces, among other things, transportation costs), readily available credit (at least until recently, when global credit markets dried up), rich agricultural research traditions, and a strong history of agricultural extension. Cheap imports are therefore dumped throughout the developing world. Legally speaking, they are not 'dumped'. Dumping is illegal under well-established international rules (Annand, 2005). Nevertheless, in point of fact—if not in point of law— dumping is what is occurring.

Looking at US exports, the Institute for Agriculture and Trade Policy (IATP) made the following calculations as to the percentage of exports that US farmers sold at average prices *below* the cost of production between 1997 and 2003: 37 per cent of all wheat; 11.8 per cent of all soybeans; 19.2 per cent of all rice (IATP, 2005, p2). Unfortunately, there is not much that poor countries can do to combat this practice. From a legal standpoint, a country must prove that they are harmed by the action in question. This is not as easy as it sounds. Cheap grain imports certainly benefit some—such as processors—which complicates the calculation. Yet there is a more practical problem that presents sufficient disincentive to keep developing countries from making too much of a stink over having their market flooded with cheap food.

In addition to their growing food dependence upon affluent nations, developing countries are finding themselves increasingly reliant upon nations and economic regions such as the US and the EU for their markets. For example, according to statistics compiled by the UK government, about 75 per cent of exports for Bangladesh are concentrated in textiles and over 90 per cent of those exports are destined for US and European markets (due, in part, to Bangladesh's cheap labor) (British Council, 2009). This dependence, however, is not reciprocal. Bangladesh exports destined for the EU totaled 5.5 billion Euros in 2008, while EU exports destined for Bangladesh total a little over 1 billion Euros (European Union, 2009). Countries such as Bangladesh have more to lose from trade sanctions than the USs and EUs of the world, giving the latter tremendous leverage over the trade policies of the former (Rosset, 2006, p42).

Box 2.2 The globalization of Ugandan Nile perch

Before the late 1980s, Uganda's fishery sector served local and regional markets. This began to change during the late 1980s, thanks to structural adjustment programmes— trade liberalization requirements that counties must follow if they hope to obtain development loans from international agencies such as the International Monetary Fund (IMF). Once open for international business, investment in the country's fishery sector soared, earning US$90 million, $101 million, $142 million, and $146 million in 2003, 2004, 2005 and 2006, respectively, which providing employment to some 500,000 people (Fulgencio, 2009, p433). The fish at the centre of it all: Nile perch. This massive fish (an adult can weigh in excess of 100kg) represents over 90 per cent of Uganda's total fish exports.[3] The fish stock, however, is becoming serious depleted. Acoustic surveys a decade ago already showed that Nile perch in Lake Victoria, the source of this fish bonanza, had dropped from 1.9 million tons in 1999 to 1.2 million tons in 2000. Two surveys in 2008 show that this figure has since plunged to 299,000 tons (Fulgencio, 2009, p434). In 2009, Uganda's export earnings dropped 35 per cent as a result of dwindling stocks (Biryabarema, 2009), the direct result of overexploitation for the international market (the Nile perch is considered a delicacy in Europe, fetching US$9 to $10 per kilogram). Declining fish stocks directly threaten the livelihoods of all those living around the lake as these fish represent not only their main source of income, but an important source of nutrition as well (Nunan, 2010).

Meanwhile, the small fishers who first profited from the fishery sector's growth are being pushed out. From an economic standpoint, full exploitation of the Nile perch, given its remarkable size, requires state of the art fishing and processing equipment and methods. Processors therefore started to vertically integrate—that is, they began to purchase their own fishing equipment and crews to obtain a greater supply (Schuurhuizen et al, 2006). Thus, while the Nile perch industry makes up nearly all of the country's export earnings, little ends up actually trickling down to the people and communities surrounding the lake (van der Knaap and Ligtvoet, 2010).

The above discussion highlights an important principle of globalization. Trade liberalization globalizes not only free market principles but also market failures (see box 2.2) (Perez et al, 2008, p6). As markets in different countries become increasingly interdependent, governments lose flexibility in establishing democratically informed domestic policy instruments, although, as just discussed, the degree of flexibility lost is far from evenly distributed. And, again, we have another example of just how unequal equal rules can be when players with different capacities are made to compete against each other.

The net result of all of this is food dependence. Between 1950 and 1970 the developing world went from taking in no grain imports to accounting for almost half of the world imports (Friedmann, 1990, p20). Harriet Friedmann (1992) discusses this growing dependency in the context of the global wheat trade. Before World War II none of the nations in Africa, Latin America or South Asia imported wheat. This changed drastically in a matter of decades. Nigeria, for instance, was entirely self-sufficient in food during the 1960s. In 1983, one quarter of Nigeria's total earnings was spent importing wheat (Jarosz, 2009). What makes this all the more remarkable is that between 1959 and 1961—as countries started to become hooked on this commodity—wheat cost considerably more than either corn (25 per cent more) or rice (600 per cent more). Countries around the world, regardless of their traditional dietary profile, began to consume increasing quantities of wheat as the century progressed.

The addiction stated with imports coming from the US. After World War II, the US had large stocks of surplus wheat due to New Deal price support programmes. The US government sought to unload this surplus without harming market prices (at the time, wheat was only second to petroleum in terms of volume traded in the international market). The US provided the developing world wheat through 'concessional sales', at a highly subsidized rate, under Public Law 480 (aka 'food aid'). During the 1950s, the US share of wheat exports grew from one third to over half of the market, with the majority destined for the developing world. Between 1950 and 1976, per capita consumption of wheat increased in the developing world over 60 per cent, while per capita consumption of cereals (minus wheat) increased 20 per cent and per capita consumption of root crops (a tradition staple in many developing nations) decreased by 20 per cent. Why did these nations choose not to invest to become food self-sufficient and decide instead to be food dependent upon countries such as the US? 'The answer', according to Harriet Friedmann (1992, p 372), 'is both material and ideological'. She continues:

> First, the USA wanted to get rid of surplus stocks of wheat it accumulated through domestic farm programmes, and this conveniently coincided with a mix of foreign policy and humanitarian

goals. The US government, through the Marshall Plan, had invented foreign aid as a mechanism to increase trade despite lack of dollars by prospective importers. In 1954 it adopted this mechanism to food aid through PL480. Second, Third World countries welcomed cheap food, that is, wheat imports subsidized by the US government, as an aid to creating an urban working class.

Directing monies away from sectors whose products can be readily substituted by cheap imports makes sense in the short term. But what happens when the river of cheap imports runs dry? Whether because of significant weather events, massive grain sales or the emergence of sectors that rely upon grain as a cheap input (such as the emerging biofuel industry), the market can never be trusted to deliver low-cost agricultural commodities year after year. Note what occurred when the Soviet Union purchased grain from the US in 1972 and 1973 on a scale never before witnessed. (Russia, coincidently, is poised to make a purchase of similar scale due to the hottest summer ever in the country's recorded history, 2010; *Moscow Times*, 2010). This sale produced sudden global shortages as prices quadrupled and food aid contributions nearly disappeared. Countries dependent upon, up until then, cheap imports found themselves dependent upon food that was suddenly not so cheap. And because they no longer had the domestic capacity to feed themselves they had no choice but to pay the higher price.

The promises of reconversion have also been short lived. Just as developing countries learned to substitute cheap imports for domestically produced grains, affluent nations found ways to substitute their own products for tropical agricultural commodities. Thus, over the last few decades, export markets for commodities produced in the poorer nations have shrunk as a result of industrial substitution. Some of the tropical commodities most affected by this process include cane sugar, which has been replaced with high-fructose corn syrup; cotton, which has been replaced by synthetic fibres; and palm oil, which has been replaced by soy and canola oils (Weis, 2007, p102).

The dependency described, however, does not just occur on the import side. Trade liberalization is making developing nations dependent on more affluent nations for their markets, which they need if they hope to see their non-traditional commodities. Take the case of the African country Burkina Faso, when its leaders took a page from the neoliberalism playbook and called upon growers to raise green beans for export rather than for domestic consumption (see Friedberg, 2003). Initially, the strategy proved profitable for the country and its farmers. Eventually, however, as farmers in other countries entered the market, conditions started to resemble those before the switch was made to non-traditional crops for exports. And the country and many of its residents returned to a precariously insecure position (see Box 2.3).

The problem—or at least one of them—with the non-traditional export market is that it cannot possibly remain profitable over the long term for the world's poor farmers. Eventually others, with more capital and better access to credit, who have witnessed this profitability from afar, will want to get in on the action. Peasant farmers thus often meet the same demise growing for the export market—the market they are asked to believe will save them—as they did growing traditional commodities for domestic consumption. Their socioeconomic position virtually guarantees such a fate under the current system.

The free market does not care for small farmers. When a country's borders are opened and the free trade process is set into motion, the sudden drop in farm gate prices immediately begins putting indebted farmers out of business. Low prices increase the minimum area needed to support a family, driving out some farmers while driving up the average farm size. As the price per agricultural unit decreases, the farmer must make up the difference by producing more units (Cochrane, 1993, pp417-436). Farmers must either (or ideally both) buy (or lease) more land or adopt productivity-enhancing technologies (e.g. higher0yielding seed). Of course, not everyone is positioned to successfully pull off this strategy. Lacking credit and capital, poor smallholders have little option but to either remain on the land and become poorer or abandon the way of life for a job in the city that may not exist—remember, in most developing countries the industrial sector is not growing fast enough to absorb the millions displaced by trade liberalization. The already well-off farmers in developing nations therefore become even more well off, while small farmers face a bleak future.

We must also remember the pressure felt by farmers from the other 'side'. Unlike most other sectors of the economy, farmers sell their products at wholesale prices but pay ritual for their inputs (Magdoff et al, 2000, p12). And over the decades, the price of those inputs—such as fuel, seed and fertilizer—has been on the rise. Farmers are therefore squeezed from both ends—by declining farm gate prices and increasing input costs.

Is food not sufficiently different from other commodities to justify policies that would exempt it from WTO requirements that everyone play under the same rules (Rosset, 2006; see also Hendrickson et al, 2001, p728)? Treating food differently, it seems to me, would make trade more fair. The hand of the free market already seems to be on holiday when it comes to production agriculture. When prices go down, a clear signal that society wants less of that commodity and more of something else (whose price at that moment is on the rise), farmers do not respond by producing something else. In fact, often they produce *more* of exactly what the market is telling them not to. The law of supply and demand has failed us when it comes to producing a self-regulating market in agriculture. In the meantime, millions have been thrown under the bus of trade liberalization for the benefit of a few.

Box 2.3 The haricot vert of Burkina Faso

Drought, crop failure and hunger plagued Western African countries during the 1960s. While the problems were nothing new to this region, the 'solution' pushed by agents both within and outside the country was. Aid monies began flowing to the region to fund the construction of reservoirs and irrigation canals. These projects sought to retain water from the rainy season and distribute it over time to maximize agricultural productivity. In addition to some rice, most of the aid was directed at producing green beans for export into the French market. The French have one of the highest rates of per capita green bean consumption in all of Europe. The *haricot vert* (aka 'green bean') is an ever present side dish, especially during the holiday season. Located in the southern hemisphere, Burkina Faso was able to supply green beans to the French during the winter holidays, when it is too cold to grow them in France. The labor-intensive nature of picking green beans also served the country of Burkina Faso by creating more jobs than many other commercial crops that where highly mechanized.

Up until the 1980s this strategy served the country and the people of Burkina Faso well, giving peasants a reliable living wage and increasing the country's foreign exchange. By the mid 1980s, Burkina Faso was the second largest African green bean exporter, behind Kenya. Yet, as happens in agriculture, market prices have since tumbled as other countries have sought a piece of the high value export pie. The increased competition has made conditions very difficult for Burkina Faso farmers. Prices have dropped. French importers no longer provide advanced financing. And endless stories are told of buyers abandoning contracted growers before harvest for someone willing to sell their beans for less, forcing farmers (or farmer co-operatives) to scramble to find buyers at the last minute before their beans spoil (Friedberg, 2003, pp454-455).

This is not a matter of breaking a few eggs to make an omelette. The question of whether trade liberalization policies are actually correlated with growth and prosperity for developing nations is an empirical one. And the data are not encouraging. An article in the *Journal of Developmental Economics* spells things out quite clearly: 'contrary to the conventional view on the growth effects of trade barriers, our estimation results show that trade barriers are positively and, in most specifications, significantly associated with growth, especially for developing countries, and they are consistent with the findings of theoretical growth and development literature' (Yanikkaya, 2003, p57). Other research, looking at sub-Saharan African economies, found little evidence that trade liberalization and the resultant agricultural exports have had a positive effect on this part of the world (McKay et al, 1997, p129). Even former US Secretary of Agriculture Dan Glickman has admitted to the failings of free market capitalism when it comes to issues of food security and international development. Noting the hypocrisy of trade liberalization arguments coming from affluent nations, Bertini and Glickman (2009, p99) write:

> No one has found a way to make the United States' own small farms competitive in a free market without public subsidies of one kind or another. Nonetheless, for decades, the World Bank and many Western aid agencies preached a rather purist version of free-market capitalism, without subsidies, as the solution to the hunger problems of developing countries. To those countries' government officials, many educated in the United States and Europe, it must have sounded like a treatise on charity penned by Casanova.

Food Aid

Famed agricultural economist Willard Cochrane (2000) made the following astute observation: whereas demand for food grows mainly with population growth, and is therefore inelastic because the stomach is inelastic, production grows much faster as new technologies increase yields and as additional land is brought into production (though, as discussed in Chapter 10, there are limits to this growth).4 The net effect is that supply will continue to outstrip demand, resulting in declining prices in the long term. Setting the wisdom of this argument momentarily to the side, Cochrane overstates the slowness by which demand for agricultural commodities grows. The biofuel industry, for one, has greatly expanded demand for grains. In addition, while the human stomach may not be all that elastic, the stomach of, say, cattle are. With the help of hormones and large doses of antibiotics, livestock have been able to consume much more grain today than they did just a couple of decades ago and produce much more meat and milk. Finally, I am not entirely sold on Cochrane's premise that the stomach is inelastic. This position seems to ignore the empirical evidence that points to how our stomachs have, at least to a degree, grown over the last few decades.

According to the US government-funded National Health and Nutrition Examination Survey (NHANES), for example, US men increased their calorie consumption from 1971 to 2000 by an average of 150 calories per day, while women increased their consumption by over 350 calories (Taubes, 2007, p250).

Criticisms aside, Cochrane's underlying point about the ever-present threat of overproduction cannot be summarily dismissed. Surplus production has plagued farmers in developed nations for well over half a century. Threats to capital accumulation were accentuated as European countries began feeding themselves as they built production capacity following World War II. By the 1950s, the stresses of overproduction were particularly acute to the world's top exporter: the US. As Cochrane reminds us, there is only so much that can be done from a policy perspective to increase domestic consumption. Our stomachs are only so big. The US National School Lunch Program (created in 1946) is an example of a domestic policy aimed at eliminating some of this agricultural surplus by way of funneling excess into the stomachs of US school children. What the US really needed, however, were alternative outlets for its surplus grain. Once the European agricultural sectors began to rebound and no longer needed (or wanted) cheap grain imports, US growers sought out new markets with the help of food aid.

In 1954, the US government created Public Law 480 (PL480) with the passing of the Agricultural Trade Development and Assistance Act. The Marshall Plan showed how foreign aid could be used to increase trade dependence despite a country's lack of money. PL480 provided a tool that could be used to flood the developing world with surplus grains without negatively affecting market prices.

I discussed earlier how a country gives up a significant degree of autonomy when it agrees to open its borders to the global market. In addition to reducing policies deemed trade distorting (e.g. tariffs), the country is often required to follow certain macroeconomic policy reforms, such as exchange rate devaluations (Peterson, 2009, pp217-218). An overvalued exchange rate makes imported goods cheaper, while increasing the price of the country's exports. Cheap food is politically popular, especially considering that peasant farmers—those with the most to gain from higher commodity prices—exist on the political margins in most countries. Then add food aid to the equation—food that is either donated or sold at prices below commercial rates. Overvalued exchange rates and food aid together exert tremendous downward pressure on domestic market prices, making it impossible for smallholder farms to make a profit. Like the import dependency mentioned earlier, this exceedingly cheap food sounds all well and good—until, that is, the food aid runs out.

For developed nations, food aid offers a means to dispose of price-suppressing surplus without causing market prices to tumble. Food aid can, however, affect the price within recipient countries. The real pay-off for donating countries, however, comes after the aid stops. Poor nations suddenly find themselves with a domestic grain deficit as fewer farms are producing what had previously been so cheap thanks to aid. Developing nations are often left with little choice but to continue their grain relationship with more affluent nations. Only now, this relationship is maintained through more formal market channels. Countries such as the US know that food aid can produce dependency. To quote Senator Hubert Humphrey in remarks to the Agriculture and Forest Committee of the US Senate in 1957: 'if you are looking for a way to get people to lean on you and to be dependent on you, in terms of their cooperation with you, it seems to me that food dependence would be terrific' (cited in Weis, 2007, p66).

There was an emerging consensus during the late 20th century among development practitioners that domestic food reserves, which could be drawn upon in the event of a food shortfall, were an inefficient distribution of resources. Better to have, it was believed, financial reserves, which could then be used to buy food, than food reserves, which require such additional capital outlays as storage and processing facilities (Jarosz, 2009, p2077). There are a number of practical problems with this strategy beyond the obvious on concerning why one would wish to make countries dependent upon others for something as fundamental as food. I could see, in the abstract, why such a policy might make sense. Financial reserves are, by definition, highly liquid—that is, they can be converted into many things very quickly. Moreover, unlike grain, money does not spoil. Unfortunately, seeing the world through abstract macroeconomic principles is like observing a country from an aeroplane at 30,000 feet: much ends up being missed that could add considerably to the situation one is trying to observe, understand and improve.

Many of the capital requirements for holding food on reserve are still needed for food aid. Countries that food aid helps the least are those lacking basic infrastructural and institutional capacities that allow for its storage and equitable distribution (Clay et al, 1999; Jayne et al, 2002). As I write these words, the one year anniversary for the catastrophic magnitude 7.0 Haiti earthquake is fast approaching.[5] The main topic of discussion on the situation in Haiti today, at least in the US, involves the snail's pace at which aid is trickling into the country (in addition to the disastrous cholera epidemic and conflict-ridden presidential elections)> More than US$9 billion has been pledged from countries around the world, but only a fraction of that has been delivered and spent. The airwaves are abuzz with people trying to figure out why, and accusatory fingers are being pointed in all directions, from the Haitian government to non-governmental organizations (NGOs). What we need to realize, however, is that good will and money can only do so much when seeking to aid a country in distress. Without already existing capacity to process and distribute aid, how can anyone expect efficient and equitable distribution, especially in the case of Haiti where whatever capacity that might have existed was destroyed by the earthquake? The same applies to food aid. Giving food without also working to build infrastructural and institutional capacities is a bit like giving someone water but without a cup to drink it from or the means to apply it to their parched fields.

A study published in the journal *Food Policy* and authored by World Bank economists examine the degree to which food aid may create disincentives to not only domestic food production (by suppressing domestic grain prices), but also in public and private investments in food production. The authors wished to determine if the benefits of food aid in addressing severe short-term hunger might be offset by the cost of increased long-term food insecurity (Ninno et al, 2007, p414). They looked at India, Bangladesh, Ethiopia and Zambia. As it turns out, their differences in population, income levels and economic structure helped to explain their contrasting experiences with food aid and agricultural development. The large populations of India and Bangladesh (1.05 billion and 144 million, respectively) make their food consumption requirements substantially greater than either Ethiopia (with half the population of Bangladesh in an area twice as large) or Zambia (with a population density one fiftieth that of Bangladesh). The demographic characteristics of India and Bangladesh indicate a greater possibility for gains due to economies of scale in marketing and storage, and their high population densities point to lower food distribution costs. Ethiopia, in particular, suffers from lower per capita income (US $100 per person) compared to India (US $480 per person) and Bangladesh (US $360 per person), which places its residents in a precarious position during periods of heightened food insecurity.

The researchers concluded that Bangladesh has been only marginally negatively affected by food aid in the long term. While food aid flows of wheat had lasted over 25 years, the country still managed to double its rice and wheat output. India experienced gains as well, but not of the magnitude witnessed in Bangladesh. In contrast, Ethiopia—the leading recipient of food aid for the last 30 years—is no more food secure today than in 1980. Three key factors were highlighted that enabled India and Bangladesh to achieve greater food security and, thus, reduce their need for food aid:

> First, Bangladesh and India maintained a political will and had donor support for long-term investments in production, including agricultural research, extension, irrigation and rural roads…Second, food aid flows were small relative to the size of total consumption… In countries where the size of food aid shipments is large relative to the size of the markets, and especially where the food aid commodity is a close substitute for major domestically produced staples, the risk

of adverse price effects on production incentives are especially great. Third, food aid inflows were channeled through a public distribution system, with adequate public storage and careful management of the timing of arrivals of food aid and the distribution of food. Food aid distributed mainly through emergency relief programs in Ethiopia has been less effectively managed. (Ninno et al, 2007, pp422-423)

In other words, India and Bangladesh attained some positive movement towards greater food security *in spite* of food aid, not because of it.

It is clearly an overstatement to proclaim that food aid, in all cases, creates food dependence. Some countries as the aforementioned study suggests have managed the perils of food aid better than others. I am also aware that the example of "Shining India" is not without its critics. Citing work by economist Utsa Patnaik, Raj Patel (2009, p30) tells of how 'statistical sleights of hand have enabled India's poor to vanish since the 1970s—namely, by lowering the official threshold of 'poverty' from 2400 calories during the 1970s to 1890 calories by 2000. As Patel (2009, p30) explains, 'around half a billion people have been written out of poverty, by the simple expedient of shifting the goalposts'.

Part of the problem with food aid rests in how it is distributed. When an emergency arises, surplus food from affluent nations is donated to relief organizations working closely with the United Nations World Food Programme. Another route is to donate food to the governments of the countries in need, who then sell the food at below market prices to raise money for general development programmes. In either case, farmers in countries receiving aid often get less for their products once the aid enters the country (Peterson, 2009, p115). Because of this, most countries, save for the US, give cash to the World Food Programme. This explains why the US leads all other nations combined in food aid shipments. From 1995 to 2005, the US accounted for approximately 60 per cent of all food aid. The remainder came from the EU (25 per cent), Japan (6 per cent), Canada (5 per cent), Australia (3 per cent), Norway (less than 1 per cent) and Switzerland (less than 1 per cent) (Hanrahan and Canda, 2005, p5). Countries other than the US are not necessarily any less giving, just giving differently—namely, cash rather than grain.

The practice of giving grain to later be sold to generate cash seems inherently inefficient on a number of levels. First, selling aid cheaply—one estimate (IATP, 2005) places the price of these sales at between 30 to 50 per cent below what the market would otherwise bear—to generate revenue for development projects minimizes taxpayers' bang for their buck. It makes little sense to sell something for between 50 and 70 cents on the dollar to generate aid revenue when the whole dollar (which previously was used to buy grain) could be given directly to those in need. Just *who* are we trying to help with food aid anyway? Are we looking to fill stomachs or pocketbooks?

Furthermore (and to respond to the two previous questions), the majority of money spent of food aid is wasted on transportation. The US Agency for International Development (USAID) food aid budget in 2005 was US $1.6 billion. Of that, only 40 per cent (US $654 million) went to paying for food. The rest was spent on overland transportation (US $141 million), ocean shipping (US $341 million), transportation and storage in destination countries (US $410 million) and administrative costs (US $81 million) (Dugger, 2005). The US government requires that 75 per cent of all food aid be transported by US flag carriers regardless of cost. Then there is the requirement that 25 per cent of the cargo must pass through Great Lakes ports. So, for example, wheat grown in Kansas might have to go first to Chicago, where it is put on a freight train, before being sent south to the Gulf of Mexico. According to the Government Accountability Office (GAO), these requirements cost US taxpayers an additional US $70 per ton in 2007 (Martin, 2010). The rationale behind this policy is national defense. Having a significant presence of US flag carriers out on the open sea enhances US military readiness. That's the argument at least. In actuality, many of the US flag carriers are owned by foreign companies with little actual military value (Martin, 2010). Food aid can thus take as long as six months to get from a US storage facility to a foreign village (Martin, 2010). In 2007, the Bush administration proposed using a portion of PL480 funds to make direct cash transfers, which would allow food to be purchased either locally or in neighboring countries. This, it was argues, would greatly reduce transportation costs—thus increasing taxpayers' bang for their buck—and expedite the allocation of aid. Congress rejected the proposal for a host of political reasons (Peterson, 2009, p115).

Former US Secretary of the Treasury Paul O'Neil expressed sentiments held by many when, referencing food aid to Africa, he exclaimed: 'We've spent trillions of dollars on these problems and we have damn near nothing to show for it' (cited in Ncayiyana, 2007). To this, Jeffery Sachs (2006, p310) responds: 'It is no surprise that there is so little to show for the aid to Africa, because there has in fact been so little aid to Africa!' Subtracting for fees for consultants from donor countries, money put towards servicing African nations' debt, and the costs of administrating and transporting food aid leaves a magnanimous sum of *6 cents* for each person in the form of actual aid. It's hardly shocking we have gotten nothing to show for our actions when the actual aid, after all the deductions are made, turns out to be so miniscule.

Notes

1. Neven et al (2009) argue that Kenyan smallholders pushed out of farming still benefit from this export strategy through the labor market (i.e. they become farm laborers). Yet, what happens when those middle-sized farms begin investing in labor-saving devices? What happens when the price of those export commodities drop as farmers, in other countries enter into the market to take advantage of premium prices? It is a lot easier to get out of farming than to get back in.

2. Neoliberalism is a political economic worldview based on rebranded classical economics (hence, the moniker 'neo'), emphasizing the sanctity of free markets, free trade and free enterprise. Chapter 10 offers a closer look at this philosophy and the problematic understanding of 'freedom' upon which it is premised.

3. See www.ugpulse.com/articles/daily/news.asp?about=Research+says+Nile+perch+fish+reduc ing&ID=6955.

4. This point draws upon what is known in economics as Engel's Law, after the 19th-century statistician Ernst Engel. Simply put, Engel's Law states that given the natural limits of our stomachs, as household incomes rise the proportion of income spent on food falls, even though (as often occurs in developing economies) actual household expenditures on food rise.

5. The event occurred on 12January2010, killing hundreds of thousands and leaving over 1 million homeless.

References

ABARE (2001) *The Impact of Agricultural Trade Liberalization on Developing Countries*, ABARE Research Report No 01.6, Australian Bureau of Agricultural and Resource Economics, Canberra, Australia.

Anderson, K., E. Martin and D. van der Mensbrugghe (2006) 'Distortions to world trade: Impacts on agricultural markets and farm incomes', *Review of Agricultural Economics*, vol 28, no 2, pp168-194

Annand, M. (2005) 'Why antidumping law is good for agriculture', in A. Schmitz (ed) *International Trade Disputes: Case Studies in North America*, University of Calgary Press, Calgary, Alberta, pp63-86

Bello, W. (2008) 'How to manufacture a food crisis', *Development*, vol 51, no 4, pp450-455

Bello, W. (2009) *The Food Wars*, Verso, New York, NY

Bertini, C. and D. Glickman (2009) 'Farm futures: Bringing agriculture back to US foreign policy', *Foreign Affairs*, vol 88, no 3, pp93-105

Bezemer, D. and D. Headey (2008) 'Agriculture, development and urban bias', *World Development*, vol 36, no 8, pp1342-1364

Biryabarema, E. (2009) 'Uganda's fish export earnings drop 35 pct in 2009', *Rutgers Africa*, http://af.reuters.com/article/investingNews/isAFJOE60SOFJ20100129, last accessed 31December2010

British Council (2009) *Bangladesh Market Introduction*, British Council, www.britishcouncil. org/eumd-information-background-bangladesh.htm, last accessed 30June2010

Byerlee, D., A. de Janvry and E. Sadoulet (2009) 'Agriculture for development: Toward a new paradigm', *Annual Review of Resource Economics*, vol 1, no 1, pp15-35

Clay, D., D. Molla and D. Habtewold (1999) 'Food aid targeting Ethiopia: A study of who needs it and who gets it', *Food Policy*, vol 24, no 4, pp391-409

Clapp, J. and D. Fuchs (2009) (eds) *Corporate Power in Global Agrifood Governance*, MIT Press, Cambridge, MA

Cochrane, W. (1993) *The Development of American Agriculture: A Historical Analysis*, University of Minnesota Press, Minneapolis, MN

Cochrane, W. (2000) *American Agriculture in an Uncertain Global Economy*, Minnesota Agricultural Economist, University of Minnesota Extension Service, No 700, http:// ageconsearch.umn.edu/bitstream/13175/1/mae700.pdf, last accessed 8 July 2010

Dasgupta, P. (1998) 'The economics of poverty in poor countries', *The Scandinavian Journal of Economics*, vol 100, no 1, pp41-68

David, M., M. Dirven and F. Vogelgesand (2000) 'The impact of the new economic model on Latin American's agriculture', *World Development*, vol 28, no 9, pp1673-1688

Dugger, C. (2005) 'Africa food for Africa's starving is road blocked in Congress', *New York Times*, 12 October, www.nytimes.com/2005/10/12/international/africa/12memo. html?ex=1286769600&en=0de1afa6dd7990e&ei=5090&partner=rssuserland&emc=rss, last accessed 19 February 2010

Ellis, F. (2005) 'Small farms, livelihood diversification, and rural-urban transitions: Strategic issues in sub-Sahara Africa', in *The Future of Small Farms: Proceedings of a Research Workshop*, International Food Policy Research Institute and Overseas Development Institute, Imperical College, London, pp135-149, http://citeseerx.ist.psu.edu/viewdoc/do wnload?doi=10.1.1.139&rep=rep1&type=pdf#page=142, last accessed 25June2010

European Union (2009) Trade Has Always Been a Principal Driving Factor of EC— Bangladesh Relations, Delegation of the European Union, www.delbgd.ec.europa.eu/en/ trade/index.htm, last accessed 30 June 2010

Fan, S., P. Hazell and S. Thorat (2000) 'Government spending, growth and poverty in rural India', *American Journal of Agricultural Economics*, vol 82, no 4, pp1038-1051

Freidberg, S. (2003) 'French beans for the masses: A modern historical geography of food in Burkina Faso', *Journal of Historical Geography*, vol 29, no 3, pp 445-463

Friedmann, H. (1990) 'The origins of third world food dependence', in H. Bernstein, B. Crow, M. Mackintosh and C. Martin (eds) *The Food Question: Profits versus People*, Monthly Review Press, New York, NY, pp 13-31

Friedmann, H. (1992) "Distance and durability: Shaky foundations of the world food economy', Third World Quarterly, vol 13, no 2, pp 371-383

Fuchs, D., A. Kalfagianni and M. Arenstsen (2009) 'Retail power, private standards, and sustainability in the global food system', in J. Clapp and D. Fuchs (eds) *Corporate Power in Global Agrifood Goverance*, MIT Press, Cambridge, MA, pp 29-59

Fulgencio, K. (2009) 'Globalisation of the Nile perch: Assessing the socio-cultural implications of the Lake Victoria fishery in Uganda', *African Journal of Political Science and International Relations*, vol 3, no 10, pp 433-442

Grindle, M (2004) 'Good enough governance: Poverty reduction and reform in developing countries', *Governance*, vol 17, no 4, pp 525-548

Hanrahan, C. and C. Canda (2005) *International Food Aid: US and other Donor Contributions*, CRS (Congressional Research Service) Report for Congress, US Library of Congress, Washington, DC, www.au.af.mil/au/awc/awcgate/crs/rs/21279.pdf, last accessed 14July2010

Hendrickson, M., W. Heffernan, P. Howard and J. Heffernan (2001) 'Consolidation in food retailing and dairy', *British Food Journal*, vol 103, no10, pp 715-728

IATP (Institute for Agriculture and Trade Policy) (2005) *Agricultural Export Dumping Booms during WTO's First Decade, Press Release*, Minneapolis, MN, 9 February, www.iatp.org/iatp/press.cfm?refid=89731, last accessed 30June2010

Jarosz, L. (2009) 'Energy, climate change, meat, and markets: Mapping the coordinates of the current food crisis', *Geography Compass*, vol 3, no 6, pp 2065-2083

Jayne, T., J. Strauss, T. Yamano and D. Molla (2002) 'Targeting the food aid in rural Ethiopia: Chronic need or inertia', *Journal of Development Economics*, vol 69, no 2, pp 247-288

Johnston, B. and J. Mellor (1961) 'The role of agriculture in economic development', *American Economic Review*, vol 51, no 4, pp 566-593

Kay, C. (2009) 'Development strategies and rural development: Exploring synergies, eradicating poverty', *The Journal of Peasants Studies*, vol 36, no 1, pp 103-137

Lewis, W. A. (1954) 'Economic development with unlimited supplies of labour', *The Manchester School*, vol 28, no 2, pp 139-191

Lupton, M. (1977) *Why Poor People Stay Poor: A Study of Urban Bias in World Development*, Temple Smith, London

Magdoff, F., J. Foster and F. Buttel (2000) 'An overview', in F. Magdoff, J. Foster and F. Buttel (eds) *Hungry for Profit: The Agribusiness Threat to Farmers, Food, and the Environment*, Monthly Review Press, New York, NY pp 7-21

Maini, K. and R. Lekhi (2007) 'Implications of World Trade Organization on dairy sector of India', in R. S. Jalal and N. S. Bisht (eds) *Emerging Dimensions of Global Trade*, Sarup and Sons, New Delhi, pp 174-180

Manson, K. (2009) 'Kenya's food miles', *Boise Weekly*, 9September, www.boiseweekly.com/boise/kenyas-food-miles/Content?oid-1168196, last accessed 28December2010

Martin, S. (2010) 'Restrictions on US food aid waste time and money', *Tampa Bay Times*, 8February, www.tampabay.com/news/world/restrictions-on-us-food-aid-waste-time-and-money/1070813, last accessed 13July2010

McKay, A., O. Morrissey and C. Vaillant (1997) 'Trade liberalization and agricultural supply response: Issues and some lessons', *The European Journal of Development Research*, vol 9, no 2, pp 129-147

Minor, N. and M. Ngigi (2004) *Are Horticulture Exports a Replicable Success Story? Evidence from Kenya and Côte d'Ivoire*, International Food Policy Research Institute, Washington, DC, www.ifpri.org/sites/default/files/publications/eptdp120.pdf, last accessed 28December2010

Moscow Times (2010) 'Ministry says it will import feed grain', *Moscow Times*, 29November, www.themoscowtimes.com/business/article/ministry-says-it-will-import-feed-grain/425151.html, last accessed 15December2010

Muuru, J. G. (2009) *Kenya's Flying Vegetables*, Africa Research Institute, London, www.africaresearchinstitute.org/files/policy-voices/docs/Kenyas-Flying-Vegetables-Small-farmers-and-the-food-miles-debate-0V6S400WZM.pdf, last accessed 28December2010

Narrod, C., D. Roy, B. Avendano and J. Okello (2008) 'Standards on smallholders: Evidence from three cases', in E. McCullough, P. Pingali and K. Stamoulis (eds) *The Transformation of Agri-Food Systems: Globalization, Supply Chains, and Small Farmers*, Earthscan, London, pp355-372

Ncayiyana, D. (2007) 'Combating poverty: The charade of development aid', *British Medical Journal*, vol 335, pp1272-1273, www.bmj.com/cgi/content/full/335/7633/1272, last accessed 3August2010

Neven, D., M. Odera, T. Reardon and H. Wang (2009) 'Kenyan supermarkets, emerging middle-class horticultural farmers, and employment impacts on the rural poor', *World Development*, vol 37, no 11, pp1802-1811

Ninno, C., P. Dorosh and K. Subbaro (2007) 'Food aid, domestic policy and food security: Contrasting experiences from South Asia and sub-Sahara Africa', *Food Policy*, vol 32, pp 413-435

Nunan, F. (2010) 'Mobility and fisherfolk livelihoods on Lake Victoria: Implications for vulnerability and risk', *Geoforum*, vol 41, no 5, pp776-785

Patel, R. (2009) *Stuffed and Starved: The Hidden Battle for the World Food System*, Melville House Publishing, Brooklyn, NY

Perez, M., S. Schlesinger and T. Wise (2008) *The Promise and Perils of Agricultural Trade Liberalization: Lessons from Latin America*, White Paper, Washington Office on Latin America, Washington, DC

Peterson, E. W. (2009) *A Billion Dollars a Day: The Economics and Politics of Agricultural Subsidies*, Wiley-Blackwell, Malden, MA

Rosset, P. (2006) *Food Is Different: Why We Must Get the WTO Out of Agriculture*, Zed Books, New York, NY

Sachs, J. (2006) *The End of Poverty: Economic Possibilities of Our Time*, Penguin, New York, NY

Schuurhuizen, R., A. Van Tilburg and E. Kambewa (2006) 'Fish in Kenya: The Nile perch chain', in R. Ruben, M. Singerland and H. Nijhoff (eds) *Agro-Food Chains and Networks for Development* , Springer, The Netherlands, pp 155-164

Taubes, G. (2007) *Good Calories, Bad Calories: Challenging the Conventional Wisdom on Diet, Weight Control, and Disease*, Knopf, New York, NY

van der Knaap, M. and W. Ligtvoet (2010) 'Is Western consumption of Nile perch from Lake Victoria sustainable?', *Aquatic Ecosystem Health and Management*, vol 13, no 4, pp 429-436

Weinberger, K. and T. Lumpkin (2005) *Horticulture for Poverty Alleviation*, Working Paper No 5, World Vegetable Centre, Shanhua, Taiwan

Weis, T. (2007) *The Global Food Economy: The Battle for the Future of Farming*, Zed Books, New York, NY

World Bank (2007) *Agriculture Investment Sourcebook*, World Bank, Washington, DC

World Bank (2007) *World Development Report 2008: Agriculture for Development*, World Bank, Washington, DC

Yanikkaya, H. (2003) 'Trade openness and economic growth: A cross country empirical investigation', *Journal of Development Economics*, vol 72, no 1, pp 57-80

Questions for Discussion

1. Dr. Carolan asks "When is a food?" not "What is a food?" What does he mean by this?

2. Dr. Carolan makes the point that his primary audience for his book and his research generally is the student—his own students—at CSU. He also goes to some length to offer respect for his colleagues in other departments at CSU. Why does his do this? How do these efforts affect his ethos?

3. Synthesis/extension question: If we consider Dr. Carolan's consideration of food as a cultural artefact that finds variable meaning depending on its context of use, how might he respond to the relationship of rural Latin@'s in in the food system as described by Elizabeth Fitting in her chapter "From Working the Farm to Fast Food and Back Again"? or by Josie Méndez-Negrete in her chapter "Desde el Corazón"?

How Consumers Respond to Corporate Social Responsibility Initiatives: A Cluster Analysis of Dairy Consumers

Marco Costanigro, Dawn Thilmany MacFadden, and Oana Deselnicub

Journal of Food Distribution Research, March 2013

This is an academic journal article written by academic scholars and published in the *Journal of Food Distribution Research*. The authors use data from a survey to assess the relative success of various Corporate Social Responsibility (CSR) activities by producers to influence consumer attitude and willingness to spend additional money to purchase a product.

A Look at Corporate Social Responsibility (CSR) in the Dairy Industry

Corporate Social Responsibility (CSR) is a formal commitment on the part of a private company to decrease the harmful effects it may have on society and the environment. Generally, specific CSR goals or actions are defined for the company as improvement or changes in specific areas that may otherwise be negatively affected due to company operations. The popularity of Corporate Social Responsibility (CSR) has increased in the past 20 years due to pressures from both the supply (forms and retailers) and demand side (consumer advocate groups, media, and stakeholders) (Oberseder 2011).

The potential for environmental externalities and the rising consumer awareness of animal welfare issues in livestock operations (Lusk et al. 2011) make the dairy industry a particularly relevant testing ground for CSR-based product differentiation strategies. According to industry sources, large distributors such as Costco and Walmart (Martinez et al. 2008) have been a major driver of CSR implementation in the dairy supply chain in an effort to reduce the risk of media scandals or other negative publicity. CSR efforts may also be driven by a desire to counter any negative stereotypes about their operations, such as the idea that large, profit-driven companies have little interest in the well-being of their employees and society in general.

CSR as a Branding Strategy to Target Consumer Activists

CSR initiatives are believed to benefit not only society and the environment, but to also create a loyal base of consumers willing to pay a price premium for CSR-differentiated brands and products. Of the consumers that we are inclined to potentially integrate CSR in their purchase decision, only a minority (21%) actually uses it as a criteria to choose among products (Mohr et al. 2001).

The lack of understanding about consumer's purchases related to CSR raises some potential questions for companies that want to market in the most effective way. Some potential questions include: Are there any clustered, like-minded consumers that are seeking a common set of CSR attributes? Do some existing labeling programs present clear signals of the CSR behaviors that "target consumer clusters" seek? And what are the purchase behaviors of the target consumers?

Data and Methods

A survey of milk consumers recruited amongst Colorado State University (CSU) personnel was carried out in the summer of 2011. A total of 96 individuals participated and the survey was administered via computer on CSU premises. In addition to a section soliciting sociodemographic information, the survey consisted of three types of tasks, which directly relate to each one of the stated research objectives:

1. In a best-worst exercise (Finn et al. 2006) participants ranked, by perceived importance, the involvement of an hypothetical dairy firm in nine alternative CSR areas of effort: animal welfare, energy consumption, water consumption, air pollution, community involvement, employee opportunities, local operation, waste management, and sustainable agricultural practices. The description of each CSR activity provided to the participants is reproduced in Table 1.

Table 1. CSR Activities Included in Study	
Dairy CSR Activities	**Description**
Animal welfare	There is a commitment to maintaining animal health through monitored nutrition and on-staff veterinarians, and reproduction by natural breeding rather than artificial insemination. Also, animals are kept outdoors on pastures rather than enclosed barns.

Energy consumption	Refers to the use of energy saving equipment in milk processing, and also to making transportation of milk to processing plants and retailers more energy efficient.
Water consumption	Implement recycling water programs through a water treatment facility and save water by using limited irrigation schedules to irrigate pastures and crops.
Air pollution	Manage the release of bovine methane by encouraging managed grazing and carbon soil sequestration. Also, decrease air pollution by making milk transportation from farm to plant and retailer more fuel efficient.
Community involvement	Company should be involved in charitable organizations, should implement volunteering days, and create and support local community programs.
Employee opportunities	The company should provide fair or above market wages, medical benefits, vacations, and retirement plans to employees. Employee advancement in company hierarchy is encouraged, as well as diversity in the workplace.
Local operation	The company uses local resources and generates local growth. The local economy is stimulated by creating jobs locally.
Waste management	Waste management refers mainly to composting solid waste to be used as fertilizer and monitoring waste runoff to the local water table.
Sustainable agricultural practices	Commitment to maintaining good soil health for a sustainable future of the business and the environment. Soil health implies practices such as the use crop rotation, using compost as natural organic fertilizer, and never using chemicals in maintaining a fertile soil.

2. Next, participants were asked to use a quantitative scale (from -5 "much worse" to +5 for "much better" in increments of one) to express how fluid milk displaying a specific label perceived to perform in the nine selected CSR areas

3. Finally, for each of the four mentioned labels, participants used a sliding bar tool (from -$2.00 to +$2.00 in increments of 10 cents) to express how much more/less they would be willing to pay for a gallon of milk displaying the label (USDA Organic, RBST-free, Validus, and Local Colorado Proud), compared to a gallon of milk without it. The exercise was then repeated, and participants were asked to estimate how much the general consumer population would be willing to pay for the label. This final step's information is the focus of a companion paper (Costanigro et al. 2012).

Findings and Discussion

The study sample statistics provided in Table 2 are comparable to the demographics for the state of Colorado provided by the US Census Bureau (US Census Quick Facts 2012). Subsequently, the cluster analysis completed for this analysis should represent similar shares of consumers who may have similar purchase motivations and perceptions of labels.

Table 2. Sample Characteristics		
Characteristic		**% of Sample**
Gender	Male	26.04
	Female	73.96
Race	White, Non-Hispanic	83.33
	Black, Non-Hispanic	4.17
	Hispanic	5.21
	Asian	2.08
	Other	5.21
Education	Some technical, business school or college	9.38
	Completed B.S., B.A., or College Work	29.17
	Some graduate work	10.42
	Graduate degree (Ph.D., M.S., M.D., J.D., etc)	48.96
	High School graduate or equivalent	2.08
Household income	Less than $20,000	2.08
	$20,000 to 34,000	10.42
	$35,000 to 49,000	18.75

	$50,000 to 74,000	30.21
	$75,000-99,000	18.75
	$100,000-124,000	7.29
	$125,000-$149,000	7.29
	Over $150,000	5.21

CSR Priorities for Consumers

The overall ranking of the CSR activities were reported in Constanigro et al. 2012 and illustrated that an overwhelming majority of participants stated that a dairy's investment in improving Animal Welfare practices was a key priority to them with respect to enterprises in the dairy sector. However, what is more interesting for this exercise is that we also find evidence of heterogeneous preferences amongst consumers. That is, a specific CSR activity may not be very important for the general population, but be extremely significant for a niche of consumers. For example, "local" was voted most important practice in 100 times (third highest in terms of "best" votes) but its overall rank is 7th because such a high share of respondents chose it as a low priority. Following Bond et al.'s 2008 work on clustering among fresh produce consumers, we sought to find similarities in individual ranking patterns between consumers as a means to identify groups of consumers (segments) with similar priorities.

In order to identify consumer segments, we used a k-means clustering technique that identifies similarities in the pattern of best-worst responses to group like-minded consumers and then named those groups based on observed patterns (Bond et al. 2008). CSR preferences within each group, as well as group characteristics, are provided in Table 3.

One result that was consistent across all consumers was their preference to buy from those who produce with some type of animal welfare certification. Beyond this general finding, two specific consumer sub-groups emerge from the results: one emphasizes local business, equal opportunities for employees, and sustainable agricultural practices; while the other prioritizes air pollution, energy consumption, water quality, and waste management. The CSR preferences of the third group (Mixed) are quite similar to the ones we previously identified for the general population, so one might consider this group as a set of "average" or "representative" consumers.

As we expect for a set of representative consumers, the mixed group represents the bulk of our sample (60%). Despite their relatively smaller household income, their average own WTP for milk labels is second highest. They are also heavy milk drinkers (72.5% drink it "often"), which is one characteristic that is likely to be particularly important to dairy processors and their retail partners. Plain milk consumption patterns of our sample are provided in Figure 1.

The first group of "niche" consumers prioritizes outcomes which the individual firm can accomplish independently (e.g., enforcing equal opportunities for their employees). We label this cluster as the "local" group since the beneficiaries of these CSR activities are more likely to be the local communities and employees of the company. The second group prioritizes more "global" or collective outcomes such as: air and water quality, energy consumption, and proper waste management, and all imply the concerted efforts of a large number of firms, perhaps including global agribusiness corporations, to lead to desired outcomes. The beneficiaries of these CSR activities are not only the communities around the firm, but also the general work population and/or global ecosystems.

One of the most interesting clusters, which could be aligned with the "locavore" movement that is increasingly targeted by food retailers, is the one labeled as local development. Some of the reasons this dairy "cluster" is of interest include their high household income, the highest average on willingness to pay (WTP) for milk labels, and the fact that 85.7% of them report drinking milk "often." However, this is a small segment (22%) of our sample, but even that share is sizable enough to represent significant buying dollars.

Table 3. CSR Preference by Cluster			
Cluster	Local Development	Global Impact	Mixed
	(22% sample)	(18% sample)	(60% sample)
Rank	1. Animal Welfare	1. Animal Welfare	1. Animal Welfare
	2. Local Business	2. Sustainable Ag. Practices	2. Sustainable Ag. Practices
	3. Employee Opportunities	**3. Waste Management**	3. Energy Consumption
	4. Sustainable Ag. Practices	**4. Energy Consumption**	4. Air Pollution
	5. Energy Consumption	**5. Water Management**	5. Employee Opportunities

	6. Water Management	**6. Air Pollution**	6. Waste Management
	7. Air Pollution	7. Employee Opportunities	7. Local Business
	8. Waste Management	8. Local Business	8. Water Management
	9. Community Involvement	9. Community Involvement	9. Community Involvement
HH Income	High	Medium	Low
	(24% over 100K, 81% over 50K)	(average 50K)	(majority 55% under 49K)
Age	Middle Aged	Young and Old (extremes, 52% under 39 yr, 33% over 50 yr)	Young (59% under 39 yr)
Education	High and low (graduate, college 67%, and the rest technical, high school only)	Generally high (graduate, college 76.5%)	Highly educated (graduate, college 83%)
WTP	Highest (avg. $0.837)	Lowest (avg. $0.525)	2nd highest (avg. $0.7)
Milk	Highest	Lowest	2nd highest
Consumption	(85.7% drink it "Often")	(47% drink it "Often")	(72.5% drink it "Often")

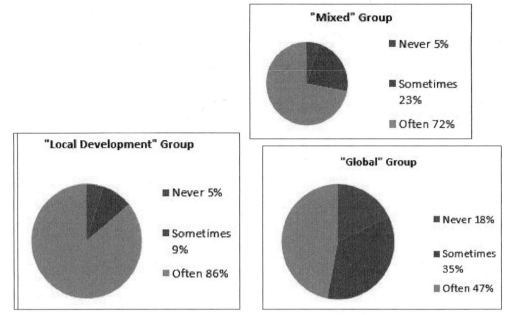

Figure 1. Milk Consumption by Cluster

Lessons on Corporate Responsibility as a Marketing Tool for the Dairy Industry

Businesses commonly seek ways to increase their competitive advantage in the marketplace, and marketing strategies often include differentiation through brands, promotions, and label information or placement in popular marketplaces.

In this study, we investigated several dimensions of consumer perceptions of CSR activities relevant to the dairy industry as a way to segment dairy buyers and identify criteria that may be effective in "branding" products toward those corporate social responsibility issues that may impact consumer buying decisions. While heterogeneity among consumers does exist, animal welfare is identified as the most preferred CSR activity by the great majority of study participants and a top priority for dairy farms. This result is not surprising in the context of increased consumer awareness of feedlot operations mistreating animals (Lusk et al. 2011).

Survey respondents were divided with respect to their CSR preferences into the "niche" sets of consumers who favor local (employee opportunities or sustainable agricultural practices) or global (air or water pollution) actions.

In short, animal welfare is an issue that is of importance and value to a fairly large set of dairy consumers, with other CSR initiatives of interest and value to smaller sets of consumers (who can be the recipient of more targeted promotion and marketing activities). So there is potential for dairy to use CSR to gain market advantage, but any firm must carefully consider how their choice of certifications, label choices, and positioning in markets frequented by certain groups of consumers will influence their success in promotion CSR.

References

Bond, A.C., D. Thilmany, and J.K. Bond. 2008. "Understanding consumer interest in product and process-based attributes for fresh produce." Agribusiness 24(2): 231-252.

Costanigro, M., O. Deselnicu, S. Kroll and D. Thilmany. 2012. "How Corporate Social Responsibility Initiatives are Emerging in the Dairy Sector: an Analysis of Consumer Perceptions and Priorities." Presented at the 2012 AAEA Annual Meetings. Seattle, WA.

Finn, A., Louviere, J. 1992. "Determining the Appropriate Response to Evidence of Public Concern: The Case of Food Safety." Journal of Public Policy 11(2): 12-25.

Lusk, J., and F.B. Norwood, F. 2011. "Speciesism, altruism and the economics of animal welfare." European Review of Agricultural Economics 1-24.

Martinez, S. and P. Kaufman. 2008. "Twenty Years of Competition Reshape the U.S. Food Marketing System." Amber Waves April http://webarchives.cdlib.org/sw1vh5d3r/http://ers.usda.gov/AmberWaves/April08/Features/FoodMarketing.htm [Accessed June 2012].

Mohr, L.A., D.J. Webb, and K. Harris. 2001. "Do consumers expect companies to be socially responsible? The impact of corporate social responsibility on buying behavior." Journal of Consumer Affairs 35(1): 45-72.

Oberseder, M., B.B. Schlegelmilch, and V. Gruber. 2011. "Why Don't Consumers Care About CSR? A Qualitative Study Exploring the Role of CSR in Consumption Decisions." Journal of Business Ethics 104: 449-460.

U.S. Census Bureau: State and County QuickFacts. 2012. Data derived from Population Estimates, American Community Survey, Census of Population and Housing, State and County Housing Unit Estimates, County Business Patterns, Non-employer Statistics, Economic Census, Survey of Business Owners, Building Permits, Consolidated Federal Funds Report. [June 2012.]

Questions for Discussion

1. What do the authors say are the corporate motivations for Corporate Social Responsibility (CSR)? Do you believe there are other motivations beyond what they state? Of the nine CSR dairy activities studied, which was by far the most important to consumers?

2. How do the authors use tables and figures to illustrate their main points? Is this an effective technique? What other figures, graphs, tables, or images might you use to amplify the points in the article?

3. Table 2 in the article provides demographic data for the individuals surveyed in the study. Do you think the results would be different for a sample population with only high school level education? For a population that was 50% non-Caucasian?

Examining College Students' Daily Consumption of Fresh Fruits and Vegetables

Patricia E. McLean-Meyinsse, Edith G. Harris, Shervia S. Taylor and Janet V. Gager

Journal of Agriculture, Food Systems, and Community Development, March 2013

This article was published in a professional academic journal entitled *The Journal of Food Distribution Research* which, according to its website, has a rich history of supporting research and educational interest in food marketing and logistics." It is an arm of the Food Distribution Research Center, a national research center whose president, according to the center's website, is Professor Dawn Thilmany of Colorado State University and the Ag Economics Department. The authors of this article are professors and scientists. According to the professional website of lead author Professor McLean-Meyinsse, she is a researcher and associate professor of agriculture economics at the Southern University Agricultural Research and Extension Center. In this article, the authors direct their research toward an audience of fellow academics and scientists who are interested in food science. Note the academic/ scientific style of writing, the use of data and charts, and the numerous references documented in the article. The research undertaken for this article was financially supported by the United States Department of Agriculture's National Institute for Food and Agriculture, and by Southern University Agricultural Research and Extension Center.

Introduction

Researchers have been suggesting for more than a decade that the United States is facing a serious healthcare crisis because of the sheer numbers of overweight and obese individuals, and the escalating costs for treating diet-related diseases. Agatston (2011) argues that unless we reverse our sedentary lifestyles and obesity epidemic, the U.S. healthcare system will go bankrupt. He also suggests that the current population of adults aged 30-45 many not live as long as their parents because of the incidences of diet-related diseases in this age group compared to the previous generations. The Robert Wood Johnson Foundation and Trust for America's Health September 2012 Report: *F as in Fat: How Obesity Threatens America's Future* (2012) also suggests that if the obesity trajectory continues, more than half of Americans will be obese by 2030, and the costs for treating new cases of diabetes, coronary heart disease, and stroke could exceed $66 billion per year. Rising obesity rates may also become a national security issue because the military now reports that 25 percent of the 17- to 24-year-olds are too overweight for military service. Further, the Department of Defense spends about $1 billion per year for weight-related health problems (Christeson et al. 2012)

Poor diets, obesity, and sedentary lifestyles have been associated with debilitating diseases such as heart disease, cancer, Type 2 diabetes, hypertension, and stroke, among others.   Consumption of fresh fruits and vegetables is frequently recommended as a viable way to attain healthier diets and to reduce diseases. Fruits and vegetables are low in fat and calories and are excellent sources of vitamins and minerals. Therefore, the dietary guidelines recommend eating a wide variety and colors of fruits and vegetables daily to provide the body with valuable nutrients such a fiber, folate, potassium, and vitamins A and C (http://www.cdc.gov). Despite these recommendations, only 23.1 percent of the U.S. population consumes the recommended five or more servings of fruits and vegetables per day.

Kiviniemi and colleagues (2011) observed lower consumption of fruits and vegetables among racial-ethnic groups when psychology distress was present. Richard, Kattelmann, and Ren (2006) studied ways to motivate greater consumption of fruits and vegetables among 18- to 24-year-olds and advanced the view that although conventional wisdom may suggest that this cohort is in good health, efforts should be made to help students to develop better eating habits because the eating patterns developed in college have life-long effects on health and well-being. Thus, teaching healthy eating habits to students should be of paramount importance. Knowledge of the daily recommendations for fruits and vegetables can also lead to increased consumption (Wolf et al. 2008). If fruits and vegetables are readily available in the home at an early age, consumption is more likely to become a life-long habit (Young, Fors, and Hayes 2004).

There is now convincing research suggesting that diets rich in fruits and vegetables can reverse, treat, or prevent diseases, and can add almost a decade to one's life. Further, vegans and vegetarians are shown to have lower incidences of heart disease, cancer, cholesterol, stroke, emphysema, dementia, Type 2 diabetes, kidney failure, and respiratory infections than the general population (Freston 2012). The challenge then is to get more Americans to move away from animal-focused diets and adopt plant-based diets. We concur with other researchers that universities are excellent settings to study eating habits and help young adults to make healthier food choices. In Louisiana, overweight and obesity rates have been increasing among 18- to 24-year-olds. Given that a large percentage of this cohort is enrolled in colleges, our study assesses the frequency of consuming fresh fruits and vegetables by a selected group of college students. The results will provide another opportunity to help students develop better eating habits.

Objectives

The study's overall objective is to examine fresh fruit and vegetable consumption among under-graduate students. The specific objectives are (a) to assess daily consumption of fresh fruits and vegetables; (b) to ascertain whether consumption varies across gender, academic classifications, and residency; (c) to explore the links between consumption patterns and participants' perceptions of their overall health status.

Methods and Procedures

Data

The study's data were compiled from a sample of 305 university students during fall 2011 and spring 2013. The survey was designed to capture student's knowledge of the information on Nutrition Facts panels, knowledge about vitamins, frequency of reading labels, frequency of consuming fresh fruits and vegetables, perceptions of health and weight, levels of physical activity, and selected demographics characteristics (age, academic classifications, majors, hometown, residency, marital status, household income, race, and gender). The data were analyzed using the chi-square test for independence for two categorical variables. The null (H_0) and alternative (H_1) hypotheses were as follows:

1. H_0: Daily consumption is independent of the selected response categories

2. H_1: Daily consumption depends on the selected response categories

Empirical Results and Discussion

Descriptive Statistics

The average age of the sampled students was 23-years-old. Freshman comprised 21 percent of the respondents; sophomores, 34 percent; juniors, 28 percent; and seniors, 17 percent. 63 percent lived off campus; 57 percent would like to pursue a career in nursing; 71 percent were women, while 87 percent had never been married. About 67 percent of the respondents perceived themselves to be in good or very good health. The results in Table 1 show that 50 percent of the students consumed no fruits and 52 percent consumed no vegetables daily, and that about 8 percent of the respondents consumed fresh fruits and vegetables at least three times per day.

Table 1. Daily Consumption Levels for Fresh Fruits and Vegetables (Percentages)

Eating Frequency	Fresh Fruits	Fresh Vegetables
0	50	52
1	29	27
2	13	13
≥3	8	9

Chi–Square Tests for Independence

Table 2 shows the cross tabulations between frequencies of consuming fruits and vegetables. From the results, 82 percent of the respondents did not consume any fresh fruits or vegetables daily. These results are statistically significant at the 1-percent level of probability. The results in Table 3 capture associations among consumption of fresh fruits, demographic characteristics, students' residence, and perceptions of overall health status. From the results, daily consumption of fresh vegetables is independent of gender, academic classifications, and residence, but depends on students' perceptions of their health. Thus, whether male or female, whether being freshmen, sophomores, juniors, or seniors, or whether students lived on or off campus, they ate fresh fruits infrequently. A closer examination of the results from Table 3 reveals that 65 percent of the respondents who perceive their health as fair or poor do not consume any fresh fruits on a daily basis. Further, 46 and 42 percent of those who felt they were in very good or excellent health, respectively also reported no daily consumption of fresh fruits.

Table 2. Cross-Tabulations for Daily Consumption of Fresh Fruits and Vegetables (Percentages)

Fruits	Vegetables					
	0	1	2	>3	χ^2	P-Value
0	82	11	49	21		
1	23	49	21	7		
2	18	42	25	15		
>3	17	25	17	41	148.303***	0.000

***Implies statistical significance at the 1-percent level of probability.

With respect to daily consumption of fresh vegetables (Table 4), consumption is also not associated with gender, academic classifications, or whether students lived on or off campus, but depends on perceptions of health status. Despite the statistically significant result, 42 percent of these students report no daily consumption of fresh vegetables. This finding echoes the warning issued by Richards and colleagues (2006) that although many students are in good health when they enroll in college, some still have undesirable eating habits. Therefore, universities should take steps to help all students to develop better eating habits so as to reduce the risks of them developing diet-related illnesses and diseases in the future.

Table 3. Cross-Tabulations between Fruit Consumption and Selected Characteristics (Percentages)

	Daily Consumption					
	0	1	2	>3	χ^2	P-Value
Total	50	29	13	18		
Male	47	29	16	8		
Female	52	29	12	7	1.073	0.784
Freshman	58	22	9	11		
Sophomore	46	34	14	6		
Junior	53	26	15	6		
Senior	44	33	14	9		
On Campus	51	31	10	8		
Off Campus	50	28	15	7	1.164	0.762

Fair/Poor	65	23	8	4		
Very Good/Good	45	32	15	8		
Excellent	33	25	17	25	13.364**	0.012

**Implies statistical significance at the 5-percent level of probability.

Table 4. Cross-Tabulations between Vegetable Consumption and Selected Characteristics (Percentages)

	Daily Consumption					
	0	1	2	≥3	χ^2	P-Value
Total	51	27	13	9		
Male	52	23	17	8		
Female	51	29	11	9	2.678	0.444
Freshman	62	21	11	6		
Sophomore	46	24	18	12		
Junior	54	27	11	8		
Senior	46	38	8	7	11.635	0.236
On Campus	49	27	16	8		
Off Campus	53	27	11	9	1.674	0.643
Fair/Poor	65	22	5	8		
Very Good/Good	46	28	16	10		
Excellent	42	33	25	0	14.528**	0.024

**Implies statistical significance at the 5-percent level of probability.

Summary and Conclusions

The study's overall objective was to examine fresh fruit and vegetable consumption among undergraduate students. The specific objectives were (a) to assess the daily consumption of fresh fruits and vegetables; (b) to ascertain whether consumption carried across gender, academic classifications, and residency; and (c) to explore the links between consumption patterns and participants' perceptions of their overall health status.

Based on the results, the sampled respondents consumed very small percentages of fresh fruits and vegetables daily. In fact, 82 percent of the respondents reported that they did not eat fresh fruits or vegetables on a daily basis. Twenty-one percent indicated that they ate fresh fruits two or more times per day compared to 25 and 33 percent, respectively at the state and national levels. Regarding daily consumption of vegetables, only 9 percent consumed vegetables at least three times per day. At the state and national levels, 21 and 26 percent of consumers, respectively, report that they eat vegetables three or more times per day. The results also suggested that only a small percentage (4 percent) of the students who described themselves as being in poor or fair health consumed fruits three or more times daily; eight percent who described their health in a similar manner consumed vegetables at least three times per day.

The United States spends a tremendous amount of its resources treating diet and health related illnesses. These expenditures are predicted to continue to rise astronomically in the future unless we change our eating habits and lifestyles. Children and young adults are the country's future; therefore, they must be encouraged to eat better by expanding their consumption of fresh fruits and vegetables. Freston (2012) suggests that in the past, conflicts of interest on the U.S. dietary guidelines committee may have prevented the government from recommending a plant-based diet for Americans. However, as the healthcare crisis deepens, obesity epidemic widens, and children's health declines, each of us may be forced to adopt some of the ideas advanced by *Food Day* regarding healthy, affordable, and sustainable foods. In other words, plant-based diet may become the norm rather than the exception.

References

Agatston, A. 2011. "How America Got So Fat and So Sick." *Prevention* 63 (10): 100-106.

Christeson W., T.A. Dawson, S. Messner-Zidell, M. Kiernan, J. Cusick, and R. Day. 2012. *Still Too Fat to Fight*. http://www.rwjf.org/en/research-publications/find-rwjf-research/2012/09/still-too-fat-to-fight.html [Accessed October 31, 2012.]

Food Day website. http://www.foodday.org/focus_areas [Accessed October 31, 2012.]

Freston, K. "Why Do Vegetarians Live Longer?" http://www.huffingtonpost.com/kathy-freston [Accessed October 27, 2012.]

CDC website. "Eat Your Fruits and Vegetables." http://cdc.gov/nutrition/everyone/fruitsvegetables/index.html [Accessed October 30, 2012]

Kiviniemi, M.T., H. Orom, and G.A. Giovino. 2011. "Race/Ethnicity, Psychological Distress, and Fruit/Vegetable Consumption. The Nature of the Distress-Behavior Relation Differs by Race/Ethnicity." *Appetite* 56(3): 737-740.

Richards, A., K.K. Kattelmann, and C. Ren. 2006. "Motivating 18- to 24-YearOlds to Increase Their Fruit and Vegetable Consumption." *Journal of the American Dietetic Association* 106:1405-1411.

Robert Wood Johnson Foundation. 2012. *F as in Fat: How Obesity Threatens America's Future.* http://www.rwjf.org/content/dam/farm/reports/reports/2012/rwjf401318. [Accessed October 31, 2012.]

Wolf, R.L., S.J. Lepore, J.L. Vandergrift, L. Wetmore-Arkader, E. Meginty, G. Pietrzak, and A.L. Yaroch. 2008. "Knowledge, Barriers, and Stage of Change as Correlates of Fruit and Vegetable Consumption among Urban and Mostly Immigrant Black Men." Journal of the American Dietetic Association 108: 1315-1322.

Young E.M., Start, W. Fors, and D.M. Hayes. 2004. "Associations between Perceived Parent Behaviors and Middle School Student Fruit and Vegetable Consumption." *Journal of Nutrition Education and Behavior* 36 (1): 2-12.

Questions for Discussion

1. The authors state "efforts should be made to help students to develop better eating habits because the eating patterns developed in college have life-long effects on health and well-being." What health issues are they referring to?

2. Since this is a scientific research article, how do the authors use survey data to make their points and justify their conclusions about student consumption of fruits and vegetables?

3. The authors never explicitly state what college the students in the survey attend. Is this intentional? Based upon the survey results of the 305 students as compared to the national averages for consumption of fruits and vegetables, what region of the country do you think the students lived in? Would the results be different for a similar college population surveyed in Colorado? In Europe? In China?

Acknowledgments

Abrams, Lindsay. "Factory Farming Is Killing the Planet: Why the Meat Industry's Future Needs to Look More Like its Past." From *Salon*, July 25, 2015. Reprinted with permission of Salon Media Group, Inc. All rights reserved.

Abramsky, Sasha. "Why Food Stamps Matter." From *The New Yorker Magazine*, Sept. 26, 2013. Copyright © 2013 by Condé Nast. Reprinted with permission. All rights reserved.

Alkon, Alison H., and Kari Marie Norgaard. "Breaking the Food Chains: An Investigation of Food Justice Activism." From *Sociological Inquiry* 79.3 (2009). Copyright © 2009 by Alpha Kappa Delta: The International Sociology Honor Society. Reprinted with permission of John Wiley & Sons, Inc. All rights reserved.

Barclay, Eliza. "More Hospitals Are Ditching Antibiotics in the Meat They Serve." From *NPR.org*, Jan. 12, 2016. Copyright © 2016 by NPR. Reprinted with permission. All rights reserved.

Berry, Wendell. "Farmland without Farmers." From *The Atlantic*. Copyright © 2015 by Wendell Berry.

Berry, Wendell. "Prayer after Eating." From *The Selected Poems of Wendell Berry*. Copyright © 1998 by Wendell Berry.

Bittman, Mark, Michael Pollan, Ricardo Salvador, and Olivier De Schutter. "A National Food Policy for the 21st Century." From *Medium.com*, Oct. 2015.

Broad, Garrett. "The Black Panther Party: A Food Justice Story." From *Huffington Post*, Feb. 24, 2016. Reprinted with permission of the author.

Caparrós, Martín. "Counting the Hungry." From *The New York Times*, Sept. 27, 2014. Reprinted with permission. All rights reserved.

Carolan, Michael. *The Real Cost of Cheap Food*. Copyright © 2011 by Dr. Michael S. Corolan. Reprinted with permission of Taylor and Francis Group. All rights reserved.

Cordain, Loren. *The Paleo Diet: Lose Weight and Get Healthy by Eating the Foods You Were Designed to Eat*. Copyright © 2002, 2011 by Loren Cordain. Published by John Wiley and Sons, 2002. Reprinted with permission of Houghton Mifflin Harcourt. All rights reserved.

Costanigro, Marco, Dawn Thilmany MacFadden, and Oana DEselnicub, "How Consumers Respond to Corporate Social Responsibility Initiatives: A Cluster

Analysis of Dairy Consumers." From the *Journal of Food Distribution Research*, Vol. 44, Issue 1. Copyright © 2013 by the Food Distribution Research Society. Reprinted with permission. All rights reserved.

Fitting, Elizabeth. "From Working the Farm to Fast Food and Back Again: Rural Mexicans in the Neoliberal Food System." From *Latin@'s Presence in the Food Industry: Changing How We Think About Food*, edited by Meredith E. Abarca and Consuelo Carr Salas. Copyright © 2016 by The University of Arkansas Press.

Reprinted with the permission of The Permissions Company, Inc., on behalf of the publisher, www.uapress.com.

Genoways, Ted. "Corn Wars." From *New Republic*, Aug. 16, 2015. Reprinted with permission. All rights reserved.

Gladwell, Malcolm. "The Trouble with Fries" From *The New Yorker*, March 5, 2001.

Grandin, Temple. "A Cow's Eye View." Excerpt(s) from *Thinking in Pictures* by Temple Grandin, Copyright © 1995, 2006 by Temple Grandin. Used by permission of Doubleday, an imprint of the Knopf Doubleday Publishing Group, a division of Penguin Random House LLC. All rights reserved.

Grant, Harriett. "Lack of Food Means Syrian Children Face 'Irreversible' Health Issues, Says UN." From *The Guardian*, Dec. 14, 2015. Reprinted with permission. All rights reserved.

Groskopf, Christopher. "Science Is Warning Us that a Food Crisis Is Coming to Southern Africa. Will We Stop It?" From *Quartz*, March 5, 2016. Reprinted with permission of Atlantic Media Co. All rights reserved.

Harmon, Amy. "Golden Rice: Lifesaver?" From *The New York Times*, Aug. 24, 2013. Reprinted with permission. All rights reserved. "Indigenous Diets Can Help Fight Modern Illnesses, Health Experts Say." From *The Guardian*, Feb. 3, 2014.

King, Jr., Martin Luther. "Letter from Birmingham Jail." Copyright © 1963 by Dr. Martin Luther King, Jr. Copyright renewed 1991 by Coretta Scott King. Reprinted with permission. All rights reserved.

Klein, Martin J. and Kristi L. Shackleford. "Beyond Black and White: Document Design and Formatting in the Writing Classroom." From *Writingspaces.org*, Vol. 2. Reprinted with permission.

Lamott, Ann. "Shitty First Drafts." From *Bird by Bird: Some Instructions On Writing and Life*. Copyright © 1994 by Anne Lamott. Used by permission of Pantheon Books, an imprint of the Knopf Doubleday Publishing Group, a division of Penguin Random House LLC. All rights reserved.

McLean-Meyinsse, Edith G. Harris, Shervia S. Taylor and Janet V. Gager. "Examining College Students' Daily Consumption of Fresh Fruits and Vegetables." From the *Journal of Food Distribution Research*, Vol. 44, Issue 1. Copyright © 2013 by the Food Distribution Research Society. Reprinted with permission. All rights reserved.

Méndez-Negrete, Josie. "Desde el Corazón." From *Latin@'s Presence in the Food Industry: Changing How We Think About Food* edited by Meredith E. Abarca and Consuelo Carr Salas. Copyright © 2016 by The University of Arkansas Press. Reprinted with the permission of The Permissions Company, Inc., on behalf of the publisher, www.uapress.com.

Morin, Roc. "The Amish Farmers Reinventing Organic Agriculture." From *The Atlantic*, Oct. 6, 2014. Reprinted with permission. All rights reserved.

Nellum, Christopher. "Fighting Food Insecurity on Campus." From *Higher Education Today*, June 29, 2015. Copyright © 2015, American Council on Education. Reprinted with permission

Neumark, Liz. "Social Justice through Food Trucks." From *The Huffington Post*, Sept. 16, 2015. Reprinted with permission of *Our Town* and Liz Neumark. All rights reserved.

Niman, Nicolette Hahn . "Pig Out" From *The New York Times*, Mar. 14, 2007. Reprinted with permission. All rights reserved.

Offutt, Chris. "Trash Food." From *The Oxford American Magazine,* April 10, 2015. Copyright © 2015 by Chris Offutt. Reprinted with permission. All rights reserved.

Penniman, Leah. "Radical Farmers Use Fresh Food to Fight Racial Injustice." From Truth-out.org, Feb. 4, 2015. Reprinted with permission. All rights reserved.

Pollan, Michael. "The Consumer: A Republic of Fat." From *The Omnivore's Dilemma.* Copyright © 2006 by Michael Pollan. Reprinted with permission. All rights reserved.

Rahkovsky, Ilya and Samantha Snyder. *Food Choices and Store Proximity.* USDA Economic Research Service, 2015. Reprinted with permission.

Roach, Mary. "The Marvels in Your Mouth." From *The New York Times*, March 3, 2013. Reprinted with permission. All rights reserved.

Saslow, Eli. "Food Stamps put Rhode Island on Monthly Boom-and- Bust Cycle." From *The Washington Post*, March 16, 2013. Reprinted with permission. All rights reserved.

Straub, Richard. "Responding—Really Responding—to Other Students' Writing." From *The Subject is Writing*, edited by Wendy Bishop. Copyright © 1999 by Boynton/Cook Publishers, Inc. All rights reserved.

"'Take My Job!' Campaign Markets Agricultural Labor." From *NPR.org*, July 7, 2010. Reprinted with permission. All rights reserved.

Tannen, Deborah. *The Argument Culture: Stopping America's War of Words.* Copyright © 1998 by Deborah Tannen. Reprinted with permission of Random House. All rights reserved.

Vernon, Rachel V. "A Native Perspective: Food is More Than Consumption." From the *Journal of Agriculture, Food Systems, and Community Development*, Sept. 9, 2015. Reprinted with permission. All rights reserved.

Wang, Ucilia. "Food Companies Are Unprepared for Water Scarcity, Says New Report." From *The Guardian*, May 7, 2015.